C0-ALN-062

Untimely Interventic

Untimely Interventions

AIDS Writing, Testimonial, and the Rhetoric of Haunting

Ross Chambers

THE UNIVERSITY OF MICHIGAN PRESS
Ann Arbor

For Sheshy

Published in the United States of America by
The University of Michigan Press
Manufactured in the United States of America
♾ Printed on acid-free paper

2007 2006 2005 2004 4 3 2 1

A CIP catalog record for this book is available from the British Library.

Library of Congress Cataloging-in-Publication Data

MK

Chambers, Ross.
Untimely interventions : AIDS writing, testimonial, and the rhetoric of haunting / Ross Chambers.
p. cm.
Includes bibliographical references and index.
ISBN 0-472-09871-3 (cloth : alk. paper) — ISBN 0-472-06871-7 (pbk. : alk. paper)
1. AIDS (Disease)—Social aspects. 2. AIDS (Disease) in literature. I. Title.
RA643.8.C438 2004
362.196'9792—dc22 2004004961

When the ear hears the tale the soul is filled with sorrow.
—from the Moussaf prayer at Yom Kippur

AIDS, like everything that appears like extermination at work, is less unsayable than it is inaudible.
—Pierre Kneip, quoted in Le Monde, *December 8, 1995*

Ein Dröhnen: es ist
die Wahreit selbst
unter die Menschen
getreten,
mitten ins
Metapherngestöber

[A muffled rumble: truth
itself has stepped
among humans
into the thick of their
flurrying metaphors]
—Paul Celan, translation modified
from that of Michael Hamburger

How do we make what we know knowable to legions?
—Douglas Crimp, Melancholia and Moralism

Preface

"Waking teaches you pain," says Paul Monette in the last paragraph of his AIDS memoir, *Borrowed Time* (342). My book too is about waking to pain. But Monette goes on to describe how, anticipating the phone call from the hospital that would bring news of his lover's death, he tried to forestall the awakening by taking a strong sleeping pill. "When the phone rang at six I drifted out of bed and went into the darkened study." And then, after receiving the news (allowing the hospital to record the message rather than taking the call in person), "I swam back to bed for the end of the night, trying to stay under the Dalmane." My book, also, is about our reluctance to awaken to pain, the pain of which we already, like Monette, have foreknowledge. It's a book, more specifically, about the messages concerning pain that try to get through to us through the fog of our cultural Dalmane. These are messages of witness, testimonial writing.

Phone calls that bring bad news, not always from the hospital, are frequent in the writing of AIDS witness; but we find the motif of the wake-up call, also awaited with dread and also bringing pain, in at least one Auschwitz narrative, Primo Levi's *Se questo è un uomo* (a title poorly translated as *Survival in Auschwitz*). Throughout nights of "alternating sleep, waking and nightmares," Levi writes (63), "the expectancy and dread of the moment of reveille keeps watch" (or in Italian, "*vigila* . . . [il] momento della *sveglia,*" *vigilare,* to keep watch, and *sveglia,* awakening, being cognates). Anticipated by the inmates, announced by the ringing of the camp bell, the moment arrives when in the block the night guard, going off duty, "pronounces the daily condemnation: '*Aufstehen,*' or more often in Polish: *Wstavać.*"

> The night guard knows [about this anticipation] and for this reason does not utter it in a tone of command, but with the quiet and subdued voice of one who knows the announcement will find all ears waiting, and will be heard and obeyed.

The message can be a quiet one—a "voce piana e sommessa" [even-toned and cowed]—because it is less annunciatory than confirmatory; in that respect it foreshadows the chastened tone in which Levi addresses his readers. In his book he wants to invite us, he says (9), not to retributory justice or chastisement, but to quiet contemplation, a "studio pacato di alcuni aspetti dell'animo umano." The translation, here, reads: "a quiet study of certain aspects of the human mind" (9); but "pacato" implies the idea of pacified, and "animo" is more that which *animates* us, as humans, than the intellect per se.[1] Levi understands that the tone of his wake-up call to us can be quiet, like the night guard's wake-up call, because the fearful implications of Auschwitz with respect to the nature of humanity are already known to us, if not acknowledged.

Yet the *strangeness* of the call, as well as its subdued tone, is what the passage about reveille in Auschwitz most calls attention to. "Like a stone, the foreign word falls to the bottom of every soul" [al fondo di tutti gli animi] (63). The voice that awakens and falls to the bottom of our spirit comes, as it were, from regions remote from everyday experience; it speaks a language whose import we grasp although it is foreign to us; it constitutes what I will call a discourse of extremity. And it is for that reason, it seems, that it persists and penetrates. The command to waken "keeps watch"; *it* does not sleep even when *we* may do so, and is capable, therefore, of returning whenever circumstances work to divert us, like Dalmane, from the pain of knowledge. Thus, having written *Se questo è un uomo,* Levi went on to write a companion volume, *La tregua* (*The Reawakening,* in what is this time a peculiarly apt English translation). *La tregua* is about the odyssey of Levi's homecoming from Auschwitz. But its epigraph is a poem dated January 16, 1946, about the persistence of Auschwitz's "comando straniero." We have returned home, the poem says, filled our bellies, and told the story. Yet:

> It's time. Quickly we'll hear again
> The alien command:
> "Wstawać."

What, then, I ask in this book, is the nature of this urge to witness, to awaken those who sleep, and to *re*awaken them, with a message of extremity that has trouble getting through the cultural haze of Dalmane—things like being comfortably at home, well fed, able to persuade ourselves the story has been satisfactorily told and is consequently "over"

—but does not lose its power to interrupt, disturb, trouble, and remind the sleepers (an anamnesis or counterforgetting in the strictest sense) of what they (we) had never ceased to know? It's as if in everyday life we all sleep, but fitfully, knowing that we are figuratively "in Auschwitz," and that however hard we may cling to our sleep, and return to it when awakened, a still but persistent voice, "piana e sommessa," remains vigilant, imperturbably ready to awaken, and if necessary reawaken us. To reawaken us to "Auschwitz" as the true context of our slumber. *That* knowledge troubles our sleep, even if witnessing's wake-up call never succeeds in truly or definitively awakening us.

Amy Hoffman was never literally in Auschwitz as Levi was; her metaphor for that to which normalcy seeks to remain oblivious is "hospital time," as she experienced it on the occasion of the death from AIDS of her friend Mike Riegle. Even though she knew Mike was in his last hours, she still managed to be asleep when the call from the hospital came:

> I'd been at the hospital all evening, and Roberta and I were going out to dinner. Our coats were on. One of us had her hand upon the doorknob, about to turn it, and the phone rang. "I'll get it," I said, out of habit, not because I thought it might be the ultimate call. I was going out to dinner. I wasn't thinking about death. Or, rather, I knew it was close, that it could happen any second, but I wasn't thinking that it might be *now* or *now* or *now*—this second. (*Hospital Time,* 77)

And even then, her cycle of awakening and reawakening wasn't over, for she had yet to discover that after a death someone ends up with the ashes. One can never get back to sleep, because "in ashes begin more responsibilities" (85). Just so, too, a phone call from a friend of her mother's is enough to remind Jamaica Kincaid, comfortably at home in Vermont, of her unbroken connection with the island of Antigua:

> I was in my house in Vermont, absorbed with the well-being of my children, absorbed with the well-being of my husband, absorbed with the well-being of myself. When I spoke to this friend of my mother's, she said that there was something wrong with my brother and that I should call my mother to find out what it was. I said, What is wrong? She said, Call your mother. I asked her, using those exact words, three times, and three times she replied the same way. And then I said, He has AIDS, and she said, Yes. (*My Brother,* 6–7)

She too, like Hoffman, her "absorption" notwithstanding, has foreknowledge of the news; but the message, here, is not only quiet and distant, yet persistent; it is also oddly indirect. Because Kincaid is in one of the periods when she is not speaking with her mother—a circumstance clearly symbolic of her exclusion of "Antigua" from her life—the message must come not only by long-distance telephone but also through a friend. Deleuze and Guattari would surely speak here of an *agencement,* the "agencing" through which messages must pass, or more accurately the agencing that constitutes them, when supposedly direct connections (an oxymoronic phrase in any case) are unavailable. Discourses of extremity inevitably rely on agencing. They come in foreign languages, are recorded on answering machines, depend on the intermediary of a friend who cannot speak their true content. Agencing is only possible, of course, because of our foreknowledge; but what makes it necessary is the ease with which we blot that (fore)knowledge out with "Dalmane."

For these reasons, too (distance, agencing), there is no closure; the message is never completed, the awakening always foreshadows a reawakening. "Le téléphone sonne. C'est fini," Bertrand Duquénelle writes, much too hopefully, at page 50 of a narrative of 116 pages, just as Amy Hoffman receives her call on page 77 of a 146-page book. Swimming back to bed after having been unwillingly wakened from his Dalmane-induced sleep by the call that he allows his answering machine to take, Paul Monette knows that he is just putting off a reawakening—"the desolate wakening to life alone—the calamity . . . that will not end until I do" (342). It is never over; there is no end to the business of waking and reawakening, just as (and perhaps because) trauma is the hurt that never heals.

Now, of all the historical traumas the twentieth century has undergone and witnessed, there are two that have particularly infamous, and as it were originary, status: the Holocaust is one, the so-called Great War the other. In his classic book, *The Great War and Modern Memory,* Paul Fussell made the claim for the originary character of the trench warfare of 1914–18; it established, he demonstrated, what were to be the major themes of twentieth-century sensibility (let's add, at least in the West). Certainly there have been wake-up calls through history; but it does seem that the witnessing writing that the Great War gave rise to, especially in German, French, and English—writing that happened before anyone knew, it seems, to call it "witnessing"—established some crucial parameters for the spate of witnessing writing and testimonial narratives that have been one of the legacies of our century, down to the AIDS writing that is my own particular corpus and beyond. Not, of course, that memoirs of trench warfare figure themselves as phone calls; but they do tend to conflate two important themes. These are the theme of the message of witness as a call from afar that awakens sleepers to pain, but of necessity goes on repeating, resonating endlessly (like a bugle call), and the theme of the dead who cannot rest or who refuse to lie down, so great is the injustice of their manner of dying. A theme of distant audibility; a theme of haunting. The French soldiers who were being herded to certain massacre at the infamous chemin des Dames (near Verdun) in 1916 made mooing and baaing noises as they moved up to the line; it was a way of signifying—since they had no other means of protest—that they were being led to slaughter. For me, at least, those animal noises resonate insistently in the first line of Wilfred Owen's "Anthem for Doomed Youth" ("What passing-bells for these who die as cattle?"), a poem written in 1917 that is possibly the paradigmatic witnessing text of the 1914–18 war, a poem in which, not at all coincidentally, "bugles calling for them from sad shires" (calling, that is, for "these who die as cattle") are nominated as a figure both of mourning and of witnessing. Those two major themes—of unjust death and of calling—thus come together and become inseparably associated in Owen's poem.

Was Owen thinking of the call known as "taps" in the United States and as the "last post" in other parts of the English-speaking world? Possibly, but not obviously so. More likely, the reference is to the bugles that at the front line sounded reveille and stand-to, wake-up calls and calls to alertness, at the gray hours of dawn and dusk when attack from the opposite lines was most likely and most to be feared. The strangeness of the "shires" from which they emanate designates them, clearly, as forerunners of Levi's alien *Wstawać* and of all the unwelcome phone calls that traverse AIDS writing—"shires," indeed, is an almost totally unexpected word in the context of the poem, so *English* is it (and thus anticipatory of the move toward England that occurs in the sonnet's sestet), but rhyming nevertheless with the "choirs" of demented shells (which themselves rhyme with passing-bells), and slant-rhyming—a practice highly significant in Owen's war verse—with words that aren't in the poem, like "shores" and also "shares" (an indicator of community). But perhaps the important point is that, if these bugle calls are wake-up calls and calls to alertness directed toward "us," the poem's living, surviving readers, safe at home "in England," the poem specifies with some emphasis[2] that they call "for them," that is, they call to us but in lieu of these who die as cattle. And so too, we may safely extrapolate, Levi's *Wstawać* calls *to* us, but *for* those he names the *sommersi,* those who have gone under in the camps. Similarly the phone calls in AIDS writing are agencings through which—even as they disturb *us* in our obliviousness—the voices of the dead, of Roger Horvitz, Mike Riegle, Kincaid's brother Devon, Duquénelle's lover Jean-François, and all the rest, continue to be heard, as if all the intervening technology spoke "for them."

Certainly Pat Barker understood things in this way, in writing her historical novel *Regeneration,* published in 1991—the title is as apt in its way as the translation of Levi's *La tregua* as *The Reawakening,* for it refers to the "regeneration," over time, of the capacity to experience pain. Barker imagines a scene, crucial to the novel, in which late in 1917, Wilfred Owen and Siegfried Sassoon work together on Owen's "Anthem." They are safe and warm in Craiglockhart, a hospital in Scotland, but outside a storm is rising, leading Sassoon to recall the misery of the men he has left in the trenches, exposed in all weathers. As the two men discuss the noise made by various weapons, Sassoon hears, not a bugle call, but a tapping sound at the window, which continues as, in due course, he retires to his room and sleeps. Barker here is conflating an episode of visitation related by Sassoon in his memoirs with the poem's interest in the sounds of war and its suggestion of their ability to reach as far as distant England, like a message of extremity. (The boom of cannon could in fact be clearly heard from the coast.)

> He woke to find Orme standing immediately inside the door. He wasn't surprised, he assumed Orme had come to arouse him for his watch. What did surprise him, a little, was that he seemed to be *in bed.* . . . After a while [Sassoon] remembered that Orme was dead.
>
> This clearly didn't worry Orme, who continued to stand quietly by the door. But Sassoon began to think it ought to worry him. Perhaps if he turned his head it would be all right. (*Regeneration,* 143)

Orme's visitation, then, is a wake-up call, but a deathly quiet one; it is a message from the dead, delivered (silently) by one of their number and speaking (silently) for them, like the bugles calling from strange shires in Owen's poem. It comes to one who sleeps warmly in a comfortable bed (perhaps indeed Sassoon is only dreaming that it has awakened him), and who seeks, in a way now familiar to us, to dispel it or ignore it by looking the other way. It produces "worry," an anxiety—as Sassoon's eventual decision to return to the front will suggest—that we are invited to understand as entirely salutary. But also, and this is new, the sleeper in his warm bed is transported by the coming of Orme to another scene, in which it is the bed that is the alien element: the scene of the front, so easy to forget when one is in Scotland.

Witnessing texts are like Orme's visit. Their uncanniness lies ultimately in their ability, not only to "return," as a ghost, and quietly to deliver strange, unwanted and unwonted wake-up messages from sites that are otherwise consigned to the extreme limits of consciousness, like a tapping at the window that causes an inexplicable anxiety, but also to produce this anxiety as of such a kind as to make us feel we have been transported *there,* to the scene of extremity, even as we continue to lie comfortably, warm and safe, *here.* The anxiety of waking to pain counts, at least for certain readers, as a vividly plausible mimesis, not just a "report" from the front or from an extermination camp or from the scene of a horrendous epidemic, but a means of "transport" able to make us feel that we are "there" when we are not. This hallucinatory effect of hypotyposis (vividness) is, of course, an exact reversal of the situation of foreknowledge that precedes the call: in one case, the context of "here" derealizes that of "there"; in the other, "there" becomes so vivid it makes "here" in turn feel like an oddity or an illusion. But in both cases the implication is of time "out of joint"; an uncanny conflation of there and here signifies also an eerie coincidence of past and present, an intimation of the untimely.

Of course, it isn't so, we aren't really there; like Sassoon, readers of witnessing texts tend to hope they can dispel the eerie impression of the presentness of the alien by just turning their head. But the impression can itself still leave an indelible psychic trace—an imprint—and thus have cultural valency. My students report something like this effect—of living the historical reality as a kind of vivid waking nightmare—when they read certain passages of Charlotte Delbo's *Auschwitz et après* (Auschwitz and after) or Tadeusz Borowski's story "This Way to the Gas, Ladies and Gentlemen," or when they view Tom Joslin's video *Silverlake Life.* One of the tasks I set myself in what follows is to explore the causes of the anxiety that can translate, in certain crucial instances of aesthetic reception, into the sensation (in Greek: *aisthesis*) of goosebumps and/or something approaching hallucination.

The dance critic Arlene Croce can be thought to have foreseen such a mode of reception, and to have sharply turned her head, when she heard of the performance of *Still/Here* that was being prepared by the Bill T. Jones dance company in 1993. *Still/Here* is about surviving in the face of terminal illness, and it was conceived in part as a response to the death from AIDS of Arnie Zane, Jones's long-term partner in dance and in life, proclaiming him to be also, in some important sense, "still here." Bill T. Jones had himself announced that he was HIV-positive. Misled by these facts, and more especially by false rumors that the members of the company were themselves all "AIDS victims," and understanding therefore—quite erroneously—that the dancers would be both cruelly overexerting their depleted bodies and performing the spectacle of their own mortality, Croce announced angrily in the *New Yorker* (December 1994) that she would neither attend a performance nor review it, denouncing "victim art" as a morbid aesthetic perversion, in which representation and its object were unduly conflated. This argument was a prescription for cultural Dalmane. The true circumstances, though, were otherwise, and they are interesting in themselves. They can provide us with an introductory example of how witnessing representations actually proceed, semiotically, in contradistinction to the rhetorical wake-up effect they are sometimes capable of exerting.

Jones had conceived a work on the theme of the commonality of human mortality. In preparation for it, he organized what he called Survival Workshops across the United States, with people already sick or dying from a range of fatal diseases. He coached these people through a series of exercises in which they were asked to translate into gesture and movement in space their feelings about illness and mortality, their understanding of the course of their lives, their image of the moment of their own future death. "I encouraged each of the group members to hold on to one individual as he or she 'walked us' through his or her life" (Jones, 253). To judge by the video documentary Bill Moyers produced for PBS, the signs the participants came up with were of the type that C. S. Peirce would have called *iconic:* a person who felt boxed in by disease drew rectangles around herself with her arms, one whose life had become labyrinthine darted in random directions. But Jones and his company then retranslated these gestures to make movements, "phrasing" them into the more fluid movements and gestures of choreography. "My own process involved the intuitive combining of the survivors' gestures to make phrases, plumbing my own body's imagination, or borrowing from existing forms—capoeira and karate among them—to create expressive dance sequences" (258). Quotations from the survivors' words, set to plangent music by Kenneth Fragelle ("Still") and Vernon Reid ("Here"), combined with video portraits (in "Here") and what had by now become extraordinarily inventive, indeed innovative choreography, to form a performance that appears to have been imagined as a long moment of *suspension,* suggestive of the state of being under suspended sentence that is survival, a suspension that Jones understood to imply the question: *When that part is over, what happens then?* (268).

The signs, that is, had by now ceased to function as iconic representations of the feelings of various individual survivors (a function still respected by the dancers in rehearsal, who named various attitudes, gestures, and movements after the survivors who had suggested them), in order to function *for an audience* in a way that Peirce would doubtless have classified as *indexical.* Indexical signs do not mimic their object through various forms of resemblance; they are indicators, "pointing" to an object that can only be deduced from the signs, in the way that a fire one cannot see, feel, or smell can be deduced from the presence of smoke. The smoke in this case is the dance, whose signs ask: when still/here is over, what happens then?—a question that can scarcely be ignored or avoided by anyone who attends a performance of *Still/Here,* although any answers one might venture will vary in style and content according to what Peirce would have called the "interpretants" furnished by the audience members themselves. Indexicality, then, is the semiotic category that governs what, in aesthetics and literary criticism (but *not* Peircian semiotics), is called symbolism.[3]

Now I am not trying to say that witnessing texts make use of indexical signs to the exclusion of other types of signs (*Still/Here* itself abounds in Peircean iconic and symbolic signs as well as indexical ones). My claim is rather that the cultural function of the witnessing texts themselves is indexical, in that their characteristic form of "aboutness" is indicative, "pointing" to an X that the culture's conventional means of representation are powerless, or at least inadequate, to reference, precisely because it lies at a point of supposedly distant extremity with respect to what the culture regards as its normal, and thus central, concerns. Such indexicality, I propose, as a pointing-towards that has an object, but an object by definition obscure, dubious, hard to envisage or realize, is inevitably experienced by its audience (to whom, as a wake-up call, the pointing is addressed) as a vague anxiety: what is being "said"? why is it being "said" so indirectly? (Imagine someone talking to you while casting sidewards glances in another direction . . .) The apprehension thus produced—I mean it in the double sense of the word: something that is *feared* is simultaneously *grasped*—is, in my opinion, the characteristic cultural effect of witnessing practices, an effect that can sometimes, as in the case of Arlene Croce's imagining of *Still/Here,* be reinterpreted as the uncanny mimeticism, the transportation into the other scene, that Barker describes Sassoon undergoing in *Regeneration.* My guess, furthermore, is that both the anxiety caused by witnessing's "indexical" functioning and its reinterpretation as hypervivid mimeticism are particularly likely to occur in cultures such as those of the West that have inherited a long tradition of understanding representation itself mimetically—as for example we do in legal definitions of testimony, in which the witness is expected to give an exact account of experience, or in the desire of many historians to recapture the past *wie es eigentlich gewesen* (as it really was).

Of course, it is not just that some cultures are more mimetically oriented than others, and thus particularly sensitive to—or squeamish about—witnessing effects. It should also be pointed out that there are cultures whose history has been of such a kind that they have tended to develop traditions of lamentation and resources for testimonial that other, happier cultures—such as those I am interested in in this book—do not *normally* have need of, and so have not (until recently) invented or acquired. Close to the cultures of the West, and so rather readily available on occasion for "borrowing" from, are Jewish culture, with its millennial tradition of lamentation, and (in the United States) Black culture, with its performance arts—blues, jazz, gospel, dance, etc.—forged in the long history of slavery and its many social sequels. Of his style of dancing, Bill T. Jones (141) recalls a dismissive characterization by, again, Arlene Croce: "He works himself into a tizzy"—but comments: "This 'tizzy' is something I have claimed as an inheritance." Similarly, in Marlon Riggs's extraordinary video, *Tongues Untied,* the collective repertoire of culturally Black performance art, including in this instance the poetry of Alex Hemphill and others, is deployed in the service of a breaking of silence—the silence surrounding white racism and Black homophobia, the silence that is both protective and damaging for those these social ills oppress, the silence that finally AIDS, functioning as a kind of last straw, leads them to break—an untying of tongues, then, that is also a call to awakening. Of contemporary Black witnessing one might readily say what Bill T. Jones says of his art (23): "Rebellion I always knew. Transgression I have had to learn."

But consider also the case of Rigoberta Menchú, whose *I, Rigoberta Menchú (Me llamo Rigoberta Menchú, y así me nació la conciencia)* founded the Spanish-language, Latin (especially Central) American genre known as *testimonio.* In her book we quickly learn that there is a tradition in her Quiché-speaking, Mayan culture of what might be called cultural induction. Babies at birth, children turning ten, couples marrying are solemnly addressed by parents and other representatives of the community, who speak to them of the dire conditions of existence, the folly of expecting one's dreams to be realized, the responsibilities one has toward others; it is a kind of lesson in the solidarity of suffering. Of one such moment, in which the post-Conquest history of the indigenous people of Central America is rehearsed, Menchú says (67): "This is, in part, a recalling of history and, in part, a call to awareness." This is a clear reference, of course, to her own coming to consciousness; but it would also be hard to define more economically the point of her having sought out the anthropologist Elizabeth Burgos-Debray in Paris, with the purpose of entrusting to her, for transmission, eventually, to a worldwide audience, Menchú's own garrulous and seemingly all-encompassing narrative about the life of her people. Her idea has been simply to extend to a cross-cultural audience—for which purpose she learned Spanish—a practice already familiar to her own people, performing in this way a form of translation and, as Jones might say, of transgression. But *recalling* history, *calling* to awareness—that is, awakening to pain—also constitute a good definition of what the genre of witnessing writing, as a whole, is all about, even though the word *witness* itself is foreign to Menchú's vocabulary.[4]

There are other cultures, though, and these are my main concern in what follows, in which the need to witness may be quite frequently experienced—as was the case in the West throughout the twentieth century and indeed the whole history of industrial and capitalist modernity—but without discursive models of witnessing coming readily to hand. These are the cultures in which drastic failures of justice, decency, tolerance, humaneness—of "culture" itself in one of its senses, in which it is synonymous with civilization—are experienced, not so much as part of an everyday experience of misery (as AIDS is added to homophobia and racism or to the harshness of ghetto existence, in urban America; or as military and judicial violence, torture and rape are added, among Menchú's people, to ordinary daily oppression and exploitation), but as something *unique,* without precedent and consequently unspeakable. Trench warfare seemed like that to all the combatants, but especially to the very young members of the officer class who were exposed alongside their working-class men to its unmitigated rigors, in the carnage of, most particularly, 1916, 1917, and 1918. The Holocaust and more generally the concentration camp system were so experienced, in Nazi Germany and then in Nazi-occupied Europe, first by its victims, and then, especially after April 1945, by a horrified and incredulous world. HIV disease, which has raged and continues to rage in many parts of the world (central Africa, South and Southeast Asia, the

Caribbean, and Brazil) as an epidemic of immense proportions that is virtually out of control, was experienced—and described in innumerable witnessing texts—as a unique visitation by members of the largely middle-class or middle-class-oriented gay male communities of large Western cities like Paris, London, New York, San Francisco, or Sydney during the 1980s and into the 1990s. These are cultures in which, simultaneously and for convergent reasons, traditions of witnessing are rare, while it remains relatively easy for "unaffected" majorities (domestic populations at the time of the Great War; those outside of the range of the Axis powers in 1939–45; nongay, non-IV-drug-using, middle-class white populations in the West) to sleep on, more or less blissfully oblivious or indifferent to, and undisturbed by, what is nevertheless *happening,* or has happened to others, at the limits of their culturally blinded awareness. And these, then, are the kinds of cultures, with special reference to the problematic situation of the writing of AIDS witnessing in France, North America, and Australia, to which my book is devoted.

I have met the missing link, writes Midas Dekkers in substance (142), and it is us. According to a widespread perception, human evolution has resulted in a hybrid species, neither simply animal in nature nor yet fully or genuinely cultured, if culture signifies civilized or humane, in contradistinction to animal. Culture, this perception goes, chronically fails us, therefore, as we lapse into animalistic behavior unworthy of our own best ideals. However, try as one might to write this problem of hybridity in terms of a nature-culture distinction, the evidence is always that the brutalities, atrocities, and acts of violence of which humans are so obviously capable are themselves the products, not of an animal nature, but of culture—of culture, that is, in the sense of the general mediator of relations, or as Raymond Williams more colloquially put it, a "whole way of life." It is culture as way of life that keeps failing culture as civilization. United States culture condones and underwrites the jurisprudence of revenge (punitive sentencing, capital punishment), the scourge of homelessness, the continuing injustices that arise from the history of slavery and the colonization of the country, and other forms of social and economic discrimination. The Great War was a product, on the one hand, of cultural phenomena—of European nationalisms, including international and colonial rivalries—and on the other of greatly advanced technological resources for warfare. The Holocaust, which is sometimes understood theologically as a manifestation of pure Evil, is unthinkable without cultural preconditions such as a political philosophy of totalitarianism, forms of racism that emerged during the nineteenth century, the economic history of Weimar Germany, and highly developed organizational and technological capacities for moving and destroying vast numbers of people. AIDS, which feels to some like a scourge of God and to others like an accident of nature, likewise has the culture of modernity as its precondition: its origins appear to lie in the colonial and postcolonial modernization of Africa, which shrank the habitat of simian species and brought them into close contact with humans, as well as in the avenues of rapid communication (highways, the movement of armies in war, air travel) that ensured the virus's epidemic and in some cases pandemic spread through human populations. HIV disease piggybacks also on poverty and what used to be known euphemistically as "uneven development," on prostitution and the traffic in women, on sexual tourism, on the drug trade (particularly the trade in heroin), on governmental irresponsibility, squeamishness, puritanism, indifference, and denial (on these factors in Southeast Asia see Beyrer). Nor would AIDS be the disease it is without the social effects of stigma, shame, and discrimination that it generates almost universally. The human animal is cultural all the way through.

But if culture (as way of life) is responsible for these kinds of failures of "culture," it is "culture" (as civilization) that requires such disturbing events to be treated, not as evidence of a chronic deficiency or of arrested evolutionary development, but as merely occasional or exceptional lapses, accidental happenings that can be explained by special circumstances and rare contingencies and are therefore able to be minimized, marginalized, dismissed, or forgotten by those who have the luxury of judging them to be remote from their own lives and circumstances, and hence irrelevant (on "states" of denial, see Cohen). What witnessing texts—like calls from the hospital, an alien *Wstawać,* bugles calling from strange shires—therefore work to require us to acknowledge is that the "alien" scene, the "other" context, is *also* a part of culture, and thus relevant to the very context in which the form of communication we call witnessing arises. Witnessing is, in that sense, an ethical practice (rarely much politicized, except in the case of the Latin American genre of *testimonio*) that seeks to inculcate a sense of shared (because cultural) responsibility that it is only too easy—for other cultural reasons—to deny. And it is because of the facility with which relevance, responsibility, and involvement can be denied—because of the ready availability of cultural Dalmane—that witnessing, like a wake-up call, takes the form of seeking to cause some *disturbance* in well-established cultural regularities and routines: routines of thought (or its absence), regularities of discursive habitus.

In Bill T. Jones's vocabulary, then, it is a matter of transgression: something grounded in rebellion but that one has to learn how to do. It requires a certain knack or skill, forms of know-how or savoir faire, but also (as I'll propose later) of making do or bricolage. Bill T. Jones's "rebellion" might be thought of, then, in witnessing terms, as a first ethical moment: that of the withholding of one's assent in the face of injustice, barbarity, atrocity, a withholding that is witnessing's essential precondition, taking as it often does the form of a desire or need, an urge or urgency, to *tell the story.* But the second ethical moment of witnessing is that of one's actual coming to witnessing, when one takes on the task of cultural transgression that is required, in an environment of complacency (the comfortable sense of being at home; full bellies; the illusion that the story has already been satisfactorily told), if one is to *get the story across.* What it takes to have the story attended to or, in the strong sense of the word, heard.

In the chapters to come I will go into some detail about the nature of the cultural transgression witnessing texts perform, using the vocabulary of a modernized version of classical rhetoric: a theory of the appropriability of genres and of the instrumentality of figuration. What I have wanted to sketch in this preface, though, is why that theory matters, why it may sometimes (often) be appropriate to disturb genre expectations, and to make use of the tricks and turns of troping, things of which honest folks are often, and understandably, suspicious. It matters because the occasions on which—with increasing frequency, it seems—"culture" lets us down are the occasions on which human culture reveals something crucial about itself: an essential fault-line running through it, or a "dark side" that is not accidental but rather constitutive, definitional. The violence "culture" pretends to hold at bay is actually something that culture is itself perfectly capable of producing, something that it does produce, qua culture, with frightening regularity. It is worth noticing, I think, that witnessing texts very rarely fall into the easy moralism of "this atrocity must never be allowed to happen again." They are too realistic, and perhaps too honest for that. Their point, and occasionally their explicit burden, is rather that such an atrocity—the same or another—*can* always happen again; it can happen any time, *now* or *now* or *now* (as Amy Hoffman puts it), and it does. *That* is what we need to know and acknowledge—if only we can be awakened sufficiently from the effects of cultural Dalmane to take it in; *that* is why the untimely interventions of testimonial are needed, *again* and *again* and *again.*

Preface

All day long, on September 11, 2001, as we waited for the president to speak and he did not appear, the journalists, thinking on their feet, told us that this was the day when America lost its innocence. Such a phrase, in theory, can only be pronounced once—or at least in relation to only one event—so it was odd that I had the sense of having heard it many times before. Didn't we lose our innocence in Oklahoma City? Or at Waco? At Columbine? Wasn't it Vietnam that dispelled our illusions? Before that Pearl Harbor? The Great Depression? Back in the nineteenth century, the Civil War had already been experienced as a loss of innocence. And if we did not lose our innocence until 2001, does that mean we were innocent of slavery?

The kind of society in which innocence is lost and regained regularly (I'm not sure there is any other) is what I call an aftermath society, one regulated by a culture in which collectively traumatic events are denied, and if necessary denied again.[5] This is the case whether the deniers be sufferers, perpetrators, or bystanders in relation to the event and whether the denial bear on the event's injustice, the sense of guilt it produces, or the pain of its aftermath. The denial can take any number of forms, from the categorical denegation ("It never happened") to the strategic *but* ("It happened, but it did not have the character that has been attributed to it," or "It happened, but we are united and strong"). Stanley Cohen has recently catalogued these forms. But denial, when you think about it, is not the same thing as the event's never having happened, or the inexistence of the ensuing pain. Denial ensures a perpetually renewable state of cultural innocence, but it does so at the cost of inevitably betraying some knowledge of the injustice, the guilt, or the pain that the act of denial fails (or refuses) to acknowledge, and of which it is, therefore, as Freud taught us, a symptom. Cohen (253) tells the story of an Indonesian student in the United States who learned of the bloodbaths in her country's postindependence history by receiving from her embassy a letter containing tips about how to "spin" this issue should it arise in conversation in her presence. So such cultures of denial are simultaneously sites of survival, in which the definition of trauma as the hurt that does not heal holds true, even in the effort the culture makes to hold its trauma at bay and assert its innocence. A sense of the pain, the injustice, the suffering, and the guilt inevitably returns, like a phone call cutting through Dalmane, or like a tacit acknowledgment piggybacking on an explicit denegation.

Aftermath cultures—a category conceivably coextensive with culture itself—are thus defined by a strange nexus of denial and acknowledgment of the traumatic such that innocence can be lost and regained over and over. For if denial functions as a readable symptom of collective pain, acknowledgment of the pain is inevitably conditioned, in turn, by the atmosphere of denial in which it arises and with which it must negotiate: the pastness of the event, its apparent insignificance relative to the affairs of the present, the obliviousness in which most people seem to manage, without difficulty, to live. Acknowledgment will therefore always seem inadequate in relation to the known magnitude of the event because it is necessarily a matter of counterdenial, involving indirection, deferment, appropriation, makeshift devices of indexicality that function—as in the case of denial—as a symptom of a certain reality, but not the reality "itself." Thus, like the affirmative statement in a negation ("No, I did not take the plums from the refrigerator"), it acquires a kind of smuggled-in quality. Monette is initially able to defer the unwanted message from the hospital by allowing his answering machine to pick up. But in so doing he ensures that the following morning, when the Dalmane will have worn off a little, it will still be, obstinately, there, although still deferred.

The survival of the traumatic, then—trauma's failure to heal—takes the form in aftermath culture of "surviving trauma," a phrase that might be allowed to imply both the fact of one's having survived a traumatic event and the contrary fact of the pain's surviving into the present, the fact that one has not survived it so much as one is (still) surviving it. In this sense, surviving trauma is an experience that is traumatic in itself, because it is the experience of the trauma's not being over when one wishes it to be in the past: as an after-math of an initial "math" (the etymological metaphor is of a second mowing of grass in the same season as the first), it is a repetition—in transformed guise—of the initial traumatic event. Thus we shall see at some length (in chapter 5) that Charlotte Delbo's title *Auschwitz et après* (Auschwitz and after) signals simultaneously that Auschwitz *is* in the past, and that between after-Auschwitz and Auschwitz there is nevertheless a kind of equivalence. The word *aftermath,* then, although it is regularly taken to refer to the sequential relation of a cause to its consequences, can also be taken to signal a strange dedifferentiation of the received categories that divide time into past, present, and future and make cause and consequences distinguishable.

And it is not solely that the past, in this way, fails to pass, but that the present itself was already also part of the past. For those who "have survived" (are surviving) Auschwitz, Auschwitz was already the experience of surviving Auschwitz (unlike the many who did not survive it), so that Auschwitz itself was a forerunner of the experience of surviving Auschwitz (not of "having survived" Auschwitz) that defines the traumatic character of aftermath. Primo Levi, for example, refers to the predictive after-Auschwitz nightmares that were part and parcel of the trauma of the camp. It seems, then, that *untimeliness* of this kind, the breakdown of reassuring categories that place trauma and survival of trauma in separate compartments, is of the essence in aftermath and consequently a prime object of aftermath denial (and hence of testimonial affirmation). Which in turn means that such untimeliness is of the essence also with respect to trauma itself, which—for those who have once experienced, and continue to experience trauma as the pain, not just of being traumatized but also of surviving a traumatizing event, of having failed as it were to succumb to it in the way that, in Auschwitz, the so-called *Muselmänner,* Levi's "sommersi," succumbed—becomes almost indistinguishable from the aftermath of trauma, and the difficulty of returning "from" trauma to an untraumatized life.

Aftermath's potential for dedifferentiation does not stop at such untimeliness, however. The class of those who "have survived" and so are surviving Auschwitz extends readily enough, not only to former prisoners but also to all those who, by outliving the camp unlike those the camp destroyed, have inherited the burden of living (in the wake of) such an event. Thus in aftermath former victims, perpetrators and bystanders, who once had quite distinct roles to play, all have in common the burden of surviving; and this is true not only of those among the bystanders who were aware of Auschwitz at the time but also of those who were unaware of it; and not only of Auschwitz's contemporaries but of members of following generations as well. All are, in a certain seemingly infinitely elastic sense, Auschwitz survivors, so that distinctions that may once have been relevant and do remain helpful, perhaps also comforting (because they tend to confine the event and its effects), tend simultaneously to break down and to blur. Similarly, too, among all these survivors, those who have taken a good strong dose of antitrauma Dalmane and those who are more readily attentive to the evidence of pain's survival have in common the conditions of aftermath that these attitudes reflect, and must acknowledge their participation in a culture that makes acknowledgers of deniers and deniers of acknowledgers. In such ways aftermath makes trouble with all the differentiating categories to which survivors might cling. Anyone's *now* has the potential to feel like an *again,* because innocence, once lost, can be and is lost again and again.

That said, the class of the former victims, from which the authors of much (but not all) testimonial writing come, has one particularizing trait that cannot be overstressed. *Their* education in trauma, unlike that of other survivors, has involved extremely close proximity, a proximity not only physical but also moral and psychological, with those who did not survive the trauma. Their preferred self-identification, then, is less with the survivors Delbo calls "the living," among whom they too live on, than with those whom the event destroyed in the most literal of senses, and who are often described therefore, particularly by victim-survivors, as its real victims. For these victim-survivors, to be surviving Auschwitz now is—as it was then—to have betrayed/be betraying those who, in Auschwitz, went under, Levi's category of "the submerged." And consequently it is to know the continuance of pain, the failure of the trauma to heal, in a way much more intense and much more troubling than others who live on are capable of imagining, because the pain of surviving is doubled by the guilt of having outlived others who didn't, with the result that those of the living who are not also surviving victims inevitably seem, to victim-survivors, uncomprehending and dismissive, oblivious of trauma's reality. Which in turn means that victim-survivors bear a brunt of denial and undergo the pain of having their own history denied, to a degree that causes many to fall silent (cf. Wajnryb) and some to turn to testimonial writing (and other forms of witness), but simultaneously leads very many among them, in contrast with those who appear to have forgotten the dead and even to be indifferent to their fate, to identify most characteristically, in their heart of hearts, with those to whom they remain loyal—as loyal as their sense of having betrayed them is intense.

And such identification *with* the dead amounts finally, for many victim-survivors, to a self-identification *as* dead. Dead because one's personal history, vividly present as it is to oneself, is bafflingly irrelevant and unreal in the eyes of others. But strangely, weirdly dead too because, unlike the real dead, one has in common with the living survivors the fact of being still alive, and of suffering all the pain of survival. "It seems to me I'm not alive," writes Mado in the third volume of Delbo's trilogy (*Auschwitz and After,* 257). "Since all are dead, it seems impossible I shouldn't be also." And in the slash in Bill T. Jones's title, *Still/Here,* it seems to me necessary to read that very *particular* pain of survival, which is the pain of a double continuity, with the dead and the living, combined with a double separation, from the living but also from the dead, with whom one nevertheless identifies and who are, so to speak, one's closest kin, as is death itself.

These survivors, like all survivors, are haunted, but unlike most of us they *know* themselves to be haunted. Their task as bearers of this knowledge, when they turn to witnessing, will consequently be one that is, for them, both doubly necessary and doubly problematic. As a matter of loyalty to the dead, the task is to give them the presence among the living that is denied them (the presence to which the survival of victim-survivors, the living dead, is witness), but as a matter of duty to the living (with whom survivor-victims share the fact of survival) it is to make perceptible to the living, despite the power of denial, the presence of the dead—and hence of death—among the living, a presence that signifies the continuance in aftermath of pain. Or, to put it another way, their task is to transmit their own sense of aftermath (as a state of acknowledged hauntedness) to those survivors who seem not to know, or at least to fail to acknowledge, that they too, as survivors, are haunted. To become the ghosts, themselves haunted, who haunt the living with their own hauntedness. To enact the dedifferentiation they suffer as victim-survivors, between living and being dead, as a dedifferentiation, rendered perceptible to the living, between the living and the dead, the dedifferentiation of aftermath as "surviving trauma."

But if testimonial writers are, in this way, ghosts who haunt because they are haunted, it becomes evident that the category of victim-survivors that they represent is extensible to all others among the living to whom the proximity of the dead, and of death, may be or become similarly palpable. To those, for example, who, still undergoing a primary trauma (people in the final stages of AIDS, men in the trenches of 1914–18, people herded into the ghettoes of occupied Poland), may feel that they are themselves already dead or as good as dead, classifiable and classified as they are, as *morituri,* among the dead although still able to act among the living (and in that sense, in the threshold situation of ghosts). These are frequently diary writers or—in the trenches, or among AIDSers in North America—poets, and their writing has the urgency that leads me to refer, in this book (see part I) to "discourses of extremity." Equally, however, those who themselves identify with those who, in this or other ways, self-identify with the dead and share with them a common trauma and the sense of a common burden, are likewise ghosts motivated to haunt because they are haunted; and such are those testimonialists who, writing in the genres I call "dual" and "collective" autobiography, share with other haunted souls and seek to make perceptible to the oblivious (who know but do not acknowledge the hauntedness of aftermath) their identificatory sense of what I will call (in part II) "phantom pain." What I think is common to all those who come to testimonial in these and similar circumstances, and what I hope will become sensible also to readers of this book, is therefore this: experiencing their own survivorhood as burdened with what Delbo calls "useless knowledge"—that is, the weight of the dead—all such haunted survivors are conscious of themselves, simultaneously, as physically marginal and/or morally *marginalized* in the space of the living (relegated to the edge of things) and *residual* in time (left over from another time because as good as dead). It is from this marginal(ized) and/or residual position—which, I hope to suggest, they seek to transform into positions of "obscenity" and "untimeliness"—that they write. Thus Harold Brodkey, for example (see chapter 1), writes as one who, still alive and *able* therefore, to write, but no longer the protagonist of his story, occupies, as he says, the position of a "rock in the garden."

But a rock in the garden that writes has odd powers. A *moriturus* like Brodkey, faced with death-at-the-door, may well be capable of giving readers a sense that what is happening to him is also happening to them; I mean that the felt proximity of death that makes Brodkey a residual figure is not without relevance to others less conscious of that proximity but to whom it can be made, through writing, as close as it is to him. Writing, that is, is capable of transforming the marginality/residuality of the witness into an experience of *liminality*—the death-at-your-doorstep effect—that can be felt, in turn, by readers. A discourse of extremity, the vehicle of phantom pain, functions, or seeks to function, for its readers, as an agent of threshold experience; it is a mediating instance that, like a ghost, makes possible, or wants to make possible, a form of contact or encounter between, on the one hand, the living—those from whom the victim-survivor/witness is alienated but who inevitably constitute the text's addressee—and on the other the phenomenon of death, with which the haunted victim-survivor/witness, already counted like Brodkey as dead, is identified. Thus it is the text that haunts, rather than the author, because it takes a rhetorical intervention to transform an author's sense of residuality into readerly liminality. But it haunts by making available to reading, in this way, the hauntedness that impels the author to write. As a consequence the textual haunting of the living by the dead may outlive "the death of the author" in the literal sense of that phrase, thanks to the same phrase's theoretical implications, as I proposed in my earlier book on AIDS diaries (Chambers 1998b).

So, setting aside for now the question of marginality and the obscene, to which I'll return in chapter 1, let me briefly point out here that because in aftermath cultures the fact of survival, as in "surviving trauma," is crucial because definitional, the category of the residual, which *manifests* survival (endows it with meaning), is both central and deeply contested. We must think in this respect not only of residual people like victim-survivors and residual phenomena like memories, but also of residual places and objects, which can be seen as either insignificant and easily dismissed (in conformity with the phenomenon of denial), or alternatively as liminal and, therefore, untimely. So too with writing, when it works to manifest survival in a culture given over to denial. Writing that seeks to liminalize the residual is readily dismissed, most usually on the grounds that its representation of events is inadequate and even suspect: it is traversed, that is, by the very effects of denial that it seeks to counter. But it can also be understood, on what are in fact closely related grounds, not as insignificant but as significant and even hypersignificant, in that it has a power to signify that operates culturally as the power of hauntedness to haunt. For the hauntedness of such writing, that is, the loss or lack that it makes manifest, derives specifically from its inability to represent, a function of the mechanisms of denial that, as I've briefly said and will illustrate at some length in this book, has the effect of making the return of the traumatic a matter of assemblage and indexicality, implying indirection and deferment, appropriation and bricolage—that is, of inflicting a kind of death on the author, understood as the master of language's power to represent.

In short, the potential power of the residual to become haunting is realized through writing that rewrites its own representational inadequacy as an index of the survival that is denied, and thus as the haunting power to become a marker of liminality. The kind of indexicality I am referring to is known in rhetoric as troping or figuration, the "turning" of speech from direct representation in the direction of symbolic utterance. It is as spectral evidence of a past that is still, surprisingly and even weirdly, present that the residual, made liminal through writing that is more figural than it is directly representational, can function culturally as a surviving indicator through which the reality of trauma and injustice, so readily denied, can be made inescapably, and sometimes very vividly, to "return" from the oblivion to which the power of denial tends to consign it, and to "happen" to those who read.

Perhaps you have noticed that the ringing of a telephone—a mostly conventionalized indexical sign—can readily be ignored and even go virtually unnoticed, although it signifies that someone wishes to speak to us. But on certain occasions—if it is in some way untimely, if it persists, for example, or occurs in the middle of the night, or seems to confirm a premonition or even to respond to a kind of foreknowledge, as in the examples of Paul Monette, Jamaica Kincaid, and Amy Hoffman that I've mentioned—it can disturb us, jolting us out of complacency and habit and into a kind of wakefulness, even though we may not have been literally asleep. The sound of the phone confirms, perhaps, a nagging anxiety, or brings sudden and unexpected awareness of danger, disaster, or loss. And some people, I among them, are particularly disturbed when they respond to the ring, pick up the phone, and hear only silence on a nevertheless open line. It is as if, in those cases, the indexical works by indicating something, let's call it "news," that, however, it does not specify, but only signals. In response to such signaling we must attend to something, but without knowing, necessarily, much more than that we must attend. When Bill T. Jones worked with the iconic representations he had learned from patients in his Survival Workshops and transformed these readily readable signs into the indexical choreography of *Still/Here,* he was quite similarly focusing our attention as spectators and directing it toward something to which the choreography referred but that perhaps neither he nor we could formulate. This something was thus rendered readable, but in a sense considerably more disturbing than the much easier interpretability of the patients' signs he had started with. I would say he was enacting as *liminally significant*—that is, haunting—the state of residuality designated by the words "still/here," of which the patients had given a less troubling, albeit quite dramatic, iconic representation.

In so doing, he asked his audience (signaled them) to attend to a signified that "lay beyond" the threshold of the choreographed gestures, movements, groupings and images, the phrasings of dance. In this he was apparently confident that we could acknowledge as (fore)known to us—recognizable and hence familiar—something that was being given to us as beyond the reach, precisely, of more conventional representations, as if the dancing was an extremely complex equivalent of one of those intrusive and untimely phone calls in the night that remind us of the reasons we have to be anxious but do not designate them. It figured for us that which eludes representation in its ordinary modes, because through denial it is lost to or lacking in those modes. For figuration is the way what poets sometimes call the "silence" that makes language haunted becomes—through language—haunting. I am committed, then, in what follows, to theorizing how it is that figural discourse, like the choreography of *Still/Here,* can give us more to be read than language conventionally permits us to say, how it utters what is unstatable, and does so by making of that inability-to-state the actual object of its utterance—what signals us to attend—as Bill T. Jones made it the object of his choreography.

Meanwhile, if testimonial writing is a way of rewriting insignificant residuality into hypersignificant liminality, it is perhaps worth pointing out that the reverse of this process of haunting will be familiar to many readers. Over a period of time, residual objects that have liminal significance can become merely insignificant. Such is the case, for example, when a person to whom we are close dies. The objects left behind—a toothbrush, say, or medical equipment, or items of clothing—acquire at first an uncanny presence. As metonymies of the person they become metaphors of the loss we have undergone, signifying simultaneously in this way both the person and the person's loss. The deceased is oddly present, *and* absent, all at once. But the process of mourning, a form of denial by which the loss is integrated into our own psychic development and ends up "forgotten," causes these haunted and haunting objects to revert, eventually, to a status of insignificance or near-insignificance. The medical equipment gets returned to the supplier, the shoes are given away, the toothbrush ends up in the trash. They have lost their liminal character and become simply residual.

Aftermath cultures, though, are melancholic in character; in them, mourning can never really be complete for the reason that trauma, although it has happened and has the status of a historical event, is never over. And we know that years later, rummaging in a little-used drawer or prowling the attic, we can come upon an object—some trinket, perhaps—that reminds us of the person who died, and be re-minded—overcome with unexpected, and unexpectedly strong, emotion. We are shaken, perhaps we weep uncontrollably, more grief-stricken than ever. This re-minding is the phenomenon that witnessing writing seeks to bring about—but it does so for people we never knew, for people who underwent extremity before we were born, perhaps, or in a remote place and under circumstances we might not previously have thought relevant to our own lives, and for whom we have therefore never really mourned. Our forgetting was only the illusion of their having been forgotten, our mourning a sham mourning. For the injustice has not been repaired, and perhaps it is irreparable. The pain survives.

Sheshy, to whom this book is dedicated, returned to me, as I worked on it, in much this way. A residual person, long forgotten, she nevertheless became for me an index of the long history of Aboriginal dispossession and suffering in my native Australia, a history I knew and thought I had grieved over but had never previously been forced to acknowledge, as personally *close* to me, until that moment of Sheshy's return, which was triggered by my reading of a report on what is known in Australia as the "stolen children"—a report not coincidentally entitled *Bringing Them Home.* In the dusty farming town in southwestern New South Wales in which I spent part of my childhood, she lived alone, an elderly Koori apparently without family or friends, in a tiny cottage—almost a shack—not far from my parents' house, amid a sea of white people (well, actually more of a puddle, perhaps). She helped my mother in the house occasionally, and sometimes babysat us kids. Her name, presumably, was Mrs. Shepherd, which points to (indexes) the generation of indigenous people who found themselves forced off the land of which they had guardianship and obliged, without access to water, to indenture themselves and work, under conditions ranging from condescending paternalism to extreme exploitation, on the new settlers' sheep-stations. I loved Sheshy. But when my family moved on—I was perhaps nine by then—I of course forgot her, as children do. And she returned, a good sixty years later, to make an untimely, spectral intervention in my tranquil affairs. I hope it's fair to say she hasn't left since.

It has long seemed to me that what we in the humanities call research, certainly the kind of research I do, is very largely a matter of educating oneself. One passes on the results in the hope that they may be helpful to others engaged in the same task. For of course others contribute to one's self-education at least as much as, and probably more than, one puts into it oneself. It is anything but a purely individual or solipsistic practice.

This book is also about education, as it happens—most explicitly so in the chapters (2 and 8) in which, symmetrically, I address the question of the witness's education (and of testimonial as an account of the education of a witness) and the issue of the kind of education in reading that might best respond to the nature of testimonial writing. The matter of my own education, however, I address here, by way of thanking those who have contributed to it, some of whom I can name, while I will have, regrettably, to leave many others unnamed. Such people are easy to recognize if not always easy to identify, so true is it that sometimes one learns best by explaining things to others, while what others teach us is usually an effect of *après-coup,* absorbed unconsciously and as it were inattentively, only to surface later (by which time it feels like a perception of our own). Sheshy, in this respect, would be my archetypical educator. But so too are all the testimonial writers whose books I've read and the growing number of scholarly writers who have discussed them, the many colleagues and friends who have asked helpful questions or made thought-provoking comments on formal occasions or over coffee, and the very large number of students who wrote diaries, reaction-papers, and term papers whose honesty helped to keep *me* honest in class, and who—with sharply angled questions and observations, with body language, and the very patience with which they heard me out—kept me on my toes in other ways.

Some of the institutions at which I was privileged to teach courses or to give lectures are the University of Toronto, the Universities of Queensland and Melbourne and Monash University in Australia, the Université du Québec à Montréal, the University of British Columbia, the University of London and the University of Bristol in the United Kingdom, the University of Colorado at Boulder, Northwestern University, Emory University, the Institut d'Etudes Françaises d'Avignon (Bryn Mawr), Louisiana State University and, of course, my home institution, the University of Michigan, which further subsidized my work by agreeing to employ me half-time for a few years preceding my retirement. But institutions, of course, are really people, and so I give warm thanks for their help and hospitality, to Roland Le Huenen, Linda Hutcheon, Anne Freadman, Peter Cryle, Helen Tiffin, Joanne Tompkins, Tony Stephens, Philip Anderson, Hector Maclean, Martine Delvaux, Sima Godfrey, Shirley Neuman, Michael Worton, Jean-Pierre Boulé, Murray Pratt, the late Jill Forbes, Warren Motte, Mireille Rosello, Michal Ginsburg, Michael Johnson, Lara Eastburn, Nathaniel Wing, Jeff Humphries, Brigitte Mahuzier, Lincoln Faller, Patricia Yaeger, David Halperin, and Tobin Siebers. People who encouraged me by soliciting work for publication include Roland Le Huenen, Michael Worton, Martine Delvaux and Nancy Miller. Some of the many students from whom I have borrowed ideas are named appreciatively at appropriate moments in what follows.

For more specific intellectual help as well as moral encouragement, let me begin by naming Keith Thomas, who has probably forgotten that he encouraged me to give testimonial poetry a place in my work (which, I know, remains haunted by the absence of Celan). It was *Testimony,* by Shoshana Felman and Dori Laub, that first interested me in witnessing writing, and I have been stimulated more recently by Shoshana's work on "trials of the century," which shows how the genre of the trial can be, and is, taken over by a witnessing function. Toward the end of my work, the coincidence of reading, in the same month, Peter Carey's *Thirty Days in Sydney* and Ruth Wajnryb's *The Silence* while team-teaching a course on autobiography with Anne Freadman and Sergio Holás helped me to draw together some final threads having to do with the character of aftermath cultures. In between, Aaron Nathan was still officially an undergraduate when he forced me to think through the implications of the "ideology of civilization" (as I, not he, came to call it). Alexandre Dauge-Roth wrote a dissertation on French-language AIDS writing from which I took copious notes and have borrowed an epigraph. I had crucial conversations with David Halperin (about "flaunting the haunt"), Tobin Siebers (about disability and indexicality), and on a number of pleasant occasions with Patricia Yaeger (about aesthetic pleasure and real pain, about trauma and survival, about *Dirt and Desire*). Vaheed Ramazani's work on the interrelation of sublimity and irony in the writing of historical pain in nineteenth-century France fed into my thinking about the nexus of denial and acknowledgment and hence underlies my conception of aftermath. Tom Trezise kindly made available to me his deeply reflective work in progress on Charlotte Delbo's *Auschwitz et après,* and Mireille Rosello bolstered my confidence when I was writing chapter 8 by permitting me to read an advance copy of her book *Postcolonial Hospitality: The Immigrant as Guest.* I do not know how to thank Martine Delvaux for the example and inspiration of her work: she is inventing a way of writing about testimonial that is itself a form of testimonial and a writing of pain.

If all these people, along with others I do not name, have constituted a kind of intellectual support team—a bit like the nurses and doctors who surround the patient's gurney in ER with a whole armamentarium of drips and manipulations and treatments—my "dial 911" or emergency response team consists of three indispensable paramedics, without whose help I could not have written this book. Steven Spalding has been an exemplary research assistant, without whose technical help the enterprise would have fallen victim to my own technoplegia. David Caron, who has a specialist's knowledge of the cultural and political scene in France, including most notably "AIDS culture," has assiduously—and tactfully—made good my informational and intellectual gaps, deficiencies, and dysfunctions, supplying references, lending books, tracking the Internet, reading drafts, correcting slips and errors, keeping me informed, and through his own work supplying me with needed frameworks of thought, notably concerning disaster and the nature of communities, including their vexed political status. Together with Alex Herrero, whom I hereby thank also as a deeply valued friend, David has kept me going, in ways small and great.

Anne Freadman, for her part, has made a contribution—also a combination of moral and intellectual support—that feels to me like a kind of coau-

thorship, although I am sure she would repudiate the
any case the book's faults are all my own). Anne is alwa
her encouragement is never empty; her criticisms are ri
formulated, and always helpful. Her own work in the
course (rhetoric, semiotics, culture) has been my most re
matters relating to genre and to the work of C. S. Peir
companion. She has been a generous reader of my m
countless conversations we have tried out ideas on each
intellectual advantage and I hope occasionally to hers.
jamin Wilkomirski, which became the fulcrum on wh
ventions turns, was written for her; a draft of the chapter
forthcoming book *The Machinery of Talk* (Stanford Un
for me a major intellectual turning point out of which
tural role of testimonial writing emerged. Inevitably,
vasive is underacknowledged in what follows—indeed
underacknowledged in what precedes; perhaps these fe
what repair that injustice.

Acknowledgments

An early version of the better part of chapter 4 appea
nessing as a Cultural Practice: Pascal de Duve's *Cargo*
of a Trope," in the *Journal of the Institute of Romance Stu*
I thank the editors for permission to reproduce this m

Sections 2 and 3 of chapter 5 are a revised version o
ries, Foster Writing, Phantom Pain," in *Extremities: Tr*
Community, ed. Nancy K. Miller and Jason Tougaw (U
Illinois Press, 2002), 92–111. I thank the editors and
sion to republish.

For permission to reproduce two photographs from
(Allan and *Candlelight Vigil)* I am grateful to Willian
Unwin. The photograph of Eric Michaels in chapter
permission of Paul Foss, of the Foundation for Intern
Inc.

"Anthem for Doomed Youth," by William Owen,
Poems of Wilfred Owen, copyright © 1963 Chatto
reprinted in chapter 3 by permission of New Directi
poration.

"Survivors," from *Collected Poems of Siegfried Sassoon*

Contents

1. Death at the Door

The trouble with death-at-your-doorstep
is that it is happening to you.
—Harold Brodkey, *This Wild Darkness*

Knocking at the Door

In August 1944, Robert Antelme was arrested in France as an agent of the Resistance and deported to Buchenwald, a political prisoner in the Reich. From there he was assigned to a work detail supplying slave labor to a factory at Gandersheim, some distance from the main camp. An intellectual with no trade skills, he was lucky to wangle his way inside the factory as a sweeper. Dirty and malodorous, dressed in rags and increasingly emaciated, the slaves were treated by the factory's civilian employees as either subhuman or invisible or both; they were given orders, sometimes curtly told to get out of the way *(Weg!),* and beaten or shouted at when they incurred anger. That was it.

As he tells it in *L'Espèce humaine* (The human race), he was sent one day to sweep "upstairs." There he found himself, cap in hand, in a large office where a woman handed him a broom and pointed at the floor. Ignored by her, he began to work. But new to the job of sweeping and perhaps also, as he says, performing a bit, he worked slowly and clumsily, moving gradually toward her feet as she stood, now looking everywhere except at him. She had "noticed" him, and finally could stand the tension no longer. "Schnell, schnell, Monsieur," she burst out (note the "Monsieur"). But Antelme continued his laborious progress until she snatched the broom and began to do the job herself, while *he* now stood in the middle of the room, hands on hips. When the floor was swept, she returned the broom; he scooped up the dust she had gathered into a neat heap, and left to get rid of it.

But he had also been told to light the stove. Now, when he returns, there are men in the room, and some of the woman's self-assurance has returned. As Antelme elaborately picks up papers near the men's feet to use in the stove, they shift position automatically, as one might brush away a fly in one's sleep—to them he is truly invisible. She, though, is "awake," as he says, and alert to what he is doing, unable either to ignore him completely or (since the whole story would have to come out) to accuse him overtly (but of what? Of deliberately needling her by doing his job badly?). As he is at last about to light the stove, she suddenly breaks off her conversation and descends furiously on him—but only to say "calmly" (getting a grip on herself at the last minute), "That will do," and to tell him to leave.

What has happened? Meeting another civilian a moment later in a hallway and being brusquely ordered out of the way, Antelme notices that now the insult "slides off" him. The curt *Weg!* meant, he knows, *You shouldn't exist* ("je ne veux pas que tu sois"); however, he reflects, "I did exist, and the insult slid off me." "Their insults can't reach me, any more than they can grasp the nightmare in the head that we are for them: constantly denied, we're still here." (But the woman, of course, came perilously close to grasping the nightmare that she would otherwise have preferred to deny. Perhaps she did grasp it.)

In 1946 or perhaps 1947 I was an ungainly adolescent, bookish and (I see in retrospect) gay-to-be, seriously out of place in a small farming town in the Northern Rivers region of New South Wales (Australia). Think Yonville in Flaubert's *Madame Bovary,* and adjust for the Antipodes in the forties, and you'll be near the mark. I had some escape hatches; they included reading, music, and learning foreign languages. In contemporary, self-consciously multicultural Australia, people carefully say "languages other than English," but *foreign* was the word back then, and that was frankly what I liked about them; they were evidence—unfortunately entirely theoretical—that other people in another environment existed.

One day that year a young woman appeared in town who was, wonder of wonders, incontrovertibly foreign. If I knew her name, I've forgotten it now. In the horrible jargon of the era she was a "displaced person" of "Baltic" origin (that there were differences of language and culture between Lithuanians, Latvians, and Estonians seems to have escaped everyone). A survivor of the camps (which camps? I don't know), she had reached Australia on an assisted passage and, after surviving yet another camp, had come, completely alone and with fragmentary English—the only person in town who was not thoroughly acculturated—to remake her life. She worked as a maid in the town's single hotel, and I can imagine now—at the time I was much too self-absorbed to do so—how lonely, vulnerable, and perhaps despairing she must have felt. But she spoke some German, the lingua franca of the camps. German was not taught at my school, and I had been learning it by correspondence. That she spoke German was the only fact about her that interested me.

I followed her around, insisting that she respond with her camp German to my own conversational gambits in student German. She did so, perhaps unwillingly—it did not occur to me to wonder what connotations the German language might have for her—or perhaps out of kindness toward a kid she may have perceived as being a fish out of water too, albeit nowhere near so lonely and unprotected as she (and certainly not an uprooted survivor of traumatic events). In my enthusiasm to practice putting the grammar and lexicon I had painstakingly acquired to use, I gave no thought whatsoever to the events and experiences she must have lived through, or to her feelings, preferences, and desires in the present. Yet, as a bright kid, I had followed the history of the war with interest, in the newspapers, over the radio, through the conversations of worried adults; and I knew, for example, what the advancing allies had discovered at Auschwitz, Dachau, Buchenwald, and the rest; I'd seen the newsreels. In the (European) spring of 1945, Australians were of course still quite concerned with the Pacific war, but that's no excuse. There *is* no excuse: what I knew of, I couldn't imagine, and I certainly couldn't connect it with this solitary woman who was so interesting and important to me because she spoke German and was the first foreigner I'd ever met.

There's a symmetry between these two stories. My story is about how *easy* it is not to acknowledge what one knows, however horrible it may be (and perhaps particularly if it is horrible), when it has happened or is happening to someone other than oneself. (Sometimes it is hard to acknowledge, easy to deny, even when it is oneself it is happening to; and to acknowledge that what is happening to others is also happening to oneself is most difficult of all.) Antelme's story is about what it takes, how *hard* it is, to break through the wall of denial and to lead human beings to *notice* the pain in which other humans are living and dying, rather than consigning it to the very edges of their consciousness. I tell the story about myself because I've come to realize that critical work always has personal underpinnings and entails emotional investments that can't and shouldn't be ignored: part of my motivation in writing this book is to make some sort of symbolic reparation for my past blindness and insensitivity. (One can't make amends, but one can acknowledge one's desire to do so.) The story about Antelme I tell, although Antelme tells it better than I, because it is an allegory of my book's subject matter, which is the act of witnessing conceived *performatively* in the context of a strong proclivity, on the part of those who understand themselves as unaffected or involved, to ignore, not only suffering itself such as Antelme's, but even the stories of suffering, as if such suffering was not also happening (in a certain sense) to them. What kind of performance does it take—analogous to Antelme's irritatingly inefficient sweeping ("je jouais," he says)—to breach the careful defenses put up by those (all of us?) who dismiss the pain of others as a sleeping person unconsciously brushes away a fly?

Yes, the book in your hands *is* mostly about AIDS writing as a form of witnessing. More particularly it is about that genre as it has been practiced in France, North America, and Australia in roughly the ten years between 1986 (when the first testimonials began to appear) and 1996 (when the arrival and relative success of combination therapy began to change the AIDS landscape, at least in the West). Yet I have been talking about the camps: not specifically about the Holocaust, but also and by implication about the Nazi genocide, carried out with unparalleled efficiency and savagery on European Jews, as well as other despised groups, Roma, homosexuals, and Jehovah's Witnesses among them. You may feel that the two—AIDS and the extermination camps—have very little in common, and I would agree with you; yet I am not mixing apples and oranges. My topic is testimonial, and I will not hesitate, therefore, to refer to Holocaust writing again; there will also be a chapter about wartime witnessing, specifically the witnessing of trench warfare in Great Britain in 1914–18. So to avoid misunderstandings, let me offer immediately a brief explanation of my practice of lumping together writing about different kinds of painful and traumatic historical experiences, since there are those to whom doing so may appear promiscuous, unjust, unwise or pernicious.

In particular the uniqueness of the Holocaust is an article of faith for some, who do not like to see it compared with other atrocities; and certainly, for whatever reasons, the Nazis' vast genocide has been for more than fifty years *the* case, at once exemplary and uniquely horrifying, around which all thinking about twentieth-century atrocity has revolved. But the twentieth century (I limit myself to that period) was also an era perhaps unparalleled in the number and variety of extreme and horrendous events and experiences to which people were subjected (I limit myself to the human species), in many parts of the world. To try to list them—the massacre of the Armenians; 1914–18; the Great Depression; the rape of Nanking; Coventry and Dresden; the concentration and extermination camps; Hiroshima and Nagasaki; Vietnam; Cambodia; brutal dictatorships in Central and South America and elsewhere (notably Africa); and so on—is a self-defeating task. (I forgot Bosnia, didn't I? And Kosovo. And the gulags; all the genocides and ethnocides of indigenous peoples in many parts of the globe; the effects of religious intolerance, racism, political terrorism, unrestrained capitalism; the pain of exile, deportation, mass migration and other displacements. Did I mention Changi and the Burma Railway?) Most of these events have been the object of witnessing writing, so that there is by now a huge corpus of testimonial texts, whose surface my research has not scratched.

AIDS, then, and AIDS witnessing figure in a long list that might go on endlessly, in part because modern history has been so prolifically atrocious and in part because one doesn't know where or how to draw a line between the (truly?) atrocious and the (merely?) horrible. Each item on the list has its historical specificity, a specificity that determines the characteristics of the witnessing associated with it in key ways. Indeed, because witnessing tends to take the form of personal narrative, and each person's experience of events like Auschwitz, Hiroshima, or the AIDS epidemic is individual, narrative accounts of historical events and experiences that we like to think of and name as units ("Hiroshima," "the Holocaust") vary strikingly among themselves. Binjamin Wilkomirski, supposedly aged at most five or six when he emerged from Auschwitz and whose memoir—now revealed to have been very probably a deluded "recovered memory"—was not published until 1995, does not and could not have the same vision of things as, say, Elie Wiesel, the authenticity of whose testimony is unquestioned despite divergences between the memoir he originally wrote in Yiddish, then rewrote in French, or Tadeusz Borowski, who was an adult, non-Jewish political prisoner and published his Auschwitz fiction in 1948, or Charlotte Delbo, who was also a political prisoner and not Jewish, but a woman, a Communist, and French and whose *Auschwitz et après* (Auschwitz and after), mostly written in the 1960s, appeared in three volumes in 1970–71. Not only the historical experiences themselves but also the accounts of given historical experiences are thus significantly different, and in many different respects, including the time and circumstances of their publication. Such specificity is a distinctive generic marker of witnessing, as opposed to, say, documentary or historical writing.

Yet the witnessing of atrocity, I argue here, is also a practice that presents significant regularities, independently of the vast range of circumstances in which people live through (or succumb to) atrocious and traumatic events and the equally large number of variables that govern the projected audience and the overall conditions of their coming to witness.[1] There is no representative subject of testimony, no story that can stand for all the stories, no experience of the atrocious that can count as exemplarily atrocious. Singularity is the general rule. But there is always an experience that the sufferer judges atrocious and is in a position to bear witness to; there is likewise the act of witness itself (for practical purposes in this book a written or filmic text), and finally there are cultural regularities in the circumstances that condition such an act as a discursive possibility—broadly speaking, the conditions of its reception. It is out of the relations (themselves variable) between these constants (an experience of a certain kind, the witnessing of the experience, the anticipated and real reception of the witnessing) that the possibility of generalizing about witnessing as a practice emerges.

Or, to put it another way, these regularities of a relational kind constitute testimonial as a genre (albeit, as we will see, a peculiarly parasitic one), and it is the genre of witnessing—rather than the occasions of witness—that is my topic. What war writers like Wilfred Owen and Erich Maria Remarque, Holocaust witnesses like Primo Levi or Robert Antelme or Elie Wiesel, and Rigoberta Menchú writing by proxy about the oppression of her people in Guatemala or AIDS writers like Paul Monette and Pascal de Duve have in common, despite the vast differences between both the occasions of their writing and the rhetorical characteristics of their texts, is that they tell a story about atrocious circumstances to an audience whose readiness to hear the story or capacity to imagine its import is dubious, given the "unimaginable" extremity of the events related but also the mechanisms of willed or unconscious rejection, the unwillingness to *hear,* that is generated in the audience by the very character of those events.

If I argue any single proposition in this book, then, it is that witnessing's generic character arises, not from the supposed "unsayability" of the event but from the presupposed cultural "inaudibility," in this sense, of the testimonial message. With respect both to the textual occasions of witnessing and to the texts themselves, we readers of testimonial narratives are all in a position that lies somewhere on a continuum between the highly "proximate" denial that Antelme experienced and on at least one occasion combatted in the Gandersheim factory, and the "distanced" insensitivity and ignorance I displayed at the age of fourteen. There is a nightmare in the head, as Antelme puts it, and it is not easy to "grasp" the nightmare; yet that's what is asked of us as readers. Nor is it easy for writers to find strategies that will make the nightmare, like death at the door, impossible to ignore because such strategies produce the sense that it "is happening"—as Harold Brodkey puts it—not only to others, but through witnessing, also to ourselves. Certainly the staging of these problematic relations in AIDS texts is determined in certain respects by the historical specificities of the disease and the social context in which it is understood, as well as the personal circumstances of the AIDS witness; but my claim is that it is also a variant of recognizably similar problems of relationality that can be seen at work in other texts of witnessing, which is why it can be illuminated by comparison with them.

Nearly all Holocaust writers are deeply conscious of the problem of what I've called their inaudibility. Primo Levi's Auschwitz nightmare is frequently cited: he dreamed that, home from the camp, he was trying to tell friends and family of the experience while those he addressed ignored him, carrying on a conversation among themselves. While still a prisoner he was thus already contemplating, at some level of consciousness, the necessity to bear witness, and already concerned, not about his ability to give an account of his experience or about the credibility of such an account, but about the problem of gaining attention for it. Not surprisingly, therefore, although the vehemence of the gesture is unexpected in so mild-mannered a writer, he opens his book with a poem that both states its crucial theme, reflected in the Italian title *Se questo è un uomo* (If this is a man), and doubles as an imprecation addressed to the inattentive reader:

> Consider if this be a man . . .
> Who fights for a scrap of bread . . .
> I commend these words to you.
>
> Carve them into your hearts . . .
> Or may your houses fall apart,
> May illness impede you,
> May your children turn their faces from you.

It's as if for Levi the humanity of the witness, whether or not "this" be a man, depends not only on having survived the assault made on it by Auschwitz, but also on the witness's report being received with due weight by its audience. Turning away, inattentive or uncaring readers commit an act of dehumanizing brutality equivalent to the conditions imposed on the inmates of the camp. And in doing so, they merit, in Levi's estimation, an equivalent punishment, in having their children turn from them, denying them their humanity in turn. The stakes of testimonial writing, therefore, are high. Just as the ordeals to which witnessing testifies put the nature of humanity to the test, so that Levi's humanity hung in the balance at Auschwitz, so too the reception of his account is a test of our humanity, which likewise hangs in the balance as we read, and hence a new (but related) ordeal for the witnessing subject. The gigantic moral experiment Levi describes Auschwitz as having been *did not stop* when the camp's gates at last swung open, releasing the prisoners. It continues, albeit in another mode, in the reception accorded the witnessing act itself. (Levi's premonition, in fact, was accurate. Now a revered classic of Holocaust writing, *Se questo è un uomo,* when it first appeared in 1947, was accorded scant attention.)

The cultural equivalence of the testimonial act and of the atrocious event or experience that it narrates is an underlying assumption and a kind of credo of most witnessing writing, as if the witness's own survival means little unless the story the witness tells also lives, in the specific sense of its being taken to heart by the audience. In much AIDS writing, the survival of the narrative is both the condition of the author's survival (the reason why an infected or dying witness does not prefer suicide to writing, for example) and itself the only form of personal survival such a writer, in the pre-1996 era, could reasonably look forward to.[2] Whence the strategic ambiguity, for example, in Harold Brodkey's sentence: "The trouble with death-at-your-doorstep is that it is happening to you." To whom is death-at-your-doorstep happening here? To Brodkey, of course. But also, putatively, to those of us who read him, by virtue of the power of Brodkey's narrative. I'll look a little later at the complexity of the passage in which this sentence occurs; suffice it to say for now that it is about the passing on of a responsibility. Unless we readers read as if "it" is happening to *us,* Brodkey himself becomes, as he bluntly puts it, "like a rock in the garden" (68), no longer even a cultural participant in history or life. It is not enough that there be a nightmare in the head; the nightmare, in Antelme's phrase, must be "grasped," grasped by those who may well believe it does not directly concern them. Witnessing, like death, comes knocking at our door: will we remain deaf, and turn away; or will we offer it hospitality? Such is the defining issue.

Signposting

Where Levi offers a curse on the inattentive reader, other witnesses may take a more urbane approach to their audience. Let's look at a photograph: it was taken by the Sydney photographer William Yang, and it opens Yang's performance piece *Sadness,* which (by contrast with Levi's initial inaudibility) had considerable cultural impact both in Australia and in parts of Asia and the Pacific basin. An intimate theatrical occasion, *Sadness* drew relatively small crowds, but it did so consistently, and it left its audience thoughtful and subdued—they were open, it seems, to the "visitation" of the event. The piece is about AIDS in Sydney and Chineseness in Australia, two delicate and touchy topics. Yang presents them simply: he shows his photographic images on a screen and accompanies them with an unassuming commentary, spoken by himself. But such simplicity, like Antelme's performance of sweeping, can be subtle, insidious, unnerving, and even devastating in its effects.

The published scenario of *Sadness* has a short preface in which Yang shows he is a thoughtful rhetorician. His desire was to "unburden [him]self of the things [he had] seen." But "'I can't do a show about death,' I said to myself, ' it's not good box-office.'" Death is Yang's topic, but if there's too much death, people won't come. The ethical purpose (to pass on a burden) has rhetorical preconditions (people's unwillingness to face the fact of death) that are inimical to it, or at least must be *turned* if the purpose is to be accomplished within the constraints of "box office." In the context of this problem the first photo the people who do come will see is crucial. What it represents is a young man named Allan in a Sydney hospital in 1988, suffering from *pneumocystis carinii* pneumonia. But representation is inseparable from signifying, as is reference from address—and as the making of a certain kind of meaning the photo functions also as an invitation. More accurately, it enacts a double invitation to its audience of spectators, an invitation first to look, and then to see. For there is more (and other) to see, the photo implies, more (and other) that it signifies, than it actually represents; and its strategy is therefore first to engage our attention and to capture our willingness to look (essentially by techniques of euphemism) and then to divert it (through a practice of symbolism) so that we are led to see more (and other) than the photo gives us to look at.

The photo is an *engaging* one at first glance. By offering entertainment and pleasure it captures my attention, and this despite the obvious gravity of Allan's sickness: he lies on a hospital bed, too fatigued to "smile for the

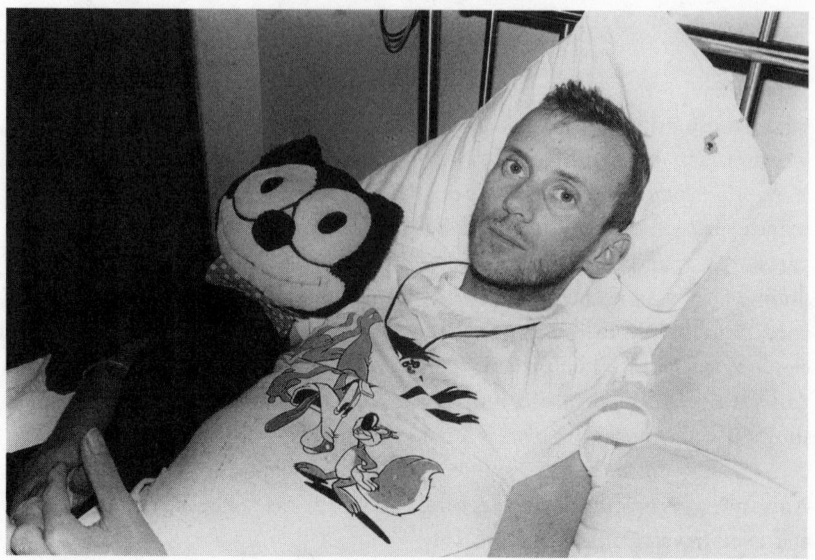

***Allan. St. Vincent's Hospital.* 1988. (From William Yang, *Sadness,* 1.)**

camera," his features drawn and his eyes rounded by fever and the incipient wasting of his face. There is a playfulness, particularly in the composition, that makes the image both amusing and intriguing to look at. Allan's face has not lost a certain youthful attractiveness, his T-shirt is adorned with cartoon characters, and at his side he grasps a large stuffed toy, almost as big as he, which I recognize immediately as Felix the Cat, another cartoon character (celebrated for his bag of tricks and his nine lives). The parallelism of the two figures, lying on the same diagonal axis that structures the image, forms a witty visual pun: the relation of the figures is mediated by Allan's grasping fingers at the bottom left of the photo and by the cartoon figures on his T-shirt (psychologically, we are learning that Allan loves cartoons, a childlike trait), and there is a striking, indeed haunting, resemblance between the two faces (Allan's almost expressionless but with large, rounded eyes, Felix's huge, staring eyes set in a flat, rotund visage, also reduced schematically to its most prominent features—ears, eyes, nose, a slit for a mouth—and with a kind of euphorically empty, "goofy" expression playing on it). My perception of the pun—the construction of a metaphor—produces aesthetic delight, not unmixed with pathos and irony (a man with a mortal illness takes comfort in a child's toy). Finally, the two pairs of eyes produce a cuteness-effect, like the big round eyes of puppies or kittens, that activates in me a sense of protectiveness and a nurturing instinct.

All this comes under the heading of *captatio benevolentiae:* my favorable attention is "caught" or "captured." But the photo's bag of tricks is not exhausted: once caught, the audience's attention has to be diverted toward a concern that's not directly represented; my look will become an act of seeing. The metaphor of the two bodies is the vehicle of this transfer (the etymological sense of the word *metaphor*). For in the act of making the punning comparison—illness has made the young man toylike; the toy, though, has a kind of dignity that's conferred by the gravity of the circumstances—my look and my attention shift between the two, following a sort of circularity that's established in the photo by Allan's fingers at the bottom, but also by the corresponding gap at the top between the two pairs of eyes, a gap bridged in the viewer's mind by the equivalence of the eyes and the fact that the two heads are situated on virtually the same plane. Connecting the two figures, then, my gaze is also led to identify a slight but significant discrepancy.

For in spite of the parallelism of the bodies, there's a difference in the directionality of each look. Allan is turning slightly to look at the camera, which by time-honored convention means that he is looking at me, the spectator, drawing my glance in a way that metaphorizes the *captatio* performed by the photo itself. Felix's eyes, though, stare straight ahead, which (given the diagonal along which both bodies lie) means that they appear to be looking away from the camera and to be fixed on something (other than the spectator) that lies outside of the frame of the photograph. In the act of realizing the metaphor and making the comparison that closes the gap between the two heads, my look and my attention are thus first drawn (by Allan's eyes) into the photograph and what it represents, then turned (by Felix's), redirected *beyond* what the photo actually represents along the vector of Felix's open-eyed stare. What is the object of the stare? What does Felix see that I am forced (looking being insufficient) to imagine? I could try to name it ("death"? "pain"? "suffering"?) but that would be self-defeating, since it's defined by the photo as a *surplus*—a surplus of signification—that transcends representation or naming. Converting my look in this way into an act of seeing (of seeing "in the mind's eye"), the metaphor begins now to function as a symbol; and this capturing and turning of attention through tropes is paradigmatic, I propose, of the indirect mode of rhetorical implication and suggestion—a mode of representation that is more and other than representation; that is, figuration—to which witnessing regularly has recourse.

Symbolism—I am using the term in the sense it has in literary study—etymologically means throwing together. It does not always employ a fully realized metaphor as its vehicle, but it does always entail a double rhetorical process, an attention-getter—such as the metaphor here—serving *also* to turn attention to an other, a more, or a beyond. And it happens, not at all coincidentally, that in just the way the initial photo prefigures, *Sadness* itself employs an attention-getting metaphor as the vehicle of a similar kind of symbolic diversion or *détournement* of attention. The components of the metaphor, in this case, are not Allan and Felix but Yang's gay "friends," afflicted by the epidemic of AIDS, and his Chinese-Australian "family" whose history of assimilation into Australian society over five generations is simultaneously a record of prejudice, oppression, and affliction. Yang was at first baffled, he tells us: he knew he had two stories to tell, but how to make them fit? "In the end, I just threw the stories together [*sym-bolein*], they were both my stories, both these diverse stories existed because of me. I was the glue." It is for us, then, the audience, to make them fit if we can, discovering (imagining) in the process the "I" named William Yang that is the only indirectly represented (i.e., figured) "glue." But being led also, through the vehicle of Yang's search for self, in the direction of more and other than that. Autobiography-by-metaphor can function simultaneously as testimonial, witnessing-by-symbol.

On the Chinese side of Yang's autobiography, his search leads to an act of injustice and a violent death: the murder of Yang's maternal uncle among the sugarcane fields of North Queensland, an act perhaps racially motivated and certainly covered up by the justice system of the day (the late 1920s)—the perpetrator, a white man, was never brought to trial. On the other (gay) side, the search culminates in a candlelight vigil, ostensibly in memory of those who have died as a result of HIV disease. But we who have worked to realize the Chinese-gay metaphor are not surprised, in the published scenario (76–77), when this nearly final photograph of the show is presented under the double rubric of *Family and Friends.* The connections between the two components of the overall metaphor—death, violent or obscene, and injustice—have become clear, if only because Yang has turned up the evidence, performing an act of testimony in a quasi-legal sense. He has photographed and shown us dusty court records discovered in a small northern courthouse, portraits of a "family" whose features bespeak assimilation or what Yang calls "Austasian-ness" (12; cf. "it takes a hundred years to get a blend like this," 29), and portraits of gay "friends," sometimes in happy groups, sometimes Chinese or Asian gay and lesbian friends, sometimes even partying, but many of them chronicled, like Allan, in their life with AIDS and their deaths. But the evidence also contains a crucial detail, a figure of absence, which performs the function of turning metaphor into symbol. Yang takes us to an abandoned Chinese cemetery in the north, where a solitary stela presents the instruction, in three Chinese characters, "regard . . . as if . . . present" (40)—an instruction that clearly applies to us as we contemplate *all* these pictures, all these portraits, many of them representing those who have died, all this testimonial evidence that therefore, like Felix's stare, asks us to see, with the mind's eye, what has been suppressed or what is no longer strictly visible.

The photo representing the candlelight vigil (followed, before the end of the performance, by only one more image, also of votive candles burning in the night, before Yang bows and kneels at a Taoist shrine) therefore signifies an invitation to "regard as if present"—the epitome of a symbolic act—all those, family and friends, whom the vigil remembers. And by extension (another metaphor) the performance of *Sadness* itself (the crowd gathered in a darkened auditorium in the presence of luminous images) exercises the same symbolic function as the vigil. It too is a wake. The dead, whom we might think buried and forgotten, do not die. Here they are, among us—or at least at the threshold of our consciousness, standing at the doorstep. Through the power of images and their appeal to our own imagination, they—the dead, the suppressed, the marginalized, the forgotten—have been made "as if present," or at least we have been led (so) to "regard"—that is to *see*—them. It's not as it would be if they were alive—injustice can't be simply canceled out—but neither can they continue to be forgotten or dismissed, as one might brush away a fly in one's sleep. The nightmare in our head is not allayed; but allaying it was not the purpose of the exercise. Instead, awakening us to it, rendering us vigilant toward it, was. Through an instrumentality of indirection, capturing and turning, metaphor and symbol, through what Deleuze and Guattari call "assemblage" or *agencement,* we've come, instead of denying the nightmare, to offer it a certain hospitality, envisioning it in our mind's eye. Might that not be what Antelme calls "grasping" it, and being "awake"?

In this book, I will propose that the modus operandi of testimonial writing is not so much directly representational (i.e. mimetic) as it is figural, and

Candlelight Vigil. **(From William Yang, *Sadness,* 76–77.)**

that its mode, therefore, is neither historical nor fictional (the two incontrovertibly representational discursive modes) but symbolic—symbolic in the sense that it produces complex indexical signs, like a stela in a graveyard, the photo of Allan or Bill T. Jones's dance performance as I described it in the preface. Such signs say: (something is) "here"—or in the case of Bill T. Jones's title and other testimonial writing (which is always about surviving)—(something is) *Still/Here.* I remarked above that representation is inseparable from signifying and that reference, therefore, is necessarily a matter of address. But the instrumentality of indexical signs lies in an address that both *attracts* attention and *redirects* it, diverting it in the direction of a "something" that the sign does not describe but only indicates, as Felix's gaze does in the photograph. It indicates the X as apprehensible (Antelme might say "graspable"), but apprehensible only "beyond the frame" and "outside of" the interaction mediated by the sign itself.

Antelme wants us to grasp the nightmare; testimonial performs a captation of attention, a sort of prior grasping at our consciousness, in order for the nightmare that it does not, because it cannot, reproduce to become graspable, by us. Its task, then, is the task of signposting. For if death is at "your" door, you may not *see* it, look as you might, unless you encounter something that testifies to its being there. Something that says "here," and points.

Turning

There's certainly some distance, however, between Yang's smoothly urbane witnessing performance and the improvisatory performance of incompetence through which Antelme drew the German woman's attention. Levi's rhetorical tactics are different again. But all three have in common the infringement of a conventional taboo through a practice of figuration or troping. In the factory, the rule is that slave labor is nonexistent, hence invisible; Antelme tropes with his body, that being the only rhetorical vehicle available to him, turning in a performance ("je jouais," 56) that emphasizes or "phrases" (makes an utterance of) his natural incompetence with brooms and signposts his own presence: "I am here." Yang infringes the showbiz rule that death is not good box office, troping the art of photography into a symbolic visitation of the dead among the living that signposts death-at-the-door. I'll return to *Se questo è un uomo* at the end of this chapter. But troping is not just ornamental here, as the pedagogical tradition of rhetoric has tended to teach since the Renaissance; it is instrumental in that it is capable of turning (Greek *trepein,* whence trope) the meaning of an interaction—Antelme and the German civilian, Yang and his audience—turning it away from the dictates of conventional propositions or expectations so that it signifies otherwise. There is thus a pragmatics of troping that permits witnessing, viewed in turn as a cultural practice, not so much to *commit* social solecisms or errors—a slave laborer drawing attention to himself, a "show" that is about death—as to *(re)phrase* such infractions as meaningful utterances; it is as if the conventions are not so much (accidentally) *infringed* as they are (intentionally) *flouted.* In terms of the relational regularities (between an atrocious or extreme object of witnessing, a witnessing text, and its audience) that I've claimed constitute witnessing as a genre, it is this rhetorical (re)phrasing of infraction into an indexical act of signposting, agencing, and redirecting of attention, that is definitional. Such, at least, is the proposition to which this book is dedicated.

Of course the practice of witnessing presents other regularities, of a "prerhetorical" and "postrhetorical" kind, that will be noticed as my argument develops. Among the prerhetorical conditions of witnessing, for example, is the fact that the witness must have *survived,* or more accurately *be surviving,* an extreme event or experience that tends, in the nature of things, to silence many or most of its potential witnesses, whether by killing them outright or by "killing" (through trauma) their motivation or ability to speak. Witnessing narratives, therefore, reflect regularly both on the implications of the witness's survival and on the birth and survival of the witness's motivation, that is, of that initial withholding of one's assent from the atrocity one is undergoing or observing that is surely at the core of all witnessing and leads to the desire to make sure both that the story gets told and that the telling of the story gets heard.

As for the postconditions, they are the conditions of a witnessing act's rhetorical *success* (as opposed to those of its rhetoricity). They include those conditions, other than purely rhetorical, that determine whether or not a given story gains access to an audience and with it the chance to affect that audience. Zalmen Gradowski, a member of the *Sonderkommando* employed to drag corpses from the gas chamber to the crematorium at Auschwitz and who for that reason could have no personal hope of living to tell the tale (members of the *Kommando* were routinely gassed in their turn), buried a diary near the crematorium in Birkenau, where it was found after the war. Less dramatically, if I am able to read and benefit from Antelme's or Levi's narratives or learn from Yang's performance, it is because—by virtue of education and social standing—they had or have access to modes of publication that make their testimonial writing available to a public wider than, say, their immediate friends and family. And if my students are able to learn about the kinds of things these witnesses seek to unburden themselves of, it's because I teach in an institution that acknowledges some educational value in their doing so. In short, cultures have important filtering or gatekeeping institutions, more or less identified in modern societies with Althusser's state ideological apparatuses, that have as one of their tasks to discriminate between what is appropriate for the members of the society to attend to and the kind of news that is best disregarded, a discrimination that is itself subject to cultural evolution and changing historical circumstances. (A major turning point in the history of AIDS consciousness in France occurred on the evening when Hervé Guibert, the author of *A l'ami qui ne m'a pas sauvé la vie* [To the friend who did not save my life], was invited to appear on the TV interview show *Apostrophes,* which thus functioned as a crucial gatekeeping agency.)[3]

The prerhetorical and postrhetorical conditions of the act of witnessing and its eventual success are important and need study; even in an initial inquiry into the pragmatics of testimonial such as this they can't be ignored. They are a topic of absorbing interest to many writers of witnessing texts themselves. But to the extent that they aren't strictly rhetorical in kind, they will not be the main focus of this book. For it is already quite rare to discuss witnessing as a rhetorical mediation, that is, in terms of the fraught relation between experiences of extremity and an audience unprepared or unwilling to do more than marginally acknowledge such experiences or to attend to their report. The model of witnessing that is most frequently active, although it may not be explicitly invoked, is rather the rhetorically naive, if not antirhetorical, understanding of testimonial as honest and direct, straightforward and unproblematic—the simple report of a reliable eyewitness—an understanding that has its roots in the conventions of legal testimony (in which an eyewitness report is contrasted favorably with hearsay evidence). The person who was present in some capacity at the events, even directly involved in them, and who gives a "plain, unvarnished," personal account of the experience, is regarded as a reliable source of knowledge, on the sole condition that the integrity of the witness be assumed, or established in some unchallengeable way. Etymologies that refer to the witness's possession of appropriate and demonstrable qualifying characteristics in the form of male genitalia "attest" to the antiquity of this theory of witnessing, with its emphasis on the idea of reliability, and hence the believability or unbelievability of the witness's report: many words in English and the Romance languages derive from Latin *testis,* and in German the verb *zeugen* (from *Zeug,* stuff)—from which *Zeuge,* "witness," and *Zeugnis,* "testimonial" derive—means both to bear witness or give evidence and to procreate, presumably on the theory that it is the male who fathers (and the female who merely bears) a child. So it is the idea of "having the right stuff"—of being legitimated to *pass on* (genes, property, and information)—that is semantically active here, and credibility is the criterion by which witnessing is judged.

Given a reliable witness, the only impediment to good witnessing that can arise in this theory is the so-called inadequacy of language. The event, that is, may have been so overwhelming or the experience so intense that the lexicon lacks suitable words with which to describe it. Hence arises the trope of "words fail me" or "I can't express"—a form of preterition—that occurs frequently in testimonial writing of all kinds, whose writers can thus be seen to subscribe to the "eyewitness" understanding of direct testimonial, conceived as the act of "telling it like it is/was," even when they may reveal themselves in other respects to be quite self-conscious rhetoricians. This theory, indeed, has the status of common sense: it is so current and widespread, so culturally dominant, that there's little point in trying to refute it. Everyone, myself included, subscribes to it on certain occasions and at least some of the time. (Historians in particular have a professional tendency to require of witnessing writing that it have credibility as documentary, and are uncomfortable with the idea that its truth might be other than factual.)[4]

In contradistinction to words that derive from *testis* or *Zeug,* the word *witness* itself, by its Anglo-Saxon etymology (*wit,* "wit," perhaps conflated with *witan,* "to know") demonstrates that we have inherited another ancient theory, grounded not in the credible eyewitness, but in the cleverness, rhetorical skill, and savoir faire of the witnessing subject as a discursive agent. This theory, however, has been somewhat submerged, and the most prominent modern alternative to the theory of direct personal report is one that refers us rather to the idea of a damaged witnessing subject. Since Freud's and Ferenczi's work on "war neurosis" (a diagnosis now generalized as post-traumatic stress disorder), attention has been increasingly focused on the concept of psychic trauma, usually associated in cases of atrocity such as war, torture, genocide, and mortal illness with physical trauma as well. This psychological approach to witnessing tends to deny witnesses their rhetorical competence because it views the symptoms of psychic trauma (which include amnesia, aphasia, mutism, lapses, and mishaps of pronunciation or articulation) as a loss or impairment of the damaged psychic subject's ability to narrate the traumatic event or experience, and indexes the trauma the witnessing subject has suffered by the degree of difficulty in narrating that the subject evidences. Here the requirement of credibility is replaced by the idea of psychic damage as itself a form of evidence; and the problem of the inadequacy of language is less an issue than is the inadequacy to the event of the witness's account of that event.

But if the witness becomes a damaged narrator who in a sense *lacks* the "right stuff," the rhetoricity of the event of witnessing requires there to be a wholly sympathetic, "healing," compensatory partnership of witness and audience, a partnership clearly modeled on psychoanalytic listening, in order for the act of witnessing to be successfully accomplished. The reader's empathy, insight, and understanding become a sine qua non, in the absence of which the witnessing narrative itself risks being dismissed, nullified, or at least disqualified as seriously inadequate. Such a theory of compensatory listening has been persuasively developed by Shoshana Felman and Dori Laub in a powerful and influential volume, *Testimony,* that has considerably strengthened the psychoanalytic theory of witnessing, notably in academic circles, and has been followed notably by the work of Cathy Caruth on trauma. Equally influential, for the specific category of illness narratives, has been the concept of the "wounded storyteller" given currency by Joseph Frank. The two most obvious deficiencies of this kind of theory, though, are the somewhat simplistic assumption that the characteristics of a narrative text are wholly and exclusively determined by the subjective nature (whether damaged or whole) of the storyteller, and the concomitant understanding of the narrative event as a wholly complicitous partnership, in which the sympathy of the audience is both indispensable and a given. Without denying the partial truth that inheres in these assumptions, nor the power of the concept of trauma, which I too will want to use, I will not be treating AIDS writing in this book as illness narrative, nor will I take the audience's sympathy as a given in the reception of witnessing narratives. Rather, my position is closer to Kalí Tal's view that there is a social "battle over the meaning of . . . traumatic experience" and that testimonial is an "aggressive act" that social convention seeks to repress (7). Indeed, in chapter 3, I'll make use of Pat Barker's extraordinary historical fiction, *Regeneration,* in an attempt to show that the supposed "symptoms" of pretestimonial or testimonial trauma are better understood not so much as impediments to communication than as readable *tropes* signifying pain, including the pain of the repression witnessing undergoes, and doing so somewhat in the manner of Robert Antelme's troping of his genuinely incompetent sweeping into an utterance that means: "I am here; you can't make me go away just by saying *Weg*!" They have a signposting function that is not reducible to their status as clinical symptom. And in chapter 6 I'll return to the issue of the symptom as trope in a discussion of Bertrand Duquénelle's *L'Aztèque,* so important is it to see that difficulty in narration can function as a sign of social opposition and a critique of cultural convention as well as of personal trauma.

In proposing a view of witnessing as the (re)phrasing of a social infraction into an oppositional utterance through the instrumentality of tropes, I want, then, to put back the wit into the act of witnessing, understanding wit to embrace a range of discursive skills that include verbal acuteness, but extend also to the "practical intelligence" of an oppositional kind that Michel de Certeau memorably describes as the opportunistic art of turning to tactical advantage—through bricolage or making do—a set of circumstances on which one does not have strategic purchase. However, it is clear that all such theories—my own, Kalí Tal's, trauma theory, eyewitness report—are themselves tactical rather than strategic, are adopted for specific purposes, and have no more than partial purchase on the "terrain" they pretend to organize and even to control or master. They are what Anne Freadman and Amanda MacDonald define as folk theories, specifying, however, that theory, as a speculative practice, may be constitutively unable ever to achieve any other status.

So let me say that in attempting to put the wit back into witness I am reacting in a compensatory way against the denial of rhetoricity inherent in eyewitness report theory and of rhetorical competence in trauma theory.

But I'm also proposing an ethical and negotiating understanding of witnessing as a friendly revision of Kalí Tal's political view of it as adversative or "aggressive"—a view that understates also the sense in which witnessing's rhetorical twists and turns may be accommodationist as well as socially transformative in intention or effect. William Yang, for example, makes it clear that for him witnessing is therapeutic and an act of "unburdening" himself—a clear reference to the psychoanalytic theory of witnessing—of what he has seen. He does not state, although it is implicit, that his unburdening is also a way of *passing on* the burden and charging others with its weight, that is, an ethical project grounded in a sense of injustice and the desire to turn audiences from their ignorance and indifference toward some form of acknowledgment of the nightmare that is—and was always already—in their head. He doesn't *state* this project, I think, because he is negotiating a quite difficult rhetorical situation—he wants to speak of death—and he knows that such terms would sound grandiloquent, especially to an Australian audience, and thus be counterproductive. Better, then, just to "throw together" the two stories, show the images, and let them work their effect, under the (rhetorical) pretense of a supposedly nonrhetorical, direct report. No need for confrontation—and, of course, better for the box office too.

But there *is* an effect, and it may be genuinely transformative. To catch the nature of the kind of practice that is witnessing, and that of the effect it produces, I need the semantics of the French verb *détourner,* which I've already used in reading the rhetoric of Yang's photo of Allan. *Détourner* can be used in the sense of turning someone away from an established or predetermined path; but it also means to appropriate or misappropriate something for purposes other than its conventional use; it can refer to hijacking a plane or a bus. Because witnessing "turns" what would otherwise be an infraction or an error, through the power of troping, into a meaningful if disturbing utterance that can participate in the exchanges and interactions that constitute culture, it is an act of *détournement* in all those senses. The culture is hijacked, its conventions appropriated for new purposes; audiences are turned from the circle of their everyday concerns toward what they may least wish to hear about, the nightmare in their heads that they have not grasped. But the effect is itself *détourné,* in the sense of the adjective drawn from the French verb, in which a road or path is *détourné* if it is all twists and turns, and a discursive utterance (say a reproach or an allusion) can be *détourné* if it is real, but passes unnoticed, or virtually so, because it is only hinted at or smuggled into the conversation. The transgressive effectiveness of testimonial writing, as a rephrased infringement of convention, generally has that smuggled-in, quasi-unnoticed quality. Wide-ranging and even combative as its effects may actually be, they are experienced more as a matter of the infiltration of culture, as Mireille Rosello might say, than as struggle or confrontation. The twists and turns of troping are at the service of an infiltration of cultural normalcy by what would *otherwise* count as an infraction of that normalcy, something that conventional writers regard as beyond its ken or at the limits of its tolerance; for what they signpost is the unmentionable, the unspeakable—that which cultural subjects shrink from acknowledging.

Witnessing, then, is an infringement by virtue of its association with what cultures regard—in the terminology I'll adopt henceforth—as *obscene.* Its rephrasing of a potential infraction into a meaningful utterance amounts, therefore, to the domestication into culture of (what culture regards as) an obscenity, a domestication that, although it flouts conventional expectations, may often go unnoticed or barely noticed. Troping is a name for the means—the *moyens détournés*—that are available to testimonial writing in order to produce that effect of cultural *détournement,* and to bring onto the "scene" of attention what a culture bans as ob-scene, not part of its scenic view.

Genre and the Obscene

As a child in rural Australia (this story predates the postwar event I related earlier and took place in Sheshy's town) I was once taken on a rabbit hunt. (Rabbits, an introduced species, were a pest: they had proliferated over the generations and were fast consuming the sparse indigenous vegetation on which sheep—another introduced species but a profitable one—were set to graze. They were routinely hunted; it was a method of pest control.) At my first sight of a dead rabbit—its small body torn and bloody, and stained with urine and feces—I turned pale, became physically ill and had to be taken home, after which the matter was never again discussed with me by my family (which was probably ashamed of my squeamishness), and rabbit hunting became a permanent but unmentioned nightmare in my head, a topic I shied away from even in thought. Meanwhile adults in the same community discussed cases of cancer in hushed, almost reverent, tones and behind closed doors—we children were "protected" from (knowledge of) cancer but matter-of-factly exposed to rabbit hunting. Go figure! These instances exemplify the cultural phenomenon that I have just designated as the obscene; and they illustrate some of the complexity of the topic. Notice that rabbit hunting had the status of the obscene in the culture of which I was a subject but not at all in that of, say, the farmers who were friends of my parents; similarly cancer, scarcely mentionable among laypersons, must have been an everyday problem that medical professionals dealt with as matter-of-factly as the farmers with their infestations of rabbits. Quite different cultures with different conceptions of obscenity coexisted within the same space—culture and cultural difference are a structural affair, not a matter of where or with whom you live.

My hypothesis is that events and experiences that are traumatic, whether collectively or to individuals, and become the object of witnessing practices have the cultural status of the obscene; and conversely, that the cultural category of obscenity defines what persons experience as traumatic. I have in mind a sense of the word *obscene* that etymologically relates it to the word *obscure:* each of these two words (and a number of others) is conjectured to derive from an Indo-European radical **sku,* denoting coverage or protection, whence Greek *skene* and ultimately English *scene.* The obscene, then, would be the "offstage" or "backstage" space that delimits, and is simultaneously inseparable from, a scene of activity on which attention is focused. The cultural obscene is "obscured" or "covered" with respect to a scene of culture, but without being discontinuous with it. And it is tinged with a sense of the sacred (Latin *obscenus* meant of ill augur), but also of stigma and abjection, both of which refer to the mixture of fascination and repulsion exerted by objects that are expelled from within the social or physical body (see Kristeva). Dubious as the etymology may be, it highlights the crucial idea that what is culturally known may not be readily acknowledged.

In order to understand this phenomenon of a cultural limit or beyond that both is and is not part of the culture, it's worth recalling the relation of restricted, or local, economies to a general or global economy that Jacques Derrida (1967) elucidates in a gloss on the work of Georges Bataille. With respect to the general economy that is global culture (in the singular), an economy that does not have knowable limits, local cultural economies—or cultures (in the plural)—constitute a set of differing restrictions of that general culture. To culture (sing.) we can apply Derrida's axiom with respect to general textuality, that is has no "outside" *(il n'y a pas de hors-texte);* we are always, from birth to death, "in" culture. Local cultures, though, have *limits* and a cultural beyond because there are other, different local cultures, all constituted as restrictions of the global culture.

I work in an "academic" culture, have an insider's sense of "gay" culture, share cultural traits with "middle class" people the world over and with people of "Australian" birth or upbringing, and so on. Such cultures don't have a physical or spatial *edge,* but are in a differential relation of "split" (neither continuity nor discontinuity) with respect to the local cultures they have knowledge of—a knowledge mediated by culture (sing.)—but regard as other. Thus, any cultural subject can become aware of the limits of her or his cultural consciousness simply by encountering, that is, coming into relation with, a culturally other subject, and it's out of this phenomenon of cultural liminality that a sense of the obscene is born.

Within culture (sing.), the other of culture—the indispensable category without which culture itself would not be a concept—is named *nature.* Names for what lies at and beyond the limits of "a" given (restricted or local) culture include the barbarous and the alien. What I call the cultural offstage, and hence the sense of the obscene, arises, however, from the knowledge cultural subjects may have, but do not necessarily acknowledge, that cultural "otherness"—what to them is alien, barbaric, and so forth—is actually *of a piece* with their own cultural identity—of a piece with because constitutive of that identity, since without restriction, and hence limits and otherness, there is no "self." For me to have a cultural identity implies also my (non)recognition that the forms of otherness I name alien or barbarian form part of that identity. Thus, the obscene becomes a liminal phenomenon, culturally speaking, in the sense that it is neither completely beyond cultural ken nor squarely acknowledged as integral to the cultural scene. More particularly, it occupies a "space" of liminality that is reserved for those culturally *definitional* events and experiences that individual cultural subjects experience as traumatic, and others treat as barbaric, hence as unmentionable or unspeakable, precisely because such happenings are felt to be "out of bounds" with respect to their own culture, a culture that is thereby redefined, by ideological sleight-of-hand, as *civilized.* Such events and experiences are *extreme,* both in the sense that they are unusually violent or grueling, intensely degrading, or profoundly unjust and in the sense that they are therefore relegated to a position at the very "edge" of consciousness, the position of that which has to be both known and, at the same time, unrecognized. That they are definitional is the conviction that underlies acts of witnessing, whose ethical task is to bring about some acknowledgment of the unrecognized.

It is helpful to describe any given local culture as a specific array of genres, where genre is understood as a conventional habitus entailing understandings and agreements that don't need to be specifically negotiated concerning the "kinds" of social interaction that are possible under the aegis of that culture. Interactions that are nongeneric in a given culture are those that are culturally "out of bounds," although they may be generic—that is, they may be regarded as appropriate—in another culture, including one quite proximate to the culture in question: I had no appropriate way of discussing rabbit hunting, although it was mentionable in any one of the genres available to the farmers who were friends of my parents. (It *became* obscene to my parents, but only in the culture of our family.) But I've already described witnessing writing both as a genre (in terms of the relational regularities it displays between an event, its witnessing, and an audience) and as an infraction of conventional expectations: it has its place in culture, as a genre; but as a genre it also disturbs social "rules" because it is "about"—more accurately, it *signposts*—the obscene. Now I want to specify formally that it is precisely as a generic anomaly that it functions, within culture, as an infringement of cultural expectations. The social infraction it commits is an infraction precisely with respect to the genre array that defines a given culture, since the (re)phrasing of infraction that is characteristic of witnessing entails the appropriation (or *détournement*) of preexisting genres—those that are definitionally *not* dedicated to the kind of subject matter a given culture may classify as obscene, but get taken over for the special purposes that are those of witnessing. Culturally speaking, witnessing is thus a genre of writing that is constitutively parasitic on other genres. It requires us, therefore, to consider briefly how and why the array of genres that constitutes a culture may be vulnerable to takeover, or at least open to infiltration, by a discourse of extremity such as witnessing writing, a figural "presentation" of the obscene that thereby itself becomes representative of the obscene within culture, intervening in the affairs of culture as the bearer of a reminder of what culture-as-civilization ignores.[5]

What genres regulate, with varying degrees of rigidity and flexibility, is the social appropriateness of discursive behavior. Michael Halliday has pointed influentially to what he dubs *field, tenor,* and *register* as the areas of appropriateness that genres regulate. That is, for a given kind of interaction, there is subject matter that is admissible or inadmissible, there are suitable and unsuitable forms of interpersonal relationality (different etiquette, if you will), and finally there are options, which may be variously acceptable or otherwise, relating to the style or vehicle of communication. If I'm carpeted (God forbid) by the president of my university in his office, the subject matter under discussion will be relatively restricted, and hierarchical niceties will be observed; I'd better not decide, furthermore, to send a friend in my place or to respond with a casual e-mail message. At a dinner party, though, things will be somewhat different, even if it is attended by the same president: jokes, first names, a relaxed conversational style, a much wider range of subject matter become possible, even mandatory (and narrow professional concerns will be excluded as unsuitable to the occasion). Given such generic regulation of culturally appropriate discursive behavior, the obscene is defined as that domain of experience or event, having historical actuality and formally recognized as real (not a fiction),[6] for which the culture finds itself, generically speaking, poorly equipped—or even totally unequipped—so that there are few or no conventions of appropriateness that might accommodate it. It is im-pertinent in the sense that it can only be "mentioned" at the price of some degree of inappropriateness or generic infraction, in respect of field, tenor, or register, and testimonial interventions, as reminders that signpost the obscene, are thus inevitably untimely incursions on the scene of culture.

This does not mean that there are *no* genre conventions of any kind that permit discussion of the obscene (which is, as I've said, an integral part of the culture that consigns obscenity to its margins). The etiquette may require hushed voices, circumstances of great intimacy and trust, "not in front of the children, dear." Alternatively, joking may be enjoined, or the kind of *avoidance chatter* in which public discourse (the media, politicians, pundits) so egregiously indulged in the early years of AIDS, and indeed still does, earning it the sobriquet of an "epidemic of signification" (Paula Treichler) or an "epidemic of interpretation" (Alain Ménil). Also, another quite proximate culture (say, working class rather than bourgeois, or that of the young as opposed to an older generation) may be less, or more, squeamish than one's own; it may be okay to talk of X at school, but not in church. There is no evidence, for example, that in Nazi Germany—where people carefully looked away, as people in contemporary cities look away from the homeless, if they chanced upon a group of emaciated, filthy, lice-infested prisoners—the bureaucracy that shuffled memos about the "transport" of "items" *(Stücke),* the police, military, and medical personnel who engaged in "actions" and "selections," or the political leaders who envisioned a "final solution," had any sense of inappropriateness or thought their vocabulary, euphemistic as it obviously was, inadequate to the realities (of persecution and extermination) they were organizing, any more than the farmers my parents knew had problems discussing the slaughter of rabbits. Himmler, it is true, made a now infamous speech in which,

without irony, he praised the men and women of the SS for their heroism in carrying out a difficult, but necessary, assignment without being able to bask in the glory of public recognition. These matters were subject to secrecy, then; but to the officials involved they were not generically obscene. However, the members of the population who were not included in the official culture and the associated command structure were in a position after the war to claim that they had not "known" of these matters because they were not generically available for acknowledgment (let alone for discussion) outside of officialdom, and were thus relegated to the very fringes of cultural consciousness, where they were "just" a nightmare in the head.

But it is exactly the proximity of different cultures and the different status of the obscene within them—adults may whisper, but children are protected, a bureaucratic culture takes matter-of-fact cognizance of what ordinary folks are expected to ignore—that makes it possible for generic arrangements (the precise structure of a given array) to *shift,* a process aided by the complexity and relative autonomy of the discursive phenomena—field, tenor, and mode—that genre regulates. A solecism with respect to subject matter may be allowed to pass, for example, if an etiquette of relationality is respected.

Indeed, the so-called rules of genre are, in reality, fairly flexible; they're more like definitions of certain regularities of practice that may admit considerable variance; and indeed—this is an axiom—even genuine rules (as in sports, or those concerning legal evidence) are never coextensive with the "games" that are actually played under their aegis. To say then that, on behalf of those limit events and experiences that a given cultural habitus consigns to its offstage as obscene, witnessing is committed to a practice of "intentional" infraction or solecism, is to imply only that it is required to "play" with the regularities of conventional genre expectations—to commit "errors" of grammar or lapses in taste; to perform exercises in inappropriateness—in ways that are initially made possible by the flexibility and "give" inherent in any given generic array.

Indeed the real problem of witnessing is rather that such generic lapses occur quite frequently in any case; and when they do they are regularly ignored or dismissed, as unintended, insignificant, accidental cultural "noise." If, through ignorance or accident, I use my fish fork to eat salad my host(ess) is unlikely to make a federal case of it—her sense of etiquette requires that the lapse be ignored, precisely because it can be regarded as a lapse. So, in order for witnessing's infractions of generic convention to be understood as intentional and hence as constituting a meaningful (if untimely) utterance, one to which it is appropriate to attend, it becomes necessary that they fall within the range of a certain metaetiquette that, quite paradoxically, cancels normal politeness rules and stretches the concept of appropriateness in such a way that it becomes able to encompass, without necessarily welcoming, an untimely intervention, as a *purposeful* infringement of what is considered appropriate. Such an infraction, having to do with the obscene, is of a different order from those violations of genre convention that are already, so to speak, "covered" by an extension of those conventions themselves (as when "politeness" requires my hostess to ignore my lapse in "etiquette").

The paradoxical metaetiquette required by witnessing is an etiquette of infraction or an art of im-pertinence, then, one that is able to signal to an audience that the speaker or writer—the rhetorical subject—is having recourse to *exceptional* means for lack of more suitable conventional ones. But for such a practice, which is witnessing's generic vocation, there are by definition no rules, and indeed no established regularities; it is bricolage and what Certeau calls an "art de faire," something that has to be made up as one goes along and hence a praxis that resists theorization because its instantiations are inevitably singular. They are without precedent, and cannot be repeated without running the risk of becoming conventional and thus losing their power, as disturbing solecisms, to index the obscene. Teenagers practice this art of the conventionally meaningful solecism when they dye their hair green or have their tongue pierced as a way of "bugging" figures of authority or maturity; but in the much more dangerous context of the Gandersheim factory, Robert Antelme's deliberately incompetent sweeping is necessarily an improvised technique, one that has to square the circle of "bugging" the German woman without incurring sanctions, and can scarcely be repeated without either becoming habit (and ceasing to signify) or—more likely—becoming recognizable as a deliberately oppositional act and incurring wrath. As it is, he is playing with fire (the woman descends on him furiously, and only at the last minute decides to dismiss him mildly). So the calculus of testimonial solecism is always a necessarily delicate one, for the "error" *must* be recognized as an intentional infraction, so that it can't be ignored or dismissed; yet for it to be received as a meaningful error, it must not—even in more normal circumstances of reception than Antelme's—provoke excessive indignation or become an object of censure (and so of censorship). Between the likelihood of being dismissed as an unimportant lapse and the danger of being dismissed more angrily as unacceptably im-pertinent and confrontational, the range of maneuver is limited. The intended infraction of conventional genre expectations, as an indexical *détournement* of its audience's attention in favor of the obscene, must itself be *détourné* in the sense of hinted at, smuggled in, not overt. A hijacking if you will, but a hijacking that slips discreetly past the antihijacking guards, getting attention but escaping sanction. Such an operation might conceivably entail some quite complicated rhetorical twists and turns, and its tricks and devices are subject to a condition of constant invention and reinvention, of permanent renewal.

Another way of describing this cultural vocation of witnessing would be to say that a *captatio*—the form of *détournement* that captures favorable attention for subject matter an audience is not predisposed to take a benevolent interest in—has to be associated with the particular act of troping that is known as catachresis. Catachresis is the name given to a kind of lexical error or making do, a form of bricolage whereby in the absence of a "proper" term another term is inappropriately, but necessarily (and hence in a sense legitimately or at least pardonably) *détourné,* turned away from its dedicated function, and pressed into alternative service. (Etymologically, catachresis signifies counterusage, although it is often translated "abuse" or "misuse.") For example, if the word *arm* properly refers to the upper limbs of humans and other primates, it is catachrestically employed by English-speakers, in a make-do kind of way, for that part of a chair on which one's arm rests (French has a proper term, *accoudoir,* for this object). Catachresis is thus a figural operation whereby a literal term is made available for other uses by means of associations that are normally metaphoric (a chair arm resembles my upper limb) or metonymic (I rest my upper limb on the arm of the chair), or of course both.

Mutatis mutandis, this is the case also when catachresis operates, as it does in witnessing, at the level of genre rather than of lexicon: it is by virtue of either resemblance or proximity or both that a conventional genre can be extended or appropriated, "turned" so as to accommodate material that is culturally obscene in that no genre was "properly" (i.e., conventionally) dedicated to it—material that was, therefore, inappropriate in every genre. And as a culturally familiar form of appropriative making-do, a catachrestic move—which may of course range from an appropriation so discreet as to escape notice to one that is very bold—has some potential for achieving a kind of legitimacy for the rhetorical subject on grounds of expressive necessity. No other means existed for saying what needed to be said; in the absence of direct means (a dedicated genre), indirect, figural means requiring reading (a substitute, appropriated genre) have been resorted to, even though these means are inappropriate. Thus catachresis can work the magic whereby an infraction is read as deliberate, but necessary, and hence as constituting, not an error and not an act of madness or even of gratuitous provocation, but a meaningful utterance that requires—not despite but because of its untimely character—to be taken seriously. The sole condition of such an outcome is, however, that the generic catachresis not become conventional (like the lexical catachresis *arm*) but retain its rhetorical character as improvisation, a discursive making do or *art de faire* that disturbs ordinary genre expectations and may well bring in its train a certain sense of anxiety. The untimely signposting of the obscene is incompatible with habits, conventions, and clichés because its crucial task is to awaken its audience from the grip of such cultural "Dalmane."

Because living and dying, for example, are closely identified (they are proximate phenomena and they resemble each other), the genre of autobiography or life writing can readily be adapted catachrestically to become an account of one's dying, an autothanatography. Because dying can scarcely be dissociated from different ways of dying, certain ways of dying regarded as obscene (dying in an extermination camp, dying of AIDS) can be smuggled into the form of an autothanatography. Finally, because dying is proximate to death itself, the autobiography of a subject dying in an obscene manner can even present itself—it is a version of the figure of prosopopoeia—as spoken with the voice of one already dead. This is the genre, a catachrestic adaptation of autobiography, of Harold Brodkey's *This Wild Darkness:*

> The trouble with death-at-your-doorstep is that it is happening to you. Also, that you are no longer the hero of your own story, no longer even the narrator. Barry was the hero of my story and Ellen the narrator. The tale was of my death among other people's lives—like a rock in the garden. (68)

Here the figure of liminality that is death-at-your-doorstep allows Brodkey to trope himself (note the past tense verb "was") as one whose process of dying is already complete. The autobiographical narrative, of which he is at once the actual hero and the actual narrator, is troped in this way as one that is being lived, Brodkey being "like a rock in the garden," by Brodkey's physician Barry and narrated by his wife Ellen. But the supposed rock in the garden is also, in fact, the author of the text, which is thus fictionally spoken by one who is dead. In that way it impersonates death-at-your-doorstep, but not the death-at-your-doorstep that is happening to Brodkey even as he writes; it is the death-at-your-doorstep that is happening, *through* Brodkey's writing, to the readers of the text, the ambiguity of the pronoun "you" being therefore crucial. What is happening to me, Brodkey implicitly claims, I can make happen to you, even though I may be at the very periphery of your consciousness like a rock in the garden, or like the dead, thanks to a text able to function as the cultural equivalent of death-at-your-doorstep.

If catachresis legitimates the infraction entailed in generic (mis)appropriation on behalf of the obscene, the logic of Brodkey's text suggests, then, that this same legitimation entails also for readers a factor of anxiety, troped here as the haunting of culture ("it is happening to you") from a position of extreme liminality, that of a rock in the garden. If witnessing writing, as a discourse of extremity, is anxiogenic, the anxiety it produces can only be understood, then, in rhetorical terms, as a function of the troubling sense of inappropriateness or impropriety, bordering on the uncanny, the "What is going on here?" feeling that can result from the practice of generic catachresis. English-speakers are not troubled by having to employ the word *arm* for the part of a chair on which they lean their elbow, but a catachresis of genre may well be a different matter, when in troubling a habitus it disturbs some basic cultural assumptions, expectations, and indeed certainties, such as, here, the "certainty" that being alive and being dead are different states. In particular, it produces anxiety as a nagging sense of inadequacy, on the one hand, and of misfit on the other.

Thus the witnessing subject, who is conscious of making do in a generic situation that is less than ideally adapted to the purpose, is led to complain of what that subject experiences as the inadequacy of language, an inadequacy experienced as all the more dramatic because the witness tends, of course, to subscribe—as everyone does—to an eyewitness, direct report theory of witnessing and to want desperately, therefore, to be able to give direct expression to the full measure of the pain and horror the text is supposed to convey. Witnesses allude very frequently, as I've mentioned, to this dilemma. Meanwhile, the audience responds with anxiety to a text that poses a difficult taxonomic, and hence also interpretive, problem: it appears to espouse a familiar genre but to be making unfamiliar and possibly inappropriate use of the genre; it feels like an error or an infraction, yet the error is apparently deliberate and designed to be expressive of a truth—a truth that can't be said, it seems, more directly. Some readers react to this elusiveness defensively and with irritation; others with pain and a sense of perhaps unfocused concern. Others again, or the same—whether indignant or disturbed—may interpret this rhetorically generated anxiety in a way symmetrical with the writer's sense of linguistic inadequacy, that is, in terms of the dominant folk-theory, and read their anxiety as a response to the vividness of representation they attribute to the text: "It was like being there," "It gave me a feeling of what *x* is really like."

If witnessing as a discourse of extremity functions socially as a form of "phantom pain," that is, of real events and historically lived traumas that are made available, but in an elusive, hard to situate, and uncanny way, to those who might not otherwise have grasped the nightmare in their heads, it is then because of its curiously undecidable rhetorical and hence cultural status, as an error that nags in this way at the consciousness because it seems not to be an error at all, but something anomalous in the way that a specter is anomalous, haunting the periphery of our safe and protected world like death at the door, with a message it intimates but does not speak. What is traumatic to the individual witness comes to haunt the social, as an anxiety of which witnessing is the vehicle; but the haunting is experienced, on one side—by the witnessing subject—as an anxiety of inadequacy (a failure of writing), that is, a sensation of hauntedness, and on the other—among the audience—as a haunting, an anxiety of elusiveness. But this last may in turn be reinterpreted so as to justify anger, denial, or rejection as a response to excess or transgression: overemphasis, inappropriate graphicness, or what in French is called *impudeur,* impudicity. The witness, that is, is held responsible for an error of taste.

My claim, then, is that this anxiogenic and spectral character of witnessing as a vehicle of the obscene arises from the "genrelessness" of obscenity, *not* from its supposed extraculturality or from the (also illusory) representational inadequacy of language. Language per se is neither adequate nor inadequate; its salient semiotic characteristic is aboutness (referentiality), not adequacy or inadequacy to an object. What makes language *feel* adequate to its users is generic appropriateness, and conversely I've argued that a situation in which generic catachresis becomes necessary generates in witnessing subjects the sense that language is inadequate to their purposes. But I've also proposed that the anxiety generated in an audience by a witness's recourse to generic catachresis, experienced as an intentional infraction of conventional expectations, may be *interpreted,* sometimes angrily, as a function of the witnessing discourse's representational vividness or exactness, that is, of an unusually successful (if not necessarily welcome) achievement of linguistic adequacy to its object. As for the supposed extraculturality of the obscene—often expressed by "un-" words like *unmentionable, unspeakable,* even *unnatural*—I've argued from the axiom of cultural globality that culture (sing.) does not admit of an outside, so that "un-" words don't describe externality with respect to (global) culture, but liminality and beyondness with respect to specific, restricted, and local cultures.

Testimonial writing is discourse, then, that speaks "from" a cultural periphery where it must make do, catachrestically, with genres that scarcely admit it. In that sense it belongs to the more general category of what I call parasocial discourse, that is, discourse that addresses a culture assumed to be general, mainstream, or dominant on behalf of subjectivities identified as marginal or (in Deleuze and Guattari's sense of the word *minor*) minoritized. It is just that witnessing is culturally rather than socially marginal: I mean that it relates to the cultural category of the obscene, even though the subject of witnessing, as a person, *may* also be a member of groups that are socially marginalized or stigmatized (including through association with the obscene, as was frequently the case with returning concentration camp survivors). Obviously, when witnessing *is* both socially marginalized by virtue of its subject and culturally obscene as a function of its topic—the case, most crucially, of AIDS writing by gay-identified authors—the task of parasocial address becomes that much more complex. Its nature as parasocial writing nevertheless resides in its vocation to bring the culturally obscene onto the cultural scene, and to claim the definitional status of what perforce registers, therefore, as liminal, diffuse, elusive, anxiogenic, or haunting.

One way to capture the nature of witnessing, then, would be to say that it is *edgy* writing. Edgy in that it is liminal, writing "from" the periphery but "in" language and genres that are simultaneously recognizable and familiar, but "turned" and strange. Edgy because it is anxious writing from the perspective of its subjects, and because it induces anxious responses in its audience. It doesn't necessarily have an uncanny effect, but the two major characteristics of the obscene—the fact that it is integral to culture and yet only diffusely "present" within culture—do suggest in their combination that something akin to the dynamic identified in psychoanalysis as that of repression and the return of the repressed (in always transformed guise) is operative. The repression is cultural in character, however, not psychoanalytic, and its return, therefore, is a social phenomenon. In coining the word *parasocial,* I wanted, therefore, to suggest, in part, a possible analogy with the events and experiences often referred to as paranormal, and in particular with effects of haunting as the manifestation of liminal areas of consciousness that, because they can be neither fully ignored nor fully identified, seem spectral and elusive, diffuse in the way that the obscene is discursively diffuse. But again, it is a cultural haunting I'm referring to, neither metaphysical in nature nor confined to the perception of individuals, but historical, and a manifestation of the "ghostly matters" about which the sociologist Avery Gordon has written compellingly—something, that is, that falls under the aegis of the *hantologie* (hauntology) that Derrida (1993) declares inseparable from every ontology. It is not surprising, therefore, in this light, that witnessing writing may haunt its readers, who find themselves unable to throw off its effect; or that haunting should be a frequently recurring metaphor in witnessing writing itself—for example, in the metaphor of death-at-your-doorstep—for its own discursive situation, as a form of parasocial discourse.

National cultures, these days, seem increasingly aware of the sense in which they are haunted, both by past atrocities and by the continuing injustices those atrocities have spawned. The list crowds the mind; it is an endless one. Germany has its *Vergangenheitsbewältigung* (dealing with the past); France struggles to come to grips with the reality of Vichy; the United States continues to live the aftermath of slavery and the Civil War; many countries, both Western and non-Western, deal and fail to deal with that of colonialism, Australia with its genocidal founding as a modern nation, South Africa with *apartheid,* Argentina with the so-called dirty war, Israel with the reality of Palestine; etc. Politicians in these countries generally seem anxious to *lay* these ghosts, exhorting people to "turn the page" and "move on," that is to forget; they themselves forget that the ghosts can't be laid without first allaying the injustices that are the present's legacy from the past, something that nations founded in violence appear constitutively unable to do, so definitional to them are violence and injustice. And, of course, plenty of new obscenities arise—AIDS is one—to haunt societies that are already haunted by those of the past. Western countries that were slow to acknowledge AIDS when it was a phenomenon of "risk groups" continue to marginalize it as an affliction of ghetto populations; and the Western AIDS writing that is my own subject matter is itself mostly oblivious of—and so haunted by—the devastating epidemic as it is being experienced in the "developing" countries of the tropical belt (much of Africa, South and Southeast Asia, Central and South America, including the Caribbean), Jamaica Kincaid's *My Brother* being a notable and very important exception, to which I will turn, albeit too briefly, at the end of this book.

So I would rather define the relation of modern cultures to the limit events and experiences that define them as an issue, not solely of memory, as is often said, but more broadly of hospitality (which includes hospitality to memories). Rather than attempting to lay the ghosts, it would be better to attend to all the obscenities, past and present, that knock for attention—in part through witnessing writing—at culture's door. Even better, to try to conceive what it would mean to open the door to them. And better still, as Derrida (1997) puts it (quoting Pierre Klossowski), to begin to contemplate the question of "prolonging the moment of the open door" [prolonger le moment de la porte ouverte]. Can we—to put it more idiomatically—not only open the door to the obscene, but also learn to hold the door open? Can we be less chary of hospitality in the future than in the past? It's possible that teaching—including the teaching of witnessing writing—holds some of the answers to that question; and I'll return therefore to the question of teaching hospitality, in the form of hospitable reading, in my final chapter. For if cultures, and notably national cultures, possess in their array a genre specifically dedicated to the relationality of culture and what is culturally other—a genre whose "rule" is precisely the suspension of conventional expectations and responses in the presence of the unfamiliar and the alien—that exceptional genre is the practice of hospitality. Testimonial texts, as untimely interventions, can scarcely *expect* hospitable reading, under pain of forfeiting the very effectiveness they derive from their untimely character. But those of us who are privileged to work in the gatekeeping institutions known as schools arguably have an ethical obligation to help the young understand why, when faced with textual indexings of death-at-your-door, *entertaining* the specter (both inviting it past the threshold and according it one's consideration) is the salutary option.

Figuration (Uttering the Unstatable)

Let's recapitulate. The gist of my argument, so far, is that contrary to received opinion, testimonial writing is not so much a descriptive practice (whether historical or fictional) as it is a symbolic practice: it has the signposting character of an indexical sign. That is, it performs a captation, capturing its readers' attention and redirecting it toward the obscene, that in culture which is otherwise culturally occulted: known but not acknowledged, or if you will, "occulturated." Since the obscene is wholly or partially excluded from the set of genres that constitutes a given culture, and so liminalized, witnessing writing is obliged to exercise its indexing function through the performance of an act of generic catachresis: in the same discursive act whereby the attention of its readers is turned in an unwonted direction, it turns a conventional genre to new purposes—indeed, these two acts are, in their effect, one and the same. But such an outcome—which amounts to the performance of an untimely cultural intervention—is further dependent on there being what I have called a metaetiquette capable of canceling normal rules of appropriateness and politeness, so that, instead of being received as an error to be shrugged off and ignored, or alternatively angrily dismissed (responses that amount to a denial of the obscene), the testimonial intervention is read instead as an intended act of im-pertinence, and hence achieves the status of a meaningful utterance. The sense of inadequacy and anxiety that accompanies such untimely interventions—inadequacy on the part of the witness, anxiety on the part of readers—is the marker of testimonial's cultural success (if that is the right word) in its function as a kind of visitation, a cultural wake-up call. And I have proposed, finally, that hospitality is the genre reserved in many if not all cultures for the kind of discursive interaction, lying outside the expectations of normal interchange, that requires engagement of this kind with the culturally "alien," an untimely intervention.

Part of this argument, as I mentioned earlier, has some affinity with Deleuze and Guattari's (1975) discussion of "minor" literature, defined as a dialectal inflection of a major(itarian) language. More specifically, though, the discursive moves I have sketched correspond to the term *agencement* that is frequently used by these authors and of which they give an account in *Mille plateaux* (1980). *Agencement* has been conventionally translated in English as "assemblage" or "device," but I also want to capture in this book another aspect of its sense by referring to it as the act of agencing. In this way I hope to suggest that the rhetoric of testimonial writing entails a depersonalization and deauthorization of the author, who as an "agencer" becomes instead the agent of an intersubjective writing/reading relation that is *other* than that of "reader" to "writer." That is, agencing writing has a signposting function such that it becomes readable much *less* as an expression of authorial subjectivity, and much *more* as an instrumentality, one that is capable of deflecting readerly attention in the direction of what—in the case of testimonial writing—is culturally obscene: the extreme event or disaster, the collective trauma that, by reason of generic unavailability, cannot be represented in mimetic fashion but nevertheless *can* be "presented," or better, *presenced* in this only apparently roundabout way.

Now Emile Benveniste accustomed us some time ago to the idea that every instance of language-use functions simultaneously as a statement or *énoncé* (that is, a "piece" of language that has structure and performs reference) and as an utterance, or *énonciation,* that is, a linguistic event mediating an interaction that entails interpretation of a hermeneutic rather than a referential kind (yes, reference is itself the product of an interpretive act). The interpretation of an utterance includes the utterance's object—the context in which the event of utterance becomes meaningful—as well as its subject (say, the psychology and/or motivation of the utterer). Agencing, in those terms, could be described, then, as the means whereby readerly (interpretive) attention is diverted both from the subject of the statement and from the subject of the utterance (i.e., from the author), so as to focus instead on the *object of the utterance,* what the event of the discourse's utterance is "all about"—something that can at best be only surmised. But what testimonial writing as an indexical practice is "all about" is what it points to or signposts: the culturally occluded obscene, something that is less "surmised" than the reader is *reminded* of its existence. To the reader it was never, strictly speaking, unknown, but unacknowledged, so that now it is "recognized," in an act of anagnorisis, a word that implies a "raising" or perhaps a turnabout of one's knowledge (or alternatively—if *ana-* is a double negative—the negation of one's not knowing). The axiom of agencing, then, is that what is referentially unstatable is not for that reason unutterable.

Many of the texts I address in this book imply or make use of a metaphor of relay in their account of what the writing of testimonial entails, or they employ other metaphors suggestive of portability, such as reporting (chapter 3) or fostering (chapter 5). Such tropes describe the witnessing writer as a mediating agent, connecting or attempting to (re)connect those who cannot speak (the dead) and those (the living) who seem oblivious to their fate, as if it were not relevant to them. But they do not imply that the author writes "on behalf of" or ventriloquizes those who cannot speak. The implication is rather that writing is an act of agencing by means of which the hauntedness characteristic of the writer's consciousness is transferred or carried over as a haunting of the reader's consciousness, a haunting that takes the form of the reader's becoming aware of the hauntedness that reader had previously been subject to but had failed to recognize or acknowledge. Writing so understood is thus not an act of representation in the normal sense so much as, through agencing, an act of counterdenial whose seat is in readerly consciousness. And it is the assemblage of linguistic or other signs that makes writing, in this way, a vehicle of return for what, by virtue of its genre apparatus, aftermath culture consigns to the liminal status of the known but unacknowledged (the obscene), that I will describe as exercising a figural function, one that does not directly represent its object so much as make it recognizable as a readable presence, and so represents it indirectly. My claim, furthermore, is that it is figuration, so understood, that legitimizes the practice of generic catachresis, causing it to be received not as an accident or an error but as meaningful in the sense of interpretable; that figuration, in other words, constitutes the metaetiquette we have been looking for. But the metaphor of relay is significant because it underscores not only the hypermediated, agenced character of figural representation—which in order to be successful must be well performed by a writer but also "picked up," as it were in a second act of relay, by a reader—but also, and as a consequence, the relative precariousness of such a rhetorical maneuver, a precariousness that is due to its inevitably roundabout and makeshift character, by comparison with the supposedly direct mode of representation—itself a contradiction in terms—that is "denied" it. For a relay can be fumbled, dropped, or otherwise misperformed; and it may even be refused.

Figuration performs a (for example, linguistic) relay because it relays the language function of stating by (and as) the language function of uttering. It does so through an assemblage or phrasing the unconventionality of which—whether it be spontaneous or calculated—produces in the reader a degree of doubt concerning its statement meaning (or content). The statement meaning of any language-use answers the question: what is this language-use *about*? Thus "It's raining" is a statement about the weather. As an utterance, however, the statement about the weather might mean something like: I don't feel up to going to the movies tonight, let's stay indoors and snuggle in front of the TV. The utterance meaning of a language-use answers the questions: why is this utterance being proffered? and (hence) what are the "contextual" circumstances that make its utterance meaningful? A figural phrasing works, then, by temporarily blocking statement meaning so that the addressee becomes an interpreter or reader, detained by the phrasing to the point of substituting for statement meaning an utterance question (why is this utterance, with its anomalous statement, being proffered?) and—in the best-case scenario—answering that question in a way that legitimizes the deficiency in the statement (i.e., it is being uttered because, to judge from the evidence, it is *about* something that it is undesirable, difficult, or impossible to state outright). Which may in turn trigger an interpretive move tending to identify (i.e., acknowledge) the nature of the statement meaning that the utterance, in this hypermediated way, has succeeded, not quite in stating but in indicating by means of its way of not (quite) stating it, thus demonstrating the axiom of agencing, that the unstatable is not necessarily unutterable.

So understood, figuration is a rhetorical realization of language use (or of the use of other signs) that produces the utterance as, in semiotic terms, an instance of indexicality—the kind of indexicality that intervenes under cultural conditions of denial as a mode of counterdenial. Figuration gains attention (achieves *captatio*) through its unconventionality of phrasing; this same phrasing then functions as an *agencement* (an "agencing assemblage") that redirects the attention it has captured. Following the direction of indexical pointing, cultural subjects, as readers, are led to acknowledge that which is liminal to the culture, and so haunts it: the unstatable. Resorting to rhetorical terminology, we might say, then, that figuration is structured like an allegory: what under circumstances of cultural denial cannot be stated, or can be stated only imperfectly, figuration nevertheless succeeds, like an allegory, in *conveying* (another word, like *relay,* that implies portability). And allegory, then—etymologically speaking otherwise (or perhaps otherness speaking?)—names the way figural language-use, as an exercise in indexicality, entails recognition of cultural hauntedness. The allegorical character of figuration is spectral in its effect.

Grace Paley (1991) has a very short narrative, "Three Days and a Question," that works out such an understanding of the reading of testimonial as attention more to utterance than to statement, more to interpretable gesture (an event) than to statable content (or structure), more to semiosis, in short, than to mimesis. On three separate days a similar event occurs. The narrator encounters, always on the street or while out and about, first an elderly Holocaust survivor, on the second occasion a young man with AIDS, and finally a Haitian taxi-driver, witnesses respectively to genocide, an inhumane epidemic, and North American racism. Each of these three has difficulties of (self-)expression, due to inadequate English in the case of the Holocaust survivor and the Haitian, and in the case of the PWA (person with AIDS) to the caution with which AIDS must be mentioned ("Carefully he says, AIDS," 53). Each is led therefore to supplement speech with the same gesture, thrusting out an arm—marked by a tattooed number, by Kaposi's lesions, by pigmentation—in the direction of his interlocutor. The interlocutor of the Holocaust survivor, who is not the narrator of the story, reacts with fear and anger. In the other two cases (in which the interlocutor is the narrator), she reacts to the PWA with embarrassment and unease (she and her friend "shift in our pockets," 54—an odd phrasing—looking for change); and then, to the Haitian, with a question. The question is addressed, however, not to the witness, but to us, her readers.

This question ("How? Why?") concerns the meaning of all three: "[t]hose gestures, those arms, the three consecutive days thrown like a formal net over the barest unchanged accidental facts" (54). But that phrase, "like a formal net," suggests that a kind of gear-change is being performed here (another mode of "shifting") and that the story-content as a narrative statement—a rehearsal of "accidental facts"—is becoming something else: the story as figuration, an agencing of the facts into a formal, that is signifying, net, "one story told" (54)—note the emphasis on utterance in the word "told," and simultaneously the elision of the authorial subject in the passive voice. This is the story as an invitation to reading. For if the narrator's questioning ("How? Why?") goes unanswered in the narrative statement (the rehearsal of facts), then perhaps the answer lies in the story's telling, its utterance. And if so, it is somewhat as if the narrator has taken on the task of repeating the three witnesses' gesture, doing so however, not by extending an arm but by proffering a story, agencing an utterance, holding out a figure (specifically, an allegory)—one that simultaneously withholds (in its statement) the very sense *it* attributes to those three gestures, and passes on responsibility, through its utterance, to its readers for interpretation of that significance.

These questions ("How?" "Why?") point us in the direction of a further significant theoretical observation concerning figuration. It is crucial, if figuration is to exercise its rhetorical function, substituting the readability of the relayed for more direct modes of representation that are culturally outlawed, for it to arouse readerly curiosity. It must be intriguing. We need therefore to distinguish between *conventionalized* tropes, whose allegorical reading has become automatic so that they no longer have the power to detain a potential reader, and figural events having a character of *singularity.* No one hesitates long over the phrase "a thousand sails," which is straightforwardly understood to be synonymous with a thousand ships. It is for this reason that, in his justly entitled *La Parole singulière*—a book, unfortunately not translated, about poetic figurality that has crucially influenced my understanding of testimonial figuration—Laurent Jenny avoids the terms *figuration* and *figure* in favor of an alternative notion of "the figural." I don't follow him in this respect because a singular phrasing is not necessarily unclassifiable and because the set of terms we have inherited from classical rhetoric, although it may need to be supplemented on occasion (cf. my discussion of stammering as a trope in chapter 3), provides a serviceable taxonomy, while the terms themselves, which sound rebarbative to modern ears but have disarmingly concrete and thus analytically helpful Greek and Latin etymologies, have a certain descriptive value. Nevertheless Jenny's point remains good. The figural assemblage capable of providing the metaetiquette that legitimizes unconventional appropriations of genre must itself be, not only unconventional, but also some sort of *trouvaille,* and as such capable of striking a reader's imagination as well as arousing curiosity.

In this respect it is figuration, as the metaetiquette of testimonial, that also furnishes the wit etymologically implied by the word *witness;* and as in the case of wit, the success of figural assemblages is conditioned on a double requirement of felicity. There being by definition no ready-made formula for singularity, no preexisting models, the figural (in Jenny's sense), like wit, is inevitably the outcome of improvisation and savvy. As a mode of bricolage it is a practical skill, like the *metis* of the Greeks, that resists theorization and can be performed with flair, or just as easily bungled. (That is why—outside of programmatic chapters such as this one and to an extent chapters 5 and 8—my argument in this book rests very largely on a series of local readings of particular examples.) But also, and again like witticisms, successful figural "solutions" can't be repeated (or can't be repeated too often) without losing their ability to intrigue the reader and produce the relay on which a response of detained, pensive, or engaged reading depends.

For a variety of reasons that include the changing character of successive historical traumas, which may render earlier rhetorical "solutions" to the witness's dilemma obsolete, as well as changing cultural conditions (Michael Rothberg, for example, demonstrates that Holocaust "representation" has been subject to modernist, realist, and postmodern moments), the genre of testimonial is always reinventing itself. But the crucial reason for the immense variety of styles and rhetorical solutions adopted in testimonial writing, as well as the range of genres that it appropriates, a variety that my few examples don't begin to do justice to, lies in the quality of singularity that is the sine qua non condition of the ability of figuration to haunt, and hence to be the vehicle of a return, through its indexical character, of what conventional culture occludes.

Witnessing writing is thus the product of a constant tension between the inevitable conventionality of "language"—whether in terms of genres or of tropes—a conventionality that makes *representation* possible, and a necessary invention or catachresis, again at the level of tropes as well as of genres, without which everything that representation "forgets," the excluded of both history and fiction as well as of everyday life, could not "return." It is surprising, perhaps, to realize that inventive devices of writing and other practices of *agencement,* a makeshift rhetoric of indexicality, hold the key to what is arguably the most important issue raised by the twentieth century's long history of atrocity, extremity, and trauma: the nature of the aftermath in which we all—all who survive—live on, and the problem, therefore, of the survival of memory. But, unless memory means only memorialization and aftermath means only forgetting, the victory of obliviousness in the form of an unchallenged and complacently denegational culture that mistakes itself for civilized, then the survival of memory—by which I mean the ability of culture's obscenities to return, and to return in a striking guise that haunts the mind, that is, our susceptibility to being reminded of what we prefer to forget—will have to depend on the availability, from generation to succeeding generation, of an art of witness—that is, of singularity—capable of keeping fresh, or of presencing, by figural means—and of re-presencing—what more conventional representations will increasingly consign to an (unpresenced) past.

That means, inter alia, that as the "original" witnesses and survivors age and die, new means of regenerating their witness will have to be found. It is partly with an eye to this problem that I study (in chapter 3) Pat Barker's historical novel *Regeneration* and its thematization of phenomena of reporting (re-porting) and repercussion (re-percussion) in relation to the war of 1914–18. For similar reasons I notice, at other places, the thematics of "relay" in a range of writing that includes Charlotte Delbo's *Auschwitz and After* (chapter 5) and the form of AIDS testimonial I call "dual autobiography" (chapter 6). And finally, I conclude the book by taking up issues concerning the teaching of testimonial writing to younger students. All these topics address crucial aspects of the problematics of memory, conceived as a *dynamics of return,* and demonstrate the degree to which testimonial writing understands itself, therefore, as a phenomenon of survival.

Lastly, however, survival, conceived in this way as the ability of the obscene to resist forgetting by returning, invites us to reflect also on testimonial as an art of untimeliness in a new and stronger sense of that word: not only the sense in which an intervention can be im-pertinent and a solecism-but-not-an-error, but also the sense to which I adverted in the preface, in which time, and the times, can be "out of joint"—Hamlet's knowledge. Our only access to the experience of trauma (other than to undergo it) is through the testimonial of survivors, who describe it, therefore, as the experience of living through (surviving) an event that feels like death, an event that for others may indeed entail their death. But if trauma, then, becomes the experience of surviving trauma, the very idea of "having survived" a trauma is seriously misconceived. The testimonials are unanimous that to "have survived" trench warfare, or the concentration and extermination camps, or AIDS, is to be *still surviving* experiences that were already themselves an experience of being, somehow, still alive although already dead. And, as Art Spiegelman's *Maus* demonstrates (see McGlothlin), that sense of surviving is not confined to the first generation. In such an experience of survival, not only does the present reproduce the past (a past that has failed to "pass") but also—this is a prominent theme in Primo Levi and Charlotte Delbo—part of the "original" trauma was the anticipation of renewed trauma in "having survived," that is, in continuing to survive it. So the flashbacks and hallucinations that form part of the symptomatology of post-traumatic stress disorder and enact most vividly the copresence of past and present, there and here, are not exceptional events of untimeliness; rather they are characteristic symptoms of a larger state of pathology or out-of-jointness, to which I give the name *aftermath,* the state of perpetually surviving a trauma that is never over.

That all who live on the planet, not just "trauma survivors" themselves, are living in the pain of aftermath is the key idea of this book, not because I have always thought so, but because such knowledge, and the desire to have it acknowledged, constitutes the principal motivation, I have learned, of witnessing writing and the reason, therefore, that underlies its rhetorical practice as an agencing of return. Such knowledge is both "useless" (Delbo's word for it) and necessary. There are those, that is, who in a situation of universal survivorhood are conscious of that situation, and recognize the untimeliness of aftermath, and those who, failing to acknowledge it, live in a falsely linear dimension of time that encourages obliviousness by fostering a belief in the distinctness of past, present, and future. Such people, faced with the evidence of disaster, are generally anxious to "turn the page," and regularly admonish those who remember to do likewise. But witnessing writing records the knowledge that in aftermath page-turning is not an option, while through its rhetorical structures—its figural assemblages and devices—it seeks to spread that conviction by making available to oblivious readers, via the experience of return, some evidence of *aftermath truth:* the truth of temporal disjointedness and the uncanniness it entails. What is that evidence? It is the reading experience produced (in an optimal scenario) by the symbolic function of figuration.

So my rough division of the chapters in this book into a group (2, 3, and 4) devoted to discourses of extremity and a second group (5, 6, 7, and 8) that takes up some of the issues of aftermath under the heading of phantom pain, is an approximation that should not be taken too seriously. My purpose is heuristic; I wanted only to indicate a difference, of an admittedly "timely" character, between two kinds of AIDS writing. A witness may write "in extremis," that is, from the midst of the situation of (initial) trauma that arises when one is surviving one's own dying of AIDS. (Similarly, Siegfried Sassoon and Wilfred Owen come to witness out of a sense of urgency born of their participation in the extremities of trench warfare.) But the alternative form of AIDS writing, the writing of aftermath, most frequently and characteristically takes the form of a surviving friend's, lover's, or relative's telling the story of another's dying, or sometimes of the epidemic itself as the writer has experienced it. What is interesting about this latter genre, however—I call it "dual" or "collective" autobiography by way of emphasizing its catachrestic and hence paradoxical character—is precisely that it often deconstructs the very distinction, between "extremity" and "aftermath" that I have just used to define it. This is most notably the case when the surviving writer is also an AIDSer (also surviving a dying) or is so closely bonded with the one who has died as to deny the difference in their identities (as, for example, in Monette's *Borrowed Time*). And consequently there is very often in "phantom pain" writing of this kind a corresponding enactment of anachronism that arises from a strong sense of repetition and return—an enactment that identifies the writing as a presentation of the untimely in the strong sense of the German word *unzeitgemäss* (not in conformity with time, or maybe: in conformity with untime), whereas "discourses of extremity" seem mainly conscious of their untimely status in the sense of their being im-pertinent or ill-timed, as in the French *intempestif.* A presentation of the untimely *(unzeitgemäss)* is, of course, automatically and by definition untimely *(intempestif),* unexpected and ill-timed, as well.

To say that phantom pain is to discourses of extremity as cultural effect is to testimonial cause would not be wrong but would nevertheless fall short of the mark, then, to the extent that untimeliness blurs and disrupts the neat temporal ordering (of past and present, trauma and aftermath, extremity and phantom) on which a cause-effect relation rests, simultaneously maintaining and dedifferentiating the terms. The sign of this blurring is the close nexus of returning (from extremity) and of returning (as a phantom presence in aftermath)—that is, of *survival* (the witness's survival, the cultural survival of pain)—to which so much witnessing writing attests. Trauma can survive culturally only through the survival of (a) witness to the pain, as the cause of an effect; yet the witness's survival of extremity, whether an existential or a merely literary survival, is itself a manifestation of the trauma's cultural return, that is, of the fact of aftermath: trauma is both in the past and not yet over; the past has not passed. And it is this baffling fact of aftermath in its untimeliness that is subserved by the rhetorical character of testimonial writing as generically catachrestic and hence figural in its mode rather than representational (more strictly as figurally rather than mimetically representational), and as having as a consequence the semiotic function of indexicality or, in another vocabulary of the symptomatic and the symbolic. The untimeliness of the writing's return in culture becomes the aftermath sign of culture's own readability.

Imagine that you are sitting in the subway minding your own business, not thinking of anything in particular. But, on the arm of a person sitting or standing near you, you unexpectedly notice the tattoo of a concentration camp survivor, or a purplish Kaposi's spot. Like the incidents Paley describes, these are sudden indexical reminders; their effect is untimely in both senses, because they yank together into a crasis of copresence contexts that are supposedly remote one from the other. Witnessing writing often makes telling use of symbolic objects of this kind (Alice's leg, in Delbo, for instance: see chapter 5), and also of symbolic spaces, like the selection ramp in Holocaust writing, or the hospital in AIDS and much other testimonial writing. More to the point, though, is that the writing itself characteristically has a similar function and exerts a similar power to remind, that is, to bring about a spectral return as a function of its own "returned," or phantom, character as figural writing.

Returning ("The Canto of Ulysses")

In Primo Levi's *Se questo è un uomo (Survival in Auschwitz),* there is a short chapter (109–15)—one of the richest and most complex in the volume, however—that can be read as defining the nexus between returning (i.e., returning "from" Auschwitz as a survivor) and bringing Auschwitz back (i.e., returning Auschwitz, causing Auschwitz to return)—bringing it back, that is, to those who were not there. Returning from Auschwitz, for Levi, is not effective unless it also realizes a return of Auschwitz itself. So it entails a project of agencing that he refers to (more simply) as telling the story, a project that he shares, moreover, with Charlotte Delbo (see chapter 5). Of course, an awareness of the unlikely success, not to say impossibility, of such a project already formed part of the ordeal of Auschwitz itself, as I have mentioned; it was the burden of nocturnal nightmares superadded to the ordeals of each day. But it seems to me that it is in the "Canto of Ulysses" chapter that Levi records his first exhilarating glimpse, while he was still in the camp—like a first glimpse of the Alps as one approaches Turin (114)—of its *possibility.* That is, the chapter is an account, readily readable as such although not explicitly so designated (that is, an allegorical account), of Levi's coming to witness following an example set, for him, by Dante's treatment of the figure of Ulysses—Homer's Odysseus—in the *Purgatorio.*[7] As such if offers an exploration of the nature of testimonial.

To return, for Levi, counts as a necessary reaffirmation of the humanity of humans that Auschwitz so radically challenged. The Auschwitz "experiment," as Levi describes it (87), was designed to demonstrate that, stripped of all the superficial signs of culture and brought to the limit of physical resistance by deprivation and exhaustion, humans become brutes, indistinguishable from animals, like the so-called *Muselmänner,* whom Levi calls "sommersi," those who have *gone under.* To return, then, is to cross in an inverse direction that limit, between humanity and animality, that the *Häftlinge* crossed, on entering the camp, in the direction of animality, in most cases never to return. But to return therefore imposes a significant revision of one's idea of what it actually means to be human, given that Auschwitz has experimentally demonstrated the falsity of the "civilized" definition of humanness that rests on culture's conventional signs, and rendered it forever obsolete. For Levi, thinking of Dante, this necessary redefinition comes like a trumpet call in the figure of Ulysses. It has to do with human inventiveness, the ability to exercise one's wits, and more specifically to exercise them in the bearing of wit-ness: telling the story, making Auschwitz return; an activity, as we've seen, that entails bricolage as a form of "practical intelligence," the ability to make use of the materials that are to hand for new and ingenious purposes to which they are not obviously adapted. In Ulysses' exhortation to his men as they boldly pass the Pillars of Hercules, the word "aguti" (signifying acuteness, sharpness, wit) rhymes with the word "bruti" (brutes), as that word's opposite. "Fatti non foste a viver come bruti," Ulysses tells his men ("you were not made to live as brutes"), going on to comment: "Li miei compagni fec'io sí acuti" [I made my companions so sharp], and Levi shows himself in the camp—I'll call this personage Primo—trying, "but in vain, to explain [to Jean] how many things this 'acuti' means" (114).

In Levi's view, then, the only possible riposte to Auschwitz's brutalizing of the human is a demonstration of human ingenuity and wit, an acuteness that one might see as exemplified, in the first instance, by Homer's Odysseus, the hero and archetypal survivor who uses his wits in order to return (to Ithaca), and who lives on in Dante's Ulysses and his praise of wit. But a similar inventiveness is exemplified also, as a kind of second-order acuteness, in Dante's bold reappropriation of Homer, his rewriting of the hero's story for new purposes, in the "canto d'Ulisse," understood as itself an example of inspired bricolage. And Levi in turn appropriates Dante's rewrite of Homer, in *Se questo è un uomo,* in a further act of ingenious making-do inspired by the unprecedented challenge of bearing witness to Auschwitz. Thus he participates in—or creates—a kind of tradition of inventiveness that reaffirms the human in response to Auschwitz and simultaneously demonstrates the degree to which the wit in witnessing is a matter of reappropriating existing culture for new purposes, that is, of catachresis—the purposes being those summarized by the word *return.* Witnessing so understood becomes a crucial practice in that, "after Auschwitz" (to echo a famous sentence of Adorno's), it restores some possibility of belief in the human again while acting—as the reminiscence of Ulysses had done for Primo in the camp—as a trumpet blast for those who sleep.

In later life Levi was to cite, as a figure for his understanding of what is at stake in returning, the old soldier in Tibullus (Elegy X), a survivor of wars who makes use of spilled wine on a tavern table to draw—poignant detail—a map of "the camps," while his companion, Tibullus's narrator, comfortably downs a glass: "Ut mihi potenti possit sua dicere facta / miles et in mensa pingere castra mero." In the same interview (Bianucci 1972), Levi also mentions Coleridge's Ancient Mariner, doggedly buttonholing the wedding guests "who don't want anything to do with him" (129), as well as—his very first example—Homer's Odysseus, willing to forgo his well-earned sleep in order to tell his tale of shipwreck at the Phaeacian court (Homer, books 6 and 7). But in the camp he had thought, not of Tibullus or Coleridge, but of Dante, and of the Ulysses canto (canto 26) of

Purgatorio, that is, of Dante's revision of Homer. Why? What underlies this unexpected visitation by Dante, I speculate, is on the one hand the radical incongruity of such an icon of high culture as the *Divina Commedia* amid the squalor of the Lager, its sheer *difference* from the camp's brutishness; but on the other the *use made of incongruity* by Dante in the astonishing exercise in appropriation and anachronism that he performs, rewriting Homer so as to substitute for Odysseus's return to Ithaca a very different history, in which return is resignified. For in Dante, Ulysses and his men are swallowed up, in open sea beyond the Pillars of Hercules, and in sight of Mount Paradise, at the pleasure of the Christian God ("com' altrui piacque," says Ulysses, as it pleased Another); so that he never makes it back to Ithaca and returns only, with his companion Diomedes, as a speaking flame encountered by Dante and Virgil in purgatory.

The implicit lesson here is that an art of ingenious appropriation and anachronism—that is of untimeliness—such as Dante's, forms the human response to disaster: the response of those who retain some semblance of humanity, and the response that affirms the value of the human. It is extremity that produces the misfit between conventional culture (say, Dante) and an experience of the obscene with which culture seems to have nothing in common, the misfit that makes the obscene unstatable. But catachrestic ingenuity such as the art of Dante can respond to disaster and its consequences by *making misfit itself into a vehicle of return.* The figure for such an art, then (a figure for figuration), is the survival of Ulysses and Diomedes as a double tongue of flame that tells a story, the story of passing a limit and of consequent submersion that analogizes for Levi the story of Auschwitz. This surviving flame thus emblematizes witnessing as a discourse of aftermath.

And in this light the "Canto of Ulysses" chapter is self-described as itself an anachronistic and untimely, double-tongued appropriation of Dante's appropriative move with respect to Homer. As such, it is a means of telling the story of Auschwitz in such a way as to cause Auschwitz to "return," of telling it, moreover, both "in Auschwitz" (to Jean) and "after Auschwitz" (to Levi's readers) so that ultimately this returning return *of* Auschwitz makes the differentiation of "in" and "after" Auschwitz moot. It is as if Auschwitz and its aftermath were so closely interdependent as to be inseparable: Auschwitz already anticipates its own aftermath, which in turn repeats Auschwitz. And Dante being both the model for Levi's move and its vehicle, it is not surprising that the name suggested by Levi for *his* act of double-tongued catachresis is allegory. The chapter figures the coming to witness allegorically, through the exemplum of Dante's Ulysses canto as an act of wit; and simultaneously it uses the canto as a figural vehicle for its own allegorical witnessing of Auschwitz, reenacting something like the semantic wrench that occurs when Tibullus's innocently used word, "castra" (military camps), suddenly reveals a capacity to evoke the concentration and extermination camps, the Lager.

One day in the camp, then, Primo is chosen to accompany Jean, a young Frenchman who is the Pikolo (the foreman's favored young assistant) of the work detail, to fetch the midday soup. This mission comes as a welcome relief from unremitting physical labor, and the spring day is warm; the two have an opportunity to walk together and to talk, like humans (not slaves). The moment is like an unwonted (untimely) incursion into Auschwitz of an after-Auschwitz mode of life, and the walk through the camp thus has a complex structural role in the textual assemblage. It binds together the witnessing of Auschwitz and, through the conversation of the pair, the exploration of witnessing in relation to a thematics of return; it alludes simultaneously to the narrative of the *Divine Comedy* (the couple of Primo and Jean replicating that of Dante and Virgil), and to the history of Ulysses' exhilarating passing of the Pillars of Hercules, followed by submersion, the cabbage and turnip soup at the end playing the role of the engulfing sea. Its ambiguity is encapsulated, furthermore, in a thematics of remembering and forgetting, for, undertaking to teach Jean some Italian, Primo is suddenly reminded of the Ulysses canto and begins to reconstitute it in his head, reproducing long passages once learned by heart and commenting on them with a kind of manic philological punctilio, while simultaneously desperate at the many gaps in his memory. The clear implication is that forgetting is the real danger of Auschwitz, the equivalent of "going under" and of reversion to "living as brutes." Both the possibility of returning one day to culture and culture's availability as a vehicle for the exercise of the human talent for wit are premised on an ability to remember, and specifically to remember culture (emblematized in Dante) under circumstances of disaster. Which means that if forgetting is what Auschwitz promotes, memory conversely names the form of return that is represented here by Primo's sudden reminiscence of Dante, his near-miraculous visitation by the spirit of Ulysses.

There is memory, then—synonymous with the possibility of survival, survival of the human, and thus of both return from Auschwitz and the return of Auschwitz—and there is everything that the soup represents. "*Kraut und Rüben? Kraut und Rüben.* The official announcement is made that the soup today is of cabbages and turnips. *Choux et navets! Káposzta és répak.* 'And over our heads the hollow seas closed up'" (115). Forgetting and submersion are related here to the Babel of languages in the camp, the mutual incomprehensibility and separation, one from the other, that divides guards and prisoners but more especially the prisoners among themselves, that is, the exact difficulty of communication that we see Primo and Jean struggling to transcend, the former using his inadequate French in an apparently hopeless attempt to initiate his friend, who knows no Italian, into the nuances and complexities of the Dante text that he has himself half forgotten.

So it is important that the text emphasizes both the incongruity of two Auschwitz inmates discussing Dante, with its implication (in view of the remoteness of Dante from the Lager) of their eventual submersion, and not only the elusiveness of the significance Primo attaches to his remembering of Dante but also the urgency he feels to transmit that (unstatable) significance to his companion, which together analogize testimonial but also seem, less optimistically, to dramatize a certain desperation and a clutching at straws on his part. Return is anything but a given: Primo's recall of Dante is imperfect, and Jean, despite his goodwill, may well fail to grasp the significance Primo wants, via Dante, to transmit. On the other hand, however, to readers of the chapter (that is, on the plane of utterance as opposed to statement), the very elusiveness of meaning acts as an indicator of allegory, as a possible figural vehicle of witnessing, while the incongruity of recalling Dante in Auschwitz functions as an irony—allegory and irony being moreover related tropes in that they are different ways of speaking with double tongue, and thus different vehicles of return. As an irony, the incongruity comments on our own easy familiarity with and unthinking acceptance of the conventions of culture (for us, that is, there is nothing strange about recalling Dante); thus it marks the distance from civilized conventions that characterizes the Lager, where Dante becomes strange. In this respect, the narrative functions as a discourse of extremity, putting us in the place of the prisoners who are surviving the trauma of Auschwitz and encouraging a form of readerly identification with their predicament. The allegory, though, signaled as it is by Primo's urgent need to transmit an elusive significance to Jean, functions rather as a vehicle of phantom pain, that is, of a return of Auschwitz within our own consciousness. The two tropes, grounded respectively in incongruity and elusiveness, form an assemblage or *agencement;* they work together to convert a text that, as statement, appears to present a situation of near hopelessness if not despair, into an utterance that can work as a vehicle of testimonial return.

Primo adverts to allegory in his brisk preliminary explanations of the *Divine Comedy* to Jean, before getting down to the real business, as it were, of the Ulysses canto. "Virgil is Reason; Beatrice is Theology," period (112). This dryness contrasts visibly, though, as the easily decodable to the unstatable, with the inexplicable significance Primo attaches to the Ulysses episode, the elusive insight he wishes to transmit to Jean, the sense of a trumpet blast that accompanies his reminiscence of Ulysses' speech to his men, and the momentousness he attributes to the famous anachronism of Ulysses' reference to God ("as pleased Another"). The text is contrasting two versions of allegory, an allegory of simple reference (a matter of straightforward equivalences, that is, of translatability), and a figural allegory that strongly resists explication because its meaning—"something gigantic that I myself have only just seen, in a flash of intuition, perhaps the reason for our fate" (115)—cannot be said, told, or translated (by Primo) and must instead be somehow grasped, intuited, or read (by Pikolo). Indeed, it is as if the very elusiveness of what Jean/the reader is invited to understand is the marker of its momentous significance, for it holds the key, perhaps ("forse"), to "il perché del nostro destino, del nostro essere oggi qui . . ." [perhaps the reason for our fate, for our being here today] (115). If there is a didactic allegory that consists (by etymology) of "speaking other" (saying Dante or Beatrice and meaning Reason or Theology), there is also an allegory of imponderables through which otherness, which cannot be spoken, achieves an utterance, an allegory in which our very destiny is at stake. The Ulysses canto, for Primo—and possibly for Jean, and even Levi's reader—is such an allegory; it is the allegory of witnessing, that is, of uttering as opposed to stating. But its mode is that of perhaps, possibly, *forse.*

The power of such an allegory, though, is that by virtue of its resistance to easy decoding it transcends linguistic inadequacy—the Babel of languages—by *alluding to* (indexing) a common destiny. The insistent shifters ("our," "here," "today") in Primo's final phrasing here (in Italian: "il perché . . . del nostro essere oggi qui . . .") could be said, I think, for here again "perhaps" is the order of the day, to enact precisely such a common destiny, by referring not only to the common fate of Primo and Jean but also to the commonality that links them to readers who are not "in Auschwitz" as they are, but in an "after Auschwitz" here-today of the readers' own, this "after Auschwitz" being linked to "in Auschwitz," however, by the power of reading. Are such readers implicated by their reading in the *same* incommunicable insight as Primo and Jean? Quite possibly not. For one thing, it is agenced for them, not by the Ulysses canto per se, but by its presencing in the assemblage that is Levi's text. What matters is the sheer fact of their being implicated. As it is for Jean to "grasp" what Primo fails to state, so it is for readers, puzzling over their own unstatable whys and wherefores—"il perché del nostro destino"—to become themselves a site where "Auschwitz," the name given to all these imponderables and unknowables, returns. And if it does, this moment of reading becomes an untimely one, comparable to Dante's anachronism and more particularly to the anachronism of using Dante to speak of Auschwitz. Thus Levi's phrasing here can be seen as the crucial instance of double tonguing in his double-tongued text; it extends the crasis (the bringing together) of Dante and Auschwitz by a crasis of Auschwitz and after.

Allegory of this kind, not so much merely resistant to easy decoding as it is ultimately unfathomable, might well be called Odyssean, in honor of Homer's man of stratagems and devices (or as Robert Fagles translates it, "of twists and turns") who is also a hero of return. For readers approaching Levi's text, and sensitive to its framing of an allegory of Auschwitz through (and as) an allegory of testimonial, the experience becomes one of apparently limitless readability. Take, for example, the allegorical relation between the incidents of Dante's canto 26 (the pilgrims' encounter with the tongue[s] of flame, the details of Ulysses' narrative about adventuring beyond the Pillars of Hercules) and what we think we know (from Levi and others) about the Lager. There is an elusive sense of fit, and a strong sense of incoherence or misfit. How to read Ulysses' passing of the Pillars of Hercules and the theme it suggests of crossing a limit or of going beyond? Should it be read as transgression, as the fate of Ulysses and his men would suggest and as, presumably, Dante intended? But why, then, does Primo interpret it so positively, as a passage from brutishness to acuteness signifying a possible return to human values (Dante's "virtute e conoscenza," "excellence and knowledge" in the translation)? And if it is a transgression, whose transgression, in Holocaust terms, is meant? That of the Nazis, who certainly crossed a limit in constructing their insane and inhumane "experiment"? That of the Jews, who we know from other writing (but not from Levi) felt variously that God was dead, or had abandoned them, or indeed was (justly?) visiting punishment on them? How does that square with the fact that Dante's God is not the Jewish God, but Christian?

For every coherence that can be constructed and seduces us into reading, there are any number of incoherences to attempt to resolve, so that one's reading becomes as involved as it is involving. Before long one is floundering in an open sea of readability that admits no possibility of closure. Levi is simultaneously enacting witnessing as a struggle to make ludicrously inadequate and inappropriate cultural instruments speak of extremity, and providing for his readers, through Odyssean allegory, a baffling experience of reading as an occasion of anxiety and puzzlement through which "Auschwitz" returns. Auschwitz, that is, as, precisely, the bafflingly incomprehensible experience ("esperienza") it was to those who were subjected to the "gigantic experiment" or "gigantesca esperienza" mounted by the Nazis. Auschwitz as, in the words of the brutal guard Levi encountered on his first day in the camp who snatched away the icicle with which he was attempting to slake his thirst, "hier ist kein Warum" (29), there are no whys and wherefores here.

Of course there is no common measure between the experience of Auschwitz and the experience of getting caught up in a complicated and ultimately insoluble allegory. If Auschwitz returns in reading, it returns not as "itself" (whatever that would mean), and not even as a representation of itself, but in symbolic guise, in the form of the experience/experimentation that is called, precisely, reading. German has a word—Levi carefully introduces it into his text, page 114—that might describe this kind of return; it is the word *Ahnung,* an obscure presentiment or foreboding (in this case an "afterboding"), an intimation or inkling. What the German woman in the Gandersheim factory experienced, for example, as a consequence of Antelme's performance of inadequate sweeping, was an *Ahnung,* some inkling of the nightmare "in her head" in the midst of which she was, also, obliviously living. Of those who are oblivious, one says exactly that they have "keine Ahnung," no inkling; and an *Ahnung* is always a bit creepy then, and notoriously hard to grasp, because it is not new knowledge so much as the return of knowledge one might have possessed, had it not been shut out or ignored. *Ahnung* in that sense is what testimonial is about.

So the function of testimonial is not to represent or to explain but to disturb and detain us, to give us pause, make us stop and become, if not pensive, then at least a bit troubled. One does not transmit an *Ahnung,* it cannot be communicated; but one *can* hope to provide the occasion of such a thing's happening to someone. Thus Primo, arriving with Jean at the kitchen, detains his friend before they join the line and the soup of cabbages and turnips closes over them; he urgently draws Jean's attention away from his daily business of soup-fetching, and redirects it toward an untimely sign, Dante's "so human and so unnecessary and yet unexpected anachronism":

> I keep Pikolo back ("Trattengo Pikolo"), it is vitally necessary and urgent that he understand this "as pleased Another" before it is too late; tomorrow he or I might be dead, or we might never see each other again. I must tell him, I must explain to him about the Middle Ages, about the so human and so necessary and yet unexpected anachronism, but still more, something that I myself have only just seen, in a flash of intuition, perhaps the reason for our fate, for our being here today . . . (115)

These supremely important whys and wherefores—"il perchè del nostro destino, del nostro essere oggi qui . . ."—respond, of course, to "hier ist kein Warum," and all the brutishness it entails. They are indeed crucial. But that is all we learn of them; tellingly, the sentence trails off into an ellipsis—the ellipsis of the unstatable?—before Primo can give substance to his "flash of intuition," and all his explanations about the Middle Ages, his glossings of the anachronism, are merely preliminaries, more the means by which Pikolo is detained, than the matter of Primo's *Ahnung.* So it seems that, finally, it is the detaining itself that signifies; and whether or how it becomes significant for Jean is ultimately up to Jean, who is about to be swallowed up, with Primo, in the soup line.

When Harold Brodkey writes that death-at-your-doorstep is happening to you, then, we can understand his elegant and striking sentence to mean, as a figure for witnessing, that an indexical sign is detaining us and signposting something about which we might otherwise have had *keine Ahnung,* no inkling. In the face of such a happening we can, like the wedding guests buttonholed by the Ancient Mariner, hurry on our way. We *are* busy people, are we not? Or we can stop, take pause, and attend to the witnessing gesture and its signposting, reading it as we may. That is what Grace and her companion, in Paley's story (a story of being detained), do while the story detains us with its own questions ("How? Why?"). For if it is true that the stakes of testimonial as a practice lie in acknowledging the commonality of the human—"our" destiny, "our" being here today—and if the corollary of that truth is that the denial of death, humanity's common fate, is therefore the root cause of discriminations, separations, injustices, and so-called crimes against humanity, then we might recall that tomorrow "he or I" (it matters not who) may be dead or, separation being death's surrogate, that "we may not see each other again." To ignore the witness, to refuse to read the witnessing gesture, is to reenact that kind of fate, to reimpose something like the very conditions of Auschwitz, in the form of separation, death's surrogate. To attend to the witness(ing gesture) is, however, not of course to overcome Auschwitz and the conditions of aftermath, but in refusing to deny death, in acknowledging its proximity (at the doorstep, tomorrow), to affirm a common link between other and self.

Part I. Discourses of Extremity

2. On Being Im-pertinent: The Ethics and Etiquette of Solecism

Joe Orton, eat your heart out!
—Eric Michaels, *Unbecoming*

A Witness's Education

It's only apparently contradictory with what I have been saying in chapter 1 about the wit in witnessing to suggest that testimonial acts always include an element of improvisation, and even innocence or naïveté. Witnessing begins in what is by definition an unreflective, intuitive moment: the moment of refusal when one withholds one's assent from something that feels too much like an atrocity, or at least a profound and painful injustice, for it to be undergone without revolt. But the counterpart of this spontaneous rejection of the intolerable—which is the desire to get the story out and tell the world—likewise depends on some unexamined assumptions: about the powers of representation, for instance, or about the accessibility of a suitably disposed audience. And such assumptions may persist in an uncalculated manner well beyond the initial moment of coming to witness and continue to motivate the witness's narrative in a "naive" way even when they turn out to have been unfounded. One sometimes does things unself-consciously that one can't, or may not wish, to account for theoretically; one can even solve problems practically that daunt analysis—indeed it happens frequently.

Certainly in AIDS witnessing there are writers who give no evidence of having ever become aware of the difficulties their assumptions background or ignore, so persuaded are they of their ability to tell the story unproblematically—to get it right, to tell it "as it is"—and so convinced of the automatic authority that accrues to such mimeticism. Such "naive" narratives find publishers and are often sympathetically reviewed; they may also reach an extensive audience. It is as if their rhetorical guilelessness was actually an asset, functioning perhaps as a token of that much desired quality, authenticity. The writing of Caroline Gréco in France *(A Dieu, Lucien)* or in Australia that of Joan Hurley *(How Far Is It to London Bridge?)* are examples. Mothers, respectively, of a son and a daughter whose AIDS deaths they recount with a sort of unprofessional simplicity, Gréco and Hurley are the authors of published narratives that were received with an uncritical acceptance that matches the spontaneity of their own writing. This does not mean, of course, that rhetorical factors are not ingredients of their success: in this kind of case, it is quite obviously the authors' social status as mothers—a status each duly claims in the narrative—that functions automatically to disarm criticism and as it were to authorize naïveté, legitimizing for many readers a tone and a register that in other circumstances might be dismissed as sentimental or ignored as trivial. Because they are mothers, their simplicity becomes a culturally appropriate performance of naïveté, and their sincerity a trope, therefore, for an uncalculated absence of concealed agendas, second messages, or complex intentions that signifies authenticity and credibility. More professionally accomplished writers and more self-conscious writers—notably those whose social positioning does not guarantee social credibility—might well envy the easy access to an audience that such unself-conscious writers can claim, as if by birthright.

To say, though, that Eric Michaels's highly self-conscious performance of witnessing in his diary, *Unbecoming,* might be regarded in some sense as naive is to risk an accusation of cultivating critical paradox for sheer paradox's sake. Yet that is what I want to propose. Unlike Hurley or Gréco, Michaels could obviously not claim anything like the kind of ready-made social acceptance and cultural authority that go with the persona of a mother. As, on the one hand, an "out" gay man and, on the other, a prominent social theorist with a "cult" following (his word) among the intelligentsia in Australia, his social status virtually ensured that his position of enunciation be construed as, at best, a marginal one. This would have been especially the case for the kind of "mass" audience that he appears to have envisaged, at least at the outset and for a considerable time thereafter, encouraged in this by his friend and co-instigator—perhaps indeed the initial proposer of the project—Paul Foss (himself the editor of a classy and highly influential, but intellectually sophisticated and theoretically oriented journal, *Art & Text*). But it gets worse. For Michaels was not only speaking in the position of an intellectual and a gay man, but far from writing like Gréco or Hurley about another's AIDS, he was writing as himself a PWA, and recording from that position the stages of his own physical unbecoming. From merely marginal on account of the first two strikes against him, his position as a man dying of AIDS becomes positively extreme. For to assume a stigma in this way (the act that Marie Maclean refers to as "delegitimation"), and to do it in an almost literal sense, is inevitably to court the misreading of its being taken as an act of self-stigmatization: not a request for attention but an invitation to be shunned. As a rhetorical act, such an assumption of stigma scarcely amounts to any kind of easy or automatic *captatio benevolentiae* such as is so readily accorded to motherhood. Rather, it counts as an error and an impudence: in the book that popularized "stigma" as a sociological concept, Erving Goffman, who is very interested in how stigmatized individuals manage their social relations, does not even foresee so ungrammatical a move. If there *is* an audience to which it might nevertheless appeal, this is likely to be anything but a mass readership; even access to a very restricted audience—one that might correspond, say, to the subscription list of *Art & Text*—is scarcely guaranteed.

Michaels's delegitimatory text, then, has to negotiate its status as a discourse of extremity. Given the im-pertinence of the author's triply marginal social status (as intellectual and theorist, as gay man, as PWA), the bland performances of naïveté possible when authors are able to take their social pertinence for granted are denied him.[1] It becomes necessary for him to assume, in both the weak and the strong senses of the word *assume,* the transgressiveness his marginal status implies, so that the display of his unbecoming becomes, ipso facto, an "unbecoming" display, unbecoming not only because it is socially ungrammatical but also because it is deliberately and knowingly so. In this way, social im-pertinence, a problem of positioning, becomes the occasion of an act of rhetorical impertinence or impudence: a way of *flaunting* one's positional ungrammaticality to which Michaels's own favored personal style—that of the tart-tongued queen, given to striking campy attitudes and claiming supposedly "dyke"-like forthrightness (*Should Have Been a Dyke* was the alternative title he toyed with)—was a natural adjunct. Michaels's carefully constructed persona in *Unbecoming*—one that he maintains with sometimes deliberate effort—is that of the "difficult patient," scathingly resistant to the discipline of the "Foucauldian holy ground" (14) that is Brisbane General Hospital—itself a model, in his own thought, for the whole social universe of Australian culture. So we are at the opposite extreme of social acceptability from that of Joan Hurley or Caroline Gréco. How then can his witnessing take itself naively for granted, as theirs does?

And yet . . . It isn't too difficult to perceive the naïveté at the very heart of Michaels's coming to witnessing. It lies, as I suppose witnessing naïveté always does, in his persistent underestimation of the very rhetorical difficulties—particularly in relation to the mass audience that he also persists in envisaging—that he was otherwise, and simultaneously, so conscious of and so adept at analyzing. Michaels was a sick man: always tired, sometimes desperately ill. If he undertook, and pursued over a period of many months, such an apparently self-defeating and thankless task, it can only have been by virtue of an act of faith on his part. But *his* act of faith could not be like the easy and uncalculating assumptions of authority that motivate writers like Hurley or Gréco; we might describe it as thoughtful, hence anxious and indeed tormented, but still an act of faith. The project itself appears to have been hatched with Foss—one has to read between the lines here—in a moment of quite spontaneous enthusiasm. Its realization, on which the diary comments reflexively from beginning to end, was obviously anything but spontaneous; Michaels quickly recognized that he had taken on a dauntingly difficult task. However, lucidly recognizing the rhetorical problem he had set himself, he went on improvising, *doing* what he could not adequately theorize.

In that improvisatory persistence lies a certain naïveté that remains faithful, it seems, to the initial enthusiasm. Obviously, a degree of improvisation was imposed by Michaels's state of health and the necessity of taking each day "as it came" that is the common fate of the seriously ill. But the writing was inevitably improvisatory also because, in Brisbane in 1987, there was a severe shortage of models for AIDS witnessing in general and for the genre of the AIDS diary in particular. Michaels had launched himself, as it were, into a genre only to discover that the genre did not yet exist: there were no predecessors known to him, no norms or guidelines to follow or transgress, no established rules to submit to, modify or disobey, no understandings as to appropriate subject-matter (what to discuss and in what sort of detail) or style (should the register be formal or informal? earnest in tone? jokey? entertaining? objective or personal? colloquial as an intimate document can be or cautious and constrained like an affidavit, a will, or some other legal document?). In short, nothing in the relationality of text and reader, no aspect of the text's structures of address, could be taken for granted in the way that Hurley or Gréco take their authority for granted. Should the reader be assumed to be hostile or complicitous, something like a concerned, interested, informed friend? Or a disgusted but perhaps morbidly fascinated bystander? And should the reader's expectations, whatever they may undecidably be, be met and satisfied, or flouted and turned? In the face of such a plethora of questions, Michaels found himself figuring out, in an (anxiously) improvisatory way—making it up as he went along—the consequences of the im-pertinence of his position and the rhetorical impertinence it implied. That is, he was writing without a safety net or, as he himself puts it, an agreed *etiquette,* the etiquette implied by any act of address, including impertinent ones; but writing nevertheless. The etiquette governing his particular deliberately impertinent performance had yet to be invented because the generic models that might normally have supplied guidelines for such a performance appeared to be very largely, if not totally, lacking. Yet, he didn't give up.

If writing that is, and remains, oblivious to generic issues and related rhetorical questions is naive, then Michaels's variety of naïveté is clearly of another order. He could not be unaware of the difficulties of his undertaking; that he nevertheless persisted in it suggests that his naïveté included, in addition to the ethical impulse to tell the story of his dying no matter what, an element that I would identify as a form of what in French is called *inconscience,* and more particularly a specific failure of awareness characteristic of intellectuals as a class. This is the naïveté of assuming that what is of interest to *them* must by definition be also a concern of nonintellectuals, including even the "mass" audience Michaels craved. Only such an assumption can account for Michaels's envisaging a mass audience but persisting, not only in writing from his position of extremity, but also, and against the advice of Paul Foss, in making the rhetorical problems of writing a diary—and more generally the necessity and difficulty of maintaining a "difficult patient" role—into something like the actual content of his writing. It is as if, pushed by the shortage of time allotted him (in 1987, no AIDS diary could be a slowly matured or deliberately elaborated work), he opted, in improvisatory fashion, to write of his concerns as they arose, almost randomly. But since the writing of the diary was itself for him a major concern, the diary itself consequently became very strongly self-reflexive, so that in practice the genre of the AIDS diary became, in Michaels's hands, that of a diary about the difficulties inherent in writing, for publication, a diary of witness in the persona of a person with AIDS.

The problem of writing, impertinently, from a position of im-pertinence thus becomes a major topic and focus of attention of a text that is nominally an account of the experience of dying of AIDS. The very spontaneity with which the diary is written makes it considerably less than a spontaneous piece of writing, one that is concerned with understanding its own deeply problematic rhetorical status as much as, and possibly more than, with doing what it is that that status might imply it should do. That's what I mean about Michaels's underestimation of the rhetorical difficulties that he so pertinently analyzes: his naïveté lies in the fact that the analysis he is so interested in actually contributes to the difficulties, particularly as long as the audience is thought of in terms of a mass readership—a fact that he, of course, imperturbably and metareflexively notes, as if understanding that he is in a hole but unable to stop digging.

In this way, intellectually sophisticated reflexivity, a display of worry, becomes a kind of place marker, within the diary, for the spontaneous naïveté, the initial innocence, quickly renounced and so never explicitly referred to, with which the diary project must have been originally conceived; that is, for the form of naïveté that is at the heart (I conjecture) of every act of witness. *That* state of unrecorded innocence has to be read between the lines, as if recorded negatively or *en creux,* in the textual self-commentary that in turn tells the story of a kind of baffled process of (self-)education: the author's many uneasy cogitations over what he has committed himself to doing. For example, in only the third paragraph of the very first entry (September, 9, 1987), I read this:

> [T]he real difficulty . . . is keeping such a journal, undertaking my diary at all. For whom do I write? And, worse yet, from what position? . . . Do I imagine such a text will be read, or even published? Necessarily, a missive (missile) from the grave (which of course solves, or at least hijacks the question of positioning). And what would be the rules governing the inscriptive practice here? . . . I shall return to these morbid reflexivities, I expect, through the course of . . . events? the disease? the plot? But not right now; right now these considerations exhaust me. (4)

The passage is a curious mixture of defensiveness and apology, genuine worry and bravado, diffidence and determination. Even as Michaels apologizes for his "reflexivities," they are naturalized as a form of morbidity, that is, a symptom of the disease that is AIDS, which justifies his persistence in them. They physically exhaust the sufferer, like a high fever or diarrhea, although this kind of cogitation is what could be called a discursive or social symptom rather than a strictly medical one. It is a function of

Michaels's illness, but only inasmuch as it positions him as an author, that is, as marginalized, minoritized, liminal with respect to a putatively general or mainstream audience and hence faced with the problems of parasociality—of minority address to a majoritarian readership—that define a discourse of extremity. At the same time, though, he is fully aware of the obsessive, out-of-control character of these "morbid reflexivities," and hence of the probable distaste of at least certain kinds of readers, even as he predicts his own recidivism. The reflexivities thus become part of the general picture of unbecoming and dis-ease the book portrays (a symptom of AIDS alongside others) as well as a part of the general unbecomingness of the portrayal; and they thus qualify as an item in the arsenal (cf. "missile") of its impertinence, even as AIDS witnessing is implicitly defined as part of the medical-social syndrome that is AIDS itself.

But notice above all the many signs of authorial self-consciousness about this reflexivity: the punning, of course, the parodic quotation of a theoretical intertext ("the inscriptive practice"), the reflexivity about reflexivity ("I shall return to these morbid reflexivities often"). I have also elided from the quotation a carefully calculated gloss on the title Michaels clearly has in mind: "perhaps bribing [the reader's] interest by inducement to trace in the prose deteriorations of judgement or style as a result of the deteriorating corpus," where "deterioration" is a synonym for "unbecoming." In a later chapter, I'll point to a similar combination of anxious reflexivity and naturalization of the difficulties inherent in AIDS writing in the texts of Bertrand Duquénelle and Amy Hoffman, who likewise treat the positional deficiency of their writing as a symptom of the social disease that is AIDS.[2] My hypothesis is that in all these authors there is a lost rhetorical innocence to be deciphered in such tormented self-consciousness, such that their writing amounts to an account of their "education," but that the loss of innocence does not preclude a certain persistence in naïveté. The signs of this persistence are the obsessiveness and compulsion, the out-of-controlness of the reflexive writing itself, which the authors naturalize as a symptom of AIDS, thus implying bitter social critique while acknowledging that, as the literary equivalent of vomit or fecal matter, it is most likely to be repugnant to any putative readership.

As a result, the "making do" character of the practice of witnessing, its striking rhetorical quality as simultaneously untutored, spontaneous, or even out of control and infinitely inventive and ingenious in its invention of etiquettes of address, can be understood as a function of the witnessing subject's own "half-baked" status as a narrator. I mean that the narrator's education has entailed the loss of innocence while precluding access to "useful" knowledge, the kind of knowledge that might permit one to know how to proceed appropriately with the business of witnessing. As an eloquent account of a witness's education in "useless" knowledge (a term I borrow here from Charlotte Delbo), Eric Michaels's diary, then, is a highly sophisticated, self-conscious account of the naively improvisatory practice that his diary writing never ceased to be. As such, it can introduce us to the improvisatory character of witnessing writing in general.

Worried by all this reflexivity, so off-putting to readers, Paul Foss early recommended a countermodel: "[H]e thinks [Joe] Orton's diary is fabulous," Michaels records, "because it is full of action: the author's always ducking off into the loo to have it off with somebody" (19). There are reasons, as we'll see, why Orton is both a suggestive and an unlikely model for Michaels, but the intuition prompting Foss's suggestion—the idea that obsessive reflexivity is an error—may well be accurate. My students—no less anti-intellectual than the next person for being undergraduates in a "quality" institution—regularly report to me that they can't "relate" to Michaels because *Unbecoming* is "too intellectual" for their taste. Because it is a thoughtful text that deliberately eschews sentiment in favor of analysis (or else dissolves it in irony), it does not conform to their idea of what an AIDS diary *should* be like. (They also sometimes declare humor to be out of place in an AIDS witnessing text; their preconceptions obviously favor something more like Gréco's or Hurley's plucking at the heartstrings than defiant texts like *Unbecoming* or an angrily satirical romp like John Greyson's film *Zero Patience.*) They are conscious, in other words, of a textual solecism but draw the line at reading the kind of statement (about anger and pain) that the offense against their expectations is attempting to make, its ungrammaticality being covered by no etiquette they are willing to acknowledge. I, on the other hand, am something like Michaels's ideal reader. It's not just that I rub my hands in delight that an AIDS author should have done so much of my own critical and theoretical labor for me. I also respond to Michaels's naively sophisticated writing, his "morbid reflexivities" and his practice of impertinence with something like the fascinated attention—a *sharing of the worry*—that he was eventually to realize (around June 26, 1988) justifies his project, but justifies it as an address to a "cult" readership in contradistinction to the "mass" following that previously had seemed so appealing (103–4). It is as if, even as Michaels's self-analysis supports and underpins my own critical project by delineating so clearly what is at stake in a discourse of extremity and the difficulties it entails, my corresponding obsession with his writing authorizes that writing retrospectively by repeating something of its dynamics, thus demonstrating the power it can exert over certain kinds of readers: those inclined, I suppose one might say, to become Michaels's intellectual *groupies.*

"Obsession" is not too strong a word, I think, for the level of my interest. For I should confess that to a degree I'm repeating myself in this chapter, and mirroring Michaels's own self-reflexive recidivism by mulling over once more here some of the issues raised by *Unbecoming* that I initially tried to come to terms with in *Facing It.*[3] His anxiety of extremity (his obsession, what he calls paranoia) has been transmitted to me as another form of obsession or paranoia, an anxiety of reception, a transmission that illustrates quite neatly the axiom that was perhaps the real subject of my earlier book, that trauma is the hurt that does not heal. It "returns," it repeats, not only as a phenomenon of individual psyches, but also in the social sphere. I don't plan to rehearse here the questions of reception I discussed before; but I will have to return to certain topics, particularly concerning the difficulties Michaels faced in his project (foremost among them the problem he defines as "tidiness") and the function of the frontispiece photo as an exemplification of his writing's impertinent rhetorical character. I'll attempt to do so as briefly as possible, and to emphasize here, more clearly than in the earlier essay, the dynamics of oppositionality that are inherent in the two moments that, taken together, define both the innocence or naïveté of Michaels's witnessing project, its essential spontaneity, and the crucial importance of his text for the critical project of my own book as an exploration of witnessing's rhetorical ingeniousness, its wit. These are the *ethical* moment of spontaneous oppositionality that underlies Michaels's conversion of his position of im-pertinence or irrelevancy into an attitude of rhetorical resistance or impertinence—his adoption of the "difficult patient" stance as an affirmation of what he calls "first principles" (97)—and the moment of intense concern over *etiquette,* the "etiquette or sense of style" he evokes in the same entry of June 21, 1988, in which ethical "first principles" are invoked. This is the etiquette that would be capable of rephrasing the solecism of impertinence in such a way that, at least for some readers, it would become readable as an utterance worth attending to; a protocol that would override conventional definitions of appropriateness in the interest of an ethical project that entails a performance of inappropriateness, an untimely intervention.

More specifically still, the story I want to tell in this respect is that of Michaels's conviction that "style" is the ingredient that gets parasocial messages, as discourses of extremity, past the cultural defenses of (in his terminology) "tidiness," so that such missives can become missiles from the grave. What does he intend, and what should we in turn understand, by "style"? I'll suggest that the brilliant art of figuration Michaels displays in the photo that serves as frontispiece to his book, standing in for a planned portrait by the famously impertinent artist Juan Davila, gives some hint of the kind of stylistic know-how Michaels had in mind. It is something that "turns" the reader and functions indexically as a daring act of *captatio,* hijacking the attention. But it is something also that can't be fully theorized and remains, as Certeau would say, an *art de faire.* As an exemplification of style, it is an art of improvisatory know-how, a cultural *practice* that retains an essential element of naïveté even as it displays stunning rhetorical skill, reflecting in this respect what I called the narrator's half-baked status as a subject of knowledge. Style, then, in this sense, is the necessary adjunct—a transmutation, as it were, of the witness's naïveté and spontaneity into an untutored, practical skill—that rescues "useless" knowledge from its uselessness, or at least transmits the anxiety it engenders so that its very uselessness becomes a cultural force.

I have a second objective, though, in returning here to *Unbecoming.* In the economy of the present book, I want Michaels's text to function paradigmatically as a narrative of education or experience, a kind of (nonfictional) Bildungsroman, and to do so not only with respect to the traumatic experience of AIDS as an educational agent, but also—and in this case perhaps primarily—in relation to the encounter with the problematics of cultural obscenity that is entailed in bearing witness to that experience. Most witnessing narrative is structured, sometimes even formally, as the story of a loss of innocence and of the painful acquisition of a certain knowledge; and if in most cases the emphasis falls naturally enough on the primary experience of trauma—and particularly so in the case of Holocaust writing—there are texts also that distribute the emphasis more evenly (Delbo's *Auschwitz et après* [Auschwitz and after] would be an excellent example). They may even lay most stress, as *Unbecoming* does, on the problems of witnessing and describe as a second but equivalent loss of innocence the acquisition of knowledge and experience—I'm looking for an English synonym for the word *Erfahrung* that Walter Benjamin employs in his famous essay on "The Storyteller"—that witnessing itself entails. In addition to *Unbecoming,* the two other texts that I will read in part I of this book (Pat Barker's historical novel *Regeneration* in chapter 3, and in chapter 4 Pascal de Duve's *Cargo vie*) are narratives of education that come under the heading of writing that is in this way supremely conscious, not only of a first trauma and a first loss of innocence (trench warfare, the onset of AIDS), but also of the similarly traumatic, and hence similarly educational, nature of the difficulties that accompany the act of witnessing itself, as the effort to bear witness to a primary historical trauma that has the cultural status of the obscene.

But the point of such writing is always that education as the overcoming of innocence, whether through the primary trauma or in the process of witnessing, does not mean that witnessing itself can be accomplished from the standpoint of something like assured or certain knowledge, the kind of "wisdom" that is achieved by the protagonists and narrators of the traditional Bildungsroman (and of its generic twin, the classical autobiography). A naïveté remains. Where Romain Gary called the historical experience of the war Europe's education *(L'Education européenne),* it was for Charlotte Delbo, in the title of the second volume of her Auschwitz trilogy, *Une Connaissance inutile,* to point out, as I've already intimated, that the knowledge acquired in such an education is "useless," and useless to the extent that it cannot be communicated to those who, as she puts it, although they are living, do not know what it means to be alive: "I learned /over there / that you cannot speak to others" (*Auschwitz and After,* 228.) The kind of knowledge that is lacking, then, is the knowledge of how to bear witness to the knowledge acquired in the primary trauma, which thus remains culturally unavailable, or at least liminal and elusive. That is why I want to insist that in witnessing narrative, particularly as it is exemplified by texts like *Unbecoming* and the others that I discuss in these opening chapters as discourses of extremity, the overcoming of innocence is always accompanied by the inevitable maintenance of a certain naïveté, since the witness is persisting in accomplishing the act of witness, but without knowing how it might be possible to do so, and relying naively, therefore, on an *art de faire* definable as the deployment of wit in the absence of wisdom.

The witness's education, therefore, is a *baffled* one; and it is the mixture of innocence and naïveté in witnesses, their half-baked status, that makes the figure of the witness a *ghostly* personage, if a ghost is understood to be simultaneously a subject of *Erfahrung* (the experience of injustice or trauma, the knowledge of death) and the site of an inability to speak that experience or knowledge, an inability that is combined—for such is what apparitions are always held to signify—with an intense desire to communicate. The witnessing figures I discuss in part I under the heading of "Discourses of Extremity" (Michaels; Sassoon and Owen in *Regeneration;* de

Duve) do understand themselves very frequently as already posthumous, or at least on the side of the dead, or—in the case of de Duve—as having "returned" from a voyage that was an encounter with death. But even when their *Bildung* is therefore an unbecoming, an *Entbildung,* and the story of its acquisition that of the becoming ghostly of the witnessing subject, their writing can still be legitimately referred to the classical conception of *Bildung* as an accession to the status of the full, and fully agential "self," however impeded or difficult that self's chances of communication may be. Their story, in other words, is more the story of their discovery of a transformation that has occurred for them in the conditions of discourse—a transformation attributable to the trauma they have undergone or are undergoing—than it is the story of a transformed subjectivity. They are in the discourse position of a ghost, but without having become ghostly as subjects of writing.

Thus these texts adhere to a conception of individual writing agency and of authorial authority that binds those of them that are written in the first person to the central convention of the genre of autobiography in its classic form: the convention of confidence in the integrity and agential autonomy of the individual writing subject. Michaels, so theoretically sophisticated, nevertheless writes as if the full responsibility for the success or failure of his witnessing project somehow inheres—and inheres uniquely—in his personal ability to get the art of im-pertinence (its ethics and its etiquette) right, and to do so by achieving the requisite style; his performance as a difficult patient is very much a solo act, and indeed the sense of his solitude is present in all but a very few pages of the text. It is individual authorship, too, that Pat Barker foregrounds in the figures of Sassoon and Owen—except that here both their collaborative friendship and the sense of responsibility each has for the men at the front, the dead and the still living, begin to suggest more strongly a shared or collective subjectivity. The poetic voice is already a plural one in this case; and as Derrida (1993) has influentially pointed out, the ghost is always (a figure of the) plural. Pascal de Duve's voice is divided, also—between his own and that of death—and he asserts that death is what speaks (or "returns") in his text. But he simultaneously claims responsibility like Michaels as an *écrivant* and asserts (contra Marguerite Duras, who believes that "to write is to be no one") that "[i]n writing one reveals oneself to oneself and to others" (*Cargo vie,* 70), thus claiming for himself the autonomy of selfhood even as death speaks in his text.

In part II, under the heading "Phantom Pain," we will encounter writing subjects, or more accurately subjects of writing, more profoundly transformed in the direction of the ghostly than are the witnessing subjects of part I. These witnessing subjects speak less "in their own name" than as the instrumentalizing agents of a discourse through which a dual or collective subjectivity—always associated with death or the dead and by definition voiceless—attempts to achieve some degree of audibility and access to some sort of hearing. The concepts of agencing and of the parasocial, which are already relevant in part I, will thus become crucial in this second part because the witnessing texts I discuss there require a critical vocabulary that does not assume or imply identity between the individual agent productive of the discourse and the subjectivity—that is, the intersubjective relations—that the discourse produces. I will propose that it is this splitting of agency from subjectivity that produces the ghostly quality of certain witnessing texts and manifests itself in writing that has (the) phantom (of) pain as its cultural content, that is, as the effect of its readability. This split of agency and subjectivity, I will suggest, underlies in particular the recurring structure of a witness or witnessing text that presents itself as ghostlike and capable of haunting its audience because it is itself haunted, for example by the collectivity of the dead.

All of which does not mean that even the most naive or innocent acts of witnessing, such as the untutored texts of Joan Hurley or Caroline Gréco, do not themselves represent, as it were in spite of themselves, acts of agencing and become bearers of phantom pain; or that considerably more sophisticated writing subjects whose "education" has been that of a double experience of personal extremity—the extremity they undergo, the extremity from which they address, in their own voice, the cultural mainstream—are not, likewise and in the same sense, bearers of collective witness. It means only that witnessing discourse varies along a continuum that has personal "voice" at one pole and acts of agencing or collective "voicing" at the other. "Voice" speaks at times *on behalf of* the otherness that is the obscene; at other times "voicing" approaches the more palpably uncanny status of *otherness speaking,* a "presencing" of the obscene.

Now we can get back to Joe Orton, whose writing, to be sure, whatever its very real qualities, makes little claim to the quality of ghostliness.

An Ethics of Im-pertinence

If Orton furnished a suggestive model for Michaels, it is because of the sheer impudence (engaging to some, offensive to many) of his performance of gayness, as a matter of cheerful promiscuity and sexual enthusiasm—always having it off with someone in the loo—in the context of Great Britain in the 1960s. Orton's impudence is rhetorically naive, or uneducated, if you will. But unlike Orton, Michaels is bearing witness to AIDS and attempting therefore to "stage-manage," as he puts it, his dying. Any performance of gayness that AIDS permits can't, at least in Michaels's experience of the disease, generate impertinence in this simple way through a display of sexual exuberance. For one thing, Michaels's energy is depleted and his libido low. In late March 1998, he describes with perverse delectation his humdrum, non-Orton-like, daily life: "I piss a lot, shit once a day, jerk off maybe once a week, and spend a lot of time on long-distance phone calls. Monday and Tuesday I teach tutes, and go in to school at least one other day a week" (78). Some months earlier, at the time he was reading Orton (November 22, 1986), the employment of a good day when he had "heaps of energy" already consisted of taking morning tea at a park kiosk with a friend ("I was quite horrible in my stage-whispered criticisms of the fat middle-class families" [20]), followed by a "jerk-off" session, celebrating a rare moment of solitude in his own apartment. "Then I watched a Deborah Kerr godawful black-and-white war melodrama on TV for the rest of the afternoon. Joe Orton, eat your heart out!" (20). Even masturbation, as it happens, will eventually fail him; and in any case he never makes much use of it as a literary resource. If sexual exuberance is, as is often thought, a significant component of gay identity (and Michaels himself argues at one point along those lines), then AIDS, which destroys the PWA's sexual energy, is the enemy of that identity, and makes it hard to deploy active sexuality as a factor of impertinence.

If an AIDS diary is written *against* everything that AIDS stands for—everything, that is, that tends to destroy the manifestation of social im-pertinence that is gayness—what, then, *can* furnish the content of such a diary? An AIDS diary can obviously not be an account of passive submission to either the disease or its treatment (medical and social) in the "Foucauldian holy ground" (14) of hospital, a merely unreactive disintegration. That, for Michaels, is a first principle. But neither can it be a narrative of active, "gay" opposition, through the kind of provocatively unbecoming sexual display that Orton specialized in. Even as his libido, his confidence, and his willpower are sapped by the effects of HIV disease, the witness as AIDS patient has to invent some other way of (being) unbecoming, another form of resistance and of stage-managing his demise. For Michaels, the answer to this problem seems to lie, quite precisely, in the difference between Orton's unreflective and in that sense naive display, which Michaels finally dismisses as "a world of abject self-deception" (25), and the more lucid strategy (not without its own naïveté, as we've seen) that Michaels finds himself adopting: the "half-baked" strategy of making the difficulties of diary-writing itself, as an attempt to assume and maintain a position of im-pertinence in the face of AIDS and all it signifies, medically and socially, into the subject matter of the diary itself. This is the difference, I want to propose, between an unreflective gesture of impudence and a thoughtful, because ethical, project, one that is equally ethical by virtue of its thoughtfulness.

The difficulties of AIDS diary writing consist both of the kind of rhetorical perplexities I've already touched on—Michaels signals these from the start—and of a whole range of social "aggravations" that threaten both the diary and its author, a topic he rapidly warms to and explores at considerable length. From disputes with neighbors, businesspeople, colleagues, and friends the list of vexations expands to include the disciplinary practices of hospital and the particularly egregious form they take when an irrational fear of AIDS is simultaneously active (much wrapping, gloving, masking, goggling, and gowning; or putting a patient with a severely impaired immune system into an infectious diseases ward). Then—Michaels having worked for five years among a group of Australian aborigines—there are the dangers to the diary project represented by the Warlpiri's adherence to their Law, particularly in respect of mourning customs that decree that all cultural productions associated with a dead person be expunged from the record; as well as by their occasional complicity with Australian puritanism and its censoring mentality. Meanwhile, at the other extreme of Australian society, there is the hypocrisy and obtuseness of a Department of Immigration determined to deport a dying man to an uncertain and virtually resourceless future in the United States.

All these forms of "aggro" are identified, as Michaels insists in the case of the hospital, with a hegemonic ideology of tidiness that seeks to eradicate—or in another scenario to consign to oblivion (which comes to the same thing)—everything that is regarded as a form of cultural dirt, that is (by Mary Douglas's famous definition), as out of place. The rebellious gay male intellectual is dirt in this sense; but so too, in white-settler Australia, is the Aboriginal culture with which Michaels feels he has important affinities and with which he is, so to speak, in alliance. The vulnerability of that which is im-pertinent or out of place to the array of threatening forces that line up under the banner of tidiness (and naturally these include some internalized personal weaknesses as well, about which Michaels also worries: occasional failures of chutzpah and a tendency to be too nice or too submissive to authority figures; self-consciousness with respect to his KS-marked body) leads him to look, therefore, for ways of ensuring the persistence of his resistance as a cultural project, one capable of surviving his own personal disappearance. These he finds in the form of "intellectual property" as a legally or culturally sanctioned mode of more than personal survival, a legacy. Thus he seeks to identify his diary, with its subject matter foregrounding his worries as a form of intellectual self-display equivalent to Orton's sexual shenanigans, with genres that might have some chance of exerting an authority able to survive the demise of their writing subject and the defeat of his personal project of opposition. In this respect, he turns in particular to the will and—another sign, perhaps, of the naïveté of intellectuals?—the academic position-paper; later he demonstrates a talent for the posthumous revenge-letter ("I have taken the Richard Nixon payback pledge," 36).

The problem, though, is that this generic proliferation in response to the threat of tidiness—the diary is part autobiography, part ethnography, part testament, part a settling of scores—in turn induces new skepticism about its efficacity as a rhetorical tactic and becomes yet another source of worry, another aggravation to contend with and to record. "It seems to be merely confusing: I leave the reader nothing generic to hang on to" (34). In combination with obsessive reflexivity, such generic versatility quickly becomes self-defeating: "[M]y own posthumous editorial voice keeps resurrecting from a cheaply ironized gallows . . . to confound utterly the cacophony of voices I employ throughout" (34). The pattern by now is familiar: the rhetorical solution turns out to be part of the self-defeating general problem of testimonial oppositionality that is AIDS. Even the conventional genres that ought to confer posthumous authority reveal their inadequacy, in the face of the particular social problems that are inherent in personifying, and attempting to present, the obscene; and finally the marginalization of the witnessing subject, whether as the (obscene) *target* of social tidiness, scheduled for elimination from the cultural scene, or as the (equally obscene) would-be *witness* to that form of injustice—whether, that is, as im-pertinent cultural object or as impertinent rhetorical subject—means that social aggravations and rhetorical difficulties eventually fuse. Intricately associated with each other, if not absolutely identical, they are aspects of the same struggle. And together they define the diary project as deeply problematic: every word of it is written under threat of extinction.

It is this position of extremity that permits us to measure the profoundly ethical character both of Michaels's decision in the first place, to embark on the oppositional project of the diary, and then of his choice to maintain the project despite the intractable problems into which it led him. His need to oppose the tidiness culture and the "Foucauldian horror show" (4) it supports is an absolutely fundamental one, a matter of axiom; the imperative to which he responds has the force of self-evidence and, as he says, of "first principles." Thus, on December 6, he reports a crucial conversation about the Immigration Department's likely refusal of his application for residency. Liz gives a lengthy exposition of the "bureaucratic logic" (24) by virtue of which it is proposed to deport him, which Michaels interrupts with a kind of condensed statement of tidiness theory: "I said Liz, stop it, *that's what made me sick in the first place*" (24; emphasis added). In other words: AIDS and tidiness are in alliance; bureaucratic logic and the disease, between them, are out to eradicate "dirt." Michaels then goes on, in this depressive moment, to sketch a slightly self-pitying version of what I am arguing constitutes his gay ethics of back-to-the-wall oppositionality: "[W]hy, because I reject nationalism and the nuclear family (for my own practice at least), [should I] have no rights, no rights at all . . . and die in a way which I, but maybe only I, believe has elements of murder?" (24–25). And three days later he returns slightly more clearly and explicitly to the topic of what he now himself identifies as a "queenly" ethics, about which one can assume he has been thinking in the interval. But here the context is "Orton's world of self-deception" (25) on the one hand, and on the other Michaels's reading of a biography of Jean Cocteau. By explicit contrast with Orton, Cocteau inspires the comment that "[i]t is the profound moral imperatives and ethical calculations that ultimately do drive great gay queens throughout this century (and the last, as far as it can be determined)" (25).

This, I would suggest, amounts to a discreetly self-referential comment, identifying the project of Michaels's diary as part of a longish tradition whose "profound moral imperatives and ethical calculations" amount to a practice of principled opposition to the values—and the lethal logic—of tidiness. The comment about Cocteau can be linked to his rejection a full six months later (June 21, just before the rhetorical breakthrough of June 26 to which I'll turn in the next section), of sentimental versions of dying of AIDS (along the lines of "great potential nipped in the bud," for example). For Michaels sentiment is not the point. "At least one reason for publishing this journal is to counter the sentimentalized narratives that seem to be all that San Francisco has been able to produce about this sequence; and to reaffirm first principles" (97). What these first principles are and why they transcend merely personal pathos don't need to be specified because for Michaels, and by this time for the reader too, they go without saying. Tidiness is murdering me—where "me," by virtue of the phenomenon of hypertypicality explained very early in the diary (7), equals gayness, hence out-of-placeness, hence oppositionality, hence the assumption of im-pertinence through a practice of impertinence. Therefore it is necessary, by categorical imperative, for me to "stage-manage" my dying into an effective counterdiscourse, one that will ensure the survival, in lieu of my person, of the oppositional spirit inherent in gayness and the century-long tradition of gay ethics. Whence the urgency, fueled by the ethical imperative, to find an "etiquette or sense of style" that will serve that end—something that on June 21 (Michaels's health has seriously deteriorated and he is deeply discouraged) looks like a serious stumbling block. The resolution of this final problem will come, however, a few days later (June 26), with the realization that a "cult" audience can initially be targeted and that a rhetoric of impertinence has some chance of getting through to such an audience.

For what it's worth, I think Michaels is correct in identifying as ethical the tradition of the great gay writers since Whitman and Wilde, or—in the lesbian branch (to which Michaels seems oblivious)—since Renée Vivien, Natalie Barney, or Colette. It is more an ethical tradition, perhaps, than contemporary lesbian and gay criticism, with its own political underpinnings, has consciously acknowledged, let alone celebrated. From Proust, Gide, and Cocteau or E. M. Forster and his group through Auden, Genet, and Hocquenguem, and from Gertrude Stein and Djuna Barnes through Wittig and Lorde, it has consisted of working to reverse conventional values: those that have given us colonialism, the great wars (and the supposedly small), the genocides and ethnic cleansings, the injustices and pain associated with gender, sexual, and racial discrimination—in short, all the major ills of the twentieth century. More specifically, this tradition has entailed an effort to revalue what those conventional values despise, marginalize, or incriminate: Cocteau casts the beautiful Jean Marais as *la bête,* Forster prefers friendship to patriotism, Genet eroticizes criminality and befriends the Black Panthers and the Palestinians. It is in more senses than one an ethics of inversion. Where the women emphasize issues of gender and sexuality, however, and espouse the body in this context of ethical revaluation, the men, it seems, often give conscious thought to colonialism, decolonization, and postcoloniality. Identified *as* dominant (white, male, colonizing) subjects, they identify *with* the "subaltern," something that clearly resonates strongly with Michaels's own interest in and affinity with Aboriginality and furnishes his specific link to the tradition.

At Yuendumu in 1982–87, working with the Warlpiri, Michaels had officially assisted (and unofficially encouraged) an extraordinary exercise in cultural self-affirmation of an oppositional kind, which was also (like gay ethical projects and in particular Michaels's diary) an example of parasocial discourse, that is, a device through which a profoundly marginalized group found the means to address a majority society in a perspective consistent with their minoritized language and culture. With ironic wit Michaels dubs this Yuendumu adventure (the creation of a locally run TV broadcasting facility) "The Birth of a Station" (84). Having participated in it, he understood himself to have an "earned, acknowledged" identity (6), indeed to enjoy "a persona and speaking rights" (100) among the Warlpiri, even as he clearly states—out of respect for the obvious truth but mindful also of the future disposition of his intellectual property, which includes *Unbecoming*—that "I am not, nor have I ever wanted or imagined myself to be a Warlpiri Aborigine" (10—shades, this time, not of *Birth of a Nation* but of the McCarthy hearings). At the same time, he realizes that in Yuendumu his specifically *gay* identity was privatized and backgrounded in relation to the prominence of this Warlpiri identification; and that this phenomenon in turn had bearing both on his appearance (how he looked) and on his attitude to his appearance (a certain narcissistic attachment, doubtless, to good looks). In Yuendumu, he says, "I stopped posing in mirrors or considering my cosmetology. I felt liberated in a sense, acknowledged that *what mirrors were available was the community itself,* and yet I was limited in my ability to read those mirrors" (58; emphasis added). This matter of appearance in relation to Aboriginal community will prove crucial, in the project of gay oppositionality that is *Unbecoming,* first in relation to Michaels's shyness about exposing his KS lesions to general view, and then in his abdication of that shyness on the occasion of his "in for a penny in for a pound" decisions of June 26 concerning the etiquette of impertinence.

But meanwhile, in April, on the occasion of a poetry reading by Mudrooroo at which he meets some "Koories from the local media association," he muses again about his affinity with Australian Aborigines:

> [W]hat strikes me again and again is that I really do like Aborigines—though that's too racist and imprecise, put that way. But they are engaged,

> in a way that white Australians tend not to be. Their circumstances are interesting, to them and to me. They tend to be kind. And no matter how hard they try, they mostly fail to be bourgeois. They are too familiar with poverty and suffering perhaps. I feel a whole lot less self-conscious about the way I look and my visible marks of disease when I'm with blacks. They seem a good deal less concerned. (84)

Having read this passage quite closely in *Facing It,* I will not go into further detail here, except to note the return of the appearance theme, but this time in the specific context of AIDS and KS, and with a hint that again it is the Aboriginal community that functions for Michaels as a friendly mirror. The passage thus outlines a complex relation entailing identification *with* Aboriginal people—or at least a kind of preferential self-association—that stops short, as it must, of identification *as* (they constitute a mirror, but one that he knows he does not read well). Taking up a hint (in the phrase "when I'm with blacks") that Michaels may have shared in the association, commonly made by North Americans, although not, I think, by Australians, of Aborigines with American Blacks (whom in fact the former tend to identify rather as honorary whitefellas), what I want to do here is to make some connections between this passage (and others about Aboriginality) and some hints in the diary that for a younger, Jewish, white, American Eric Michaels, a crucial model of style—style as a way of living and a social attitude, but also style as a performance practice—was furnished by Afro-American culture. "But really the privileged position of blacks always remained in the definition of what was cool, what was sophisticated, in language and performance, at least for my (and adjacent) generations of white Americans. Blacks seemed to have everything we tried for and lacked" (52). If there is some transfer, doubtless two-way, between this long-term admiration and style envy of his in relation to Blacks and Michaels's often expressed, and always carefully worded expressions of affinity with the Australian indigenous people with whom he had worked on a parasocial project, then perhaps we can glimpse in the connection one of the deeper sources of his thinking about the "etiquette or sense of style" entailed in an ethical and therefore rhetorical project of impertinence, consistent with the tradition of a gay ethics of inversion. This is the thinking that emerges finally, in the entry for June 26, in the context of a photography session with Penny Taylor, which seems to have been for Michaels a kind of exercise in the "mirroring" of his AIDS-marked self and hence the "stage management" of his death.

For partial confirmation of this hypothesis, we can go back to the passage dated December 9 about Orton, Cocteau, and the "profound moral imperatives and ethical calculations" of the great gay queens. An ethical project of this kind, Michaels adds, is "the only justification for wearing Chanel black and a single string of pearls. It is the only note that can be struck when you lean against the piano, to sing . . ." (26). Here queenly ethics, campy gay male drag and gender-reversal, and the style of Black performance (jazz or blues) come together in a prototype for the performance (the unbecoming performance of unbecoming) that *Unbecoming* will be. Only the (key) element of Aboriginality is missing. Can it be, then, that the crucial event that was finally to bring about the stylistic amalgam that emerged in June was the "Aboriginal anti-demonstration" in Sydney on the occasion of the bicentennial Australia Day of January 1988? In his long entry for January 26 (44–48), Michaels calls this demo a "collective counter-expression" (45) and sums up his own experience of it as a "good vacation" (48)—a vacation from Brisbane, a vacation from tidiness, even a vacation, perhaps, from AIDS. It was the occasion of a brief reunion with Paddy Jupurrurla and "the other Yuendumu people" (47) that gave Michaels great joy. "A wonderful, wonderful afternoon for an unreconstructed hippy like myself" (46). And as late as August 10, two weeks before his actual death, he will be daydreaming, therefore, of returning to die in Alice Springs, within reach of Yuendumu, and commenting that *that* would be a way of dying with "more style than lying here and being bored to death" (125).

So, if the ethical task of achieving, and maintaining, a presence of the obscene—of gayness, of AIDS, of death—in a culture fully seduced, as it seemed to Michaels, by the sirens of tidiness implies a rhetorical problem of etiquette or style, we should not be surprised if the resolution of this apparently intractable issue turns out, in the end, to involve a complex or amalgam of different modes of stylistic performance in which we can identify the unreconstructed hippy, the queenly and the Black, while the Aboriginal "inability to be bourgeois" is prominent and probably determining. What still remains to be solved, though, is the problem of audience. How, within the tidiness culture, to find a group of readers who might respond to such a style and be hospitable to the antitidiness message it implies? A group able to read what it means, moreover, for a white bourgeois intellectual to espouse such a style and message? And there remains also the fact of Michaels's own growing diffidence, almost a failure of nerve, as his health fails. There is a subterranean link, perhaps, between his residual shyness about his personal appearance, not fully abolished until June 26, and his growing uneasiness throughout May and June about the felicity conditions, and hence the feasibility of "any, assumedly posthumous, project" (97) such as the diary. By the end of May, as he gets weaker and his mood slips into despondency, he admits to a temptation to "give it all up," a temptation that amounts to the moral equivalent of suicide—abandonment of the ethical project, an admission of defeat. "What makes me think I have to stage-manage this as well? I'm sure death itself is the simplest thing in the world. The choice seems to be merely this: to arrange everything, to maintain a morbid fantasy of control, or simply give it up and let it go. The latter looks more and more appealing" (93).

Now, we might notice, it is no longer the "reflexivities" of writing that are morbid, but the urge to pursue the ethical project. It is as if AIDS had now infiltrated the project itself, like the virus investing a T cell, and gotten the better of it.

An Etiquette of Impertinence

"But you don't die, at least right away" (94). In a sense, it is AIDS itself that comes to the rescue, AIDS "the disease of a thousand rehearsals" (94) that brings you close to death and then brings you back to face life (with AIDS) again. Ten days after the crisis of June 5, when Michaels said to his doctor: "It's getting nasty. Can you get me out of this now?" he is reporting, thanks to treatment, that it "seems a bit unsporting to terminate, mostly out of boredom." There are people to "hang out for," and writing to "try to finish up if I can motivate myself at all" (94). Soon thereafter we learn that there have been long autobiographical sessions with a tape recorder and a discussion with Paul about "publication strategy" (96, June 21), even though self-confidence is still lacking: "[B]ut again, I mean, after all, who is she? who, indeed, does she think she is? What could possibly justify all this attention?" (96). As this last question suggests, the problem remains that of audience; still thinking, presumably, of a popular audience, Michaels wonders why he or his diary should claim "mass" attention. But further taping continues, with John von Sturmer now (June 22); and when, shortly afterward, Peggy Taylor relays John at the bedside, the diary entry for June 26 begins as a substitute and supplement for the "tapes we were making" (103). So there is continuity between the taped autobiographical sessions, the diary project, and, finally, the photo session on which the June 26 entry also reports. Throwing his concern about appearance to the wind,

Michaels has sat, we learn (not without surprise), for a number of shots, "[a]ll nude to the waist down [*sic*], featuring the cancer lesions most prominently." The defiant spirit of the difficult patient is back: "There goes Michaels, terrorizing the ward again!" Furthermore, "my reservations about the etiquette of stage-managing my own demise" have vanished. "In for a pence [*sic*] . . ." (103). (These slips and lapses of English are poignant and suggestive in light of the social solecism Michaels knows these pictures commit: "Paul always incites me to such scandal," he reports, perhaps a bit disingenuously.)

The photographs are intended, indeed, partly to provide "'specimen' shots" and partly "to serve as graphics if needed" (i.e., as illustrations to the diary). The specimen shots were "for Juan [Davila] to work from for the portrait" (presumably a predictably scandalous cover portrait, the idea of which had been cooked up in discussion with Foss a few days earlier). But in the event, it is one of these "night-flash" pictures that serves as the diary's frontispiece and substitutes for the imagined portrait; it is published, as the Australian edition carefully points out, "by permission of the author," that is, as part of an agreed strategy and not by editorial whim. In short, there has now been a complete return of Michaels's confidence; this return of confidence harks back to the conversation with Paul, but derives too from a crucial modification in Michaels's thinking. The problem of the projected audience has been resolved: "Now I see the advantages of being a cult figure, writing for a specialized audience, circulating in these very restricted orbits" (103). The advantage is that this restricted audience "may be just the folks I wanted to talk to" (104)—those likely to respond with at least curiosity and perhaps interest, even engagement, to the kind of impertinent performance Michaels understands his unbecoming to demand, as an ethical matter, but which corresponds also to his personal stylistic preferences.

The required etiquette, in other words, entails selecting an audience for whom impertinence is likely to function both as confrontation or provocation, a matter of flaunting, *and* as *captatio;* or as Michaels puts it more cautiously, "[Y]ou can at least pretend that they're a bit less likely to be the ones to turn you in to the mind police" (104). What's more, "there is an interface between the small-scale public media and the mass . . . so that even if Paul is right that these diaries get a wider than cult reading, no worries mate" (104). It is not simply that it is still possible, therefore, to reach a mass audience, but more profoundly that the dangers attached to targeting and attaining such an audience—"the worst of the possible consequences of being discovered (so longed for in my youthful quest for stardom)" (104)—have now been "escaped." I take this to mean that any temptation to put a damper on the im-pertinence of the content and the impertinence of the style out of concern for mass taste has been averted, thanks to the obligatory prior passage of the text through the intelligentsia, with whom Michaels knows that it is fairly safe for him to be himself. "And that's why Juan can paint the cover and I can call the thing *Unbecoming* (though I still like *Should Have Been a Dyke*), and we can throw the whole bucket of blood up. I have the satisfaction, my anger transubstantiated" (104).

In both the Australian and the American editions, the cover art reproduces Hugh Steers's *Blue Towel, Red Tank,* which is in perhaps more allegorical than metaphorical relation to Michaels's text. The volume is dedicated, in the Australian edition, to the memory of Terry Bell, a pioneer of the AIDS battle in that country; in the American edition, two further names have, significantly, been added: those of Hugh Steers himself and of Richard Kemp (Michaels's physician at Brisbane General). The reader encounters the frontispiece photo of Eric Michaels, nude "to the waist down" and showing prominent KS lesions, on the page immediately preceding the dedication, in the Australian edition, and on the page following it in the American. After the shock of this encounter (or these encounters) with memento mori, some relatively more lenifying front matter then intervenes between the frontispiece and the text, of which it functions as a graphic *mise en abyme* (i.e., a part of the text emblematic of the whole). There is a foreword (by Paul Foss) and an introduction (by Simon Watney) in the original edition and, in the American edition, a preface by Michael Moon as well as the foreword and introduction. Although it is clear that Michaels gave his imprimatur to the photo, he may or may not have anticipated the cushioning effect that this proliferating prefatory matter inevitably introduces for the reader. What I notice, in any case, is that student readers rarely refer to these intervening materials, but seem unable to discuss Michaels's text without returning, again and again, to the frontispiece.

It is lit with a flash, so it is one of the Friday evening shots, as opposed to the Saturday morning garden shots that Michaels describes as "more aggressive and more elaborate" (103). Yet it is hard to imagine a photographic portrait more complexly readable (i.e., "elaborate") or more rhetorically provocative ("aggressive") than this. Michaels sits slightly slumped, his whole upper body exposed to show his lesions, the torso and arms pas-

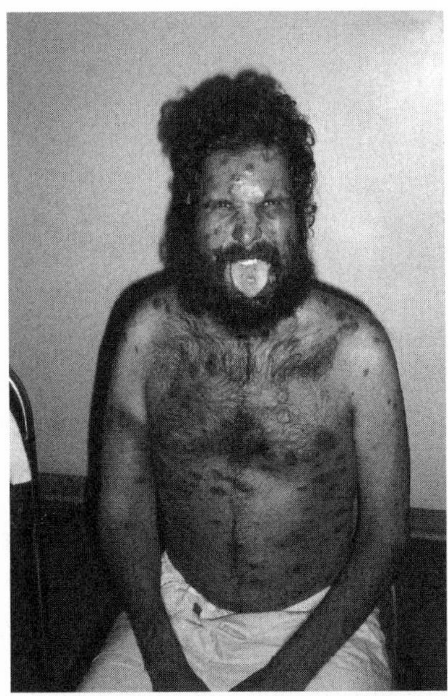

Eric Michaels, Brisbane, June 26, 1988.
(From Eric Michaels, *Unbecoming*, viii.)

sive, the face contrasting by the intensity of its expression, framed by a head of wild hair and an unruly black beard. On his fully extended tongue he displays a prominent KS lesion, which catches the light of the flash and forms both the photo's *punctum* and its *studium* (see Barthes, 1980). The expression, which at a very casual first glance might be mistaken for a broad grin, proves on closer examination to be one of fury, so that the odd contrast with both the more relaxed body and the fleeting hint of laughter in the openness of the face intensifies the effect of concentrated rage, which is particularly readable in the eyes. It's as if the whole of Michaels's determination, will and aggressiveness is channeled into the narrowed eyes and broadly extended tongue, where it is caught and immobilized by the flash, so that this intense facial expression seems to escape linear time and to be making a permanent effort to obtrude, in untimely fashion, out of the photo's two-dimensional plane and into the three-dimensional world of the observer, that is, into the posthumous future to which Michaels's thoughts, we know from the text, were quite single-mindedly turned. Meanwhile the more relaxed gestures of the portrait—the ghost of a grin, the slumped body—represent, as it were, more contingent and even personal moments in the text: Michaels's impishness, his moments of weakness and defeat. For this is certainly a portrait of a body in the process of its unbecoming.

But its style—plain to the point of take-it-or-leave-itness, unsentimental to the point of bleakness, aggressive to the point of concealing, at least momentarily, its elaborateness and complex readability—makes it rhetorically strong: both impertinent (as the extended tongue obviously indexes) and curiously engaging, in the strongest sense of that word (from which, however, I don't exclude the weaker meaning). In other words, an etiquette is at work, for I find myself unable to dismiss the photo's impertinence, as I might simply ignore some man who put his tongue out at me in the street, and move on. Rather I become interested in it; like my students in class, I am led by it to read and reread the photo. For if this picture is impudent, aggressive, confrontational—in-your-face as well as take-it-or-leave-it, which is a rhetorical definition of the act called flaunting—it is also impertinently im-pertinent, not so much ignorably irrelevant as interestingly incongruous, and so somewhat comparable, for example, with Primo Levi's symptomatic redeployment of Dantean anachronism discussed in chapter 1, in that, once it has caught my attention (the function of impertinence), it produces the quality of inexhaustible readability (the function of im-pertinence). It becomes hard for me to *stop* reading, as if my attention had become permanently diverted. This attention takes the form, simultaneously, of an anxiety and an obsession, something that, as previously mentioned, reproduces Michaels's own worry about the status of his text but also ensures that, posthumously, his text remains culturally active, obtruding, like the extended tongue and the intense eyes of the photo, into a "cultural future."

Because it is both the photo's *punctum*—it catches attention by its impertinence—and its *studium*—the place where its incongruity is concentrated—the tongue is where any, inevitably incomplete, reading of the photo should begin. The genre of this image is to all intents and purposes that of scientific illustration, the "specimen." It has the look of a picture taken in the interests of medical science, to demonstrate what a case of Kaposi's sarcoma looks like. The patient has been asked by a physician (or a technician) to put out his tongue so as to make the lesion clearly visible, and the patient, as a disciplined subject, is submissively or at least cooperatively complying. Or so it would seem were it not for the intensity in the eyes, which—as an incongruity in the medical context—requires us to read the extended tongue otherwise: not as a sign of compliance but as an act of impudence. Michaels's own struggle with the powers of discipline and his persistent rebellion are thus encapsulated in the tongue, as the picture's *studium;* and it is done through a figure of readability that can be identified as syllepsis (etymologically "taking together"). Syllepsis occurs when a sign signifies two different meanings—or, as here, stands for two sets of values—concurrently. Compliance and noncompliance, referring respectively to the genre of medical illustration and its subversion—its appropriation for other purposes—produce the solecism of generic catachresis. And the (indexical) object of the readability that is thus produced, that is, what can't be directly stated but only made available indirectly, through a "rephrasing," would have to be named as the pain of Michaels's situation: the way he lives his dying, is forced to live his dying, in and as an anxiety of im-pertinence. The effect of the syllepsis is somewhat comparable in this respect to Walter Benjamin's famous understanding (in "Theses on the Philosophy of History") of *Dialektik im Stillstand* or frozen dialectic, which is also a "flash" that gives insight into the darkness and pain of history.

But if syllepsis is the figure by means of which the generic catachresis of this image (as an adopted but adapted example of medical illustration) is performed, "turning" it to witnessing purposes rather than scientific or disciplinary ones, the photo also performs another syllepsis, this time relating to subgenres of scientific illustration, and similarly analyzable as performing a *captatio.* This second syllepsis is the vehicle through which Michaels enacts, in another dialectical "flash" of readability, the rhetorical project of capturing readerly attention and involvement through the photo itself, a performed act of impertinence: the effect Barthes calls *punctum.* If there is subversive catachresis of the genre of scientific, specifically medical illustration, one may also hesitate sylleptically between medical illustration as a subgenre of the scientific (in which Michaels has the persona of a "patient") and a second subgenre, in which he—a professional ethnographer photographed by another professional ethnographer—becomes a "native." This is the subgenre of anthropological illustration. More specifically, through this second syllepsis of the subgenres, the AIDS patient comes to exhibit, simultaneously and interchangeably, some of the characteristic signs of Aboriginality and becomes a (certain kind of) Koori, like those with whom, in the text (84), he claims an affinity (an affinity, let me recall, that stops short of identification-as while implying an identification-with). In my experience, viewers of the photo will often spontaneously say: "He looks like an Australian Aborigine," and there are probably many more who think it without voicing the perception. One of my students, who had skipped the prefatory matter but looked at the frontispiece, reported in class that he had thought Michaels was an Aboriginal anthropologist who had worked with the Warlpiri in that capacity; the student had gotten well into the text on that assumption without encountering any problems, only gradually realizing his "error." When realization finally hit, he had experienced the flash of syllepsis with considerable intensity, and expressed astonishment that such a confusion was possible. (The pronoun *I* being in the linguistic category of the "shifter," autobiography in fact lends itself rather easily to sylleptic shift.) It became necessary for me to explain that Michaels was not necessarily claiming an "Aboriginal identity" in the photo any more than—my student's error notwithstanding—he does in the text.

If Michaels were claiming Aboriginal identity, that would be much more than an act of impudence on his part. It would entail grossly racist insensitivity of a kind that modern anthropologists, sensitive to such issues, are particularly anxious to avoid. In fact, the impertinence is more subtle. The syllepsis of AIDSness (in medical terms) and Aboriginality (in anthropological terms) functions as a particular kind of categorical error, an illegitimate crasis or stammer such that the separability of the categories is denied without their identity being affirmed, in what Gilles Deleuze (1993) calls a "synthesis of disjunction." And to the extent that this stammer gives evidence of being deliberately committed, it constitutes an impertinence—the impertinence indexed by the outstretched tongue.[4] The root of this impertinence lies in the fact that a supposed categorical error that denies the separability of categories, but does so as it were accidentally, must now be reinterpreted as an actual affirmation of their inseparability, and indeed in this case as a personal assumption of their inseparability—a crime against tidiness and its logic of separability. Michaels's gamble, to which he committed himself on June 26, 1988, is that for a certain kind of audience, such an impertinence can function as a *captatio,* arousing interest along with an anxiety of readability in those "folks" whom it selects from the mass as being those "I wanted to talk to" (104). What does it mean, they are led to ask, that the anthropologist and the native, AIDS and aboriginality are being folded in this way into each other?

As an interpretive matter, one might claim, for example, that where medical illustration produces AIDS as a pathology of the biological body, this picture with its syllepsis of the subgenres has the effect of suggesting, without quite stating, that Aboriginality is an equivalent pathology, this time of the social body, being regarded in the Australian national culture as a kind of disease, and as subject therefore, like AIDS, to being tidied out of the way. In a further extension of this logic, the reversibility of this metaphoric equivalence between the medical and the social might be taken to imply that AIDSness is itself, like Aboriginality, not only a medical matter but also a cultural pathology in its own right. If Aboriginality becomes interpretable as a kind of scabrous disease, AIDS in turn becomes a social and not merely medical pathology: and both forms of pathology, therefore, are subject to "treatment" at the hands of the tidiness culture that produces these definitions. For example, the policy of allowing Australian Aborigines to "die out," which was historically advocated and very nearly achieved in Australia, has its counterpart in the suspicion often voiced in the 1980s and still harbored in some quarters, that governments were inactive in the struggle against AIDS because they welcomed the epidemic as an opportunity to rid their nations of unwanted groups such as homosexuals, drug users, or ethnic minorities. Such paranoid beliefs have their roots in real histories, and like Michaels's belief that the hospital that put him in an infectious disease ward was out to murder him, are not easily refutable; there is evidence in their favor.

Now I am not guaranteeing this interpretation of the image, but attempting to illustrate the uncontrollability of the readability that its indexical character unleashes. For readers who succumb to the *captatio* of the impertinence, the sylleptic incongruity invites interpretations that, paranoid or no, reproduce the kind of anxiety of im-pertinence that Michaels describes as having constituted his experience of dying of AIDS. For such readers, though, defined as a group by their susceptibility to the effect of the outstretched tongue, the image's *punctum,* there is a second anxiety, which is that of being—like the addressees of Michaels's posthumous revenge letters or the friends publicly blamed in the text for the errors and inadequacies of their care—targeted and accused. The outstretched tongue is pointed at me; I am the object of its impertinence; I must thus ask myself whether I am not guilty of complicity in the tidiness culture's depredations, and an accessory, therefore, to a murder. The categorical solecism or stammer produced by syllepsis breaks the tidiness rule that items of a paradigm cannot co-occur (an anthropologist is not a native, a white AIDS patient is not an Aboriginal) and substitutes a regime of uncontrollable readability for the kind of directness of communication tidiness would prefer. But the reader who has been (self-)selected from the mass by responding to the tongue's *captatio* must ask, not only: What does this image—or this text—mean? But also: What does it have to do *with me*? Why am *I* accused? And to feel accused is to know that one is not uninvolved; it is to be *engaged*.

Thus the final categorical breakdown performed by the impertinence of the image of im-pertinence is that of the separateness that is axiomatically held to distinguish (in tidy fashion) a reading subject, by definition a member of the tidiness culture, and the im-pertinent, impertinent, and, in short, unbecoming object of reading, the tidiness culture's unkempt, wild-eyed, bespotted other. The text's rhetorical unbecomingness plunges the reader responsive to its *captatio* into an experience of the unbecoming of tidiness itself, because the reader is forced to acknowledge the phenomenon of reading as a matter of relationality. This is the relationality at which Michaels's extended tongue in the photo hints so strongly, as a figure for both the im-pertinence and the impertinence of not pathological but pathologized speech, straining as it does to escape the plane of the photo, and to reach into—to engage—the world of the photo's viewer or *Unbecoming*'s reader. To the reader who identifies as the addressee of the image, of the text's impertinently pointed tongue, it signifies that such a photo, such a text, *cannot be held at arm's length.* Thus, for such a reader (let me stress one last time that not all readers can be expected to respond, or to respond in this way, the etiquette is not all-inclusive), the text's photographic and verbal impertinence has the effect of transforming the textual subject's im-pertinent cultural status into something more *pertinent* to that reader than the reader may have wished to acknowledge, but certainly already *knew* (that is, of which the reader had the foreknowledge on which witnessing always counts). "I have the satisfaction, my anger transubstantiated," as Michaels puts it (104). But for me, as this targeted reader, my careful protections against the untidy, the unbecoming, the obscene, and the untimely have collapsed. Why indeed *should* I have protected myself against them, though, unless I knew all along that they were there, already a part of me?

A Symptomatology of Culture

In Australia, there is concern about the environment, as elsewhere in the world. But this concern also takes a more local form: how to protect the often unique indigenous fauna and flora of the country from the depredations of imported species? This is of course an entirely legitimate preoccupation, the effects of past errors being everywhere to be seen. The worry, however, sometimes reaches a pitch of anxiety that suggests it should be read, also, as a cultural symptom: a displacement, perhaps, of deeper fears concerning *human* immigration. (For many years, passengers on incoming international flights to Australia were ceremoniously sprayed for bugs—much to their surprise and amusement—before being allowed to disembark.) Since 1788, when the so-called First Fleet arrived in Botany Bay and a colony was established where Sydney now stands, there has been a national immigration history of violent appropriation, on the one hand, and of the denial of hospitality on the other—a form of "tidiness" in Michaels's sense of the word. This history begins with the forced migration of a population of English and Irish convicts, under military escort, to an inconceivably remote penal colony; it merges seamlessly into the white settler's relentless eviction of the Aboriginal people, who appear initially to have sought to welcome them, from the land that defined their cultural identity. This eviction was an act of ethnicide bordering on genocide, that responded brutally to the indigenous people's attempt to apply laws of hospitality and to accommodate the newcomers within their own classificatory systems. Ignoring their status as uninvited guests (not to say invaders), and failing to understand either the Aboriginal relation to the land or the hospitality that was being extended, the settler society declared the land uninhabited *(terra nullius),* giving itself a license in this way to attempt to wipe out the original inhabitants by means not infrequently direct and conscious, but no less lethal for being mainly indirect, unconscious, misguided, or unintended. Within a few generations this tidying attempt had come perilously close to succeeding.

At midcentury, a wave of Chinese immigration associated with the gold rush (the wave in which William Yang's ancestors reached the country) exacerbated the racism and xenophobia of the white settler culture, whose object extended now from Aborigines to immigrants from East Asia and the Pacific, and in due course, albeit a bit less virulently, to those from West Asia and the Mediterranean basin. The notoriously rigid and hypocritical White Australia policy emerged, and was not officially abandoned until a generation ago, when quite suddenly, under new historical conditions, Australia became an officially multicultural nation. That rancorous hostility to nonwhite people nevertheless continued to smolder in many sections of the population was demonstrated, however, by the emergence and sudden popularity of Pauline Hanson's One Nation Party in the 1990s; this party's policy statements showed clearly that the hostility continues to embrace both Asians ("Chinese") and indigenous Australians, as if these were somehow one and the same in their otherness. This is the historical and cultural frame in which the peculiar pointedness of Eric Michaels's association of his AIDS with Aboriginality in the frontispiece portrait of *Unbecoming* becomes apparent.

He is alluding to Australia's immigration history by daring to hint at a conceivable counterhistory. In this counterhistory, institutions like the Immigration Department would have inherited something like Aboriginal forms and practices of hospitality, as opposed to settler-invader attitudes and customs. A diary entry for June 22 (just before the photography session) makes this idea explicit. "I reckon," Michaels says, using a characteristic Australianism, "I reckon—and this has Warlpiri sources too—that dying here does give me certain Australian 'citizenship' rights" (98). Blandly assuming the *pertinence* to government and bureaucratic policy of what he broadly hints are Aboriginal beliefs, he commits the *impertinence* of proposing a thesis that for two hundred years has been unthinkable in the settler society, with its racist investments and its tidiness culture: the thesis that Aboriginality has prior rights in Australia. In the year of the Bicentenary, that is his version of the Aboriginal countercelebrations he had enjoyed participating in in January, and at which he had the pleasure of an all too brief reunion with Warlpiri friends, including Paddy Jupurrurla (44–48). So the argument is not just that Michaels has a classificatory name and speaking rights among the Warlpiri (he has experienced their hospitality), but also that his AIDS and his death confer on him the equivalent of *land rights* (the Aboriginal version of "citizenship")—the land rights of which his friends were unjustly and summarily divested by the newcomers of 1788. Thus, he is claiming the right not only not to be deported as an undesirable alien, but also to have, like Paddy and the other Warlpiri, a "cultural future" (cf. the title of Michaels's ethnographic monograph on the "Birth of a Station": *For a Cultural Future: Francis Jupurrurla Makes TV at Yuendumu* [Melbourne, 1988]). His claim, he implies, is of equal legitimacy to the political claim to land rights that as he wrote was being contemporaneously pressed with vigor by Aboriginal activists and advocates, in the political sphere and in the courts. (The claim was to be vindicated, shortly after Michaels's death, by the landmark *Mabo* decision of 1992, which finally repudiated the infamous doctrine of *terra nullius.*)

Michaels, then, is taking an ethical position—making a claim for justice—in relation to the question of hospitality. He is asserting the superiority of Aboriginal practices and understandings and their continuing relevance to, as well as their historical primacy in, Australia; and he is implying the moral indigence of a settler society and a racist culture that are contemptuous of Aboriginality and willing, "therefore," to deport an AIDS patient to an uncertain future in another country, out of tidiness, while simultaneously being hypocritical enough to add the rider that he not be moved unless and until his health improves. (Notice that this rider holds a kind of Damoclean sword over the dying patient by threatening dire consequences should he get well: it is a disguised expression of the desire for Michaels to die, somewhat reminiscent of those pundits who, after a century of virtual genocide, felt free to lament—also prematurely—the passing of the Aborigines.) This, then, is a society that treats cultural otherness as obscene, and the obscene as something to be ignored—tidied out of sight—when it cannot in good conscience be eliminated.

Now the confrontational character of Michaels's impudence—which has visible affinities with gay "attitude" and Jewish chutzpah as well as with U.S. Black style and the historical Aboriginal persistence in claiming a cultural future—puts him at one extreme of an etiquette of im-pertinence that can be understood as polarized. He is at the confrontational end of a certain spectrum of possibility, as opposed to the infiltrational end. Likewise, his brilliant handling of the figure of syllepsis produces a rich and complex readability that I have tried to explore in some detail because it is rarely matched in its exemplary character—its striking indexicality—by other texts. His writing is not alone, however, within the Australian context, in exploiting rhetorical effects derived from the perception of a certain cultural proximity between the obscenity of AIDS and other manifestations of social marginality and/or the category of the subaltern. Indeed, the sense of such a proximity seems characteristic of some of the most prominent Australian AIDS writing, and symptomatic or definitional, therefore, in respect of the national culture. It is as if the model of a parasite-host relation presented by HIV disease (understood, that is, as an "invasion" of the body and a "threat" to or an "attack" on the immune system) acquires particular cultural relevance in the context of the national history of inhospitability in the name of tidiness I have just sketched. This suggests that AIDS writing, with its rhetorical practice of proximity, can be read, inter alia, as a symptomatology, but less of AIDS itself, than of the supposedly healthy or "seronegative" society in which AIDS has the status of an obscenity.

In *Sadness,* for example, already briefly discussed (chapter 1), William Yang "throws together," sym-bolically, stories of his gay friends, impacted by the epidemic, and those of his Chinese-Australian family, subjected over generations to the ordeals of immigration, then of assimilation, then (in Yang's own case) of self-rediscovery or reinvention, ordeals that are encapsulated in the history of Yang's murdered uncle and of the nephew's recovering of that obfuscated history. The relation, says Yang jokingly, is that of "guilt by association" (13). The joke is mild, the wit less mordant than Michaels's, the *captatio* it performs closer to a conventional *captatio benevolentiae.* This is wry humor rather than impertinence or confrontation, as befits the more general audience Yang seeks to address, and the looser associationism of symbolism as opposed to syllepsis, a looseness that likewise allows more room for a variety of audience responses by positioning the addressee less pointedly than does Michaels's outstretched tongue. It could even be argued that, in associating AIDS with Chineseness (by contrast with Michaels's provocative association of it with Aboriginality, and guilt by association notwithstanding), Yang is actually piggybacking AIDS, the relative newcomer to the category of the obscene, on the category of Chineseness that, after generations of assimilation and in the context of contemporary Australian multiculturalism, now enjoys greater cultural admissibility and indeed respectability, at least among the young, urban, educated folk who attended performances of *Sadness.* Nevertheless, by virtue of the history of inhospitability to which it refers, the joke still has a sting, and the symptomatological character of the gay/AIDS-Chinese proximity it presents is inescapable.

About the urbane and gently ironic writing of John Foster in *Take Me to Paris, Johnny!* something similar might be said. This is the story of John's "cross-class, cross-colour, same-sex relationship" (49) with Juan, a refugee from the homophobia and racism of revolutionary Cuba, and of Juan's death in Melbourne from the effects of AIDS—the relation of similarity/difference between the two first names being emblematic of this text's participation in the genre I call "dual autobiography" (see chapter 6) as well as of its interest in a thematics of proximity. But this is writing that, while remaining within the scope of an etiquette of im-pertinence, self-consciously eschews impertinence itself; it occupies the opposite end of the spectrum of possibilities from Michaels's performance. The text is both complicitous with and expectant of complicity from a readership that is assumed to be as squeamish about the obscenity of AIDS as the couple of John and Juan is itself represented as being. For, unlike Michaels's, this is a story about the denial of AIDS, described as an unspeakable horror that creeps up on a couple who are mutually complicitous in their failure to acknowledge its reality (and indeed, in retrospect, its fatality). Only toward the end does the disease outwit their defenses and become undeniable.

This story thus parallels the history of European Jewry, faced in the 1930s with Nazi anti-Semitism but still taken by surprise, in the 1940s, by the "final solution"—a history to which the book alludes, in part through references to John's research as an academic historian of modern Germany and in part through a running parallel, anchored in an epigraph from Cabrera Infante, that links Nazi anti-Semitism with Cuban homophobia. If Foster's audience is assumed to be naturally as horrified by AIDS as are John and Juan themselves, his readers are also assumed to be horrified by the horror with which the "inherent" crime of homosexuality (or that of blackness) is regarded in Cuba and elsewhere; and if not by that, then by the horror that the crime of being Jewish inspired in Nazi Germany. There is thus a kind of mounting scale of associationist piggybacking-by-proximity, like the opportunist piggybacking of AIDS and gayness on Chineseness that seems to operate in *Sadness* (where the case is less clear, however, and somewhat closer to Michaels's more daring and provocatively incongruous association of AIDS with Aboriginality). The taken-for-granted obscenity of AIDS piggybacks here on homosexuality and race, assumed to be regarded as less obscene by a larger number of people, and these piggyback in turn on the cultural respectability of Jewishness and the virtual outlawing of anti-Semitism that has taken place in the cultural mainstream, in Australia and elsewhere, as a consequence of the Holocaust. And the book's rhetoric turns, therefore, on the assumption that there is a significant difference, supposedly recognized by the book's addressee as well as its narrator and characters, between AIDS, as a "genuinely" obscene phenomenon that it is natural to wish to deny, and other categories like homosexuality, color, or Jewishness, that are understood to be shunned, denied, or persecuted only as a consequence of unacceptable prejudice. It is in this sense that, by contrast with *Unbecoming*'s provocative deployment of Aboriginality, *Take Me to Paris* is complicitous with the audience it addresses, rather than impertinent or confrontational. But it nevertheless seeks, ultimately, to "unveil" AIDS—to make it a readable object that readers of the book cannot avoid contemplating.

In this respect, the crucial technique of association by proximity is that of framing, the *parergon:* without a frame, there is no "work" *(ergon)* as such, and the supposedly subsidiary frame is therefore constitutive of the work, and part and parcel of it. An account of John's visit to Cuba after Juan's death begins and ends the story of their relation—itself a parable of proximity, involving a gay white Australian academic of middle-class status and a young, black, *loca,* Cuban refugee who is virtually a street kid when John meets him one day outside the New York Public Library—and of the death of Juan, which is the occasion of the framing trip to Cuba. Because John undertakes the Cuba trip in order to bring news of Juan's death to Juan's mother in Guantánamo, and because he shrouds the reality of his AIDS from her, as Juan himself had done ("It was enough to say that he had died of a virus for which they could find no remedy," 8), the frame narrative functions as an anticipatory *mise en abyme,* doubling the euphemistic rhetoric of the main story. But because this frame also explores the homophobic and racist discrimination, bordering on persecution, that caused Juan to flee Cuba and implies a parallel with Nazi Germany, the frame narrative simultaneously both sets in train the story of Juan's life (for he was not to escape either homophobia or racism by fleeing Cuba) and sets up a contrast with the hospitality Juan was finally to find—Immigration Department suspicions notwithstanding—in Melbourne, thanks to John's love and the affection of a small circle of friends. "Cross-class, cross-colour, same-sex love" has power against social injustice, if not against the horror of AIDS; such is the burden of the central, framed, story.

Apart from this visit of John's to Juan's mother, bringing a photograph of her son's tombstone—a visit that is therefore a metaphor for the book's own bringing of unwelcome news to its readership—the book offers a number of other models for its rhetorical practice and narrative method. Juan's dancing—it was contrary to revolutionary principles for him to train as a ballet dancer in Cuba—is one of them; his quilting (117) is another: the fabric of his life has to be pieced together, in love and mourning, from the gaps and evasions of his own face-saving reticence. But two conventional genres are particularly interesting models, if only because their relevance to Foster's text is distributed, roughly speaking, between the frame narrative and the framed story, respectively, while they are relevant, however, in an oddly contradictory way. One is the usually euphemistic genre of the obituary or the epitaph, alluded to in the frame by the tombstone photo John takes to Guantánamo (it says only that Juan Gualberto Céspedes "died" on April 17, 1987). On his deathbed, Juan had wailed (in unusually formal English): "I have accomplished nothing," thus pronouncing his own epitaph. John had attempted to respond with a corrective obituary formula of his own: "There has been us" (196). As an expansion of both of these formulations, the book thus situates itself, especially through the frame, as a monument—like a tombstone—to the significance of the couple's achievement, and as a complementary gesture of posthumous salvage, demonstrating the courage, spirit, and integrity of Juan's fatally damaged existence, and doing so in the reticent and euphemistic spirit of obituary remembrance.

But it is also—and this is the second generic model—a kind of coming-out narrative, in which Juan's self-protective "shrouding" of his life (17) in the face of the "blame that had vaguely attached to him ever since his difficult birth" (9) is both respected and simultaneously countered, by an equally cautious unshrouding of Juan's life and of the reality of his AIDS as that which, in the end, cannot be denied. This is the business of the main story. Although no one can bear to face this reality, its truth must nevertheless emerge. And thus are defined both the function of the central story and the problematics of the etiquette of im-pertinence as Foster, at the opposite extreme from Michaels, conceives it and deploys it (framing and framed story combined) in his narrative. "I was disturbed by the decisions that the disease was forcing on me," he writes (172), "uneasy with the interventions and subterfuges, the disclosures and withholdings that it seemed to make unavoidable." His anxiety about disclosure matches Michaels's about the stage management of his death, except that whereas the one is concerned to find a style that will legitimate the impertinence, the other is concerned with filtering and withholding, the necessary shrouding of the very unshrouding he must nevertheless accomplish. And it is in the somewhat oxymoronic character of such an undertaking that the complementarity of the obituary monument and the coming-out narrative—and hence of the framing and framed narratives—is made manifest.

John's countermodel of the cautious unshrouding his narrative attempts is described—in terms like *assaulting, battering, ambushing, stunning*—when he gives an account of the locally famous "Grim Reaper" advertising campaign that was authorized in Australia, by ghastly coincidence, in the weeks preceding Juan's death by the National Advisory Council on AIDS. "They confronted you with this fantastic, cowled creature, socket-eyed, and scythe-swinging, knocking down its victims like pins in a bowling alley" (177). But Juan, John writes, knows that "AIDS is not like that" (178): AIDS does not batter, but creeps up on you, silently and imperceptibly infiltrating your defenses. How to unmask it, then, but nonviolently, without "stunning" people with images of horror, and in a way consonant with AIDS's very nature, as a kind of clandestine, creepy, but subterranean presence? A first answer is given by Juan's dancing:

> That was the last time Juan danced. He was a star that night, and he shone more brightly because his sickness was evident. He no longer attempted to mask it, but drew attention to himself as if to say, "This is my coming out." People asked each other, "Is it cancer?" They asked me, "Is it terminal?" They couldn't bring themselves to say, "Is it AIDS?" They had never seen AIDS. No one in our circle had seen it. Only Juan, who had nursed Jerry on his death-bed. (146)

Juan, who knows, must therefore be the teacher, and *his* preferred vehicle, dancing, suggests that although John's writing must make his sickness "evident," must unmask and draw attention, making Juan a star, it must also do so through a discourse that is inexplicit, that creeps up on one, as AIDS does, leaving *open* the baffled questions asked in its presence by those who do not know. Irony, it seems, is the trope in Foster's writing that best matches these requirements; irony in this text is the anti–"Grim Reaper" device that models itself on Juan's dancing, shroudedly unshrouding, "outing" AIDS but doing so in the euphemistic language of obituary and cautiously respecting the nature of the disease by respecting at the same time the reader's denial of its reality, thus countering denial but without confronting or condemning it. If syllepsis, in Michaels's performance, is a kind of ethnic drag, like donning "Chanel black and a single string of pearls" when one "lean[s] against the piano, to sing" (*Unbecoming,* 26), irony is the "dance" Foster performs as a writer. His mode, then, is not the impertinence of drag but the reticence of the shroud, which both decently conceals and inescapably reveals the obscenity. Like AIDS itself, as Foster, instructed by Juan, knows and understands it, irony's mode, as an etiquette of im-pertinence, is infiltrational, not confrontational in "Grim Reaper" fashion or impudent as Michaels's drag performance is.

Irony is pervasive in *Take Me to Paris;* but, again speaking roughly, one can say that its distribution, between the framing and the framed narratives, corresponds to two different forms of irony, each of which presupposes a complicity between narrator (as ironizing subject) and reader (as the decoder without whom irony fails or fizzles). The efficacity of "rhetorical" irony as a trope lies in its ability to select a readership complicit with the ironizing subject because able to perceive a discrepancy or split between the semantic content of a statement (i.e., of the plane of *énoncé*) and the implication of its being uttered (on the plane of *énonciation*). Such a complicity rests, in turn, on shared ideological presuppositions that constitute a kind of foreknowledge of the unstated. Thus, Foster's ironies appeal most obviously to a liberal-minded reader capable of measuring the discrepancy, for instance, in the comment concerning Juan's ejection from the Cuban National Ballet School, that "the most noble principle of collectivism dictated that he should be removed" (17), or the observation that in so-called special military reeducation units ("more simply known as concentration camps"), "*locas* had a curious habit of subverting the education process, so they were given separate instruction and helped to learn by beating" (18). These are the kinds of ironies that proliferate in the frame narrative, very largely concerning Cuba. But they recur in the framed story whenever Cuba-like situations arise, as in the comment on the Australian Immigration Department's skittishness about admitting a former Cuban citizen (not coincidentally also black and gay) that is implied by a description of Juan and John "lying on the beach at Wilson's Promontory undermining national security" (84). These are not subtle ironies, nor do they need to be. We can notice, too, that one does not need to share Foster's liberalism, but only to recognize it, in order to be drawn into the complicity entailed in recognizing such ironies. For the function of Foster's rhetorical ironies is to select readers likely to be sympathetic with Juan, as a persecuted figure of subalternity, so that the sympathy can then be transferred to, and maintained in, the unshrouding of Juan's AIDS, an unshrouding that will be largely the work of the framed narrative and of what is called "dramatic" irony. The liberal readers selected by the text's rhetorical ironies are, precisely, those most likely to grasp the symbolic implications—that is, the historical significance—of the incongruity that is a successful "cross-class, cross-color, same-sex" couple (49). Irony is the mode of agencing that selects them, just as, in Michaels, syllepsis selects a not dissimilar class of readers as the best, because most receptive, target of its impertinence.

It is dramatic irony, however, that works in the framed narrative—the story of the couple and of Juan's death—as a gentle unshrouding of AIDS. The form of complicity produced by dramatic irony depends less crucially on unspoken but shared ideological presuppositions than on the shared access of readers (or in the theater, spectators) and of an ironizing narrative instance to knowledge and an understanding of the life circumstances (or "fate") of characters that is denied the characters themselves (or to which, at least, the characters are relatively blind). Thus, if Juan and John are mutually complicitous in their blindness to Juan's AIDS and shroud from themselves the obscenity that is nevertheless stalking them, reasonably alert readers are tipped quite early to what the characters ignore and the narrator knows. Such readers can attend, sympathetically, to the features and processes of the psychological denial they perceive the couple to be acting out, both individually and together. But by the same means, these readers have been simultaneously maneuvered into acknowledging the obscene reality that, under other circumstances, the text assumes, they would prefer to ignore. They can hardly withhold sympathy from the blind or semiblind characters with whom they share the need to deny AIDS, but they are themselves unable to deny, as the characters do virtually to the end, the obscenity that has now infiltrated their consciousness, as a function of their ironic dissociation from characters with whose denial they are simultaneously complicitous.

In the calculation of this effect Foster's silence about his own infection is a crucial element. It is easy to miss the only hint he gives of his own illness: John fetches a beloved jacket from home for Juan to be buried in, and comments: "[I] made my last trip, *on his account,* back to the hospital" (199; emphasis added). By shrouding in this way his own AIDS, Foster produces John, the narrator, as a figure of easy identification for the reader-addressee who is presumed to be, like John, white, literate, middle class, and, unlike Foster, HIV-negative. This is the figure who represents the ironizing textual subject with whom the reader shares a complicity in both the rhetorical and the dramatic irony: his HIV status being, as it were, ignored, only his gayness marks him as "different." (Of course, there is an unmistakable hint, since John does fleetingly acknowledge his AIDS, that the reader may also be infected, as John is, whether unknowingly, unconsciously, or through being in a state of denial. That is the irony of the irony.) One consequence of this easy identification of the assumedly white, middle-class, literate, and HIV-negative reader with John is that the reader is thereby invited to share in John's love for and admiration of Juan, that is, to reenact the dynamics of the cross-color, cross-class, same-sex relationship—a dynamics to which the Immigration Department itself, functioning here, as it does in *Unbecoming,* as the key gatekeeper institution of Australian society when it comes to extending or refusing hospitality to the obscene, is willing to give its blessing, *precisely because it is ignorant of Juan's AIDS* (as it was not ignorant in Eric Michaels's case, and in the way that an only moderately inattentive reader can be ignorant of John's/Foster's AIDS in reading *Take Me to Paris*).

But a second consequence is that the assumptions underlying the history of immigration in Australia—that it is white Australians who are, as it were, "uncontaminated" while all others are marked, subject to stigma and associated with the obscene, or in short *abject*—are involuntarily and

perhaps unconsciously reproduced in the pattern of complicities that the text's ironies, rhetorical and dramatic, both solicit and produce. In this respect, there is an evident contrast, at the level of tactics and the etiquette of im-pertinence, with Eric Michaels's upfrontness about his AIDS status and association of his own person, as a PWA, with Aboriginality. The price to pay for an etiquette of the im-pertinent that is gentle, infiltratory, and reader friendly—more opportunistic than impertinent or confrontational—turns out, predictably enough, to be a degree of conformity with reader prejudice concerning the nature of the obscene: not only is the desirability of its being shrouded reaffirmed, in conformity with the dictates of tidiness culture, but also its identification with otherness as opposed to one's own supposedly uncontaminated self. Michaels, by contrast, does not pander to the supposition that AIDS is alien and other because he understands "untidiness," like Aboriginality, to be integral to the tidiness culture: it gives him "citizen rights." That said, both texts function, however, as does *Sadness* also, through their enactment of im-pertinence in rhetorical practices of proximity, as symptomatologies of a culture that is profoundly inhospitable to what it classifies as other than culture: the supposed "outside" of culture that is nevertheless, and for that very reason, crucial to its self-definition, and hence internal to it.[5]

But it is precisely because AIDS writing is culturally definitional in this sense, as a symptomatology of a supposedly healthy society that nevertheless unhealthily denies what is most crucial to it, that such writing is so risky. It seeks to hit a nerve—the very nerve of which culture is necessarily most protective. At both ends of the spectrum of possibilities that is the etiquette of im-pertinence (and not solely at the infiltrational or conciliatory end), the strong possibility exists, therefore, of such writing's being neutralized. For if tactics of infiltration risk *reinforcing* the exclusionary cultural pattern they seek to elude through their practices of shrouded unshrouding, as *Take Me to Paris* does, confrontational texts like *Unbecoming* run the equivalent if opposite risk, if "style" should fail, of *provoking* that exclusionary effect, and of being simply rejected. The end result, in either case, is much the same. The slightest miscalculation—whether of complicity at one end of the etiquette's range, or of provocation at the other—can cause a witnessing text to fall victim to what Michaels understands (I'm not sure this is true of Foster) as the lethal power of conventional culture. This is a power that is lethal not only to the Juans of this world and to rebellious subjects like Michaels, who *offend* it, but also to those who, like Foster, court their own self-erasure, running the risk of going too far in the direction of compromise, and thus of *comforting* the forces that respond to manifestations of cultural obscenity by obliterating it (whether it be by erasing it from consciousness or by eradicating it from the world). The two poles that set limits to the range wherein an etiquette of im-pertinence can come into play, offering it only a very narrow band of testimonial efficacity, are thus the risk of failure through assimilation to conventional culture, and the risk of rejection by that culture, each of which spells the demise of the witnessing mission through the consequent failure of testimonial troping to function as an indexical sign.

Between these two poles of possible failure, then, seeking to infiltrate at one end and to confront at the other, witnessing writing navigates. It seeks a "style" or an "etiquette" that would authorize a delicate balancing act, that of gaining cultural recognition for the culturally im-pertinent without compromising the force of the im(-)pertinence by provoking the response that, whether through absorption and assimilation or through rejection and exclusion, would neutralize it. This balancing act is, of course, exactly that which defines figural writing having the character of semiotic indexicality, as these terms were understood in chapter 1. An indexical must gain attention, but not to the extent of losing its pointing function; equally a figure becomes unreadable, qua figure, when statement-content disappears altogether or utterance-effect becomes absolute. Thus, there is always some degree of infiltration in confrontation, and of confrontation in infiltration; always a component of cultural conformity even in confrontation, and of unconformity in infiltration. Texts may polarize within the limits of this range, as I have suggested *Unbecoming* and *Take Me to Paris* do, but they share the constraints on rhetorical feasibility (the sense of solecism and the necessity of an "etiquette") that the range defines, constraints that determine testimonial's acts of cultural *détournement* as themselves *détourné:* indirect, elusive, hard to track and easy to overlook. The task is always a delicate one, and the wonder is that success is possible at all. The extent to which witnessing writing succeeds must always be measured, therefore, against the very high probability of its failing.

I have laid a rather heavy weight of exemplarity on *Unbecoming* in this chapter, viewing it as exemplary in respect of the spontaneity, naïveté, and improvisation that, along with wit, go into witnessing; in relation also to the problematics of im-pertinence (with its ethical entailments) and of impertinence (with its rhetorical dilemmas) that frames, defines, and limits the social effectiveness and cultural impact of witnessing texts; and finally in relation to the symptomatological character of AIDS writing in

Australia. But what makes the text crucial, from the point of view of this book, is its understanding and articulation of the degree of risk-taking, and of the relatively limited range of options for rhetorical success, that inevitably accompanies witnessing, as a practice that is always to some degree improvisatory—and always potentially wrong-footed, therefore—to the extent that it is obliged to negotiate with conventions and expectations that are inimical to its purposes.

3. Stuttering Rifles, Stammering Poetry: Reporting from the Front

What am I supposed to do with this gob-stopper?
—Pat Barker, *Regeneration*

What Is a Symptom?

In *The Differend,* Jean-François Lyotard finds himself at one point (paragraph 148) reduced to metaphor. He is addressing the idea that genre is an exclusionary phenomenon, and wants to describe it as a kind of spell (my word) that exerts its charm over everything it touches, or in Lyotard's vocabulary, over the "universe" that sentences "present." This universe consists not only of the sentences' referent but also of the intersubjectivity of addresser and addressee; all are under the sway of genre. Lyotard doesn't use my metaphor of spell or enchantment, but resorts instead to the idea of seduction, which perhaps seems better suited to imply that everything in a given "phrase universe" is drawn by a kind of unconscious consent into the ambience of generic conformity, thereby leaving a residue of alternative possibilities, an extrageneric surplus to which the universe in question is oblivious. But seduction isn't quite the right word either, because it suggests the initiative of a seducer, the agent of an intentionally seductive act. Consequently,

> The idea of seduction needs to be extended. A genre of discourse exerts a seduction upon a phrase universe. It inclines the instances presented by this phrase toward certain linkings [*certains enchaînements*], or at least it steers them away from other linkings which are not suitable with regard to the end pursued by the genre. It is not the addressee who is seduced by the addresser. The addresser, the referent and the sense are no less subject than

> the addressee to the seduction exerted by what is at play [*en jeu*] in a genre of discourse. (84)

Even the seducer, in this understanding, is seduced.

If, then, we are under a spell or subject to a seduction whenever genre intervenes (that is, under every possible regime of discourse, there being no sentences that are not subject to genre), there is only one way we can become aware of our subjection to genre. The spell is broken when genre's ordinary workings break down or encounter a hitch; and such accidents occur, Lyotard explains, because there is sometimes something to be said, the "phrasing" of which (its putting into sentences or *mise en phrases*) is not permitted by any one of the whole set of genres that are available. This situation is what he calls a *differend;* it is a generic stand-off. What is couched, for example, in the political or journalistic language of "declaration" (e.g., "The war in France has become a senseless slaughter and peace should be negotiated"—this being the burden of the "Declaration" that Siegfried Sassoon attempted to publicize in the summer of 1917) *cannot be heard* by those to whom it is addressed: say, middle-class English readers in 1917, perusing the *Times* over their breakfast eggs. It cannot be heard, except as madness, because they are under the seduction of a genre array that excludes the possibility of such a declaration's being made in the newspaper or in Parliament by insisting on phrasing warfare exclusively in the lexicon of patriotism and heroism. Thus there are warlike genres and also realist genres, but war is not a recognizable topic in realist sentences, and realism cannot occur in the genres reserved for speaking of war.

> In the differend, something "asks" to be put into phrases, and suffers from the wrong of not being able to be put into phrases instantaneously. This is when human beings who thought they could use language as an instrument of communication learn through the feeling of pain which accompanies silence (and of pleasure which accompanies the invention of a new idiom) that they are summoned [*requis*] by language, not to augment to their profit the quantity of information communicable through ordinary idioms, but to recognize that what remains to be phrased exceeds what they can presently phrase, and that they must permit idioms to be instituted that do not yet exist. (par. 23, 13; transl. modified)

Neither blunt declaration, then (a realist mode that does not admit warfare as its subject matter in the England of 1917) nor the register of heroism, glory, and love of country (the sole generic register in which it is permissible to report on warfare) are able to capture the "something" that is asking to be put into sentences. For *that* a "new idiom" is required; the alternative is to suffer the pain attendant on the silencing of something that asks to be phrased.

Lyotard does not discuss the nature of new idioms in *The Differend,* but in *The Inhuman* explores the category of the aesthetic sublime as a way of eluding generic constraints. Here, I am theorizing witnessing writing as a Lyotardian "new idiom"—one that is invented, in relation to the category not of the sublime but of the obscene, as a product of generic catachresis. And the story Pat Barker tells in her remarkable historical novel *Regeneration* (part of a trilogy set in England during the final years of the 1914–18 war)[1] is that of a differend arising in English culture as a result of the events in France—the slaughter of English, French, and German soldiers on both sides of the trenches that formed the front—and of the emergence, under those circumstances, of a new idiom through the invention, out of the conventional genre of (in particular) the poetic elegy, of a poetry of modern warfare. And such poetry is one of the sites, I would claim, where modern practices of witnessing can be seen, retrospectively, to have emerged. (I mean that these practices appear to have emerged without a name, that is, as a new idiom apparently without generic attachment, the sense of the word *witness* not yet having been "extended" for that purpose. The historical subjects—writers and readers—who were part of the universe "presented" by these new sentences, sentences of which they were simultaneously the agents, could not be aware that they were, precisely, bearing witness.)[2]

As a historical fiction, and indeed a kind of archaeology of testimonial, *Regeneration* is a work of metawitnessing, then. It tells the story—a kind of Bildungsroman—of the poets and simultaneously infantry officers Siegfried Sassoon and Wilfred Owen, who came to witness in the circumstances of "useless knowledge" (Charlotte Delbo's term) that for them arose out of an experience of incompatibility. This was the incompatibility of their experience in France, as something requiring to be phrased, with the only genres available in the England of Lloyd George for presenting warfare. But it is, of course, axiomatic in this study (see chapter 2) that witnessing is always in some degree metawitnessing, an account, like a Bildungsroman, of the experience—the education—entailed in coming to witnessing. What *Regeneration* demonstrates is, in a sense, the converse of that axiom, that is, that metawitnessing, in turn, functions (as I hope my own work of more theoretically oriented metawitnessing does) as itself a mode of witnessing. To describe the difficulties of witnessing is also a way of bearing witness to that something that asks, as Lyotard says, to be phrased wherever there is a generic differend. Since the American war in Vietnam, in which the Pentagon discovered the power, in particular, of TV reportage to "bring the war into the living rooms" of the nation—that is, to *presence* its horrors, as opposed to just presenting them, for millions of domestic viewers—the "small" wars of the West (innumerable interventions in Africa, the war in the Persian Gulf, subsequent bombardments of Iraq, NATO's offensive against Serbian-dominated Yugoslavia . . .) have been fought under regimes of such strict information control as to recall, uncannily, the kind of information blackout that prevailed in England, with respect to the war in France, in 1917: not the absence of information (casualty lists were published, battles were reported), but the absence of its readability, by virtue of the substitution of received genres for what was asking to be phrased, the casting of a kind of generic spell that excluded the presencing of the war (the ironic point of Remarque's title, *All Quiet on the Western Front*). That my students are ready to affirm that the Vietnam War did away with the kind of thing Barker describes, but reticent about acknowledging the relevance of her text to, say, the Gulf War (which not coincidentally was being fought as she began work on the novel),[3] is evidence, I think, that *Regeneration* is doing contemporary witnessing work—necessary but difficult because of the resistance it encounters—in its own right. But I'll concentrate in this chapter on the novel's metawitnessing character as an account of the difficulty of reporting from the front in the England of 1917, and of the new idiom that emerged in war poetry as a way of phrasing, under the conditions of the generic differend, what was asking to be said.

The novel is very largely set in a hospital: Craiglockhart in Scotland, where officers suffering from "shell shock" (in Freudian terms, war neurosis, today known as post-traumatic stress disorder) rested up and were given psychiatric treatment. A few episodes are set in other military hospitals as well. Hospitals, which were once places where the indigent went to die, have become crucial gatekeeping institutions in modern society, places where death is kept at bay, both in the medical sense that individual lives are prolonged there (sometimes by heroic means), and in the cultural sense that the existence of hospitals enables people to go about their ordinary lives without encountering (as was once the case) frequent reminders of mortality. Accordingly, they are a recurring topos in the various forms of witnessing writing I take account of in this study. In AIDS writing such as Eric Michaels's (chapter 2), the hospital is a figure for a whole society; alternatively it may be treated as a liminal site, as for example in Amy Hoffman's *Hospital Time* (chapter 6), where it figures the marginalized community of those touched by AIDS (the dead, the ill and dying, those who care for them). Hervé Guibert's memorable summary judgment, in *Cytomégalovirus,* "L'hôpital, c'est l'enfer" [Hospital is hell], captures both the marginalizing and the universalizing conception of the institution. As for the literature of the camps, it similarly treats hospital (the *Rewier,* the *Krankenbau*) as both liminal—the last station before either selection or death, and in either case what camp slang called exit via the chimney—and broadly representative of the "univers concentrationnaire" (Rousset) as a whole, that is, its epitome: if a few days' respite can sometimes be obtained there from unremitting labor, it is also, in its own right, a place of severe deprivation, and haunted by the likelihood of arbitrary death that every inmate lived with. Finally, in the writing of the 1914–18 war, in which the place of encounter with death is of course primarily the front, hospitals (and hospital trains) are more often places where an incongruous side-by-sideness occurs as returnees from carnage and death, still haunted by that experience, find themselves dealing, almost without transition, with the imperturbably civilized life of those behind the lines. Men traumatized physically and mentally from their experience of war are suddenly in the position of awkwardly conforming, or attempting to conform, to conventions of decorum that make them feel dislocated. They are in a state of double disconnection: the front is distant, home is unreal. (For more on the hospital as between-site and its relevance to the reading of testimonial writing itself, see chapter 8.)

So the "survivors" are described in Sassoon's 1917 poem of that title, itself written at Craiglockhart:

> No doubt they'll soon get well: the shock and strain
>   Have caused their stammering, disconnected talk.
> Of course, they're "longing to go out again,"—
>   These boys with old, scared faces, learning to walk.

But what is notable about this poem about men shattered by "shock and strain" learning to "walk" again in the world of normalcy is that its own speaking subject seems no less disconnected than the stammering talk it attributes to the survivors. The poem's diction varies between free indirect discourse ("No doubt they'll soon get well"; and later "they'll soon forget their haunted nights"), ironic quotation ("longing to go out again"), and, in the last line ("Children, with eyes that hate you"), strategic employment of an ambiguous "you" that could refer either to the poem's "I" or to its addressee, or to both. The effect is to present the poem's speaker as dissociated from the very language in which the poem is couched, and thus from the addressee, "you," who is associated with this language through the ironic quotation and, more subtly, the free indirect discourse. But the speaker is detached as well from the "survivors" themselves, who are described in a somewhat distanced perspective and in the third person as "boys with old, scared faces" and, later in the poem, as "haunted" in their "cowed / Subjection to the ghosts of friends who died." This somewhat clinical language contrasts, by implication, with their "stammering, disconnected talk," with the result that the speaker is associated, through an imposed and alien but nevertheless common language, with those from whom he rhetorically dissociates himself, while he is dissociated, also by that language, from those—the "survivors"—with whom the poem is nevertheless in sympathy. (I quote this poem in full at the end of section 2 of this chapter, where I will return to it to show that it also incorporates a stammer of its own. It is thus itself self-identified as a survivor poem, not just a poem "about" survivors but an aftermath text in which voices of denial vie with something—the stammer—that opposes denial.)

Craiglockhart during the period of Sassoon's residence there—the period of his meeting with Wilfred Owen, of the two men's friendship and of their joint elaboration of a poetry of war witnessing exemplified by Owen's "Anthem for Doomed Youth"—is the locus, then, of *Regeneration.* But Barker makes the hospital both a liminal place, as it is in Sassoon's poem (a place of dislocation), and a figure for British society as it was in 1917, a pathologically split society both haunted by the war and intent on *not knowing,* a society under the spell of genres like those Sassoon parodies that excluded recognition of the war's reality. In the novel's topography, the geographical separation of Great Britain from France by the English Channel figures this ideological insularity of British society with respect to the reality of trench warfare, its determination not to know what it is doing to a generation of "boys with old, scared faces." At the same time, the narrowness of the Channel and the relative ease of communication between Britain and France suggests the actual proximity of what the society held at arm's length (letters, newspapers, and packages reached the front within twenty-four hours; officers could dine in Mayfair or attend Covent Garden and be back in a dugout a day or so later). A particular sign of that proximity and a phenomenon often mentioned in memoirs of the period was the audibility of the cannon from the shores of England, which stands in the novel for the haunting of this placid society, deeply attached to the mental and material comforts of middle-class well-being, by the unthinkable extremity of events and experiences occurring within its earshot but, as it were, ignored and unheard. And the cannon also suggest the possibility of there being nevertheless a report from the front—understand "report" as both the sound of an explosion and a mediated but reliable account—that might achieve audibility and an audience, and thus actualize the hauntedness to which British society, oblivious under the spell of its genres, was subject.

Craiglockhart, then, is England: a place physically distant from the front but in moral, mental, and psychic contact with the war it bends its efforts to "forgetting," and consequently a haunted space, appropriate for the emergence of a "new idiom" capable of phrasing what is actively asking—despite its exclusion, despite the spell cast on all—to be said. The men's neurotic symptoms, "caused," as Sassoon's free indirect discourse states, "by the shock and strain"—not only the stammering and stuttering, but also the amnesia, the hallucinations and flashbacks, the nightmares, everything the hospital seeks to cure—of course call out for treatment. But they are also, perhaps, as the poem further suggests by its speaker's own alienation and discomfort in language, signs that something is asking to be phrased that cannot be said, the means of saying it being unavailable. The symptoms of neurosis are also indications that something is seriously wrong socially.

To those under the spell of warfare's restriction to heroic and patriotic genres, the symptoms of shell shock—say, stammering, disconnected talk—can only be understood as a sign of madness. They do not otherwise "make sense," and Craiglockhart is there (at least in the case of officers) to attempt to cure the madness and return the patients to the front. As a social institution, its task is thus to protect English society from a certain threat: the evidence such symptoms present that something is asking to be phrased that would, if it could be heard, dispel the general state of seduction, break the spell under the effects of which the society lives. For in France, as the characters are aware, shell shock is a natural, that is, healthy response to extreme and traumatic circumstances, a sign of good sense. Only in England does it become an illness to be cured, and by the same token, the sign that something in the society itself is awry, the evidence that a nation capable of sacrificing its own young to the interests of its peace of mind—an untroubled conscience, the maintenance of mental, physical, and moral comfort—is a pathologically and perhaps criminally self-complacent society, one that is unaware of the extent to which it is itself both murderous and mad.

Taken, then, not as a liminal place where victims of shock and strain are cured so that they can return to the shock and strain, but as a microcosm of England itself, as an unhealthy and dangerous (i.e., haunted) social formation, the hospital, as Barker's novel presents it, asks questions concerning the status of the symptom. What *is* a symptom? Of *what* is it symptomatic? Can the attribution of symptom-status itself call, on occasion, for a symptomatological interpretation? In this light, the false diagnosis of war neurosis that lands Sassoon in Craiglockhart—Sassoon who is a healthy man even by the criteria of his physician—for having attempted to protest the conduct of the war becomes an indictment: it is the symptom of a society so seduced by its own genres that it will savagely repress any manifestation of what those genres exclude. And the question then becomes how to save such a society from itself, how to make such a symptomatological reading available to a society that is actively engaged, through its hospitals, in repressing the significance of the signs of trauma that it so industriously, and caringly, seeks to heal but entirely fails to read. How to activate, how to *presence,* the haunt.

These questions about the status of the symptom govern two of the main narrative strains of the novel. Sassoon's physician, Dr. W. H. R. Rivers (an eminent neurologist and ethnographer drafted as a psychiatrist) will evolve, in the course of his relation with his pseudopatient, from taking a therapeutic perspective on symptoms (as demanding treatment and if possible cure), to a symptomatological understanding of the hospital's purposes as themselves signs of social pathology. "A society that devours its young deserves no automatic or unquestioning allegiance" (249). Meanwhile Sassoon and his new friend Wilfred Owen will develop a form of writing that has the characteristics of the symptom—poetry like "Survivors" that is made, rhetorically, to stutter and stammer—but which, by virtue of its status as writing, can function symptomatologically, rendering a diagnosis of what ails a society by making readable to that society that which, in the symptoms of trauma, is asking to be phrased. By becoming a symptom, not of individual or personal neurosis, but of the chaos and carnage of the trenches—of everything England is otherwise so thoroughly disposed to ignore—it makes readable what cannot be said: not only the pain and trauma of the sufferers but also the tragic error of the society about itself. This is an example of the new idiom that Lyotard sees as the only alternative to situations of generic differend; it contrasts, therefore, with Sassoon's failed "Declaration," which participates *in* the differend. This second narrative, of Sassoon's and Owen's joint coming to witness, and the questions it presupposes concerning the nature and possibility of symptomatic writing, will interest me in what follows.

Instead of inviting cure, and with it the silencing of what the symptom bespeaks, can the symptom become itself, not a way of speaking directly (a possibility the situation of differend excludes), but a way of making readable what is at stake when there is a differend? And if so, how? Can literary discourse (with its ready-made readership), be made to stutter and stammer symptomatologically? Can the stammering, disconnected talk diagnosed in Sassoon's poem as caused by the shock and strain of war (a diagnosis the poem may or may not endorse) become, rather, a device of readability and a rhetorically significant practice of writing, a way of "putting into" sentences, and making present to readers, what cannot otherwise be said to them? In "Survivors," to return now to that poem, we can see something like such a literary form of stammering beginning to emerge. It has to do partly with the disconnection of the speaking subject from the language he produces (since a stammerer stammers because what is required to be said in given generic circumstances does not have the speaker's adherence: stammering is a sign that the spell of genre is inoperative or dysfunctional). But there is a recognizable mimesis of stammer, also, in lines like 7–8, disconnected as they are by enjambment, centered on the word "shatter'd," and splayed by an Owenesque half- (or slant-) rhyme:

> and they'll be proud
> Of glorious war that shatter'd all their pride.

Here there is a disjunction—a minidifferend—between the free indirect discourse of "proud / Of glorious war," which appropriates the idiom of patriotic heroism, and the declarative (realist) statement "war that shatter'd all their pride," a disjunction that is amalgamated into a kind of stammer—technically, a crasis—by means of the word *war* that is common to both segments. Deleuze (1993) would call it a disjunctive synthesis *(synthèse de disjonction).* A similar disconnect (as colloquial American speech calls such an effect) is manifest too in the rhymes *cowed/proud* and *died/pride,* the conjunction of which justifies, and anchors in the poem, the (therefore) "accidental" half-rhyme, a moment of "noise" in its formal structure, of *proud/pride.* At this moment, the speaker's speech—from which his own dissociation is quite elaborately mimed throughout the poem—reproduces, then, the stammering, disconnected talk that is thought to be a symptom of neurosis. But it "turns" that talk in such a way that it now asks to be read according to another set of semiotic understandings, that is, in the way that one reads a poem, whose formal characteristics are understood to signify even when they may mime accident or noise.

The issue, then, with respect to the symptom, is the question the novel puts into the mouth of Prior, under the stress of shock and strain, just before he lapses into the amnesia, his own symptom of trauma, that has brought him under Rivers's care. Prior is a relatively secondary character in *Regeneration* who will become central to the remaining two novels of the trilogy. His question is "recovered," because he has forgotten it, through hypnosis, in the course of which he relives the moment when a shell struck his trench, leaving "not much that was recognizable" of two men. Prior stands with a human eye in his hand. In the crude idiom of the front he asks: "What am I supposed to do with this gob-stopper?" (103). That the gob-stopper is an eye is relevant, particularly, to *The Eye in the Door,* the suggestion being that there is an equivalence between surveillance (a theme of that novel) and discursive stopping of the gob as modes of repression that, in wartime Britain, go hand in hand. But the question about the gob-stopper is crucial, also, to *Regeneration*'s concern with discursive issues: the status of the symptom as that which stops the gob, and the psychiatric practice of treating traumatized "survivors" so that, their symptoms disappearing, their gob is stopped again (even though they may now speak fluently), the significance of the symptoms having been erased along with the cure of the patient. Through Prior's question, the novel asks what we are supposed to do with these two forms of gob-stopping (neurosis and its cure). And it suggests what can be done, instead, with speech that is neither cured, in this sense, nor yet *fully* blocked (as it is in the case of Prior's amnesia), but "recovers" the significance of the blocking from the forgetfulness to which it has been consigned. That is, it asks what can be done through *impeded speech.* Is something lost when such speech becomes fluent again? Can (a literary enactment of) impediment itself be made to function rhetorically, and to bespeak (to make readable) what the cure of impediment hustles—as in Michaels's analysis of the culture of tidiness—out of the range of discursive ken?

This is a question, or a set of questions, to which Gilles Deleuze and Félix Guattari, using a different lexicon (that of the becoming "minor" of dominant languages) have given profound thought in their work, both separately and together. In particular, Deleuze's last book, a collection of essays entitled *Critique et clinique,* invites us to rephrase the question of the symptom as gob-stopper in terms of the relation of the clinical (the domain in which impeded discourse is a symptom) to the critical (the domain in which it functions symptomatologically). But in case anyone should think that either Pat Barker or I, interpreting her novel, is committing a severe anachronism in "projecting" this question, of obviously contemporary urgency, onto the period of 1914–18, it is worth pausing briefly to mention that the critical force of the supposedly clinical was already articulated in the clearest possible way in Rebecca West's first novel, published in 1918: *The Return of the Soldier.*[4] (West, then aged twenty-four, was of exactly the same chronological generation as the young men who were sent to the war.) A soldier suffering (like Prior) from amnesia looks blankly at his superficial, snobby, and supercilious wife Kitty and the fashionably decorated home she has made for him. Instead, he recalls only his love for the socially unsuitable but life-affirming Margaret—this is a very Nietzschean novel—in whose company he is relaxed, happy, and alive. Amnesia, in this case, has restored a broken continuity between his idyllic prewar affair with Margaret and the traumatized present (the war, his marriage) that he does not recognize. Thus, the narrator specifies, he has attained something "saner than sanity," and moreover his symptom makes readable something that he would not otherwise have been able to put into language. "His very loss of memory was a triumph over the limitations of language which prevent the mass of men from making explicit statements about their spiritual relationships" (33). The impediment of amnesia is not *the* impediment; rather the "limitations" of normal language (and the habits of conventional culture) are.

Of course, Chris has to be cured; he must be returned to his legal relationship with his wife and the class duties it entails. It is this cure that, remarkably, West's novel equates metaphorically with returning to the trenches. The cure that, at Craiglockhart, would have returned him to the front, returns him, instead, to ordinary upper-class domesticity, the nature of which, however, is described by the carnage in the trenches (so that it is not a hospital that functions here as the defining metaphor of modern society but the front itself). "When we had lifted the yoke of our embraces [those of Kitty and the narrator greeting the now cured Chris] from his shoulders, he would go back to that flooded trench in Flanders under that sky more full of flying death than clouds, to that No Man's Land where bullets fall like rain on the rotting faces of the dead" (187). These are virtually the last words of the narrative. It is hard to imagine a harsher indictment of social ill health than this, and it is certainly significant that it is the judgment of a twenty-something author, put into the mouth of an also young, female narrator.

The judgment is matched, though, for bitterness, by the revulsion of Rivers, a man in his sixties and deathly tired, at the end of *Regeneration.* Rivers too indicts a society that constricts its members and concomitantly "devours its own young":

> He remembered telling Head how he had tried to change his life when he came back from Melanesia for the second time and how that attempt had failed. He'd gone on being reticent, introverted, reclusive. . . . Now, in middle age, the sheer extent of the *mess* seemed to be forcing him into conflict with the authorities. . . . A society that devours its own young deserves no automatic or unquestioning allegiance. Perhaps the rebellion of the old might count for rather more than the rebellion of the young. (249)

In making this weary judgment about the relative merits of the rebellion of the old and the rebellion of the young, however, Rivers is discounting the form of rebellion that Sassoon and Owen, two young men, have been concocting together, as it were under Rivers's very nose, at Craiglockhart. Rivers had earlier noticed that Sassoon had cured himself of a "terrible period of nightmares and hallucinations" through writing war poetry: in other words, the "determination to remember" and the "will to convince civilians that the war was mad" (26) that such writing betokens (writing that includes but is not restricted to the "Declaration"), offers a form of therapy superior to Rivers's own methods. Quite unjustly, then, Rivers is now restricting Sassoon's rebellion to the failed Declaration. (Owen, even younger than Sassoon and the stammerer of the two, is not Rivers's patient, so it is more understandable that Rivers should be unaware of his writing.) It is not the rebellion of the old, however—a rebellion only projected by Rivers—but the rebellion of the young, as inventors of a new idiom of impediment that is an early historical manifestation of the modern phenomenon of witnessing writing, that Barker's novel describes. And Barker describes it, *not* as a form of successful personal therapy, but as the turning of a clinical phenomenon to a critical function, the invention of a literary symptomatology that addresses a society so under the restrictive seduction of its genres that, without knowing it, it is devouring its young. Far from committing a historical anachronism, then, she is identifying, through Rivers's only partial insight into what is at stake, a historical moment and a generation responsible, in view of the trauma it underwent, for the emergence of issues in culture, and corresponding cultural practices, that have proven crucial throughout the twentieth century.

Very early in the novel, Rivers tells Sassoon that, in his opinion, the young man is suffering, not from war neurosis but from "a very powerful *anti*-war neurosis" (15). Rivers's crucial error lies in the paradox that he "cures" Sassoon's antiwar neurosis, leading Sassoon eventually to return to the front. Rivers thus demonstrates complicity with a society that devours its young. But in a way that Rivers does not grasp, Sassoon and Owen, meanwhile, are doing something quite different with the gob-stopper of their antiwar neurosis. They are channeling it into the invention of a new idiom that is symptomatic in the manner of shell shock itself, of shell shock as an antiwar neurosis, and instituting a literary symptomatology that is a paradigmatic form of modern witnessing.

Stuttering and Stammering

There is an ideal of effortless, unimpeded speech, in which everything works smoothly. Sentences develop coherently, word by word, phrase by phrase. They hang together effortlessly, one with another, whether it is I who am linking them or an interlocutor who is responding with other sentences to "mine" (the sentences, that is, that present "me"). The phrase universe—I as addresser, the addressee, the referent—adheres seamlessly to the sentences, and they to it. It's not just that they say what I intend and what the addressee expects to hear; what they say is what wants to be phrased. This ideal of perfect fluency (rarely if ever achieved) describes the state of seduction that arises under a perfectly functioning genre regime: language itself is seduced into a seamless efficiency. Military discipline, insofar as it is discursively realized, is the best example I can think of of such a state of achieved seduction. Subalterns know exactly what to say and how to say it ("Yes, sir!") in the presence of superiors; no one says anything unexpected or departs from the prescribed manner; everyone is so thoroughly rehearsed that they adhere to the situation of discipline as if it were entirely natural, although as the product of intense "training" it is obviously the contrary of natural. Through discipline hierarchy is enforced in discourse and in turn enforces the discourse. There is no disjunction; no one feels the need of another genre; nothing asks to be phrased that isn't phrasable.

On the other hand, a stammerer is a speaker who is *not* seduced by what a given genre may require (provide) in the way of phrasing. I may be ashamed of, or guilty about, what I am saying or the fact of saying it; I may disbelieve what I am trying to mouth; I may be speaking without authorization in the presence of superiors. My dissociation from the generic situation produces a halting, impeded delivery; the sentence proceeds by fits and starts; by the same token, my addressee's uptake is less than assured in proportion as my take is unclear; reference itself becomes dubious. The disjointedness of the sentences coincides with a sense on my part of dissociation and on my interlocutor's part of unease, while the unproblematic attribution of "reality" to a generic world crumbles. Another set of generic understandings and arrangements would be required—but that other genre is not available, either because it does not exist, or because I am ignorant of it, or because the hierarchical circumstances forbid my having recourse to it. Stammering is thus closely related to the differend as a sign of *another message* asking to be put into sentences, but unable to be realized phrastically, because of generic insufficiency, deficiency, or unavailability, *except* (but it is a crucial exception) in the form of a disturbance in the sentences that *are* produced, of "noise" in the discursive apparatus that "normally" runs so smoothly.

I've been using the word *stammering* (as most of the theoretical literature appears to do) as a catchall (or "generic") term; but it is worth distinguishing now between the two versions of stopped gob, or forms of discursive noise, that are stammering and stuttering. *Stuttering* emphasizes noise in its literal sense: the term refers primarily to the explosive force of an iterative articulation in which a word or phrase has to be "forced out." Stammering, on the other hand, emphasizes noise in the informational sense: it refers to the disconnectedness (Sassoon's word), the disjointedness, or (Deleuze's term) the disjunctive synthesis that arises from the impeded production of a (therefore) ill-formed sentence. Stammering disrupts the fluency and smoothness that are the effects of generic seduction. The common collocation of "stuttering and stammering" (cf. German *stottern und stammeln*) is itself, by these definitions, more a kind of stammer (a disjunctive synthesis) than a kind of stutter. But that is because it proposes the equivalence of the terms that it disjoins. For both forms of noise, the explosiveness of stuttering and the disjointedness of stammering, betray a certain discomfort, on the speaker's part, with respect to genre—a failure of the spell that produces fluency and, with it, comfort—and both transmit that discomfort to an audience that feels betrayed in its expectation of easy coherence and smoothness, the effects of seduction. There is always, in the case of stammering and stuttering, some sort of misfit, incongruity, or lack that dispels the easy conjunctions (of language segments themselves; of language and speakers of language; of language, speakers, and universe), the sense of natural fit that is characteristic of generic ease. Something "else" is asking to be phrased, which the genre(s) can't accommodate. A crasis (mixture, amalgam) is jamming together, uncomfortably, as in a portmanteau word (beloved of Lewis Carroll, that arch-stammerer), things that don't "go" together, that don't "fit": different messages, a message and a genre that is "wrong," different genres (neither of which is the "right" one), the requirements of the genre apparatus and a speaker's knowledge of something surplus to that apparatus. If syllepsis (see chapter 2) describes a *smooth* operation of "taking together," as in a stylish pun, stammering and stuttering make "impossible" puns—they are the signs of the disruption of fluency that results from an enforced collocation of incongruities, or indeed incompatibles. So I'll continue to use *stammer* as the general term, reserving *stutter* for texts that are literally noisy (e.g., by onomatopoeia) as well as informationally so.

But Pte Callan, in *Regeneration,* doesn't even stutter or stammer. He suffers from mutism (something Rivers muses, that is characteristic of "other ranks"; it is the officer class that stammers). For Callan, the disjunction between the sayable and his experience is complete; there is no question of "something 'asking' to be phrased," as Lyotard puts it, because he is literally speechless. Dr. Yealland treats this speechlessness, then, as if it were a case of "dumb insolence." He cures Callan of his "shell shock" by attaching electrodes to his vocal organs and administering electric shocks—an exact, "civilized" equivalent of the trauma that has silenced him—for as long as it takes for Callan, first, to stammer out painfully, and then to articulate clearly and fluently, what it is that Yealland wishes to hear him say. That is, a genre is imposed—the genre defined by what Yealland is willing to hear—and it is imposed by disciplinary techniques that amount to a form of torture, so that we see here, in this "extreme" case, the equivalence that Barker's novel is proposing, only slightly less explicitly than Rebecca West's, between English society in its state of gob-stopping seduction and the world of the front, each of them traumatic in its way. All alternatives to Yealland's requirements are relentlessly excluded, until they become unimaginable (that is, they are repressed, consigned to oblivion, they can no longer "interfere"). "You must speak," Yealland explains at the outset, "but I shall not listen to anything you say" (231), which means: I shall hear only what is said in the genre I wish to enforce. At the end, when Callan can indeed speak, the following exchange exemplifies the success of the method:

> "Are you not pleased to be cured," Yealland asked.
>
> Callan smiled.
>
> "I do not like your smile," Yealland said. "I find it most objectionable. Sit down."
>
> Callan smiled and the key electrode was applied to the side of his mouth. When he was finally permitted to stand up again, he no longer smiled.
>
> "Are you not pleased to be cured?" Yealland repeated.
>
> "Yes, sir."
>
> "Nothing else?"
>
> A fractional hesitation. Then Callan realized what was required and came smartly to the salute. "Thank you, sir." (233)

What is instructive, here, from the point of view of testimonial writing, is that, between the two extremes of mutism on the one hand and generically enforced fluency on the other, stammering (more specifically in this case stuttering) is presented as intermediary. It is a form of (impeded) speech, but/so not of a kind to satisfy the requirements of Dr. Yealland, who wants fluency.

> "Go on repeating the days," Yealland said.
>
> "S-s-s-sunday. M-m-m-m-m-monday. T-t-t-t-tuesday . . ."
>
> Saturday came at last.
>
> Yealland said, "Remember there is no way out, except by the return of your proper voice and by that door. I have one key, you have the other. When you can talk properly, I shall open the door and you can go back to the ward." (233)

Callan is declared cured, then, only when *all* the signs (first his stutter, then his smile) of his discomfort in the genre whose enforced "seduction" Yealland is bringing about have been made to disappear and he speaks "properly." Fluency and ease in speaking are thus described by Barker as products of constraint and discipline—not the natural and healthy phenomena one might like to think but forms of violence that repeat the violence of the war itself. And witnessing's alliance with impeded speech is thus demonstrated to be the only mode available—along with the "smile" of irony, perceptible everywhere for instance in Sassoon's "Survivors"—that is not either silence or collusion with the imposed genre spell—the "proper" voice, the "proper" speech—that, precisely, witnessing writing seeks to break by the improprieties it commits.

Dr. Yealland is not a fictional invention of Barker's. His methods, as her "Author's Note" specifies, are described in his 1918 book, published by the respectable house of Macmillan, *Hysterical Disorders of Warfare.* She wants us to know that she is not making anything up. At the same time, the allegorical intent of this episode (her own witnessing mode) is patent here. The situation of discursive control that prevails in England and excludes all improper messages pertaining to the reality of France, give or take some stammering officers convalescing in more benign circumstances than those allowed Callan, is not essentially different—the form of silencing that Sassoon's "Declaration" undergoes being a case in point—from the one that Yealland enforces in the "electric room." It is significant, therefore, that Rivers—an embarrassed and dissociated witness to Callan's cure (by this time, late in the novel, he has long developed a stammer of his own)—recognizes his own therapeutic methods, and those of his Craiglockhart colleagues, in Yealland's brutal treatment. Apparently more benign and kindly, they do not differ in their ultimate effect; and Craiglockhart is thus no less allegorical of England than is Yealland's appropriately named National Hospital in London:

> Just as Yealland silenced the unconscious protest of *his* patients by removing the paralysis, the deafness, the blindness, the muteness that stood between them and the war, so, in an infinitely more gentle way, *he* [Rivers] silenced *his* patients; for the stammerings, the nightmares, the tremors, the memory lapses, of officers were just as much unwitting protest as the grosser maladies of the men. (238)

The "cure" of Sassoon's antiwar neurosis—the very sign that he is not ill—is, again, the exemplification of this perception.

But the class differences of which Rivers is so conscious—as conscious, here, as he is coming to be of the discursive control exercised by English society at large and in little by Craiglockhart—are also significant from the point of view of the possibility of a witnessing literature that would be a writing of stammer. For while class difference participates centrally, as Rivers understands, in the general system of control (it is something like the social equivalent of the hierarchy enforced by military discipline), it also offers, in a way that Rivers seems unaware of, a breach in that system of control, through which the discourse of impediment that is witnessing writing might penetrate and break the spell, or at least disrupt some of the comfort the spell engenders. For stammering is a "symptom" of English middle-classness, particularly among men (that is, it is also a gendered symptom, and a symptom therefore of discomfort in the apparatus of gender). This class phenomenon is independent, at least superficially, of stammering's position as part of the symptomatology of shell shock: it existed before the war and it exists in people (e.g., Rivers) not directly exposed to trauma at the front. It follows that if witnessing writing is to symptomatize the reality of the trenches by miming the "stammering, disconnected talk" of the "survivors" of war, such speech is already, as it happens, *naturalized* in the English middle (and upper) classes, where it has the status of a by no means unfamiliar abnormality or breach of the fluency ideal. It is a symptom, there, of discomfort in the class (and gender) system: a system of social "kinds" that is, arguably, homologous, therefore, with the more specifically discursive set of genres that warfare disrupts.[5] The implication is that, for the middle and upper classes, there is a daily, home-based trauma of genre (including but presumably not restricted to gender and class—one thinks also of the repression of homosexuality) that is an entailment of genre's seductiveness, a trauma whose nature is revealed by the trauma of war, which produces similar symptoms. Yealland's method of treating those symptoms is simply an exemplification of the daily trauma at home; and war poetry that stammers will have an uncanny familiarity, therefore, when it is read on what is aptly called the "home front." Domestic foreknowledge of stammering and what it signifies becomes the Trojan horse through which witnessing writing can infiltrate culture, and haunt it.

But the class character of stammering also offers insight into another question that is inevitably raised by the writing of Sassoon and Owen. Why poetry? Why (in addition to the fact that the two are poets by vocation) is poetry—and in the case of Owen's "Anthem," the poetic elegy, the defining genre of English Romanticism—the genre that is first turned to the purposes of witnessing, in the historical context of the war, by being made to stammer? The prose memoirs of Sassoon, Blunden, and Graves, like the writing of Jünger and Remarque in Germany, did not appear until well into the 1920s; only in France is the pattern broken by the publication (and to be fair, the rapid translation into English) of Henri Barbusse's remarkable reportage, *Le Feu* (Under fire) as early as 1916. (Apollinaire's celebratory war poetry—an episode in the long story of the fascination exerted in France by the dark sublime—is another instance of French particularity in this respect.) Barker's novel offers no explicit commentary on this question, but it isn't difficult to supply some of the missing context. There was a much larger readership for poetry in 1917 than is the case now. At the same time, since poetry assumes forms of literacy that are normally acquired only through education, that readership was mainly middle class. And the reading relation, in the case of poetry, was understood, as it had been throughout the nineteenth century, to be a "private" one, involving a certain intimacy of reader and text—and unrelated, therefore, to public sphere discourse (publishing a "Declaration," having questions asked in Parliament, and the like).

Part of the class system as it flourished in this era had to do also with respect for the privacy of middle-class people, combined with a deep mistrust of the loyalty of the working class, understood to be prone—as of course the Russian Revolution of 1917 "proved"—to the virus of socialism (and hence internationalism and pacifism), and so kept very much under surveillance. The correspondence of "other ranks" at the front was subject, for example, to careful censorship (performed by their officers), the only alternative being the infamous Field Service Post Card, which censored the other way, by imposing certain phrases and excluding others (a card that was much parodied, therefore, by young officers like Sassoon and his friends). By contrast, officers' correspondence was on the "honor system," and Owen, for example, wrote to his mother, frankly and graphically, about conditions at the front throughout the war. Although it was published, readily purchasable at bookstores and widely read, poetry must have been classified generically, then, as more like the private affairs of trustworthy middle-class people as discussed in letters and conversation, than the kind of thing that would stir up trouble among workers and other ranks. It thus had a potential for cultural infiltration that letters themselves, as a genuinely private genre, could not match. Owen himself articulates something of the belief that poetry, as a lyric genre, is private when, in his first conversation with Sassoon in Barker's novel, she has him declare it to be "the opposite" of war. "S-something to t-take refuge in" (84). He is thinking of his beloved Keats and Shelley. But to the extent that the only existing models for war poetry, apart from Sassoon's earlier efforts, were Tennysonian or, at best, Kiplingesque, he is not far from truth in respect of war poetry as well.

The question "Why poetry?" raises a second set of considerations, however. Are there reasons why poetry, as a linguistic mode, might be particularly suited to being made to stutter and stammer? This question makes it necessary for me to open a longish theoretical parenthesis, following the foregoing historical excursus, before returning to the novel. I'll begin by recalling Roman Jakobson's description of the "poetic function" of language and will take on board also the sense of the word stammering *(bégaiement)* as it is employed by Deleuze and Guattari, notably in Deleuze's (1993) essay "Bégaya-t-il" (He stammered), as that sense is amplified by Lecercle. Jakobson draws attention to the significance of the fact that language works simultaneously on two "axes": an axis of combination, actualized in the speech chain (or syntagm) and governed therefore by conventions of syntax, and an axis of selection, through which particular words are chosen from an available paradigm to fill specific syntagmatic slots. Only one member of a given paradigm can be selected for a given slot, a constraint that—interestingly, in the present context—the fashion for deploying slashes and parenthesized alternative morphemes in much contemporary critical writing is attempting to loosen (it makes the language stammer). As a normative sentence proceeds, however, the range of paradigmatic options, that is, of possible selections, narrows from slot to slot, as in the sentence: "If my mother (not *your brother* or *their neighbor*) could hear you (not *see us* or *understand George*), she (compulsory pronoun selection after "mother") would be turning (not *revolving* or *spinning* or *jumping for joy*) in her . . ." At the end of this sentence, there is really only one word that can be selected for the final slot (although, of course, for bathetic effect I might select *bathtub* rather than *grave*). At this point, the effect is that of Lacan's celebrated upholstery tack *(point de capiton),* retroactively fixing, or pinning down, the whole sentence. Part of this normative system of sentence coherence has to do also with a call-and-response sentence structure ("If my mother . . . , she would . . ."), referred to in rhetoric as theme and rheme, or alternatively protasis (proposition) and apodosis (restitution, giving back). Finally, it needs to be added—something that standard accounts often omit—that such internal sentence coherence is ultimately an effect of genre, exactly like the take/uptake relation between sentences that genre also regulates (see Lyotard; Freadman 1988, 1990). A sentence that is appropriately put together for genre A may not "make sense" in genre B, a different "phrase universe."

According to Jakobson, the poetic function of language arises when the paradigmatic selections made at different slots along the axis of combination are *themselves* members of a paradigm, so that a principle of similarity (Jakobson says "equivalence"; one might also say substitutability) is "projected" onto the syntagmatic chain. His most striking and memorable example is the political slogan "I like Ike" (note that the poetic function is exemplified by poetry but not restricted to genres conventionally understood to be poetic). It is this projection of similarity onto the syntagmatic axis that contains the potential for making language stammer, for similarity (understood as a paradigmatic "belongingness" of one word or group of words with another) is a function, among other things, and as has already been noted, of genre. Stammering arises, however, when there is a linguistically manifested differend between different segments of a syntagm, say the protasis and apodosis of the "same" sentence. That is, groups of words that do not "go together" generically are treated as being paradigmatically related for the purpose of constructing a sentence. Take *life* and *death.* Are they members of a paradigm? Certainly. Can they be combined or mixed (conjoined by crasis) in the same genre? Not necessarily. In a ghost story, yes (the ghost is a walking crasis of life and death). In the phrase universes of realism, though, life and death can't be amalgamated because they are regarded as incompatible opposites. So a sentence like "If my mother were alive, she'd be spinning in her grave" (which I adapt from one of Lecercle's examples) is an incongruous, that is, stammering, sentence because, by a perversion (turning) of the poetic function, sentence segments that imply the relevance of two different genres are combined, paradigmatically, as the call and response of a single sentence. "If my mother were alive, . . . she'd be thoroughly disgusted" is a thoroughly realist sentence: it presupposes the incompatibility of being alive and being dead. "If my mother knew what you are doing . . . , she would turn in her grave" is a thoroughly fantastic, ghost story sentence: it considers being in the grave and knowing what someone is doing to be compatible. Combine the generic premises of realism and the fantastic, as phrase universes, and the sentence stammers. The effect is one of genre syllepsis, equivalent to selecting two different paradigm-members for the same slot in a sentence.

Notice that, because the sentence segments are paradigmatically related but generically incompatible—they refer to different phrase universes—neither genre actually prevails: there is mutual interference between, in this case, the realist and the fantastic genres that are indexed by the two segments of the sentence, and there is no other genre in which the incongruity might be resolved. So the sentence lacks an upholstery tack. This is the sense in which a sentence stammer is a minidifferend, and its effect, of course, is to invite reading. Its (in)coherence suggests that something—some kind of *Ahnung* (cf. chapter 1)—is asking to be phrased to which neither genre is adequate—something that needs, but does not have, a genre of its own and can only be agenced into readability, or presenced, by the device of the stammer. In a poem from *Schneepart,* Celan writes of "die nachzustotternde Welt / bei der ich zu Gast / gewesen sein werde" [the world that can only be stammered over (stuttered over) of which I shall have been a guest]. And in the poem that furnishes one of the epigraphs to this volume he writes of "truth itself" as a distant, muffled rumble ("ein Dröhnen"), "stepping" among humans "mitten ins / Metapherngestöber," amid the flurrying metaphors. This "world," this "truth," is what the flurry of a stammering sentence—a miniature snowstorm or *Schneegestöber* of discourse—seeks to presence, like the distant rumble of cannon from France, heard on an English coast.[6]

Reintroducing now the distinction between stammering and stuttering, we might say, then, that where a "stammering" sentence is the result of an *extension* of the poetic function, by a kind of syllepsis, to generically different paradigms in such a way as to produce informational noise, literary "stuttering" is a *concentration* or an *intensification*—a jamming together—of the poetic function that produces literal noise. "I like Ike," Jakobson's condensed example of the poetic function, is already a stutter, in this sense, although I wouldn't call it a stammer. Let me illustrate stuttering further. It happens, to take a tendentious example, that English is a language rich in stutterlike words (which form a paradigm, therefore), words that resemble "stutter" in their phonetic conformation. *Stammer* itself is one such stutterlike word (so, contrary to my earlier remark, "stuttering and stammering" *might* be better described as a stutter than as a stammer?). Others include *stopper* (as in gob-stopper), *spatter* (as of blood), *patter, shatter, titter, twitter, tittle, tattle, rattle* (all words that have "iterativity" as a seme—but if I continue I'll reach *kettle* and *settle, cattle* and *battle,* which don't). Stammerlike words, oddly, are rarer, but they include *glimmer* (and *glamour*). A poem that contains a high concentration of stutterlike words and stammerlike words (Owen's "Anthem" is such a poem) will be a stuttering poem, as will any poem that overdoes the poetic function. "Anthem" stutters in this way, overdoes the poetic function, because it produces noise onomatopoeically, as a "report" of the "rifles' rapid stutter" at the front, an iteration of their explosiveness in speech. And if the poem is simultaneously the site of a generic differend, combining—say—elegiac sentence-segments and segments that are incompatible with elegy (because they imply the impossibility or incongruence of the idea of mourning), it will be, also, a stammering poem; "Anthem," as we'll see at some length, is also such a poem. It both stammers and stutters.

Sassoon's lines from "Survivors"—let me quote them again:

> (. . .) and they'll be proud
> Of glorious war that shatter'd all their pride.

—incorporate a stutter-like word in "shatter" and stutter also on proud and pride (cf. elsewhere "dreams that drip," "grim and glad"). But they stammer in that the segments "proud / Of glorious war" and "that shatter'd all their pride" seem to hail from two different and incompatible phrase universes of war writing; on the one hand the conventionally poetic, together with the genres of patriotic public rhetoric, and on the other private genres like conversations among soldiers, or in some cases letters home (Owen's to his mother, for example), or letters among friends (like those of Sassoon and his group), in which declarative realism is permitted. Notice in particular how the word *shatter*—at the center of its pentameter, where it almost rhymes with "battle" in the same position in the following line while recalling "stammering" from line 2—encapsulates the poem's generic stammer: its spelling ("shatter'd") refers to conventional poetic diction, but it is a stutterlike word that signifies violent disjunction. As such, it is the poem's affective and rhetorical kernel. It has the status of the poem's "symptom." But what it symptomatizes in the poem requires us to read *it*—the poem—not so much as a clinical symptom of war's shock and strain, but as socially symptomatic: a sign that something is being phrased, through literary invention, that on their own, neither clinically shattered speech nor the conventionally elevated language of literary heroism can say. Something that becomes readable only in a new idiom that arises, critically, as simultaneously a poeticization of shattered speech and a shattering of the language of heroism.

Survivors

No doubt they'll soon get well; the shock and strain
    Have caused their stammering, disconnected talk.
Of course they're "longing to go out again,"—
    These boys with old, scared faces, learning to walk.
They'll soon forget their haunted nights; their cowed
    Subjection to the hosts of friends who died,—
Their dreams that drip with murder; and they'll be proud
    Of glorious war that shatter'd all their pride . . .
Men who went to battle, grim and glad;
    Children, with eyes that hate you, broken and mad.

Craiglockhart, October 1917

Reporting

Completed in September 1917, shortly before Sassoon dated "Survivors" from Craiglockhart in October, Wilfred Owen's "Anthem for Doomed Youth" had gone through a number of drafts, which attest to the struggle Owen had in inventing a new idiom. Two of these drafts, the first and the last, carry penciled emendations in Sassoon's hand, a fact acknowledged by Owen as if to authenticate the evidence of their collaboration. These drafts are the historical point of departure for Barker's fictional account of the two men's work together.[7]

Anthem for Doomed Youth

What passing-bells for these who die as cattle?
    Only the monstrous anger of the guns.
    Only the stuttering rifles' rapid rattle
Can patter out their hasty orisons.
No mockeries now for them; no prayers nor bells,
    Nor any voice of mourning save the choirs,—
The shrill, demented choirs of wailing shells;
And bugles calling for them from sad shires.

What candles may be held to speed them all?
    Not in the hands of boys, but in their eyes
Shall shine the holy glimmer of good-byes.

The pallor of girls' brows shall be their pall;
Their flowers the tenderness of patient minds,
And each slow dusk a drawing-down of blinds.

Barker's account of the genesis of this poem is part of her more general account of various historical repercussions of the distant war in English society: in this respect the poem is like the emancipation of young working women (Sarah, Madge, and Betty), a certain reemergence of homosexuality, or Rivers's rethinking of the nature of his own culture—all topics the *Regeneration* trilogy explores quite carefully. Such repercussions occur, the book suggests, even in a country otherwise subject to a status quo firmly anchored in denial through generic seduction. There is thus a converging "evolution" in each poet's "point of view" (82) about poetry as a result of their experiences of the war; it culminates in "Anthem," in which the conventions of poetry—specifically, of the Romantic elegy—are pointedly *questioned* ("What passing-bells. . . ?" "What candles?") and at the same time *superseded* as the din of "battle" (a rhyme word significantly absent, however, from the text) invades the poem in the literary form of its own onomatopoeic stuttering diction. England does change, then, in response to war's reality. But the modernization that English poetry undergoes through the coming to witness of Sassoon and Owen is particularly significant because, while the poem itself indexes one of the changes, its genesis also offers a key to understanding the *process* of change as a cultural phenomenon. Distant repercussions of the agony in the trenches (I use the word *re-percussion* advisedly) make themselves felt, and re-verberate (beat again) like so many re-ports of explosion: sounds "carried" over a distance—from the front—to explode "again." The poem whose iterative status I am emphasizing is not the war; it signifies as war's cultural effect, a phenomenon of aftermath.

If I speak of reverberation, though, it is because the joint evolution of the two poets itself reverberates. It is parallel but also complementary: in the same movement whereby Owen comes to a poetry of witness, evolving forward, so to speak, Sassoon evolves backward: he responds to that poetry, even as it is in the process of being invented, by a becoming-haunted and a becoming-ghostly of his own that is the turning point of his decision to return to France. Thus a suggestive equivalence is proposed between going back (as Sassoon resolves to do) and, as Owen learns to do, moving forward through a poetry of witness that makes the war hearable in England *per medium* of its stuttering and stammering. The novel can be thought, then, to be proposing an understanding of cultural repercussions as reports, in the curious double sense the word has: etymologically a carrying back, but semantically a carrying across or forward, and so—etymologically again—a second sounding (or reverberation) of what has been experienced in another place. (For the relevance of reporting to the dynamics of apostrophe, see chapter 4.)

Notice that Sassoon's decision to return to the trenches does not mean that he is abandoning the duty of witness, but only that he has abandoned the supposedly direct method of the "Declaration" in favor of something more indirect or (as one could say in French) *reporté,* deferred. He is submissive to the discipline imposed on him, and at the same time planning to continue the work of witness; rather than expressing his views through rebellion, however, he will haunt England from France, in the way that, in his Craiglockhart poem "Sick Leave," the "nameless dead" are described as haunting *him.* They come in his sleep, they "whisper in my heart; their thoughts are mine." In "Sick Leave," it is those haunting figures that the haunted "I" of the poem enjoins himself to rejoin:

> I think of the Battalion in the mud.
> "When are you going out to them again?
> Are they not still your brothers in our blood?"

Rivers is only slightly off track, then, when he conjectures at the end of the novel that Sassoon "is going back with the intention of being killed" (250). It is rather that he is returning, to die or not, but with the intention of haunting. He wants to be one with the dead, and through that oneness with the dead to haunt the living as they do. The deployment of pronouns in the last line of "Sick Leave" is accordingly even cannier than the ambiguity of the "you" of address in "Survivors," an ambiguity "Sick Leave" repeats ("eyes that hate you" there; "still your brothers" here). For a more complex movement is sketched, *back* referentially to "they" (in France), then *forward* to the "you" of address (in England)—the "you" that is the reader, through the "you" of "I's" self-address. This is the reverberating movement of a report. And the double inclusiveness of the last pronoun in the line, "our"—signifying both "I"-and-"them" and "I"-and-"you"—drives home the implications of this shuttling, back-and-forth movement. The blood that *I* share with them is also the blood that *you* share with them (as you do with me, and as I do).

A report, then, reverberates because it is a sound—specifically the sound of an explosion—that *carries* (back and forth) over a considerable distance; mediation is of the essence in any reporting. Similarly, the French verb *reporter,* which means to carry forward (as in a ledger) or to postpone or defer (to carry something forward to another date) is an etymological doublet of *rapporter,* to make a report of or give an account of something. To the extent that reporting or reportage continues to imply, in both languages, this etymological sense of portability—carrying back, carrying across, over, or forward—these words can serve to define witnessing as, in effect, the product of a double shuffle (or reverberation), between reporting as a mode of referentiality (referring back to France) and reporting as a mode of address (carrying the reference forward). The carrying back shuffles because it implies a movement forward, and carrying forward, enacted in poems like "Survivors" and "Sick Leave" as a double take on "you," shuffles because it functions also (from "you" through "I" to "them") as a referring back. Because it is doubly split, then—by the I-them of hauntedness and the I-you of (self-)address—the lyric "I's" subjectivity becomes the haunted/haunting agent of a reporting that itself haunts, while the stutter or stammer in the poem (of which the double take on "you" is thus an exemplum) is the very sign, therefore, of the poem's reporting status. Through the explosiveness of its stuttering diction, the text is a report of the war (its stuttering carries back to the din of battle through the figure of onomatopoeia), while the iterativity of its stammer is the sign of the double portability, of reference and address, of which the poem is an operator. And it is in this way that the symptom of hauntedness—"their stammering, disconnected talk"—comes to function symptomatologically, as a haunting. It does double duty, as a repercussion of "shock and strain," but one that carries forward, as the report of a distant explosion, to disturb a complacent society. And a hospital like Craiglockhart—intermediary between the war and the society whose complacency it also actively subserves—is the most likely place for such a shift (the shuffle or reverberation between the symptomatic stutter and the symptomatological stammer) to occur.

It is these issues of reporting that are implicitly in play in Barker's fictional tracing of the interpersonal reverberations (poetological but also erotic, although not sexual) through which the friendship of the two young poets leads to the creation of a new poetic idiom, exemplified by Owen's "Anthem." Throughout the trilogy, it is through an exploration of the actual fungibility of the social "kinds" that English society treats as autonomous that Barker demonstrates the repercussions of war on that society—whence the centrality of Prior (who is both bisexual and an officer of working-class origins), and in *Regeneration* of the cross-generational, father-son friendship of Sassoon and Rivers that is at the novel's heart. But it is only in the narrative concerning "Anthem" that she addresses discursive genres as such and their adaptability, in a narrative that tells the story of Owen's coming to witness, Sassoon's decision to return to France, and their collaboration on Owen's poem.

Each episode of this narrative addresses the phenomenon of reporting from a different angle. First is that of the war's repercussion in English poetry, that is, the shift in its character that "Anthem" exemplifies, its abandonment of Romanticism and the modernization of its diction in the form of the new idiom elaborated at Craiglockhart. Then comes reporting in its referential, carrying-back aspect: "Anthem" as a poem in which, through the stutter of its onomatopoeia, the din of war becomes audible. Finally there is the carrying-forward aspect: at the same time as its stutter brings about Sassoon's decision to return to France and to witness from there, the iterativity of the poem's stammer brings "the monstrous anger of the guns" within earshot of English domesticity. Through publication, the repercussion of war in the poem has repercussions of its own. Sassoon's offer to have "Anthem" appear in a paper aptly named *The Nation*—which ends the narrative—is thus crucial, if only because this act countermands, so to speak, the failure of his "Declaration" to *carry,* that is, to find an audience. By contrast, the personal "revelation" (157) Sassoon has experienced—the revelation of what poetry can become; the revelation of which the poem is a vehicle—is here carried forward and extended, by becoming culturally available.

It is by virtue of its publication, for example—but here we leave the narrative proper for the domain of its implication—that the poem's reporting function can be continued, through another link in the reporting chain, by Barker's novel. For in these episodes Barker reveals herself to be an extremely careful and perceptive reader of the poetry of Sassoon and Owen; but because her narrative thus constitutes a reading of their work, it becomes in turn an act of reporting (of referring back and carrying forward)—a witnessing act, then, that repeats and carries forward their own. *Regeneration* thus situates itself as one of the cultural reverberations both of the war itself and of what happened at Craiglockhart in the fall of 1917.[8] And by this I do not mean that it is what Dominick LaCapra (1998) would call an act of "secondary" witness, although it does certainly acknowledge the primacy of Owen's and Sassoon's experience and does not claim primacy for itself, any more than their poetry does. It has the status of a report. As a *historical* novel, it fulfills the historian's supposedly secondary task by performing a kind of "archaeology," going back to the past. But as a historical *novel,* it functions as their writing does, as a report of an event that it carries forward—an event that it doesn't represent, mime, imitate, or reproduce for us, its readers, however, but can only presence more uncannily, as that which haunts its text as a phenomenon of readability, and so haunts us. (Its witnessing of the war in France through a narrative focus on the war's repercussions is, of course, a way of signaling, in this respect, its status as report.) But consequently *my* reading, in turn, of Barker's reading is yet another reverberation, repercussion or report, even though my intent, in the first place, is quite technical and critical. My report will consist of attempting to make explicit what Barker's narrative implies, as a reading of (the genesis of) "Anthem," about the relation between the fungibility of kinds/genres and the emergence of a new, in this case poetic, idiom.

I will be guided in this project by the idea that "Anthem" is a poem that both stutters (onomatopoeically) and stammers (poetically); and that the stammering in the poem converts a minidifferend or generic antinomy (that of elegy and realism) into a catachresis of genre that functions so as to make readable—to carry forward or report to an audience, symptomatologically—that something asking to be phrased, of which, in Lyotard's analysis, the differend is symptomatic. By catachresis, I'll argue, the Romantic elegy becomes "not-elegy" (what Ramazani calls "modern elegy"); and by not-elegy I'll understand a discursive formation that stages its own makeshift character, symptomatologically, as neither an elegy in the conventional sense nor yet not an elegy. It is neither an elegy nor not an elegy because it is a way of mourning (by failing to mourn) those who, on the battlefield, die deprived of mourning "as cattle," *and* those whose survivorhood is defined by their inability appropriately to mourn them. Together it is these two groups that form the category the poem anthems as the "doomed."

In the subheads that follow, the genitive should be taken, then, as respectively subjective and objective. "The writing of a poem" means how the poem came to be written (section 4) and the poem's character as a writing having the character of readability (section 5). Barker's fictional narrative of a genesis (her implied reading of the poem) will suggest a reading of the poem as writing, for which I take the major responsibility.

The Writing of a Poem: Genesis

The first episode in the narrative of the poem's writing (80–85) is that of the meeting of Sassoon and Owen. In May 1917, Sassoon had published *The Old Huntsman,* a collection of verse that contained some of his early war poetry, including a line (about "Bert's" having "gone syphilitic") that had caused a slight scandal. "I had trouble getting them to print that," Sassoon recalls (81). Intimidated and stuttering badly, Owen now brings five copies of this volume to Sassoon, asking that they be signed for his family. Naturally the conversation turns to poetry, its nature and relation to the war; and it becomes clear that each man's position is in the process of changing. Sassoon is tending more and more in the direction of realist frankness about syphilis and the like, while Owen's taste favors the Christian symbolism, and the thematics of sacrifice and redemption, of Sassoon's earlier poems. Slightly irritated and faintly condescending, the older poet explains that his book "isn't putting one point of view, it's charting the—the *evolution* of a point of view" (82). Owen, for his part, surprises Sassoon by the realism with which he writes to his mother, but clings to an idealist view of poetry: it is "the opposite of all that," and "S-something to t-take refuge in" from the war (84). Yet, the text notes, he is already abandoning this position even as he defends it. The suggestion is that "Anthem" will be an outcome of the evolutionary process the war is bringing about in each man's thinking, and something of a combination of Sassoon's preference for realism and Owen's stammer—a stammer of hesitation and embarrassment (with respect to infringements of generic convention), but also an indicator of mutability, complexity, and ambiguity. "I see we got to the slaughterhouse in the end," will be Sassoon's approving comment when finally the first line will have evolved from "What minute-bells for these who die so fast?" to "for these who die as cattle?" (154). And the stammer will be transformed from a personal symptom to a figural assemblage.

Meanwhile, where the poets' affinity is most apparent is in their shared sense that in France one is "too *healthy,*" as Sassoon says, to think about metaphysical themes (like redemption) or the politics of pacifism—the implication being (Nietzsche is in the background) that these understandings are not soldierly responses but are symptomatic of English unhealthiness. They agree too—something that makes the nape of Sassoon's neck crawl—that the trenches are a haunted place; Owen recalls an impression that the skulls visible in the wall of a trench are "men from Marlborough's army" (83), and Sassoon describes a vision in which he found himself projected into the future: "a hundred years from now they'll still be ploughing up skulls. And I seemed to be in that time and to be looking back. I think I saw our ghosts" (84). It is to this eerie place, then, "with the limbers against the skyline, and the flares going up," haunted by the dead of the past but where the living too are future ghosts, that Sassoon will soon opt to return, as if answering an uncanny call (the call, in part of Owen's poem).

For in the second episode (140–45), Sassoon makes a return visit to Owen, "on the run" from his roommate's Theosophy (English unhealthiness) and remembering the realism of "the last poem he had been shown" (141). Owen shows him an early draft of "Anthem," which determines the topic of conversation—via a discussion of line 2—as noise, and specifically the noise of war. A crucial distinction is first worked out, however, between the (poeticizing, patriotic) genre implied by the phrase "the *solemn* anger of *our* guns," which Sassoon dismisses as "War Office propaganda," and the alternative phrasing Owen is considering: "the *monstrous* anger of *the* guns" (emphasis added), which is simultaneously accusatory and generalizing, implying that the war is a humanitarian disaster. This distinction—to make Barker's point explicit—entails a turn from conventional war poetry to witnessing writing; so it is worth adding what is not said by either of the friends, that the word "solemn" also subscribes too much to the atmosphere and lexicon of elegy, which the poem is already invoking ("What passing-bells. . . ?") only to deny, or to question, its relevance. "Solemn" blurs the contrast, on which the poem's witnessing status depends, between the tokens of mourning and the murderous guns. "Monstrous" must therefore win out over "solemn" despite Owen's hesitation—he is again in the process of abandoning the position he defends. It is a corollary to the correction that seems more obvious to both, of "our guns" to "the guns." "If it's 'the,' it's got to be 'monstrous.'—Agreed" (141–42).

Here the character of the poem is established: at this stage, it is a not-elegy for those who, dying "in herds" (the phrase anticipating the slaughterhouse that now replaces "so fast"), do not benefit from any other form of mourning. Attention consequently turns from the guns to the noise of war: that which both denies the possibility of mourning and offers the only form of "passing-bell" granted the dead. Onomatopoeia in something like its etymological sense (word-making) becomes the issue because it is understood, implicitly, that the poem must be the verbal equivalent of the noise that embodies not-elegy; it must be a report from the front. But line 3 of the completed poem ("Only the stuttering rifle's rapid rattle") is not yet in place,[9] and the future poem's "patter"(ning) as poetic stutter is adumbrated, in this first draft, only in the contrast of the passing-bells and the shells at, respectively, the beginning and end of the "stanza" (line 7 in both the draft and the final version, the draft having a seven-plus-seven configuration). So it is to the issue of the kind of noise that shells make that Sassoon and Owen turn. They work for a half-hour or so.

> At one point, Sassoon looked up and said: "What's that noise?"
>
> "The wind." Owen was trying to find the precise word for the noise of the shells, and the wind was a distraction he was trying to ignore.
>
> "No, *that.*"
>
> Owen listened, "I can't hear anything."
>
> "That tapping."
>
> Owen listened again. "No."
>
> "Must be imagining things." Sassoon listened again, then said, "They don't *wail,* they hiss." He looked at Owen. "I hear hissing."
>
> "*You* hear tapping." (142)

Sassoon is established here as the haunted one of the two, and Owen as the maker of the noisy poem—the poem that haunts. The wind is a "distraction" to Owen—"noise" in the sense the word has in information theory—because he is working on making a verbally noisy poem, in the same sense: a text that will be generically noisy as well as a site of noisy onomatopoeia, with a view to gaining a cultural hearing. Meanwhile, it is Sassoon who hears the tapping. But an equivalence is established between the tapping—sign of Sassoon's hauntedness—and the onomatopoeic noise in the poem by the final exchange: "'I hear hissing.'—'*You* hear tapping.'" Sassoon is hearing the noisy report from the front that the poem, in turn, will carry forward, the one haunted the other haunting.[10]

For now, retiring for the night, listening to the storm, thinking of the weather in France, still hearing the tapping, his mind "filled with memories of his last weeks in France" (143), Sassoon is ready for visitation. He wakes "to find Orme standing immediately inside the door. He wasn't surprised, he assumed Orme had come to rouse him for his watch. What did surprise him, a little, was that he seemed to be *in bed.* . . . After a while he remembered that Orme was dead" (143). I've already commented (in the preface) on this moment as a wake-up call, and on its eerie conflation of *here*

(England, the living) and *there* (France, the dead) in a moment of vivid hypotyposis. Its incongruity and untimeliness can now be described, then, as also a Deleuzian disjunctive synthesis, having the structure of a poetic stammer. So it is important that the text distinguishes this particular phenomenon from the hallucinations and nightmares—the symptoms of neurosis—that Sassoon had experienced the previous spring. "His nocturnal visitors [in London] had come trailing gore, pointing to amputations and head-wounds. . . . This had been so restrained. Dignified. And it hadn't followed on from a nightmare either" (144). Not only is the experience of a different quality, then, but its effect is a clarifying one; it has symptomatological implications rather than merely symptomatic significance.

For, rushing the following morning to "report" this visitation to Rivers and finding him already departed (on what is as good as "sick leave"), Sassoon views himself, as he shaves, as a ghost: "He looked at his face in the glass. In the half light, against white tiles, it looked scarcely less ghostly than Orme's" (143). And as he does so a memory stirs, of himself as a child, his pale face framed in a dark, oval mirror, on "the day his father left home" (145). That is, his becoming-ghostly—recall the "boys with old, scared faces" of "Survivors"—is a function of his hauntedness (of "cowed / Subjection to friends who died") and a consequence or entailment of Orme's visitation; but that hauntedness is itself a sign—the sign of something of which the conduct of the war is more an effect than a cause. It is the sign of a defection that is intergenerational in import. For if the world has become absurd, if ghosts walk (intimating, as in *Hamlet,* that time itself is "out of joint"), it is because behind the gore and agony of the war lies a betrayal of the young by authority—by the nation, society at large, the Father. Those whom the haunted, and therefore in turn ghostly, witness is called upon to haunt are therefore the elders who do not *know* they are haunted, and cannot hear the message asking to be phrased: members of the generation that not only devours its children but does so unwittingly. Rivers, for Sassoon, is a "substitute father" (145) who, on a personal plane, can be forgiven his remissness; but Sassoon knows now (it is a function of the divide between generations) that his place is in France, with the dead and those of the living who are themselves future ghosts. Orme's coming to him, together with Rivers's absence as addressee of Sassoon's report, implies Sassoon's return, performing the carrying-back part of the function of reporting in response to Orme's carrying forward of hauntedness.

But it also implies inventing a new idiom, capable of carrying forward in poetry the haunt that Orme performs, carrying it forward from Craiglockhart (from the "survivors" whose friends have died) to a society of older survivors, whose "paternal" obliviousness it might, Orme-like, penetrate. Orme's visitation is triggered by the poem on which Sassoon and Owen are working, but its character ("restrained," "dignified," but also clarifying, revealing, symptomatological) also makes it more a figure for the possible effect of ghostly writing than a symptom of neurosis. We can expect, then, that the poem in turn will not only carry back to the war (its stutter, like Orme's tapping, harking back to the monstrous anger of the guns, the wail of the shells, and the rifle's rapid rattle), but will also enact in its writing a forward movement like Orme's. And it is this aspect of the poem's reporting, which has to do more particularly with its stammer, that Barker alludes to in the third and final episode (156–58) of her account of the writing of "Anthem."

What is at stake in this final meeting of the two poets, who discuss the now completed poem (and this time we do not learn in whose room the conversation takes place or consequently who is visiting whom), is the meaning to be given to what Sassoon identifies almost immediately as a "contradiction" in the poem's thematic structure. Significantly, he does this almost in the same moment as he recognizes the poem as a revelation, as if its success as a "new idiom" and its contradictoriness are connected.

> "It's better, isn't it?" [says Owen.]
>
> "Better? It's *transformed.*" [Sassoon] read it again. "Though when you look at the *sense* . . . You do realise you've completely contradicted yourself, don't you? You start by saying there is no consolation, and then you say there is." (157)

Owen's response to this observation is equivocation: it's not consolation, he says, but "pride in sacrifice"; and he goes on to point out a similarly (non)contradictory passage in Sassoon's own verse (as if Barker were presenting whatever it is that is at issue between them as a general marker of the new idiom they have invented, without their having themselves fully recognized its character). Furthermore, Sassoon notices that his friend has lost his stammer and has "the self-confidence to contradict his hero" (157), which further suggests that "contradiction" is characteristic of the now self-confident idiom that has come into being, however, through so many drafts that Owen has "lost count" (156), and through so many stages of diffidence, hesitation, and disagreement. More particularly, one might imagine that Owen's stammer has now migrated, in the form of "contradiction," into what is, nevertheless, *confident* verse.

Since Sassoon's comment ("You start by . . . , then you say") implies that the alleged contradiction is structural, some formal observations are relevant. The poem, which has always had fourteen lines, is now clearly a sonnet, although the disposition of the octet (4 + 4) and the sestet (3 + 3) makes it, perhaps not coincidentally, more like a "French" sonnet (4 + 4 + 3 + 3) than a conventional English or Shakespearean one (in which the sestet has a four-plus-two structure). The pentameter rhythm is slowed and disturbed in places by trochees ("sad shires," "girls' brows"), and the last line is actually stretched into a hexameter by its three accented monosyllables: "And eách slów dúsk a dráwing dówn of blínds." These slight irregularities notwithstanding, we are well within the tradition of English verse; it is *that* tradition, as Sassoon's remark points up, that is being made to stammer here through the mapping of a thematic disjunction onto the formal equilibrium of octet and sestet. Sassoon is not upset by the poem's onomatopoeic stutter (the "sound" as opposed to the "sense"), and even less by its realism ("I see we got to the slaughterhouse" [157]); it is the contravention of the lyric convention of coherence or "unity"—unity of theme, tone, and mood in harmony with unity of structure—that bothers him. Since it is in the octet that consolation is denied and in the sestet that it—or at least Owen's "pride in sacrifice"—is affirmed, the contradiction is actually underlined, rather than obscured, by the sonnet's conformity to a traditional configuration.

But let us look more closely, and in particular at the rhetorical effect produced by the fact that the balance of octet and sestet is underscored by the question-and-answer form of the protasis and apodosis in each: "What passing-bells. . . ? / Only the monstrous anger of the guns," etc.; "What candles. . . ?/ Not . . . but . . ." This questioning-and-responding form produces a degree of ambiguity, in each case, that inflects the more obvious contradictoriness Sassoon detects between octet and sestet, inflecting it quite affirmatively in the case of the supposedly disconsolate sestet—yes, there *is* a sort of consolation—while the emphasis in the octet falls more on the negative: no, there is *no* consolation (except the monstrous anger of the guns). Because of this ambiguation of the contradiction, the sonnet's characteristic move is as much one of mitigation and dedifferentiation as it is one of contradiction; the no-consolation is mitigated, but so too is the consolation. I will argue in the next section that if the contradiction of octet and sestet enacts the dynamics of stammer as a differend writ small (both denying and affirming elegy as the possibility of mourning), the ambiguation has the effect of making the poem readable, rather, as stammering in discomfort with its own generic misfit, that is, with its undecidability as a product of catachresis, not-elegy.

For Sassoon's "contradiction" is more accurately an antinomy, a conflict between two equally legitimating "laws," and in this case, the legitimating laws are regimes of genre, specifically the assumptions of realism (no consolation) on the one hand—that is, of genres like letters and private conversations, where frankness is assumed—and, on the other, those of elegy (mourning brings consolation). To the degree that there is conflict there is differend, bespeaking something else that is "asking" to be phrased. But to the degree that the contradiction is ambiguated and the conflict mitigated, there is a turning of the genre of elegy into what I have called not-elegy: neither an elegy nor not an elegy. Where the stammer of differend is symptomatic, then, carrying back to the trauma and pain to which it refers—which in this case means not only, as Lyotard says, the pain arising from silencing but also the pain of the thing itself, the trauma of warfare, that is asking to be phrased—the stammer of generic discomfort, indexing an awareness of solecism, is symptomatological because it produces readability, defining a new idiom that carries forward and presences both the pain of the silencing and the pain that is silenced. It does so by piggybacking on conventions—the sonnet, the elegy, the poetic—that are familiar to all readers of English poetry, readers who might otherwise have remained oblivious to the pain that not-elegy presences.

Thus the poetic stammer, as opposed to the painful stammer of differend to which it alludes, becomes an occasion of actual pleasure, the pleasure attributed by Lyotard to the invention of a new idiom and acknowledged in Barker's text by the satisfaction she attributes to the two friends as they read the completed text of "Anthem" and comment with varying degrees of modesty and excitement ("it's better"; "it's *transformed*"; "a revelation") on its success. And aesthetic success, in turn, implies publishability: a not-elegy carries forward a report from the front, through its readability, in a way that is not open to, say, a plain "declaration," which can only be embroiled in the dynamics of differend, or even to a merely contradictory poem. To recapitulate, then, before moving on to a closer analysis of the poem as not-elegy: the poem both enacts a contradiction (or stammer) in the configuration of octet and sestet, and within each of these two segments (and hence between them) converts that same contradiction into something more ambiguous, a stammering that corresponds to the complex poetic mood of not-elegy; and it is this ambiguation of contradiction that I understand, therefore, as the operator of generic catachresis—what Eric Michaels (chapter 2) might have called its etiquette—and a marker of the poem's open-ended readability. "Anthem" can go to *The Nation.*

The Writing of a Poem: Analysis

Contradiction to Catachresis (Call and Response, 1)

As the staging of a differend, the sonnet mixes syntagms appropriate to elegy ("What passing-bells for these. . . ?"; "voices of mourning"; "What candles may be held to speed them all?"; "drawing-down of blinds") and words derived from the lexicon of elegy ("bells," "orisons," "prayers," "choirs," "holy," "good-byes," "pall," "flowers") with assertively realist declaratives, localized in the octet: most notably, "these who die as cattle," "the monstrous anger of the guns," "the shrill, demented [choirs] of wailing shells." These last redefine the trappings of elegy, which in the questions of lines 1 and 9 the poetic subject seems to desire, as "mockeries." What is being called for, it seems, would be a form or mode of mourning *like* passing-bells and candles, but more appropriate to "these who die as cattle" than the rituals associated with elegy. This would constitute a form of (not-)elegy that would not be a mockery. At first glance, it is true, the question-answer structure, especially of the octet, declares such a resolution of the desire for elegy with the unsuitability of conventional ritual to be an impossibility. What passing-bells? None (the guns continue imperturbably, there is only their monstrous anger). On second thought, though, the word "only" introduces the possibility of an alternative reading. "Only the monstrous anger of the guns . . ." says that there are no passing-bells. But it simultaneously suggests that the guns, the rifles, the shells, each making their own form of noisy racket, *could* be candidates—they are the only candidates there are—for the role of alternative to the passing-bells and other trappings of elegy. And since the apparatus of elegy is not only absent but also unsuitable, the weaponry might also be more appropriate than is elegy to the case of "these who die as cattle." In short, the noisy armaments might be available, catachrestically, as a means of making do where the forms and modes that are conventionally dedicated to the purposes of mourning demonstrate their inadequacy. What passing-bells? Well, the guns, rifles and shells are not passing-bells; they are weapons of destruction that wreak terrible carnage. But perhaps they can be made to serve.

Moreover, the poem that stutters like the rifles' "rapid rattle" and patters out its own "hasty orisons" by wailing with "the shrill, demented choirs of . . . shells"—the poem as report—can be understood likewise to be describing itself, by virtue of its own noisy status, as a possible candidate for the role of elegy-substitute: not elegy at all, but nevertheless some sort of elegy, and the only kind of elegy that suits the circumstances. As a not-elegy in this sense, it is more appropriate, less of a mockery, than elegy itself would be, since it makes use of the weapons of destruction that are the "only" means of mourning there are. It uses them, not for their proper purpose (of carnage), but in a consciously makeshift way, as precisely a form of (not-)elegy. That is, both the conventional genre of elegy and the weapons of mass destruction are being subjected to a practice of catachresis here, and turned from their expected use, the outcome being the poem. In this respect, the bugles of line 8 are emblematic. Realistically, they are sounding reveille or stand-to, not the last post; they are allied with the guns, the rifles, and the shells as part of the noise of war. But "calling" as they are "from sad shires," they irresistibly evoke the possibility of their becoming instruments of mourning: their mournfulness suggests the grieving of which "these who die as cattle" are deprived by the conditions of trench warfare, but without their ceasing to be part of the noise of war. And the poem itself, as a report of that noise that poetically enacts as not-elegy the rifles' stutter and the monstrous anger of the guns, also "calls" as the bugles do, but from "sad shires" of its own—shires defined by the deictic "these" (not "those") of line 1 as a place where one is in physical proximity or moral solidarity with the slaughtered, that is, from the front (whether literally or metaphorically). The front is that place where the rifles' stutter and the bugles' sound is recruited by the poem—the site of a becoming-elegiac of war's own indifferent noise—into a call of its own.

But if the poem calls, will it be heard? And if so, by whom? And where? The sestet—which can now be seen to function in the poem's own configuration as a response to the call articulated in the octet—begins to suggest answers to such questions. For it is here that the emphases of the octet are reversed while being ambiguated in their turn. Where the octet's most obvious sense is the denial of consolation, the sestet affirms instead, as Sassoon noticed, that there *is* a kind of consolation and a way in which the slaughtered *are* mourned—a way somewhat closer, moreover, to the conventions of mourning that are associated with elegy, without actually corresponding to them. For, symmetrically with the way the octet takes away all possibility of consolation only to give it back in an unexpected way, the consolation the sestet offers takes away what it apparently gives. There is consolation, but it is inadequate; it is inadequate because it is "only" an improvised, substitute making-do, or catachrestic mode of mourning. *Not* candles in boys' hands but only the good-bye glimmers in their eyes are holy, and shine "to speed them all." The *only* pall for the dead is pallor, that of girls' brows, and their only flowers "the tenderness of patient minds." The answer the poem provides for its initial question: "What passing-bells for these. . . ?" is thus, finally, *only* mourning-substitutes: the glimmering of good-byes and the patient, long-suffering tenderness resumed in the image of the drawing-down of blinds, itself in metaphoric equivalence with "each slow dusk." And if the rhythm of this last line evokes dirges and funereal music (a melancholic "anthem"), the sense refers to a slow and patient, inconclusive fading (like that of a Scottish twilight, or "gloaming"—cf. "glimmers"), a fading in which the poem also participates. It is as if the existential "passing" of the survivors constitutes, in the end, the (passing-)bell, the slowly tolling mode of mourning, for which the poem's initial question asked. As such, it contrasts with the "hasty orisons" accorded "these who," in the poem's first draft, "die so fast," whether it be in the form of the rifles' "rapid rattle" or of elegiac candles to "speed them all."

This final mode of mourning is obviously different from the conditions of warfare evoked in the octet as the "only" form of passing-bells accorded the dead; and it is more like passing-bells than are the noisy weapons of war, or indeed the glimmers in boys' eyes. In this it constitutes an ultimate response, itself mediated by the boys' fleeting good-byes, to the call enacted by the weaponry of war and onomatopoeically reported in the octet. But the difference is now only that between a slow dying that constitutes survivorhood as (not-)mourning, and a fast death that goes unmourned (except, precisely, by not-mourning, and by the poem as not-elegy). It is the boys at the front who mediate this difference, as do catachresis and making-do themselves, which form the topic of both octet and sestet, call and response. Like the noise of war as a model of (not-)elegy, good-bye glimmers and pallor and patience, as modes of (not-)mourning, are "only" makeshift, unsatisfying, and—although more suitable than elegiac mockeries and more like conventional mourning than the noise of war—ultimately inadequate. Partaking of *both* these modes of catachresis, enacting simultaneously a call and a response as not-elegy, the poem links the two, carrying back to the dead and carrying forward to the survivors. And it unites the dead and those who survive to (not-)mourn them in the single category of the "doomed" that it anthems.

But it resolves nothing. The mourning in boys' eyes and on girls' brows is an unconsoled and unconsolable mourning; it lasts a lifetime and, like a long slow dusk, it is itself equivalent to a way of dying. It is, in Freudian terms, more like melancholia than it is mourning proper; such melancholia is the only form of mourning there is when soldiers die as cattle amid the noise of war, just as the noise of battle, taken up into a poem, is their only elegiac passing-bell. Such not-mourning, as described in the sestet, corresponds, then, to the not-elegy as it is figured in the octet; it is both not-elegy's own prevailing mood, and at the same time the only response to its call. Only the sense of irreparable loss suffered by the dead soldiers' companions in the trenches and by their female coevals at home responds to the bugles' calling "from sad shires"; but the survivors themselves, whether "boys" or "girls," are deprived *in* their mourning as the dead are deprived *of* mourning. The bond between them is close. And it is thus that the poem finally becomes an anthem (or not-anthem: a hymn but more of loss than praise) for "doomed youth"—that is, not only for "these" who die at the front but also for all (including the poem itself) who are denied the ability to mourn them in the way that they should, properly, be mourned. As a not-elegy it is about the dead; but as a (not-)anthem, it is "for" two groups: "these" who die without passing-bells, and the survivors who (as "these" implies) feel close to them. The anthem is a not-elegy for those who live as well as for those who die. So the poem is unresolved, it remains contradictory as Sassoon says, it stammers, because the mourning of "these who die as cattle"—unmourned as cattle are unmourned—is never over; and it is never over because mourning itself, in that circumstance, becomes a makeshift substitute for proper mourning.

Because the poem is in not-mourning for both "these" who die and "these" whose mourning is without consolation, the last-minute change of title, from "Anthem for Dead Youth" to "Anthem for Doomed Youth," has particular significance. Where "dead" refers only to the young men slaughtered at the front, "doomed" includes the dead but also both groups of survivors whose proximity to them—spatial as well as moral in the case of the boys, moral only in that of the girls—condemns them to a form of pain, the pain of being unable properly to mourn, the pain of being haunted, that associates them with those who haunt because they die in circumstances that prevent them from being adequately mourned. In the novel, Barker attributes this change of title to Sassoon, although the handwriting on the draft is, to my perhaps untutored eye, clearly Owen's.[11] "He thought for a moment, crossed one word out, substituted another. 'There you are,' he said, handing the poem back, smiling. 'Anthem for *Doomed* Youth.'" (158). It is, then, as if the poem has undergone a double expansion: from a not-elegy for the dead to an anthem for the doomed (the movement from the octet to the sestet), but also from the doomed in France (the boys) to the girls in England, doomed too, and associated with the survivors at the front through the quality of their not-mourning. This second expansion is the work of the sestet. But there the poem's expansion, its reporting movement, which has reached across the Channel, stops. For where the word "doomed" annuls distinctions between those who die and those who survive, between boys and girls, and between France and England, the word "youth" in the title restricts the category of the doomed to the members of a single generation. If the call in the poem's octet is responded to, *intra*-generationally, in the sestet, the sense in which the poem itself might be heard as a call, and responded to *inter*generationally, and its movement of reporting continue, goes unaddressed. Indeed, it seems to be excluded by the specification in the title that the anthem is "for" doomed *youth.* Should we consider Barker's attribution of the title change to Sassoon, in combination with Sassoon's offer to have "Anthem" published in *The Nation,* a way of both noting the poem's pessimism with respect to any further extension of its power to report, and of countermanding that pessimism? And is it further implied that the poem's inability to resolve is a function of uncertainty respecting the ability of its call to be heard and responded to outside of the generation of the doomed?

Not-Elegy and Anthem (Call and Response, 2)

An anthem, I suggest, can be "for" a doomed generation—that is, written in honor of that generation, and intended for that generation—without its ability to *carry* being restricted to the generation for which it is written. "Anthem for Doomed Youth" laments the doomed and implicitly praises them—as a manifestation of "pride in sacrifice." But (it is a consequence of the reference-address nexus that grounds the dynamics of reporting) one must also ask for whom the anthem is performed. Who, in other words, is the audience of the dedicatory act by which the poem declares itself an anthem "for" doomed youth? And what, more particularly, is the status of the elders who are so pointedly excluded from the ranks of the doomed, as if *their* survivorhood and mourning were different in kind from that of youth? The very pointedness of this exclusion argues, I propose, that it is a mode of address, and I will try to suggest that such a mode of address amounts to an act of haunting. As in Sassoon's poem, all survivors are haunted—not just the "doomed" or the "shell-shocked" among them—and like the double take on "you" that Sassoon exploits, Owen's poem too has shuffling devices or devices of reportage, the dedicatory title among them, that transmit the haunt from those who know themselves to be haunted, as their not-mourning indicates, to those who may not know that they are haunted, and remain oblivious to the pain of the doomed—those, that is, who are content with (or seduced by) elegy and able to mourn without difficulty, whose mourning is not poisoned by the sense of waste that, in the preface he drafted for an edition of his poetry that he never saw, Owen called the "pity" of war.

I see two ways in which, by designating itself as utterance, "Anthem" alludes to its audience; in each case, though, the assumed relation of the implied audience to the poem is curiously unspecific. The first is the deictic "these" that has already been mentioned as entailing proximity on the part of "I" to the referent, "these who die," and by implication also on the part of the "boys" and "girls" who are included in the same, extended, referential gesture as the dead. But deixis (pointing) is the emblematic gesture of reporting because it inevitably associates address (forward) with reference (back) : one points at something for the benefit of someone. Thus it implies, in addition to the relation of speaker to referent, an intersubjective relation of addresser and addressee and a presumed relation of the addressee to the object of reference. Had line 1 read "for *those* who die as cattle," it could have been readily deduced that the speaker and the addressee are in a relation of proximity, and that what they share is a distanced relation to the referent. "These," though, does not permit judgments either about the nature of the addresser-addressee relation or about the relation of the addressee to the referent; in each case they *could* be proximate, but may equally be distant. And the weight of lyric convention tends to suggest, at least at first glance, that the poem should therefore be understood as a private monologue, a meditation on the speaker's part, that is not so much addressed to readers as they are invited to "overhear" it.

In this respect, though, the generic designation "anthem" in the title—the second way in which the poem implies an audience—may have as one of its functions to relate the poem less to lyric introspection than to a tradition of ritual choral music (cf. the "choirs" in lines 6 and 7), one that implies performance for an audience that participates responsively. Because the poem is a substitute anthem for the "choirs" that are otherwise supplied only by the shrill, demented wail of the shells, "anthem" would be Owen's way of designating the poem's generic indeterminacy as not-elegy, drawing attention to its catachrestic status. The effect of the title would then be self-deprecatory in respect of the poem, and (given that anthems are church music) derisory in relation to the ecclesiastical gestures—passing-bells, orisons and prayers, choirs and candles—listed in the poem as mockeries. But an anthem is nevertheless a hymn of celebration (Owen's "pride in sacrifice" is relevant), and as such it has an antiphonal structure, as does the poem (structured by call and response in the relation of octet to sestet and by question and answer in each segment)—a structure that extends readily, I suggest, to the relation of poem to audience. That is, the poem itself becomes a call that *awaits* a response (although it does not necessarily predict one), because the antiphonal structure of anthem presupposes and implies a "responsive" audience—the "congregation" participates symbolically, if not actually, in the hymn. The etymological collocation of *anti* (against) and *phoné* (voice) from which the word *anthem* derives—a collocation normally understood to refer to a harmonious dialogue or exchange of voices—might in this case be interpreted, it is true, as implying warring voices, differend, catachrestic ambiguity, the stammer of not-elegy, and thus thought to express a degree of anxiety on the poem's part concerning the actual relation of its call to a supposedly answering response. For the titular phrase "anthem for doomed youth" is concordant with the deictic "these" in that it specifies a referent and the nature of the relation of subject of enunciation to the referent (proximity in one case, pride and praise in the other), but merely implies an addressee or audience, without committing itself as to the nature of the relation linking either speaker and audience or audience and referent. A call implies a response; but if it remains unheard—if the congregation fails to participate in the anthem—it may well go without a response.

But if the poem can be understood in this way as a call that expects a response or a question awaiting an answer, then the calls in the poem (those of the bugles) and its questions ("What passing-bells. . . ?" "What candles. . . ?") become signifiers of the poem's own calling and questioning, as these are addressed—perhaps somewhat dubiously—not to those it hymns but to an audience of those who are, precisely, *not* members of the category of "doomed youth," but in a relation to those "for" whom the poem is written that is like that of congregation to choir. These addressees are asked to consider the question of their responsiveness—the nature of their relation to the anthem and participation in its not-elegiac mood—and more particularly the degree of their equivalence or nonequivalence, as survivors, with those in the poem who respond to "these who die" with good-bye glimmers, pallor, and patience, the drawing-down of blinds. For it is not just that in the course of the sestet the category of youthful survivors undergoes a kind of expansion (a poem set in France moves from battlefront good-byes on the part of boys, across the Channel to England, where it embraces girl not-mourners as well as boys, and domestic settings as well as the front). It is also that time slows (or expands): the boys' good-byes glimmer fleetingly in accordance with the "hasty," "rapid" conditions that prevail at the front, but survivorhood in England becomes a matter of patience and "each slow dusk." As the poem enacts a movement of reporting, carrying across, over or forward, its range thus extends spatially and expands temporally, so that this movement—bridging the Channel, embracing the genders—irresistibly suggests the possibility of further portability as time goes on. The very stretching of the last line, its lengthening to a slow, insistent hexameter, tends to suggest this extensibility, as if the poem ended on an ellipsis or an et cetera, without truly ending at all. Its rhythm is that of funereal music; its failure to resolve is that of the poem as not-elegy—the endlessness of not-mourning; its fading, though, while it may suggest an uncertain voice petering out or stammering to a stop, a sign (like stammering) of uncertainty about audience, also invites continuation, somewhat as, in the dynamics of asyndeton (see chapters 5, 6, and 7), an interruption implies relay, picking up, portability; the inevitability of something continuing, like the reverberations of a report. That something which continues, of course, is not-mourning.

By the same token, the categories of referent and addressee begin to blur, finally, as they do already in the sestet, in favor of the larger category of *those who respond.* In this light, survivors, who include boys and girls, embracing the genders, might also include, embracing the generations, their elders. If the anthem is "for" (in praise of, in not-mourning for) doomed youth, the range of audibility of its calling and questioning—that is, of its address structure—may exceed in this way that of its internal reference; the poem may also be "for" (initially in the sense of addressed to) those who, without being youthful, might still be considered "doomed"—doomed, that is (and whether or not they are aware of it), to a painful survivorhood. For where youth is a restricted category, that of the doomed is potentially universal; it could include all who, surviving the dead like the boys and the girls in the poem, find themselves also, like them in all but their youth, condemned to live on, deprived and unconsoled. Rivers, in Barker's novel, becomes such a survivor, for example. In order to hear the poem's call and respond to its questioning, it would be enough for such survivors to realize both of what doomed survivorhood consists (melancholy, the inability to mourn except in the form of not-mourning), and the fact of their own participation in such a form of survival, whose marker is the mood of not-elegy. It is enough for them to realize, as Rivers does in the case of Sassoon, their own proximity both to the speaker of the poem and to "these" of whom he speaks; to realize, that is, their own hauntedness. It is enough, in short, to respond to the poem's call in order to join its range of reference, the doomed whom it anthems and laments. And, of course, vice versa.

What, for example, after the "boys" and "girls" of the poem, of the very next category of the deprived and unconsoled: the grieving mothers and fathers who are parents of the dead, but also of the doomed (and share, in that sense, in their doom)? But the category of kin extends, in turn, to the nation and beyond. For who is not, like the boys and girls, a survivor, but like the parents a survivor both of the dead and of those whom the poem names as doomed? When Barker has Sassoon offer to have "Anthem" published in *The Nation* and, virtually in the same gesture, modify the wording of the title so as to replace "dead" by "doomed," she is having him imply a certain commutability of survivorhood and doomedness, and this commutability implies in turn an open-ended portability of the poem's range, such that its address to survivors becomes coterminous with its referencing of doomedness. It is for every thoughtful reader to ponder the issue of what it means to outlive both "those who die as cattle" and a whole generation forced to survive the loss of what makes living worthwhile. Among survivors, there are only those who know this, and understand themselves as proximate to doomed youth, because doomed as they are, and those who do not—and remain unaware of their hauntedness.

The poem, in short, asks some persistent and penetrating, but "silent" (unformulated) questions—silent because it relies on me, as its reader, to reformulate the questions it does pose, together with their answers, in ways relevant to my own situation of survivorhood. This—its potential for endless reverberation—is its method of haunting, in which it is much like Orme standing quietly and wordlessly just within the door of Sassoon's room. It can afford to be dignified and restrained, like Orme, because its method, like his, is one of implication and infiltration, dependent on my foreknowledge of what it (therefore) does not need to say. But if, like Sassoon, I am conscious in even a small degree of some of the implications of my own survivorhood—what it has cost others for me to be in the position of having outlived them—then the poem's call can scarcely be ignored. "[That Orme was dead] clearly did not worry Orme, who continued to stand quietly by the door, but Sassoon began to think it ought to worry him" (143). Carried forward by the poem to its first readers, as an effect of its reporting, the questions continue to carry over in this way, even as the reverberations and repercussions of the 1914–18 war have partly merged into, and partly been muffled by, the reports of later events. Thus they reach readers who are alive today, their urgency unabated—perhaps even increased—even as the poem itself, in its mild modernism, begins to look increasingly, at least to hasty readers, like a period piece. (My deictic "today" responds, across generations and into the future, to Owen's inspired "these.")

In the preface he rough-drafted for the publication of his collected war poems (a publication he did not live to see), Owen again deployed some significant deixis. "These elegies," he wrote, "are to this generation in no sense consolatory. They may be to the next" (31). Whatever he may have meant by this (that?) last sentence, I have to say that, although I was born long after Owen was killed in early November 1918, a week before the armistice, I do not find his "elegies" consolatory at all. Neither, it is clear, does Pat Barker, whose novel devotes itself to *regenerating,* for us, now, the pain of 1917. A pain that has not ceased to have repercussions, whose reporting continues to reverberate.[12]

4. Twisting a Trope: Reading and Writing Extremity

Ils parlent parfois du sida, très mal, à qui pire pire. Ils ne remarquent pas (ne suis-je pas le nain secret?) que l'ignorance et le simplisme des uns m'énervent, et que l'intolérance des autres me révolte.

[They sometimes talk about AIDS, very badly, outbadlying one another. They don't notice (am I not the secret dwarf?) that the ignorance and simple-mindedness of some are irritating and the intolerance of others revolting to me.]

—Pascal de Duve, *Cargo vie*

Travel

Fourteen ninety-two. A man whose name, in his native Italian, means "pigeon" sails from Spain on a voyage of discovery from which he was to bring back to Europe the astonishing revelation of a New World, mixed up in his mind with the splendors of Cathay. As his first name predicted, Cristoforo Colombo took Christ to the New World but, as many historians think, he brought back the syphilis spirochete, which then rapidly spread through Europe, and even reached Japan. Other historians, though, think Columbus took syphilis to America, along with other European diseases that rapidly decimated the indigenous population.

Nineteen ninety-two. In the year of the Columbus quincentenary, a young man of Flemish origins, whose name might mean "the dove" ("duif" in Dutch, "colomba" in Italian),[1] embarks from the port of Le Havre, to cross the Atlantic on a cargo ship and return to France, after touching at Fort-de-France and Pointe-à-Pitre in the French West Indies. It was May 28, Ascension Day. He took with him the virus that causes AIDS, HIV, as a kind of stowaway, both in his body (it had already entered his brain and caused a severe encephalopathy) and on board, the captain, crew, and fellow passengers being unaware that a *sidéen* was among them. And he brought the AIDS back, this messenger dove, as a revelation to Europe: not just a message of "AIDS awareness," but also the revelation of a New World opened up by viewing life in the perspective of death. A message not unlinked to sacrifice, as the reference to the Pascal lamb in the young man's first name foretold.

Like Columbus's, de Duve's message comes in the form of a logbook: "un journal de bord: ce sera aussi un journal de corps et un journal de coeur" [a logbook: it will also be a body diary and a journal of the heart] (11); it is published under the title *Cargo vie.* Like the work of Hervé Guibert and Cyril Collard, it was an important vehicle of AIDS witness in France, reaching a wide audience. The virus Pascal took to America and brought back, transformed into a viral message—for, as he put it, "VIH, c'est un peu toi qui écris ici" [HIV, you're pretty much the one doing the writing here] (13)—has spread. Meanwhile he died, in April 1993, less than a year after arriving back in Le Havre on June 22, 1992. For reasons that will become evident, *Cargo vie* has not been translated into English.

The story I wish to tell—contributing a bit, I hope, to the spread of this viral message—is not specifically about this fascinating parallel between de Duve's voyage and Columbus's, present in the text as a submerged pun; but it is about the pattern of departure and return, the dynamic of leave-taking and revelation, that *Cargo vie* enacts. De Duve's voyage is a voyage into the domain of the sacred, where an immanence that is Life meets a transcendance that is Death (47), and then back with its message of revelation. And his text correspondingly entails some rhetorical voyaging, enacted (as I want to show) most particularly in and through the figure of apostrophe, a "turning away" *(apo-strophein)* or leave-taking that constitutes a message directed toward those away from whom one turns. We have already encountered the text's key apostrophe—"VIH, c'est un peu toi qui écris ici"—which I might well have chosen as the epigraph for this chapter. But there are many other apostrophes in de Duve's text, almost as many as there are puns. They include apostrophes *to* one *from* whom the writing subject turns away (de Duve's former lover, "E."), and a recurrent refrain of address *to* AIDS as "sida mon amour" [AIDS my love] that enacts a turning away from E. but also from all, except fellow *sidéens,* who constitute the book's audience. It's the significance of the alliance of apostrophe and punning in this book that I want to explore.

Apostrophe, like all tropes or "turns" of speech, is a mode of rhetorical indirection. It enacts the knowledge on which Columbus acted, that it is possible, and sometimes opportune, to travel West in order to arrive (back) East. "Ma vie," de Duve wrote (24), "n'aura été qu'un très court circuit. Je fonce, mais je fonce" [My life will have been just a very short circuit. I'm going down, but I'm plunging ahead]. The circuitous, even when it is "very short," can turn *foncer,* sinking, bottoming, into *foncer* in the sense of charging or pouncing: achieving one's goal by the most direct route, and a way of going down without—as Levi might have said—going under. How are we to understand this paradox, caught in a pun?

Equivocation

"Le silence éternel de ces espaces infinis m'effraie" [The eternal silence of infinite space strikes awe into me]. Blaise Pascal, to whom Pascal de Duve's first name points as his last alludes to Columbus, is another predecessor whose most famous *pensée* furnishes a subtext of *Cargo vie.* As a "journal de bord" in another sense, the logbook of a voyage to the *edge* (French *bord*) and back, *Cargo vie* has thematic affinities with the celebrated thinker of the "two infinites" as well as formal resemblances: a collection of fragments and jottings (dated and carefully ordered, however, as the logbook format requires), *Cargo vie* is a set of "pensées de Pascal" for the era of AIDS. And like Blaise Pascal's text also, it has an apologetic purpose: it aims to penetrate the complacency and upset the "ignorance and simple-mindedness," not to mention the "intolerance" and homophobia, of which Pascal de Duve encounters manifestations whenever his fellow passengers talk about AIDS. Where they vie with one another in speaking "ill" of it—as if their conversation was a little epidemic of *mal,* in the word's many senses (evil, wrong, ill health among them)—de Duve will speak *well* of it. That is, he will speak of it as a form of health, he will say good things about it, he will write of it efficaciously, as an "écrivant" as opposed to an "écrivaniteux" (52). He will awaken people from their complacency. For where Blaise Pascal condemns the human proclivity for *divertissement,* Pascal de Duve invents a small, Pascal-like, metaphysical parable of his own, in which he describes humanity as so many cattle, put out to graze by a "mysterious peasant, who then immediately vanished." What should we do? "Paître ou ne pas paître, telle est la question. Et la plupart paissent placidement sans trop s'interroger" [To graze or not to graze, that is the question. And most graze placidly without asking themselves too many questions] (33). "Paître ou ne pas paître" refers punningly, of course, to the famous question of Hamlet's monologue: to be or not to be, in French "être ou ne pas être." It is this bovine complacency, this cud-chewing placidity, that needs to be awakened, de Duve understands, to something like Pascal's *effroi* in the face of infinity, a sense of awe and wonder, if humanity is truly to *be.* That is what is at stake in speaking "well" of AIDS, exercising the function of *écrivant.*

Enter now Baudelaire—and behind him, in more shadowy fashion, Galileo Galilei, the "starry messenger" *(siderius nuntius)* who first shook human complacency by revealing earth's marginal place in the solar system, and was thus a predecessor of Blaise Pascal. Baudelaire's 1857 verse collection, *Les Fleurs du mal* (The flowers of evil) clearly posed the question of how to speak *well* (in the form of "flowers") of that which is ill, evil, wrong, and painful: *le mal.* And he did so in the context of the pusillanimity and hypocrisy—the ability to ignore the reality of evil—of which Baudelaire's liminal poem, the famous "Au Lecteur," accused his readers. Baudelaire, who has a bird's name *(beau de l'air)* was like Pascal (that's Blaise Pascal) in his desire to communicate a certain experience of the *gouffre,* or abyss; but unlike (Blaise) Pascal and like Pascal de Duve, he defines the problem of evil, and the problem of bearing witness to evil, in the context of general complacency and *inconscience,* as the characteristic problems of modernity. And his title, *Les Fleurs du mal,* defines the problem of witnessing as a puzzle entailing incongruity and equivocation.

In 1841, Baudelaire made a voyage to the Indian Ocean, from which he returned with a tropical version of exotic beauty and sensuality that revolutionized French poetry and furnished a vision of the "ideal" that, in Baudelaire's dichotomized worldview, counterbalances *spleen* (the domain of depression and evil), somewhat as *fleurs* counterbalances *le mal* in his title. He also brought back from his long voyage a fascination with birds, as winged messengers of beauty too often constrained by earth and earthboundedness. In an anthology piece dating from this period, he describes the albatross as a bird that soars free, "prince des nuées," but when captured, becomes an ungainly object of mockery: the poet too is an albatross, "ses ailes de géant l'empêchent de marcher" [his gigantic wings prevent him from walking]. Years later, in a poem written in 1859 that became another anthology piece, a swan in an urban gutter is described as a figure of exile: "comme les exilés, ridicule et sublime" [like exiles, both ridiculous and sublime]. These birds thus illustrate a problem that can be called the problem of the pigeon and the dove: the proximity of pigeon and dove is incongruous—but it also suggests a kind of solution to a problem of expression, the possibility of bearing witness to that which is ugly in a language of beauty. That is, it suggests the possibility of an equivocation. In Mauritius, Baudelaire would surely have learned that the island had been named "Isle of the Swan" by its Portuguese discoverers, who—lacking a word for the ungainly, earthbound dodo they found there—had recourse to the compromise of catachresis, a perfect model for a poet in search of a way to turn the ugliness of modernity into poetry, and to reconcile *le mal* with the "flowers" (of rhetoric) inherited from the past.

Baudelaire figures explicitly in *Cargo vie* as a poet of the sea ("homme libre, toujours tu chériras la mer!" [Free man, thou shalt ever cherish the sea] [105]). A little more discreetly, the opening and closing liminal poems of *Les Fleurs du mal* are also invoked, one in praise of voyaging to the *edge* ("Le Voyage"), the other ("Au Lecteur") an acerbic attack on readerly hypocrisy. But if, like Columbus, Baudelaire enjoys the role of predecessor and his subtextual presence in *Cargo vie* is pervasive, it is because his collection illustrates the inevitable rhetoricity, the compromises and equivocations, to which the task of witnessing condemns an aerial messenger or *siderius nuntius,* the bearer of a revelation addressed to ordinary, placid, cud-chewing humanity—famously apostrophized in "Au Lecteur" as "Hypocrite lecteur,—mon semblable,—mon frère!" [Hypocritical reader—my likeness—my brother!]. Indeed, the apostrophe itself illustrates exactly such a rhetorical compromise, since it acknowledges that in a world subject to the reign of *le mal*—where the Devil exercises a kind of Oriental despotism—poets are necessarily brothers in hypocrisy to their hypocritical readers. If there is a difference between Baudelaire and de Duve in this respect, it is not at the level of the equivocations enforced by the task of bearing witness, but lies rather in the fact that where Baudelaire's problem is to find a language of beauty in order to make *le mal* readable, de Duve must work to make the revelation concerning the nature of existence—the heightened sense of living that he owes to AIDS, as an approach to death—available to an audience so plunged into complacency that it not only ignores the viral presence of AIDS in its life, like the passengers and crew of the ship unaware of the "stowaway" among them, but also resists the revelation of beauty that Pascal knows AIDS, as *le mal,* can simultaneously provide. If the ship on which de Duve travels is the vehicle, for him, of a voyage of discovery, it is also a "ship of fools" in which the viral presence both of *le mal* and of beauty—which, for him, is the *same* viral presence—seems condemned to remain clandestine.[2]

It is the emergence of that viral presence from its clandestinity, and the role of equivocation, not only in de Duve's characterization of that presence (as simultaneously "sida mon amour" and "sida mon calvaire," "AIDS my love" and "AIDS my Calvary"), but also and more particularly in the process of its emergence, that I want to trace in this chapter. The Columbus-like round trip of discovery and return maps a structure of indirection that is homologous with the mode of rhetorical indirection through which the traveler-become-messenger seeks, viruslike and following the example of Baudelaire, to infiltrate the defenses of his own version of the hypocritical reader, the hypothetical reader, who will be directly addressed (but can one directly address a reader who remains hypothetical?) only a few lines before the end of the text. That reader will be asked to make a choice, by naming the cargo ship on which the voyage has taken place: ship of fools or voyage of life? But this invitation to choose is in fact only the last of de Duve's many equivocations, since it pretends to attribute freedom to a reader who must *already* have made the desired choice, the title of the book the reader holds being *Cargo vie,* the Cargo Ship of Life. So the whole exercise—the equivocation whereby a round-trip voyage and an indirect mode of address do duty one for the other—has been designed to make sure that, by the time the reader reads the words in which the reader is addressed as hypothetical, that reader is no longer hypothetical but real—a reader who not only empirically *exists* but has also been rhetorically *reached* by the message of revelation. Thus the emergence of the viral messenger from clandestinity is matched by, and of a piece with, a symmetrical evolution in the reader, who emerges, as the narrative develops, from behind the defenses of placid, cowlike grazing in order to confirm at the end, that "our" ship, the ship of humanity, is, notwithstanding appearances, a ship of life, not a ship of fools—one to which the sidereal message (the message of the stars and the message of *le sida,* AIDS) is crucial, and indeed definitional.

I will not attempt in what follows to catalog the many ways in which de Duve's text can be described as equivocal. It equivocates generically (between logbook and the *pensées;* the literal voyage, the voyage of discovery, the mythic voyage to the edge, and the encounter with death; the discovery narrative and the ship of fools story). It equivocates thematically ("sida mon amour" and "sida mon calvaire"; the approach to death as an experience of the sacred, the sublime, the obscene; de Duve's fainting fits, the effects of encephalopathy, and his proclivity to awe and wonderment in the presence of the vastness of sea and starlit sky). Finally it equivocates rhetorically, in the relation of text to addressee, which is the form of equivocation I will mainly consider here, in looking into the significance of de Duve's punning text and the uses to which it puts the figure of apostrophe, which I will describe as an equivocation of address. But I will also relate this last practice—the rhetorical equivocation by which turning away *(apostrephein)* functions in a roundabout way as a mode of address—both to the thematic equivocation by which a round-trip voyage is made to link, in two directions, the sphere of the living and the sphere of the beyond (an approach to death; a return bearing a viral message), and to the generic equivocation by which autobiography shades into thanatography. My reader should bear in mind, also, that practices of equivocation exist along a continuum between an equivocation of copresence (in which both propositions—say, ship of fools and ship of life, or "sida mon amour" and "sida mon calvaire"—are mentioned) and an equivocation of suggestion, in which one proposition is implied by the other. So copresence equivocation, in fact, tends to shade into suggestion equivocation; equivocation itself equivocates. Equivocation by suggestion is what in English is called double entendre and in French *équivoque:* although the "suggested" element need not necessarily be sexual, it will normally be more of the order of the unmentionable or the obscene than is the "suggesting" (or suggestive) element, which cleaves to the order of the sayable. A dove harbors a pigeon as a swan may refer to a dodo and as, in Baudelaire, the beauty of poetic language may be the catachrestic vehicle for insinuating knowledge of *le mal.*

In Pascal de Duve's case, a copresence equivocation (of ship of fools and ship of life, or of literal voyage and mythic voyage) functions as part of a rhetorical apparatus designed to gain the attention of those placid, bovine readers who are confined to the ship of fools and in danger therefore of missing out on life's most significant experience. But one may think it serves also—that is, equivocally—as the suggestive vehicle of an equivocation by suggestion in which "sida mon amour"—AIDS as the life-enhancing experience of an approach to death—stands in for "sida mon calvaire" as the dove harbors the pigeon and poetic beauty the presence of evil. And if a hypothesis is etymologically an underlying proposition, we can say in that case that the "hypothetical" reader to whom de Duve appeals at the end (a substitute for Baudelaire's "hypocritical" reader) is one who is not only hypothesized by the writer, but also is (hypothesized as) capable of formulating hypotheses, that is, of detecting in the text its unformulated but underlying propositions. Such a reader will have been trained, so to speak, to read the text's *équivoque* by reading its equivocations. The "hypothesizing" reader hypothesized in this way by the text will thus be, as Baudelaire might say, *frère* and *semblable* to the equivocating and equivocal writer. As an allegory of its own rhetorical circumstances, *Cargo vie* is about Pascal de Duve's search for, and roundabout approach to, such a fraternal, and I will say loving, reader.

As the French sense of the word *équivoque* demonstrates, equivocation has had a bad reputation. In classical rhetoric it is recognized as the figure of amphibology (throwing both ways), but it appears always to have been treated with suspicion and regarded as a tricky practice bordering on deception, a device of sophistry. Yet equivocation is also the art of the diplomat, and it is an indispensable resource, especially to those on the weaker side of an argument, in circumstances where a delicate negotiation between remote and apparently incompatible positions has to be "finessed." In that respect, equivocation may be the only alternative to stand-off or differend. For one who, like Pascal de Duve, wishes to bear witness to an experience of extremity that is doubly disturbing to the bovine—because it is extreme, and because the extremity implies the obscene—and who, furthermore, wishes to do so without provocation or impertinence à la Eric Michaels, a double practice of equivocation recommends itself. An equivocation of copresence can reconcile AIDS as an exhilarating experience of the edge with the attachment to mental comfort, the complacency and ignorance that prevail on the ship of fools. But simultaneously, and especially for a suitably "hypothetical" reader, the dimension of pain and suffering, the ordeal that the exhilaration entails, can also be suggested by a second-order equivocation, or *équivoque.* De Duve's wager, in *Cargo vie,* is that certain readers, among those willing to be drawn out of their bovine somnolence by a promise of wonderment, will prove also to be "loving" readers, responsive to the equivocation of suggestion and able, therefore, to grasp and empathize with the pain out of which the book is written.

This is as much as to say that, where Eric Michaels challenges the reader he addresses and Wilfred Owen, in "Anthem for Doomed Youth," positions the reader as a kind of parent (see chapters 2 and 3 respectively), *Cargo vie* is not only a logbook and a collection of *pensées,* but also, and at its deepest generic level, a kind of love letter, addressed fraternally—like a message in a bottle—to whoever will prove able to respond to it, that is—in the strong sense of the term—to *read* it. The book is in many ways a meditation on the power of the letter. It refers to the power of letters—the letters of the alphabet—to dissolve and recompose themselves into puns that change the significance of things; and to the power therefore of the literal to signify other and more than it says. But it refers also to the power of epistolary texts, going beyond the literal in this way, to get at the *heart* of things, by revealing (without saying) what is in the writer's heart and touching the heart of a receiver. It would not be an exaggeration, therefore, to say that, if Pascal de Duve travels—becoming a second Columbus or a new Baudelaire, a *siderius nuntius* and the author of his own *pensées de Pascal* concerning the experience of the edge—it is in order to put between himself and an audience at home the distance that makes it possible to exert the power of the letter, and through that power to flush out of the apparently indifferent, self-complacent, ignorant, and inattentive audience the ideal reader to whom his logbook—"livre de bord, de corps et de coeur"—is addressed. The body leaves for the edge that the heart may return, not literally, but letterally. For apostrophe as a form of equivocation is all about leaving in order the better to return.

Apostrophe

In Greek, there are two forms of the verb to turn: *trepein,* from which we have inherited the word *trope,* and *strephein,* from which comes *apostrophe.* Apostrophe is the trope that consists of turning away; but the turning away that is apostrophe is a turn or trope of speech, a message that seems always addressed *to* someone while being directed *at* someone else. More technically, it equivocates between statement and utterance, since the addressee named—as it were in the vocative case—in the statement is other than the actual receiver addressed by the utterance. Conflating the "I" of the statement with the subject of the utterance, the recipient of the message is led to wonder what it means that the speaker is addressing the audience by turning away from it: that is, to read.

The first set of apostrophes to examine in *Cargo vie* is the series that predominates at the start, addressed (in the statement) to Pascal's lover, who abandoned him, "suivant le principe de la méthode *couard*" (a play on cowardice and *la méthode Coué,* self-delusionary optimism), at the onset of his illness. Since E. is himself seropositive, his inability to deal with AIDS in any shape or form, including his lover's illness, is a striking exemplification of what I would describe as cultural unwillingness or inability to take cognizance of the obscene. In rejecting his lover Pascal as a PWA, E. is denying the AIDS that circulates already, in viral form, in his own body; and in this respect he is like the passengers on the ship who cannot imagine that their banana boat is a *cargo mixte* in more senses than one, transporting AIDS along with the rest of its cargo. E. thus makes seropositivity itself into a figure for the relation of a social formation to the category of the obscene; he stands in for, let's say, France in the era of what was called *dédramatisation,* a metaphorically seropositive country that knew it was seropositive, in the sense that it harbored AIDS, but "played down" that knowledge, hoping "selon le principe de la méthode *couard*/Coué" that it would *go away.* "Tu faisais toujours," Pascal says to E., "comme si le sida n'existait pas. Le sujet était tabou" [You always acted as if AIDS didn't exist. The topic was taboo] (49). Pascal's apostrophes to E., then, are something like zero-degree apostrophes, since the split they imply (E. is other than the text's readership) scarcely conceals—indeed it makes more easily recognizable—an also implied relation of metaphorical identity.

These apostrophes, accordingly, enact Pascal's turning away from E., who has turned away from him. They enable the speaker simultaneously to indicate that he is similarly turning away from a society that practices the "méthode *couard*" as E. does and, via the address to E., to direct a message—a message of rejection—that embraces the whole society of denial and occultation for which E. stands:

> E., I'm taking away with me your letters, all your letters; the photos too, overflowing as they are with a life that is now deceased. Their funeral bier is a cardboard shoe box [which Pascal plans to drop overboard one night, burying E.'s letters, and E. with them, at sea] . . . and I'll go through this ritual sea-burial [*enmèrement*] so that the past will rejoin the past, bobbing for a brief moment on the foam before it sinks forever. (35–36; see also 107)

"Je procéderai à cet *enmèrement* rituel . . ." These "letters" will be buried at sea/in the mother, only to dissolve and be reconstituted, as a kind of pun on themselves, in the love letter that is Pascal's diary. But the spelling of "enmèrement" (as opposed to *enmerment* as a pun on *enterrement*) also tends to obscure or euphemize, with an allusion to motherhood, the nevertheless easily readable *équivoque* or double entendre whereby *enmerment* suggests *emmerdement.* Pascal is saying, not only "E., je t'enterre" [E., I'm burying you], but also "E., je t'emmerde" [E., I shit on you]. (And concomitantly: France, I reject you.)

That said, however, the memories that linger of the one-year relation with E. visibly serve as a first model for the relation to AIDS that now replaces those supposedly rejected memories, a relation that is also enacted—"sida mon amour"—through apostrophe. "E., do you recall those long nights of mad lovemaking, which reached an apotheosis [as] Mozart's Requiem hallowed us, saluting in us two worn-out heroes glorifying life?

Those were magical dawns when I addressed you as 'Vous.'" (25) Love on the rebound takes the same form—Eros or Life sanctified by Thanatos—as the love affair that was, in retrospect, only a first approximation, an anticipation of the new splendor Pascal now celebrates. And as the dynamics of apostrophe requires, de Duve can turn away from E. and enact his rejection, but only by turning toward one who is preferred, but also stands in for, the figure whose rejection is now being signified, the (statement-)address to AIDS being readable as an (utterance-)message of rejection to E., and beyond E. to the society that denies its own seropositivity. In this case, though, the preferred figure, boldly and scandalously, is the virus and the syndrome it causes (de Duve understandably identifies them, given his directly virus-caused encephalopathy) that *ought* to be the object, not of veneration, but of loathing. The writer personifies both through apostrophe, writing *VIH* or *sida* (without articles) as the grammar of the vocative requires: "Cher, très cher VIH, voilà encore que tu m'enfièvres, comme seul toi peux le faire" [Dear, beloved HIV, there you go setting me on fire (with fever), as only you can do] (41), or "Sida mon amour. Toi au moins, tu me resteras fidèle jusqu'à la mort" [AIDS my love, you at least will remain faithful to me unto death] (84). And thus a whole series of apostrophes like these—mainly introduced by an insistently returning refrain of "sida mon amour"—reiterate the status of this turning toward AIDS, through various forms of insinuation, as an explicit counterpart to the turning away from E., with whom the syndrome is always favorably compared. For example:

> AIDS my Calvary, AIDS my love, with you I have a personal relationship I don't plan to run away from. (84)

> AIDS my beloved, I love you. I worship you as much as I loathe you [Je t'adore autant que je t'abhorre]. (104)

The question, then, for de Duve, is not whether the beloved to whom he turns, in preference to E., is loathsome or an object of veneration: the implication of his equivocation (i.e., it doesn't matter whether I adore or abhor; *adorer* and *abhorrer,* in their pronunciation, are separated only by one phoneme) is that the difference is an insignificant one, by comparison with the disgust he feels for E., and for the society he is simultaneously shunning. Readers of these provocative apostrophes must therefore ask themselves either what intensity of experience justifies the turning away that is being enacted (and of which they too are an object), or what profound disgust, with respect to those who are being rejected, motivates it, or both. And, as a result, any complacency on the reader's part will have been disturbed, perhaps even dispelled, in favor of an active engagement with the text and what it means, a reading.

Not coincidentally, furthermore, turning toward HIV/AIDS also means turning toward people with AIDS, as another part of the message of rejection directed at those who, like E., cannot live with the disease and try to ignore the obscene. Conscious of the scandalousness of his preference, de Duve finally offers a justification of his obsessive refrain of "sida mon amour." The passage opens as if intended for all who might be shocked: "Sida my love, how dare I write this impassioned cry?" (96). But it quickly turns out to be itself an apostrophe, the statement of which is addressed more specifically to de Duve's fellow *sidéens,* as if the risk of alienating *them* were his only concern. It is their attention he wished to draw to the heightened consciousness, the feeling of wonderment the disease can confer on those willing to face it:

> Open your eyes and wonder at the great things and especially the small, all the things that those . . . for whom Death is distant and abstract cannot truly enjoy as we can. AIDSers of the world, let us be intoxicated by this privilege, the better to combat our sufferings, which I have absolutely no wish to minimize.

The dynamics of address are very legible here. The statement celebrates a kind of privilege conferred by AIDS on those for whom Death is not distant and abstract; it is the utterance that redirects the message concerning this privilege to all the text's readers, a category that certainly includes many for whom Death is distant and abstract, many of those who are described elsewhere (31) as throwing out the diamond with the bathwater and who are in danger of dying without having lived.

For de Duve is justifying one provocative apostrophe by repeating its dynamics in another, turning here not to "sida mon amour," however, but to his "brothers and sisters in misfortune," and addressing them in language reminiscent of Marx ("Workers of the world . . .") and Baudelaire (the author of a celebrated poem in praise of intoxication, "Enivrez-vous!"), as if they alone, the class of people privileged by the access to wonderment afforded them by their illness, were also those alone likely to be shocked by a loving address to AIDS. Again an audience is being produced as the recipient of an implied message of rejection, but this audience is addressed as if its members were incapable, unwilling, or unworthy to receive the message intended for PWAs, their assumed imperviousness to shock being taken as an indicator of their inability to attain a state of wonderment, and vice versa. This rejected audience, in the terms of another of de Duve's puns (see 92), is thus the mass of those who act, like E., as if they were non-*sidérables* (not subject to astonishment/acquiring AIDS) and who are not so much incapable of becoming *sidérés,* therefore—that is, struck with amazement at the beauty of life through consciousness of the proximity of death—as they are incapable, through the force of their denial, of even becoming aware of that potential. These are figured by the passengers on the ship of fools who sprawl asleep in front of the ship's VCR (38) while one of their number prowls the decks alone, struck with wonderment at the vastness of the sea and the night sky, or who, contemplating the ship's rust over predinner drinks, fail to perceive the significance this manifestation of entropy might have for them: "Our vessel is infested almost all over with rust as by a parasite, notably on the stern upper deck, where it draws brownish extraterrestrial continents on a green background. This rust is the ship's living memory. No other is affected by it in the exact same way" (33). These extraterrestrial continents, this living memory, are not for all; the marker of the ship's living individuality is invisible to all who cannot recognize in it their own conditions of existence. Conversely, those who can—if such there be—are potentially *sidérables.*

Readers of the text, then, as the actual recipients of de Duve's (utterance-)apostrophes, have an advantage in this respect over the ship's passengers and the impervious masses they figure. Unlike them, a reader is in a position to connect this passage about rust with Pascal de Duve's understanding of AIDS the beloved, as both that which opens vast "extraterrestrial continents" of experience and that which defines a living identity even as it destroys the sufferer.

> If I love my AIDS, it is not solely because it causes me to live more intensely than ever: I love it too because it is *unique.* It is, in a certain fashion and if I dare say so, my "own." No two AIDS cases are identical. Its forms are infinitely rich. In this, my AIDS "overdetermines" me, it offers me an extra dimension of uniqueness. It is something like the pathological counterpart [*revers*] of my unique being. (70)

One of the few meditations on AIDS in the volume that is not couched as an apostrophe, and whose address to the reader is in that sense direct and undisguised, this passage signifies clearly that the syndrome is not only, like love, a state of grace—"a species of grace that, for those who attempt to face up to things, sharpens the lived experience of wonderment until it becomes quasi-permanent" (44)—but also, because of the unique way it identifies living with dying, like rust eating a ship, a factor of identity: "Il m'est . . . 'propre.'" (70) And it is as encounter with death and factor of identity that AIDS can be the making of a writer. That is what it means to be *sidéré*—a word that literally means to be struck by a heavenly body, metaphorically means struck with wonderment or awe (thunderstruck), and punningly means overcome by *le sida,* AIDS. "Having been *sidérable* a long time, and now being completely *sidéré,*" de Duve writes, "I am not terrorized by AIDS, the thing that is the cause of my writing, of my writing precisely this" (92). And "this" can be taken to refer either to *Cargo vie* as a whole, or to the puns in the sentence just quoted, or to both. But to be *sidéré,* and thus a writer, a writer of "this"—the deictic implies an address—is therefore to address a reader conceived, unlike the ship's passengers, as potentially *sidérable,* a possible (hypothetical) brother or even lover for the writer in the uniqueness the state of being *sidéré* confers on him.

It is finally as a writer, then, that de Duve, the *sidéen,* functions as a stowaway on the ship of fools, its unnoticed and unacknowledged parasite or "secret dwarf" (38); but as a writer, too, that he is both a lover of AIDS and in search of a reader. For E. did not cause him to write, except for love letters that are now dismissed as so many "dérapages désacralisants" [sloppy errors that destroy the sacredness] (18), and which more importantly never brought forth a reply, indeed were never so much as acknowledged by their recipient. AIDS, though, is the occasion for another kind of letter, both a love letter ("lettre d'amour") to AIDS and a bitterness letter ("lettre d'amertume") to E., that is a "lettre d'amourtume" (24). The brilliant portmanteau word both captures the dynamics of apostrophe—love in one direction, bitterness in the other—and fuses it into a condensed stammer, as if writing itself had been struck by lightning. "Ein Witz ist ein Blitz," according to Dan Mellamphy, is an axiom of Friedrich Schlegel's: wit is a lightning strike.[3] To the extent that Pascal's "lettre d'amourtume" coincides with the text of *Cargo vie* itself, the phrase suggests that writing is the place—a place struck by lightning, *sidéré*—where the trope of apostrophe might become reversible and twist back on itself; and it asks whether the writing of *amourtume* can achieve, from its reader, an acknowledgment or response—tantamount to recognition of the obscenity that is AIDS—of a kind that love letters to E. failed to elicit from their own recipient. Can Pascal's voyage and the writing that is its counterpart have the roundabout power of transforming readers like E. into readers worthy of the traveler's/writer's love? Readers capable, themselves, of being "smitten"?[4]

For writing, we learn finally, is not a solipsistic activity, although it may, and in the case of de Duve's journal-writing on board ship it does, occur secretly. One writes as a matter of self-definition, to be sure, but also, de Duve says, to reveal oneself to others:

> "*To write is to be no one,*" writes Marguerite Duras (alias no one therefore). Obviously I don't agree. In writing, one reveals oneself, to oneself and to others. (32)

Who then, it becomes necessary to ask, are these others to whom the writer, an unrecognized figure on the ship of fools, turned passionately toward AIDS in his apostrophic turning away from the fools, nevertheless wishes to reveal himself? The readers of the text, who are also the readers of his apostrophes, are not necessarily identical, it seems, with those who are rejected as hopelessly incapable of recognizing their own *sidérabilité;* and apostrophe equivocates, therefore, not only in respect of addressees but also in respect of those who are rejected. If Pascal's declarations of love for HIV signify rejection of E. and of those on the ship of fools who are like E. in their denial of life's extremities, those declarations (which at first seemed attributable to the dynamics of rebound) might now be able, Columbus-like, to turn back on themselves, and return as a message of love directed toward a human, not viral, audience capable of being receptive to it? In whichever direction the message turns, something "returns" in it as the possibility of its being, hypothetically, read. Thus, in the final apostrophe to de Duve's "Dear, and above all extremely hypothetical reader" (116), it is easy to catch an echo of the earlier address to AIDS as "Dear, beloved HIV . . ." (41), such that "très hypothétique" reads as if it were a synonym for "beloved" [très cher]. But in the address to AIDS we already perceived reminiscences of the apostrophes to E., memory-laden rejections that they were; and these in turn return, therefore, in the final address to the hypothetical/beloved reader. If writing's turn back to the reader *repeats* in this way—with a twist—its initial turn away from E., it does so on the supposition, then, that something has been transformed as a result of the voyage: something in the writing first of all, but correspondingly—and by virtue of the power of that transformed writing—something in the reader who is both still equatable with E. and no longer like him.

What "returns" in the writing is, of course, the impact of limit experience, the loving encounter with AIDS that de Duve portrays as sideration, a species of grace, a revelation of selfhood, an affair of the heart, and a voyage to the edge. We need to pause, therefore, at this point, to consider a little more closely de Duve's understanding of writing in relation, not yet to its reader, but to its primary apostrophic addressee, "sida mon amour." By virtue of a new equivocation, writing is described as having the double sense that the phrase "the writing of AIDS" captures, since the ambiguous genitive means both (subjectively) that it is AIDS doing the writing and (objectively) that the writing is about AIDS but done by a human agent, a writer. It is because of that double sense that AIDS writing—the phrase is another equivocation—can become the turning point and the point of return, the "lettre d'amourtume," where the trope of apostrophe is able to twist back from the edge and return to its reader, but charged with a new import, loaded with new cargo. One name for that new charge is HIV, as if the title *Cargo vie* entailed a bilingual pun and had "cargo VIH" as its underlying proposition.[5] But the other name that de Duve gives it is death: death is AIDS writing's viral load. In every sense, the "smitten" writing of the "smitten" AIDSer, a *sidéré,* seeks out a reader who is both "smiteable" *(sidérable)* and able to recognize, through Pascal's experience and his *pensées,* that reader's own "smiteability" *(sidérabilité).*

Writing

"Writing," de Duve writes, "is sovereign, splendid, and mysterious; its opposite is *écrivanité*" (52). The pun (on *écrivain,* writer, and *vanité,* vanity) is glossed as follows:

> Those who write should be more mindful of the ultimate blank page that ends their books. It symbolizes everything that falls short, everything that goes too far, everything that is sloppy. (52)

The apparent perfection of certain writing merely masks its emptiness, whereas genuine writing, conscious of its imperfection, is writing whose writer is aware of its relation to death, the ultimate blank page. "Sus aux *écrivaniteux,*" then, "je préfère être qualifié d'écrivant" [Down with vanity writers, I prefer to be designated a writing agent] (52).[6] As opposed to those who are at best "écri*vains*," the writing agent or *écrivant* is the writer courted by Death and working with Death in close collaboration. For Death is an artist, and to René Char's observation that "with Death we have only one recourse, to make art first," de Duve responds, picking up on Char's probably unintended and unconscious ambiguity (or equivocation?):

> Death is already making art in me—is my AIDS anything other than its work in progress? It's not up to me any more to make art before Death does. It's up to me to make art *at the same time* as Death—and to do so by exploiting Death, without emotional complications [*états d'âme*] or shamefacedness [*vergogne*] of any kind—the price to pay is already high enough. (87)

But if Death is an artist, then so too is the writer. De Duve understands himself, not just as Death's amanuensis, as the word *écrivant* might suggest, but as having an autonomous identity and exercising an agency that is capable, as he says, of "exploiting" Death's work, even as that work is pursued in his body and reveals that very identity, in the way that rust and AIDS do. What makes writing sovereign, splendid, and mysterious, then, is finally an act of collaboration—indeed a manifestation of couplehood—that in turn depends on an ability on the writer's part to acknowledge the work of Death in his person, and to incorporate it into his writing.

Two successive short entries—readable, unlike most of de Duve's *pensées,* as forming a logical sequence—draw the connections between love of AIDS (and the superiority of such love over the affair with E.), and the collaboration with Death (in the form of AIDS) that is writing:

> For as long, at least, as this narrative continues, I am carrying out, double mouthful by double mouthful, a hunger strike [*grève de la fin,* an end strike]. Tiny little beasties, lined up by the millions, you occupy my brain and take care of it. But with what a blaze [*avec quelle flamboyance*].
>
> HIV, you're pretty much the one doing the writing here. (13)

HIV, that is, takes care of the writer's brain (*l'occupe,* keeps it occupied, and *s'en occupe*), as E. refused to do. In doing so, it is the occasion for a hunger strike on de Duve's part, an act of personal will that is simultaneously what Samuel Beckett might have called an endgame: it is an end strike. De Duve participates enthusiastically, then, in his own dying, taking double mouthfuls or gobbling it down (as the expression "mettre les bouchées doubles" implies), even hurrying it along. For, "to put it *simply,*" he writes elsewhere, "I'm getting my gray matter gobbled [by HIV]" [je me fais bouffer le gris du cerveau] (27; emphasis added). Better to eat doubly (in a final hunger strike) than to get eaten, simply, by the virus.[7] In the first instance, striking provides a form of sustenance and can be participated in greedily, "à bouchées doubles"; in the second, one just disappears. Notice that the apostrophe *to* HIV, here, actually enacts this collaboration *with* HIV. It does not only address the virus as a way of turning away from E. and those like him; the act of apostrophizing itself, that is, its utterance, brings the apostrophizing subject onto the stage and thus distributes the function of writing between the two agents, one of whom is the addressee of the statement (HIV, you are doing the writing)—but with a significant restriction ("c'est *un peu* toi qui écris")—while the other is the subject of the utterance, whose participation is no less actual and indispensable for being tacit. "Un peu" is concessive ("you're pretty much the one doing the writing") but also distributive (as in "you are doing a little of the writing," and I the rest). Like the apostrophe itself, it is the vehicle of an act of equivocation, then, that accords Death responsibility for the work in progress, its "oeuvre en création" (87), while reserving a portion of agency to the human actor, the *écrivant* whose agency is also contributing a mite to the common task.

This sentence thus begins to make equivocation look like both the mode through which Death's presence in the text is enacted and the marker of an artistic collaboration between Death, in the (equivocal) guise of HIV/AIDS, and the author as writing agent or *écrivant,* the agencer of Death. The pun on *grève de la faim* that opens the paragraph "here"— "VIH, c'est un peu toi qui écris *ici*"—is like the pun on *sida, sidérable,* and *sidéré,* then, that leads in another place to an acknowledgment that AIDS is "the thing that causes *me* to write, to write precisely *this*" (87; emphasis added). The pun's presence is not accidental; rather it is the very sign that "it is up to me to make art *at the same time* as Death." And we can say, therefore, that punning (and more broadly paronomasia) invades de Duve's text in the way that rust parasites a ship—drawing brownish images of "extraterrestrial continents" (33), simultaneously new worlds and starry messages—and in the way that HIV's teeming millions of "tiny beasties" occupy his brain, preoccupy it, and "take care" of it; but also with a different sense. If puns and wordplay mark the text as the site of the writing of AIDS, in the sense of the writing of AIDS that AIDS performs, they signify also that de Duve has discovered a writing of AIDS—that is, a way of writing (about) AIDS—that is uniquely and identifiably his own, "proper" to him.

They are the marker, that is, of viral writing, an *écriture parasitée,* traversed by the static of happenstance that makes words accidentally resemble one another, as for example *virus* and *survie,* survival, do (51), or in Latin *credere,* to believe and *cor-dare,* to give of one's heart (10), or again *la mort,* death, *l'amour,* love, *l'amer,* that which is bitter, and *la mer,* the sea (33 and passim). What information theory understands as so much noise in the channel of communication, something that is normally backgrounded in favor of the unequivocal transmission of meanings, here becomes foregrounded, as the indicator of Death's presence (the inevitable blank page), and as the sign, therefore, that "this" is not *écrivanité* but the work of an *écrivant,* collaborating with Death precisely so as to interrupt, through equivocation—the scrambling of significance—the placid transmissions of sense that exclude acknowledgment of Death's presence in life. Punning, then, is what happens when "letters" are thrown into the sea of Baudelairean freedom *(la mer, l'amer, l'amour, la mort)* in a form of *enmerment* that mixes and recombines them into new, and inspiriting significance. But puns and wordplay do not imply a Mallarméan "illocutionary disappearance of the poet," or the writer's becoming no one à la Duras. For the *écrivant,* as Death's collaborator, is taking double mouthfuls as a way of end-striking, and as an alternative to the "simple" fate of allowing himself to be gobbled, passively, by Death. This double-mouthing (punning, equivocation) entails active authorial agency in the collaboration with Death. Thus, throughout his text, de Duve makes himself responsible, in a way that challenges the Mallarmé-Duras tradition of *écriture,* for *taking* the puns furnished by the randomness of language (by Death) and "exploiting" them *coolly* ("sans états d'âme ni vergogne"): that is, for setting them in a verbal environment that makes them signify, and indeed goes far toward specifying what they signify. In this way he ensures that his collaboration with the viral infection that overtakes language reveals a voice that is his own, conferring on him a personal identity that can be revealed to others. But also, and to take the argument further, if he opens himself up to Death in this way and becomes the site where Death pursues its "oeuvre en création," it is so that his writerly voice can function as the indispensable vector or vehicle, the crucial agent of an agencing through which the work of Death that is the punning, equivocal text can be made available to others, along with the revelation of his identity. That is, his writing transforms Death's work-in-progress (de Duve's AIDS) into a message—a message in which Death has been disocculted and become readable, if only its readers are willing, in turn, to open themselves to its infection, to acknowledge themselves as *sidérables.* The form of equivocation that is his partnership with Death becomes the equivocal and equivocating text, a "noisy" message studded (French *étoilé*) with puns and having the potential to disturb the placid world of the (unequivocally) bovine by discovering within it bearers of *sidérabilité,* readers.

With this turn of the writer, not away from but toward his audience, apostrophe, one might say, has—rather circuitously—come full circle. The address *to* AIDS has merged into a collaborative writing, *with* AIDS (a merger enacted in the key apostrophe: "VIH, c'est un peu toi écris ici"), and in that form is now directed *back,* toward the living, as an agencing through which, in virally infected language, Death speaks—the pigeon readable in the dove. The Baudelairean hypocritical reader has become de Duve's hypothetical reader, hypothesized, that is, as capable, in turn, of hypothesis—of entertaining the supposition, the underlying proposition, that broaches the cultural immune system and opens the possibility of the reader's sharing with the writer, as his "frère" and "semblable," the condition of *émerveillement:* amazement, wonderment, awe, sideration. Call it HIV, or Death; the sublime or the sacred; the infinite; it is the conversion of the reader to sideration—a metaphorical seroconversion—that counts, for de Duve, as more important than the actual object of wonderment. But the condition of that reader's conversion from hypocritical to hypothetical is necessarily a certain disoccultation of the self, through writing, on the part of the author, since it is exactly that occultation, or his acquiescence in that occultation, that produces the ship of fools where hypocrisy reigns and prevents it from becoming a ship of life. The writer, in other words, must step out of the ship-of-fools role of "secret dwarf" in order to reveal himself to others, and do so not just as a member of a generic category, the *sidéen* (which he knows would provoke a fright and panic on board [34]), but as the absolutely unique figure that AIDS has made of him: AIDS's lover, Death's collaborator and messenger, the bearer of an extraordinary privilege as well as the subject of a painful ordeal. A figure, that is, who can be loved, but who, in order to do so, must reveal himself to an also unique reader capable of loving.

Such a disoccultation, on the writer's part, will entail his abandonment also, now that they have done their work, of practices of indirection and equivocation. As a reader, initially standing with the grazing cows, I have found myself both rejected and addressed by de Duve's apostrophes, and consequently intrigued. My attention has been caught, a *captatio* has occurred. Why is this speaker so ostentatiously and indeed scandalously turning away from me? And turning toward an obscene object, AIDS or death? Now he is actually collaborating with the obscene, making striking puns, producing a form of viral writing, of noisy language that is directed back toward me even as it bespeaks the very "hypothesis" I did not wish to entertain. And I am discovering, as a consequence of this indexical practice, that the obscenity was always within me, as a potential for wonderment, like rust in a ship or virus in the bloodstream or accidents of language, disregarded and unacknowledged. The time is thus ripe for the writer's practice of apostrophe to reveal itself for what it has always been, less a turning away than a visitation in disguise—an unwonted incursion into the peaceful meadow from which I had, in fact, never successfully banished it.

If prosopopoeia is the name for that form of mask-making (of indexing) which is necessary for a "voicing" of Death to occur in the language of the living, and for the obscene to achieve social recognition, then apostrophe as it has been practiced here is a form of prosopopoeia. It has taken the form of an elaborate feint (the move in war or in combat sports whereby one pretends to retreat, or to look in another direction, the better to return in force); in that respect, it demonstrates the degree to which agencing can be a matter of calculated maneuver. But now it is time for the agencer to unmask himself, leaving us with the mask itself—his writing as equivocal act of agencing—as the readable sign of the ultimately unstatable object to the edge of which his round-trip voyage brought him.

Return

The ostensible reason why de Duve keeps his condition a secret on board his ship is that cargo vessels do not accept seriously ill passengers because there is normally no physician available to treat them. He manages to protect his position as *passager clandestin,* or stowaway, in spite of the fevers he is subject to and the severe fits in the course of which the world is drained of color before he loses consciousness—counterparts to the raptures of wonderment that the approach of death inspires. The ignorant and homophobic conversations to which, as a result, he is privy, the "hateful and cynical pronouncements" (85) he hears, do not encourage him to confide in his fellow passengers. But on two occasions in the course of the voyage he does make a self-revelatory move, and these two episodes function therefore as embedded versions, or anticipations—technically *mises en abyme*—of what will eventually be the relation of the text's viral writing to its hypothetical reader(s). These episodes of disclosure are complementary in that in the first Pascal declares his status as PWA to a fellow passenger, while in the next he transfers his love relation with HIV back toward a fellow human being (who happens to be a crew member on the ship of fools).

In the first episode, a passenger named Nicole receives a letter that she is specifically instructed not to read until she is off the ship, on her way to Venezuela. She has demonstrated her worthiness to receive Pascal's revelation—the letter is in some respects a condensed version of the diary itself, from which it quotes—by showing interest in and empathy with him as well as concern about his health. She "takes care" of him, as E. didn't and as the others don't, most notably on the occasion of a terrifying descent into the engine room in the course of which Pascal comes close to fainting in public: this descent into the ship's underworld, ironically known as "Paradise," allegorizes the voyage itself as an exploration of the edge. Nicole's support of the sufferer thus earns her his confidence. "I can tell you now," he writes (57), "that I am the bearer of a heavy secret, which I will reveal to you because you are worthy of it." She has passed a qualifying test for the position of reader, been selected from among the fools as "worthy" *(digne).* But clandestinity is preserved by the double envelope in which the letter is placed, and the instruction: OPEN ONLY ON THE PLANE (61). Nevertheless, at lunch that same day the passengers joke about Pascal's peeling sunburn: he is changing skin like a snake, and revealing a new face to the world. "It is true: my blistered face is preparing to change its skin. What they don't see is that my heart is peeling too" (63).

The moment for his heart to reveal itself, after his face, comes—still in an ambiance of some clandestinity, however—on the morning of the ship's arrival in Le Havre, at the end of its return journey. This, we know, is both a return to the point of departure and a "return" in the sense that something previously unacknowledged, if not repressed, the underlying hypothesis the text's hypothetical reader will be asked to take cognizance of, is ready to emerge. The visitation Pascal now performs enacts this dual return. Soon after leaving Le Havre on the voyage out, he had had an erotic dream starring the ship's radio operator, "a young lad with very short black hair and eyes as blue as the sea at its bluest" (21). Now, on the last day, he repeats, by visiting Sparks's office, the visitation his unconscious had earlier "permitted itself" (21) under cover of sleep: "I paid a short visit to the radio operator, at once to make his acquaintance and to bid him farewell"

(115). As the leave-taking that is apostrophe implies a return, so the return itself signifies a leave-taking. But *this* leave-taking does not function, like apostrophe, as a turning away or a rejection; rather, a bit flirtatiously, it is a getting-to-know-you at the same time as it is a farewell, and an emergence from secrecy, a self-unmasking that models *Cargo vie*'s own address, as a leave-taking, to its hypothesized reader, and describes it as revelatory.

Between the two protagonists of this lived "erotic dream" (21), there is an immediate and spontaneous complicity, in which Pascal rejoices. "We moved spontaneously, the better to enrapture me, from the ceremonious 'vous' to the more complicitous 'tu'" (116, one recalls what was said of E., and of the "magical dawns in which I addressed you as 'Vous'"). The spontaneous complicity recalls the friendship with Nicole, but friendship here has also undergone an erotic reconfiguration, so that it recalls also, with reversed signification, the figure of E. But because the self-revelation—again as in the case of Nicole—remains under the sign of leave-taking, no sexual joining will occur. This visit is a message of reconciliation that takes the form of departure and death, and its vehicle, therefore, is not sexual congress but writing and reading. "Without his suspecting in the slightest that I was about to skip out on him, he went into the next room for a moment. Before slipping away, I left him a brief note in Morse code on his desk" (116). The vocabulary recalls E.'s unceremonious dropping of Pascal, but Pascal's "slipping away," in which he substitutes a text for his person, is also an unmistakable anticipation of de Duve's imminent death, an event that can go unnoticed because it is the textual message, about life, that matters. But the message about life is also a "billet," a love letter, addressed to a new lover, other than E. and other than AIDS, in terms that partly resemble those of Pascal's enthusiastic apostrophes to AIDS, but also encourage the lover to live life (*not* to throw out the diamond with the bathwater, *not* to die without having lived). "YOU KNOW, THROUGHOUT OUR VOYAGE TOGETHER, I HAVE GREATLY LOVED YOU BECAUSE YOU HAVE CAUSED ME STRONG EMOTIONS. MAY GOOD WINDS SPEED YOU IN LIFE" (116; of course all the second-person pronouns are in the *tu* form).

This double language, repeating the praise addressed to AIDS throughout the diary but "returning" the apostrophe as an address to the living, makes the Morse message another embedded model or *mise en abyme* of *Cargo vie.* But, as the letter to Nicole was protectively enclosed in a double envelope, the message to the radio operator remains coded, albeit in a form (that of Morse) that is not very hard to break: again, a process of selection is occurring. Both of these messages occur on board the ship, where secrecy is the rule for Pascal and clandestinity is required, given the inescapable presence of "fools," even when he is personally opening up to others. When de Duve finally turns to his hypothetical reader, however, as he will in the paragraph immediately following the account of his visit to the radio operator, he continues to employ precautions, signifying clearly that it is still a matter of discovering an appropriately complicitous, caring reader among the mass of bovines. Thus, the reader is addressed in apostrophe form (suggesting that the recipient of the utterance may differ from the addressee of the statement), and de Duve sets the reader a kind of qualifying riddle or enigma. At the same time, however, and because this is the key moment of self-unmasking, he departs very largely from his cautious practices in the direction of openness and immediacy, hinting very broadly at the riddle's correct answer so as to ensure that the reader will answer it right. For *this* reader, as I pointed out earlier, is assumed to have already passed the qualifying test imposed by the rhetorical roundaboutness and double-mouthing of the diary—its out-and-back voyaging, its apostrophes and other equivocations—and to have arrived at its last page as now, *the* reader, Mr. (or Ms.) Right. This last test, therefore, is pro forma:

> Beloved, above all extremely hypothetical reader (what will become of these pages? . . .), please choose the name of my cargo ship, which is now more or less yours. But I would be so happy for you to call it LIFE. (116)

Yet equivocation remains. The longish parenthesis I have elided in the above quotation is filled with dickering on de Duve's part over whether to publish the diary and make it available to others, or whether to keep it as a purely personal record, that is, whether to respect the conventions of the diary as *journal intime,* or to adapt it into a text of witness, which of course assumes a more or less public readership: "what will become of these pages? Shall I reveal them as a book [*les livrerai-je*] one day to someone other than myself, I who will really need them to remember, and to draw from them the strength to continue the fight?" It is as if de Duve remains uncertain, even at the moment when he writes his envoi to the reader—whose existence thus remains hypothetical, in the sense of dubious, to the last—whether the "ship" he is on—the world—is exclusively a ship of fools in which his writing is condemned to remain secret, and of purely personal value to himself alone, or whether, as his experience with Nicole and the radio operator has suggested, the ship of fools *also* contains readers on whom he can count: readers who are on the same ship—as one says "on the same wavelength"—as he is. That is why the telltale marker of equivocation, "un peu" (which this time I have translated "more or less"), recurs when the reader is invited to name the ship: "mon cargo, qui est maintenant un peu le tien." The echo of "VIH, c'est un peu toi qui écris ici" [HIV, you're pretty much the one doing the writing here] (13) is unmistakable. As de Duve protected his identity as a writer even in collaboration with Death's "oeuvre en création," he here protects his identity in the very act of complicity the text's relation to its reader presupposes, leaving it slightly open whether or not the reader *is* "on the same ship" as he.

As readers, then, dear reader (I am addressing those who hold de Duve's book in their hands and those who are reading my essay), we still have some choices to make and some questions to ponder, even though the choice of the ship's name *has* in fact been made and the decision to publish taken. These gestures, on de Duve's part, imply his confidence in us. But are we equal to it? Is it possible to be, or to become, the reader de Duve desires? Or does his apostrophic address, in this case, imply that the true addressee—the ideal reader of its utterance—is always another? De Duve's confidence in us, I think, is not so much misplaced, although it most probably is also that, as intended to sow in the actual, empirical reader seeds of doubt, uncertainty, and anxiety. Anxiety, that is, concerning the reader's capacity to respond as required; to match the extraordinary vision of life that the text proposes—that is, to respond with the love de Duve demands. The point, though, is that such anxiety is itself, not only most probably the best we can muster in the way of a response, but also itself already preferable to the placid grazing of complacent human cattle. If we are to be the "hypothetical" readers the text appears to envision, perhaps the deepest meaning of that adjective is finally that we should be prepared to abandon certainty, an uncertain, exploratory, consciously tentative and hypothetical reading being, in the end, the very sign of love the text actually calls for; or at least a response that is neither placid nor hypocritical.

For, equivocal to the last, the text itself does little to encourage any certainty as to the actual nature or reality—the authenticity, if you will—of the object of de Duve's visionary enthusiasms, which should logically be the object of any complicitous or loving reading of the text. In one of the longest passages in the volume (a little more than a page in length), de Duve condemns Jean-Paul Sartre as a *believer:* he "*believed* in the non-existence of God *in the same way* as his adversaries (for example the Christian existentialist Gabriel Marceau) *believed* in His existence" (40). Against Sartre, or Marceau, and relying on Kant, de Duve favors "intellectual humility" on the subject of the sacred, and describes himself, somewhat oxymoronically, as "resolutely agnostic—an 'abstentionist purveyor of wonderment [*émerveilliste abstentionnel*]'" (40). Resolute agnosticism and abstentionist *émerveillisme* lead, not surprisingly, to a somewhat equivocal conclusion: "That way, I can at least be certain of not making an error, while keeping my Mystery." On the question of whether there is, or is not, in reality a sublime point, defined somewhat as in surrealism as the point where the opposites (in this case living and dying) coalesce, de Duve offers no guarantees whatsoever. Instead, he gives us *edge* discourse, a "livre de bord" in the form of a discourse of extremity. Such discourse, visionary as it indubitably is, is also "abstentionist": it takes away what it gives in the same moment as it gives it, because the issue of the object of vision is not, for de Duve, the real question raised by a language of wonderment.

That question is rather the question of extremity, and of limit experience, of whose existence there can be no doubt. Vision is like the enlarged eyes that de Duve sees when he looks in the mirror: "My face is often bloodless, precadaverous, and always emaciated and bony, . . . contrasting with my huge, staring eyes, wide open on a World that, as I prepare to disappear, leaves me more and more wonderstruck" (83). Of these eyes, he had earlier written:

> It is an optical illusion, but disease does appear to enlarge my eyes, making them stare as if startled, but also hungry to see, astonished—the World and its mirror. In reality, I think eyes do not change size in the course of a lifetime. If I am correct, emaciated patients and tiny newborns thus share the strange radiance of apparently huge eyes. At each of life's extremities, the wonderment is one and the same. (17)

If this passage equivocates, it is with respect only to what these huge (-seeming) eyes signify: it is both tempting and erroneous to perceive them as guarantors of the visionary, and de Duve is expressing in this way the strength of his desire for the sacred to be a reality while simultaneously pouring cold water on it, as an "illusion d'optique." What is not illusion, though—and here there is argument and affirmation, not equivocation: "In reality, I think. . . ," "If I am correct . . ."—is that the illusion of enlarged eyes, itself clearly a metaphor for the discourse of wonderment, is an indicator. It signposts, indexically, the extremity of which wonderment is itself a product: "Aux deux extrémités de la vie, un même émerveillement." So the suggestion is, first of all, that emaciated patients are exactly like newborns, in that they are seeing the world fresh and new, undisturbed by the force of habit; in each case, their privilege is that of an "étrange rayonnement d'yeux," eyes of extraordinary radiance, but also eyes *capable of radiating* strangely (as if endowed with "x ray" vision or some other form of transcendental sight). However, and second, the word "extremity," here, begs to be understood, more equivocally, in a second and even a third sense. In a first, chronological sense, it refers quite obviously to the two "ends" of a lifetime, birth and death, beginning and end. But in spatial terms an extremity is an edge or a limit, and Pascal de Duve is, in fact, *not* experiencing death per se so much as he is engaged in the experience of *approaching* Death, a limit experience.

Thus the extremity in which he finds himself, the extremity indexed by the wonderment and awe he records, is synonymous with crisis and intensity, and is opposed, therefore, not chronologically to an in-between experience of midlife, but philosophically, ethically, and aesthetically, to "middling" experiences of existence, in the sense of the mediocre: the experience of those whose life is lived as unremarkable and who remain oblivious to the possibility of wonderment. In this respect, his experience is not strictly symmetrical with the newborn's, then; and this is the case because, where the newborn is, in chronological terms, at the beginning of a presumably normal life-span, he as a *malade amaigri* faces the end of his existence without having lived a normal span of years. Extremity, for him, is an existential fact as much as a temporal one because it interrupts life, so to speak, abnormally or at least unduly and unexpectedly; it is a crisis of malady and so an encounter with *le mal.* It is of the order of the obscene. And if, as a consequence, that untimely encounter engenders a wonderfully heightened perception of the world, an excited participation in living, and a rhetoric of wonderment—according to the axiom: "at each of life's extremities, the wonderment is one and the same"—these epiphenomena are also, for de Duve but not for tiny newborns, and as Baudelaire's title puts it, *les fleurs du mal.* They are catachrestic, like calling a dodo a swan. It is as flowers of *le mal* that we are therefore invited, by this passage, to read them. Wonderment is a symptom of extremity, which is not just death, life's natural end, but also dying before one's time as a limit experience, a voyage to the edge and an untimely visitation. And the question of reading wonderment has slipped accordingly, from that of the authenticity or illusoriness of wonderment's object, on which de Duve is agnostic, to that of the underlying ill of which wonderment is an index, or a kind of symptom, a point on which he is unequivocal.

This means not only that we *can* read wonderment uncertainly, but that we must. For, as an index of extremity, the capacity for wonderment comments on the stolid complacency of "middling" existences, in which people graze their life away in pasture without ever having lived. But it thus alludes also to a third possible sense of the word *extremity,* which indicates not only a temporal end, and a personal crisis arising from an experience of intensity, but also and finally the cultural banishment of extreme experience, which is consigned to a *finis terrae* of extremity reserved by culture for that which belongs beyond the pale, a surplus that transcends the limits conventional culture assigns to itself. It is here and in this way that the extreme becomes, not illusory (for it is certainly real), but undescribable, and simultaneously unknowable, albeit not unacknowledgable. If the object of visionary wonderment is quite possibly illusory (only the wonderment itself, as an indicator of extremity, being indisputably real), it now becomes clear that the cause of which wonderment is a consequence, and that which "returns" in a discourse of wonderment, likewise provokes uncertainty. This is because, as *le mal,* it is culturally obscene, so that the only mode in which it can be apprehended is one of indirection. The form of readability that characterizes discourses of extremity makes them an *indexical* sign, pointing in the direction of an object that is otherwise undeterminable.

It is here—in this sense and in this way—that reading and uncertainty actually become synonymous. It is not now that a reader may hesitate over whether to give credence to an object of visionary wonderment that may or may not be illusory, but that uncertainty becomes definitional with respect to readability when the object of reading is of the order of the obscene, at the extreme limit of culture. And so, having unmasked himself with all necessary prudence—to Nicole, to Sparks, to the hypothetical reader—as his voyage turns and returns, nearing its end, Pascal nevertheless maintains the equivocation and apostrophe of his text—both the markers of its readability and the generators of that readability—until the very last line. His abstentionism, the marker of his agencing role, prevails in this way to the last. And as readers we have now to negotiate, not only our relation to the object of wonderment, but also our relation to the underlying cause of which the wonderment is a consequence or epiphenomenon. And this in turn means that we must face, as a final undecidability and perhaps the text's most deeply underlying equivocation, the question of the relation between the (obscene) underlying cause, described to us as real, and the (sublime or sacred) object of wonderment, which is much more uncertain.

This, not coincidentally, is also the key theological question: that of the relation of the sacred to evil, *le mal.* The one has been given to us as the, possibly illusory, object of Pascal's vision, the other as the certainly real, but only readable, object that the text, as a discourse of extremity, presents as its very raison d'être. Are we then reading the one when we read the other? And who can know? *Cargo vie* twice cites Kant's *Critique of Pure Reason* as a book that, "carefully read" [bien lu], counsels agnosticism and "postulates intellectual humility about these things" (40). We could hardly be advised more clearly—less equivocally—that *Cargo vie* itself, carefully read, postulates, and seeks to promote, uncertainty in its reader, notably as a function of the double object it gives us to read—the sacred and the obscene—and the question of the relation between these two elements. Such uncertainty, though, can scarcely be equated with the placidity of a certain "don't know, don't care" agnosticism; it acquires urgency from the very context of extremity in which it arises; and thus it shades, given the necessity of "intellectual humility," into anxiety, which is manifestly what de Duve means by a *resolute* (not wishy-washy) agnosticism.

So when the last entry of the book turns out to be a quotation from Nietzsche—and moreover a quotation in the form of an apostrophe—readerly caution is advisable. One should, above all, refrain from leaping to conclusions. The entry reads in its entirety: "'I love thee, Eternity!' (Friedrich Nietzsche)." The quoted text is printed in italics, the parenthetical attribution to Nietzsche is in bold, and is set below the quotation, so that the whole looks less like a final entry than an envoi or terminal epigraph to the text as a whole. The echo of the many apostrophes to AIDS in the book is unmistakable, and it would be easy simply to assimilate this last apostrophe to them—*except* that it is a quotation, and a (pseudo)envoi. Is the author assuming Nietzsche's apostrophe here? Or does his quoting reserve the possibility of his distancing himself somewhat, in abstentionist fashion, from its apparent import? Why end a book that raises such crucial issues with a quotation from another author? And of course, we also know enough by now to be aware that, in any case, something inevitably returns in apostrophe that makes its apparent address and therefore its significance subject to caution, independently of whether it is quoted or not. The knot of undecidables in this moment—what returns in the address to Eternity and why is the address to AIDS reiterated here? To whom is the utterance, as opposed to its statement, addressed? What is the point of de Duve's assumption of, or failure to assume, the Nietzsche text?—constitutes, I speculate, a final address to the reader; that would be why the entry resembles an envoi (itself a form of apostrophe). And what these undecidabilities *say,* I think—that is, I hypothesize, for they say without saying—is: dear reader, dear and especially very hypothetical reader, *keep the hypotheses coming.* For they, and the urgency of the questioning to which they respond, are all we have as an alternative—the alternative of anxiety—to the placidity that causes people, like cattle, to die without having lived.

Grisons-nous! . . .

I proposed in chapter 2 that much Australian AIDS writing addresses, sometimes provocatively and sometimes more discreetly, a national anxiety about otherness, both internal (Aboriginality) and external (immigration); and I suggested that this deep cultural anxiety is a legacy of settler-colony history, in which AIDS writing is thus a contemporary intervention. In the national culture of France, firmly associated in almost doctrinal fashion with the history of the Republic (which has been in part a colonial history), it is not difficult to detect a continuing strain of obsession with purity, which in turn generates both a fear of, and a fascination with, the phenomenon of contagion. There is some concurrence of opinion that these cultural traits have their source in the Revolution of 1789, and more particularly in the revolutionary Terror of 1793.

Faced with "traitors" within and "enemies" without, the Terror had recourse, in an effort both to galvanize the nation and to protect the Republic, to a rhetoric of revolutionary sublimity, a hyperbolization of fetishized abstractions of which echoes can readily be detected in French political discourse today. This rhetoric was backed by a darker form of sublimity: a bloodbath of legalistically sanctioned and administratively rationalized death that was made possible by the invention of the guillotine, an invention that identifies this orgy of killing as a specifically modern phenomenon, since the machine was the first to administer death on an industrial, as opposed to a merely artisanal scale. But the final sanction of these horrifying developments was not legalism but the orgy of joy the executions unleashed in the crowd. That is, the perceived threat of a contagion capable of destroying the supposed purity of the Revolution finally gave rise, at the other end of a chain of effects, to another form of contagion in the intoxication or *griserie* that gripped the crowd, a phenomenon of *liesse populaire* that has remained attached, for better or for ill, to the idea of the

Republic—in the eyes of its disapproving opponents as well as in the minds of its friends—for more than two hundred years. The repressed of Republican ideology *returned,* in transformed guise, as orgy.

In this way, France's abrupt accession to modernity took place in circumstances that were firmly grounded in Enlightenment values but also launched a kind of historical "flight forward," fueled by a dynamics of disenchantment (there is no purity) and of attempted reenchantment. My colleague Alina Clej is engaged in a diachronic study of this "long shadow" cast by the revolution, one that centers on the phenomena of addiction and intoxication; while another colleague, David Caron, has shown (Caron 2001) how a discourse of malady and contagion has played itself out in the history of French anti-Semitism and homophobia since the accession to power of the Third Republic, and continues to determine the politics of immigration and of AIDS in France, as well as official policies toward emerging "communities"—whether Islamic, Jewish, or gay—that are regarded as potentially dangerous to Republican purity. I am drawing, too, on Marie-Hélène Huet's fascinating work on the revolutionary sublime, as well as on a special number of *L'Esprit créateur* on contagion, edited by Mireille Rosello: see in particular her stimulating introduction. And finally I refer the reader to Richard Burton's extraordinary study of the French political tradition of the bloodbath, and of the "sacralization of suffering" (Burton, 180) that it has entailed.

In the context of this puzzling feature of modern French culture, it seems possible to say, first, that Pascal de Duve proposes love as an antidote to AIDS, and second that he defines love—his model for reading—as a mutual *griserie,* a *griserie* that is, so to speak, an orgy of hypothesizing, so that contagion is both a negative force (AIDS, *le mal*) and a positive response. As we have seen, when he apostrophizes his "brothers and sisters in misfortune," his recommendation is *grisons-nous* (an echo, as I've said, of Baudelaire's famous "Enivrez-vous!"), and even *grisons-nous de griserie:* "let us become intoxicated on this privilege [the privilege of *griserie,* in the form of wonderment], in order the better to combat our sufferings" (96). To AIDS he says: "There you go setting me on fire [with fever], as only you can do" [Voilà que tu m'enfièvres . . .] (41). He memorializes long nights of lovemaking with E.—a now rejected memory but nevertheless the archetype experience that frames de Duve's relation to AIDS as well as to his reader—as rendered "sacred" by Mozart's Requiem. And as a gloss on the comment that those nights achieved their apotheosis in magical dawns "when I addressed you as 'Vous,'" he adds this encomium to love as *emotional contagion,* grounded in the illusion such contagion produces of "divinity":

> It was only very late [in the affair] that I dared to call you *vous,* when I sincerely believed the whole thing was somehow divine—when I sincerely believed it couldn't have been merely coincidence that, without the slightest prior agreement, we would suddenly burst into sobs of happiness and emotion, at the same moment, tear for tear. (25)

De Duve was a Belgian citizen, but an inheritor of the French cultural tradition through the French language; his celebration of love as a form of *griserie* and of *griserie* as a form of contagion that is an antidote to another form of contagion, may well account for his book's success with French readers at the same time as it baffles and sometimes dismays non-French readers (and many AIDS activists in France), who expect a less equivocal condemnation of AIDS and its sufferings, and indeed of *le mal.*

For *Cargo vie* is one of three cultural interventions which, in the early 1990s, succeeded in grabbing the attention of the French "general public" for AIDS—something that, during the preceding decade (the period of governmental *dédramatisation* when AIDS was presented, less as a public health threat, than as a strictly private affair between the ill and their physicians) seemed impossible. (Of course, there were other important factors at work as well, including the politicization of AIDS by the National Front, the "polluted blood" scandal, and the work of ACT-UP Paris.) The other two best-selling cultural bombshells of this crucial moment were Hervé Guibert's autofiction *A l'ami qui ne m'a pas sauvé la vie* (To the friend who did not save my life), and Cyril Collard's also autobiographical novelization, *Les Nuits fauves,* from which the author drew the wildly successful film of the same title (in English *Savage Nights*). Guibert might be said to be a practitioner of the "dark sublime" more than of *griserie* as such; but in Collard both contagion and intoxication are literalized: his bisexual, HIV-positive hero's "rage to live" expresses itself in his addiction to fast cars, drugs, and raunchy nights of cruising the Seine embankment, but also in the *entraînement* that leads him—quite casually and naturally, and almost without thought—to have unprotected sex with his new girlfriend Laura, putting her at risk of contracting the virus, and doing so as a sign of his love. "I loved her," he says simply, as if that was all the explanation needed.

(AIDS is, of course, an infectious disease, more properly a syndrome, *not* a contagious one. But the reason it is so widely feared has everything to do with a mythic belief in its powers of contagion.)

In the general cultural context I have sketched, what the three authors who presenced AIDS in the French cultural consciousness have in common—and in this respect I should also mention Christophe Bourdin's autobiographical "novel" *Le Fil* (The thread), which similarly was widely read when it appeared in 1994[8]—is that they subscribe, with minor variations of emphasis, to what, for simplicity's sake, and taking advantage of Rimbaud's international fame, I'll call the "Rimbaud syndrome." This syndrome (before AIDS I'd have called it a "complex") combines the charm exerted by the figure of the "rebellious angel"—young men of ambiguous, androgynous charm (sometimes themselves bisexual), seemingly intent on a short but intensely lived life, and whose attitudes defy the conventional mores and values of their society—with the cultural attractiveness of intoxication, *griserie,* and the dark sublime: what Baudelaire, an earlier hero of this cultural tradition, would have called (in direct reference to Blaise Pascal) *le gouffre,* the abyss, and what in this chapter on de Duve I have been calling "the edge," and "extremity." At the time of France's (still incomplete) shift from giving AIDS the kid gloves treatment or "playing it down" to more engaged and enlightened policies, this combination—the figure of the rebellious angel as simultaneously lovable and the bearer, even the purveyor, of contagion—functioned, I think, as the culturally recognizable "figure" (in both senses of the word) that proved capable of bringing the obscenity of AIDS onto the cultural stage.

As a counterexample from the same period one could cite Bertrand Duquénelle's extraordinary memoir, *L'Aztèque,* which was relatively little noticed when it appeared in 1993 and has now gone out of print (whereas Collard, Guibert, and de Duve are in readily available paperback editions). *L'Aztèque,* which I discuss in chapter 6, visibly alludes to the Rimbaud syndrome, but—it seems—with too much acerbic intelligence and too little indulgence in *griserie* or the dark sublime, too little coquetry, also, with the reader, for it to have achieved success. And conversely, by the time Guillaume Dustan appears on the Parisian scene (see chapter 7), the cultural climate will have changed dramatically, thanks in part to the introduction of combination therapy in 1996 and in part to the historical emergence of a recognizable "gay community," complete with rainbow flags, centered in the Paris neighborhood of the Marais. Dustan's cultural reference is far less to mainstream French cultural and literary traditions (although his work does unmistakably reference eighteenth-century *libertin* writing) than it is communitarian: identified, that is, with "international" (sc. American-style) gaydom, albeit with some recognizably French twists (irony, for example).

"Mainstream," in France, tends to imply high-cultural and literary manifestations more than it would in the United States, but the Rimbaud syndrome has relevance in both high and popular culture. It is certainly not coincidental, for example, that TV appearances (in the case of de Duve and Guibert), an autothanatographical video entitled *La Pudeur ou l'impudeur* (in Guibert's case; see Boulé 1995; Chambers 1998), and in Collard's case the fact that he starred as himself in what was in all possible senses "the film of his life" contributed very materially to the success of their cultural interventions in a quite broad cross-section of the public. All three writers were very photogenic, and Guibert and Collard in particular were much photographed—groping for an analogy through which to describe their attractiveness I come up with Leonardo di Caprio playing Rimbaud in Agnieszka Holland's film, *Total Eclipse.* Each appears to have practiced an art of personal seduction on the public stage that was a counterpart to the seductiveness of their own writing and that in each case had, at its heart, a certain performance of vulnerability, combined however with a "rebellious" refusal to be helpless. This resourceful vulnerability in turn entails a proclivity to a perhaps strategic self-exposure, which can be made to resonate both with the etiology of AIDS and with the social pariahhood PWAs, in France perhaps more than elsewhere, frequently endured. "Long before my positive test results," Guibert writes, "I'd felt my blood suddenly stripped naked, laid bare. . . . From that moment on, I would have to live with this exposed and denuded blood . . . when I'm walking on the street, taking public transportation, the constant target of an arrow aimed at me wherever I go. Does it show in my eyes?" (*To the Friend,* 6). And vulnerability is certainly the central topic of Guibert's novel, which is very largely about the betrayals suffered by a man with AIDS. Viewers of *Les Nuits fauves* will recall the moment when Jean (played by Collard) seduces Laura (and a good proportion of the audience) by "doing his possum face" (and English readers will be reminded that the expression "playing possum" refers to a way of exposing one's vulnerability, in hopes of survival, by performing a simulacrum of death). Finally a theme of vulnerability runs through de Duve's self-presentation and eventual self-exposure in *Cargo vie:* it is in his physical frailty and fainting fits, in his sensitivity to slight and rejection as well as to beauty and the sensation of life; and it is in his desire to be "taken care of"—the response for which he praises AIDS (13) and rewards Nicole with his trust. Rebellious as these angelic figures are, they simultaneously present themselves as wounded, then, and turn their woundedness into a mode of seduction.

AIDS, that is, is their *mal du siècle.* For there is clearly here a reversion to the constructions of the Poet—think of Byron, Chateaubriand, or Lamartine—that made the "male malady" (as it has been tellingly rebaptized by Margaret Waller) so fashionable in the post-Napoleonic generation of the Restoration and the July Monarchy. Not coincidentally, this was the era also when the technique of marketing poetry through widespread distribution of flattering portraits of poets was invented, a technique that worked particularly well when the poet was masculine but young, melancholy, brooding, and, of course, vulnerable. One can be more specific, though, as to the French literary traditions of the last two hundred years on which this successful AIDS writing of the early 1990s—successful in the sense that it drew popular or mainstream attention—was drawing, traditions that, taken together, can be thought to have constituted a recipe for the etiquette of im-pertinence in the modern context. Three such traditions, closely interrelated and for all of which Rimbaud is an exemplary figure, seem to me to be particularly relevant; and I'll close this chapter by evoking them very briefly.

The first of these—something that appears to have been quite particular to writing in France—is the prosopopoeic turn given to autobiographical writing so as to frame the autobiographer's voice as in some sense posthumous: a voice from beyond the grave. Chateaubriand's *Mémoires d'outre-tombe* (Memoirs from beyond the tomb) is of course the canonical reference; but no less cogent is a related strand of male autobiographical writing, in which it is the death of the writer's "self," and the consequent discovery of another world beyond the world of everyday rationality, that is celebrated. The disorder into which the final books of Rousseau's *Confessions* collapse may well have been the progenitor here; but at midcentury (roughly contemporaneous with the appearance of the *Mémoires d'outre-tombe*) it was Nerval's *Aurélia* that set the standard. This is the autobiography of one whose mind has succumbed to (what is called) "madness," an autobiography whose narrative structure Nerval specifically compares to the ancient epic topos of the "descent into the underworld" (which itself was readily conflated by nineteenth-century writers with Orphic myth). Rimbaud's account of his own period of poetic madness and metaphysical as well as social revolt, *Une Saison en Enfer,* clearly echoes Nerval's text; and so, at a further remove, does de Duve, suggesting the homology of his round-trip voyage to the edge with the structure of the descent into the underworld through the episode of the passengers' visit to the engine room, while simultaneously giving us to understand that Death participates in the author's writing as an at least equal partner, and indeed that, since his brain is being devoured ("bouffé") by the virus, HIV is itself "pretty much the one doing the writing" in his case. Guibert recalls the topos also, by staging his writing as a form of suicide experiment (Chambers 1997) and a farewell symphony (chapter 7). And because the well-publicized actual (as opposed to literary) deaths of all three of these French AIDS writers supervened shortly after publication of their work (and in some instances preceding it), they have all involuntarily repeated the gesture by which Nerval literalized the prosopopoeic character of *Aurélia* by committing suicide between the appearance of the first part of his text and that of the second, whose proofs he did not correct (so that to this day the text remains marked by the disorder that recalls his death). In Collard's case, his death in 1993 coincided with the announcement that *Les Nuits fauves* had been awarded four "Césars" (French Oscars), and followed closely on the release of the film the previous fall in cinemas throughout France. Walter Benjamin remarks in his essay on "The Storyteller" that death is the sanction of the storyteller's art; in AIDS writing, the "death of the author" (Chambers 1998b)—a phenomenon that is of course definitional of writing in general—was, before 1996, all too easily literalized in this way; but the literalization sometimes lent extraordinary authority to acts of witnessing, and in Collard's case, seems to have made his testimonial intervention impossible to ignore.[9]

The remaining two traditions can be addressed more briefly, since they are both implicit in what I have said of the prosopopoeic autobiography (or autothanatography). These are the traditions of the dark sublime, most famously represented in France in the work of Georges Bataille and Antonin Artaud, and of *écriture* (writerliness) or the linguistic sublime, a tradition which has run from Mallarmé (and his Romantic and post-Romantic predecessors) through Blanchot and Derrida to the *Tel Quel* writers and Gilles Deleuze, all of whom were influenced by Bataille and/or take Artaud as a crucial point of reference. The young AIDS writers of the 1990s are thus direct cultural inheritors of these two traditions, or this single tradition, for which Rimbaud is again a paradigmatic figure—but the Rimbaud, in this case, of the programmatic letter to his friend and former teacher, Demeny, known as the "Lettre du Voyant," with its two sloganlike formulations: "Je est un autre" [I is an other] and "Trouver une langue" [we have to find/invent a language].

What is common to the two traditions is the cultivation of limit experience as an alternative to the mundane, the conventional, the instrumental or utilitarian, together with a consequent belief in and promotion of excess, surplus, going beyond the boundaries of the "ideological"—what Bataille both eroticizes and sacralizes as "sovereignty"—understood as a way to promote the expansion and liberation of subjectivity through practices of sublimating depersonalization. That which—to the constructed, "ideological" formation that is a person—looks like the greatest evil—*le mal*—is *umgewertet* (Nietzsche's word, referring to the reversal of all values) so as to become, instead, the source of liberating sovereignty in *griserie.*[10] We have seen de Duve simultaneously yielding to the attractions of such thinking and resisting certain of its premises (clinging to the personhood of the writer even in collaboration with death, proposing "intellectual humility" and agnosticism in the face of claims to divinity and the sacred). And more generally I think it might be argued that what most unites writers like de Duve, Guibert, and Collard—in many respects extremely different one from other—is finally that they each seek to make AIDS the occasion of an *Umwertung,* a reversal of values or ethics of inversion (chapter 2) through which *le mal* can become a source of (at the very least writerly) sovereignty, in Bataille's sense, but *without the sacrifice of personhood* (and indeed, in the cases of Guibert and Collard, while retaining a certain narcissistic focus on the person and the personality of the author). *Griserie,* but without loss of personal identity.

Along with the performance of vulnerability, this narcissistic focus in combination with the cultivation of forms of *griserie* is perhaps something inherent in the Rimbaud syndrome. But I think it could be described also as a recipe for cultural haunting, "French style," in which two apparently contradictory gestures—a voyage "out," so to speak, and a voyage "back"—are enacted in a way that synthesizes them, or seeks to synthesize them: I mean the dissolution of self inherent in sovereignty, and the return of the messenger (Greek *angelos,* de Duve's/Galileo's *siderius nuntius*) as the bearer of contagion. More particularly this synthesis would be a way of haunting "*gay* French style"—as exemplified most tellingly for me in Guibert's video diary, *La Pudeur ou l'impudeur* (see Chambers 1998). By this I mean that it haunts in the way that such haunting could be imagined in a social and cultural context in which AIDS was still very largely *privatized,* both politically and culturally, as was homosexuality; so that French homosexual

PWAs found themselves very frequently forced to deal with a situation of the most intense solitude, a solitude more intense than was—and still is—suffered by their "sisters and brothers in misfortune" in countries where established communities were able to take some of the responsibilities for support that were shirked by governments, public health systems, and frequently biological families as well. This burden of solitude, I submit, is thematized implicitly in all these writers as the form of woundedness that makes them seductive, but seductive as bearers of contagion.

It was difficult in such circumstances to imagine ghostliness and haunting as plural, rather than singular; or to think of the ghost as a figure for a sense of collective injustice, as Derrida understands it in *Specters of Marx* and as I will interpret testimonial haunting in part II. Rather, I suggest, it is the sense of solitude in these writers that reads—somewhat unfairly—as narcissistic focus on the person, and as resistance to the depersonalization inherent in the *griserie* of the sublime even as that *griserie* is embraced. Texts like those of Collard, Guibert, and de Duve seem to me both to *assume* (in both senses) the solitude of the PWA in person, and to seek to *transform* that solitude, through the culturally available vehicle of the Rimbaud syndrome, into, simultaneously, an experience of sovereignty or *griserie*—the experience whose probable illusoriness de Duve is so mindful of—and a way of achieving, thanks to the seductive figure of the rebellious angel, a social presence—an agency and an impact—of a kind that was denied the privatized individual PWA. An agency, an impact, and a presence that, now, can't be ignored or denied, and that are capable of surviving the author's personal demise, at the price of his becoming a textualized phantom.[11]

Part II. Phantom Pain

5. Orphaned Memories, Phantom Pain: Toward a Hauntology of Discourse

> She wishes that the dead were not quite so dead.
> She also wishes that the dead were not quite so alive.
> She thought that dead people should feel more dead.
> —Lily Brett, *Too Many Men*

Aftermath Writing

For writers like Michaels, Sassoon and Owen, or Pascal de Duve (part I), personal survival is scarcely an issue. They write from the very thick of events that they judge will destroy them; and what concerns them is rather that there be a readership for what they write. In what I've called discourses of extremity, the problematics of survival is thus a problematics of readability. In aftermath writing, however, which shares this problematics of readability with discourses of extremity, the paramount question is that of what it means to survive a traumatic event or experience, that is, to outlive those who have been destroyed by it while finding oneself, nevertheless, closer to the dead in experience, knowledge, and sympathy, than to those whose lives have gone on, and continue to go on apparently unscathed and unaware. There is, in other words, a problematics of the witness's survival in its relation to what I'll call the survivorhood of others. And this problematics is coextensive with a rhetorical problem: how to parlay the hauntedness of one's relation to the dead into a haunting that will affect the living, waking them from the self-absorbed ignorance in which they live. This last—the problem of the survivor as agencer of a haunt that brings into relation the living and the dead—is the question on which I concentrate in this chapter. I'll describe it as a problem of relay, the agencing of phantom pain, and of agencing as a matter of flaunting one's hauntedness.

On the face of it, the three texts to which I'll refer are a heterogeneous group. One is a Holocaust memoir that is generally thought, except by its author, to be spurious—a case, it seems, of deludedness rather than of fraudulence. The second is not strictly a Holocaust memoir (its author was in Auschwitz-Birkenau as a political prisoner), but it is regarded as one of the major testimonials we have to the horror of the concentration and extermination camps. By contrast, the third is a protest—in the form of a satirical fable with singing and dancing—against the "culture of certainty" that, during the 1980s especially, transformed the AIDS epidemic in North America (and elsewhere) into an epidemic of blame. My purpose in putting together this mixed bag is not to be provocative. But, before turning in the chapters to come to two particular forms of the writing of aftermath that the AIDS epidemic has generated (the "dual autobiography" in chapter 6 and the "collective auto/biography" in chapter 7), I want to illustrate here the very large range of cultural manifestations that can be described under the rubric of aftermath writing.

What such manifestations have in common is their concern with the state of *hauntedness* that corresponds to an experience of trauma as that which fails to end, but continues to repeat and to return, even when it is supposedly "over." All denials notwithstanding, Auschwitz is still with us; so too is the epidemic; and (as *Regeneration* suggests) so too is the 1914–18 war. My reader will readily supply other examples. But it is not this hauntedness per se that distinguishes survival from survivorhood so much as the awareness of it that dogs "survivors" (in the form of a consciousness of their being haunted by the dead), and the denial on the part of the "living" of their own hauntedness—their denial of the relevance of that which haunts to their own lives. The rhetorical task of survivor witnessing as aftermath writing is therefore so to *convey* its own hauntedness that the injustice that haunts the witness (the trauma of the event, the deaths of those who did not survive) is *recognized as haunting,* also, by those who read the witnessing text. The text becomes the vehicle that relays hauntedness as a haunting.

This relay is achieved, I'll propose, by bringing into alignment, thanks to the instrumentality of *figuration* as a mode of indexicality, that which is inadequately represented in the text-as-statement and that which is produced by the text-as-utterance as the object the reader is called upon to interpret. That which language cannot *say* (but only signify) becomes that which is given to be *read,* and can therefore be acknowledged although it cannot be known. The object is presenced, but not made present as it would illusorily be in an act of mimesis; it has the reality, and the elusiveness, of the experience known as phantom pain. What Charlotte Delbo calls "useless knowledge," what, I'll suggest, "Binjamin Wilkomirski's" *Fragments* manifests as orphaned memories, and what finally John Greyson's film *Zero Patience* symbolizes as the zero degree of hauntedness/hauntingness, is what the gesture of direct reference can only manifest as lack. It is only through the readability of the figural that the lacking object can come to be recognized, in the spectral form I call phantom pain. To mobilize once again Derrida's punning axiom (there is no ontology without a hauntology), it becomes clear that a rhetoric of witnessing in the mode of aftermath—but discourses of extremity also work as aftermath writing when they are read—must be a hauntology of discourse: an exploration of the sense in which discourse, being haunted, also haunts.

Because trauma repeats and returns even when it is supposedly over, aftermath writing as a hauntedness that haunts has a double character of untimeliness. It is both an exploration of survival as the experience of untimeliness—that is, of a baffling experience of time as, conjointly, the separation of past and present and their continuing copresence (e.g., in the form of flashback)—and an art of untimely intervention, seeking to introduce an awareness of untimeliness into a culture that prefers to live in time as if the past had no place in the present and did not haunt (i.e., inhabit) it. It thus turns survivorhood into survival for those who become its engaged readers. A hauntology of discourse, then—and this is as true for discourses of extremity when they are read as it is for the larger category of aftermath writing—will be a rhetoric of untimeliness as an art of the inopportune and the im-pertinent (cf. the meanings of French *intempestif*), grounded in a symptomatology of what in German could be called *Unzeitgemässigkeit,* untimeliness as a lack of common measure *(Mass),* an out-of-jointness, between time and "untime" in societies that are haunted but seek to ignore their hauntedness.[1] Where the generic catachresis that is characteristic of witnessing is the sign of its *intempestivité* (for if no genre is appropriate for the obscene, there can be no right time for it either), it is an engaged reading that supplies the "measure" (a word I find also in Delbo) capable of making the phenomena of *Unzeit* recognizable within time—an experience of the "uncanny" whose vehicle is the symbolic, that is, the figural. That is why in this chapter I'll seek to describe figuration as the "relay" that, by indexing pain, *conveys* hauntedness, carries it over, and permits it—in the best possible scenario—to become haunting.

Who's There?

"Who's there?" is Bernardo's anxious question at the beginning of *Hamlet,* as he stands guard on the haunted heights of Elsinore. Of course it's a defining question for the play; perhaps too it's the question the condition of hauntedness regularly requires us to ask; certainly it's the question I'm led to formulate in response to the *Fragments* affair.

Commentators have mainly discussed the affair in two ways. It's seen first as a matter involving the perhaps fraudulent, more probably deluded, "borrowing" (Ganzfried) of the identity of Holocaust survivor, and hence—this being the second issue—as a problem in the ethics of authorship. Without denying the significance of these and other questions the affair raises, I would like to reframe the discussion and ask what it means for a culture of aftermath to be haunted by a collective memory—the memory of painful events that few, if any, living members of the culture may have directly perpetrated or suffered from in their own persons. In particular I want to raise the issue of what it might mean for an individual to confuse the collective historical consciousness concerning outrageous events with painful personal memories; and to confuse them to the point of being *inhabited* (i.e., haunted) by the events *as though* he or she had actually lived through them. In short, I want to view the case of this text as symptomatic, but culturally symptomatic as much as personally so.

Fragments was published in 1995 under its original German title of *Bruchstücke* and rapidly translated into many other languages. The English language version by Carol Brown Janeway appeared in 1996; it bears a subtitle that identifies the text generically as memoir, *Memoirs of a Wartime Childhood.* In all versions the author's name was given as Binjamin Wilkomirski, and indeed the text purports to consist of Wilkomirski's scattered and elusive memories of having been a small Jewish child in Nazi-occupied Latvia and Poland, including his internment in Majdanek and then apparently Auschwitz-Birkenau, before he was finally brought from Cracow to an orphanage in Switzerland at war's end, and eventually adopted by foster parents whose name he took.

Early readers, myself included, found in the book deeply moving personal testimony concerning an aspect of that atrocious historical period of which, for painfully obvious reasons, there is virtually no direct personal record: the experience of the infants and very young children who were caught up and brutally destroyed in the Nazi extermination machine. But some of the book's most powerful and moving passages are actually in the last third of the narrative, when the scene shifts from wartime Poland to Switzerland in the immediate postwar period. Having perfectly internalized the rules of survival appropriate to the Lager, the child Wilkomirski now finds himself in a terrifying new situation, more terrifying even than the extreme vulnerability of his situation in the camps, because it seems to him unreal and a pretense. He knows only the rules of survival that pertained in Auschwitz, but the world in which he moves both resembles and does not resemble the camp. Thus, his environment, reassuringly familiar to us, has become, for him, more frighteningly alien than the camp itself because it is the environment of aftermath: it continues the camp, but in unfamiliar guise.

These are passages to which I'll eventually return, because what they describe is a condition of hauntedness—the hauntedness of a placid and supposedly peaceful Switzerland to which, in the consciousness of the young Binjamin, Auschwitz and all the conditions of the *Endlösung* nevertheless remain fully and uncannily *relevant.* The Lager is present, actual, and active—but spectrally so, because the continuity and connectedness between Switzerland and Poland that the relevance presupposes go unrecognized, and indeed are energetically denied, by virtually all, whether adults or children, who surround the child. Hence the child's sense of Switzerland's unreality. All survivors of extreme and traumatic events or experiences report a similar sense of dissociation from the supposedly normal life that surrounds them. But for Binjamin the sensation of normalcy's unreality is exacerbated because, precisely, he has never *known* this "normal" life that he is suddenly expected to recognize and embrace.

So, at least, *Fragments* could be read until 1998. In that year it was revealed that the book's author had the legal identity, not of Binjamin Wilkomirski but of Bruno Dössekker, born in Biel (Switzerland) in 1941, the illegitimate child of a Swiss mother (see Ganzfried). Originally Bruno Grosjean, he had lived first in orphanages and foster care before taking the name of his foster parents and becoming Bruno Dössekker. He could not be identical with Wilkomirski. This bombshell provoked an immediate hue and cry, during which Dössekker has steadfastly—I'm tempted to say obstinately—clung to the claim that he is Binjamin Wilkomirski, a claim he grounds in the fragments of memory that inhabit his consciousness and in a distinction he had made in the afterword of *Fragments:* "Legally accredited truth is one thing—the truth of a life is another" (154). Dössekker, it seems, *trusts* his memories. He trusts them more than he trusts bureaucratic paperwork; and he trusts that *they* identify him as Binjamin

Wilkomirski. It's fair to say that few now follow him in this belief. But also, few believe him to have been insincere or duplicitous in claiming the existential, if not legal, identity of Wilkomirski.

Whether or not the impersonation resulted from fraud or delusion, the scandal, of course, arose from the fact that the identity of Holocaust survivor had been successfully appropriated. Such a fact seriously challenged the historical and sometimes metaphysical uniqueness that is attributed by some to the events variously known as the Destruction, the Holocaust, the *Endlösung.* But the confusion about what it meant that Wilkomirski was Dössekker who is not Wilkomirski was compounded by the difficulties that now emerged concerning the book's actual genre. *Fragments* claimed to be memoir, but it could not now be regarded as autobiographical, since the memories are not Dössekker's but Wilkomirski's, who however apparently never existed and can't therefore be the book's author. The "autobiographical pact" (Lejeune) was violated. But on the other hand *Fragments* could not readily be regarded as historical fiction, in the manner of, say, Hersey's *The Wall* or Styron's *Sophie's Choice,* if only because the author (whether Dössekker or Wilkomirski) steadfastly continued to identify it as autobiography. No one has asked whether the existence of such a generic solecism might not be the sign of something more than a merely personal aberration, or whether the personal delusion might not be a cultural symptom, the evidence of a certain collective pathology. Such a pathology, I wish to suggest, might be the condition of a society subject to a troubled collective memory, and suffering from a haunted historical consciousness. To my mind it is as if the book functions, through a kind of lapsus or *Fehlleistung* on Dössekker's part, as a species of testimonial, but in a way and a sense different from the intention to testify that its deluded author has claimed. Not so much Dössekker's delusion as the hauntedness of a culture of aftermath in which such a delusion is possible is what *Fragments* appears to bear witness to.

In the fall of 1999, following the advice of a professional historian (Stefan Mächler),[2] publishers began to withdraw *Fragments* from circulation, following the example of the original publisher, Suhrkamp. On November 2, Schocken Books announced that it was suspending publication in the United States. One may speculate about the pressures, legal, political, or otherwise, to which the publishers were yielding. If my hunch has some merit, a major, if probably unacknowledged, part of their motivation may lie in the desire characteristic of the living, when the dead are restless and specters roam, to *lay the ghost.* As a haunted text—the text of

Bruno Dössekker, a writer who is inhabited and indeed (it seems) possessed by the remembered identity of Binjamin Wilkomirski—*Fragments* is evidence of a haunted society, in which an individual can mistake the collective consciousness of a painful past for a personal memory. As such, it makes a hauntedness that was easy to ignore more difficult to deny; the ghost must be laid. For if it is easy not to believe in ghosts, it is hard not to be troubled by them, and by the questions they raise. Acting as gatekeeper institutions for their various societies, the publishing houses have understandably—if regrettably—attempted to block the awkward questions *Fragments* raises, beginning with the question of haunted identity: Who's there?

Ghosts are not easily laid, however. The reason for this is that what their presence signifies is the sense the living have of an injustice that has gone unrepaired (and may indeed be irreparable). It always seems easier to lay the ghost than to repair the injustice—but "seems" is the operative word because ghosts ultimately refuse to lie down and be still, for the very reason that the consciousness of injustice, otherwise known as a sense of guilt, inhabits the living, not the dead. However much, like Lily Brett's character in this chapter's epigraph, we may think that the dead should feel less alive and act more dead, they remain restless because the living remain anxious, being prevented by guilt from completing the normal process of mourning that would lay them to rest. They keep returning, as revenants. Take the short item that appeared in the *New York Times* of November 3, 1999 (B4). Under the heading "Publisher Drops Holocaust Book," it announced the withdrawal of *Fragments* the previous day.[3] In the words of the *Times,* the book was withdrawn because of "evidence that the account was no more than a vivid fantasy." Do we think it was the fantastic character of the fantasy or its vividness that was judged to be at fault? For not surprisingly perhaps, but certainly very symptomatically, *Fragments* remains a "Holocaust book," to the *Times,* even as the headline reports its having been "dropped." And in the very sentence that announces Wilkomirski's fallacious existence (as "no more than" a vivid fantasy), a ghostly "Mr. Wilkomirski" walks. "The report concluded," says the *Times,* "that Mr. Wilkomirski had not been a Jewish orphan but a Swiss-born child named Bruno Dössekker." Here is evidence of the difficulty of laying ghosts.

True, it's the hasty prose of a sloppy journalist. But the paralogism, which is a bit like disbelieving in ghosts but being troubled by them, is startling. There is a stammer of sense here that can't be attributed to Dössekker's personal delusion. And what makes the sentence even more unsettling is not just that Wilkomirski survives as the subject of the clause that expunges him, but also that in surviving he is favored with an honorific "*Mr.* Wilkomirski," as if *he* were the adult, while Dössekker the putative author of the book and a grown-up, becomes just Bruno, "a Swiss-born child." Each appears to have changed status with the other. Who then, one may ask, is being referred to as "the author" in the sentence that follows? "People with knowledge of the report said that when confronted with its findings, *the author* declared defiantly: 'I am Binjamin Wilkomirski.'" What matter who speaks? was a brash question much bandied about in theoretical circles in the 1960s; but the evidence of the *Fragments* affair is both that it *can* sometimes matter very much to whom speech is attributed, and that in haunted societies the attribution can be a somewhat rough-and-ready affair, given the difficulty of responding to the question of spectrality—Who's there?—and the unwillingness of ghosts to submit to our desire and to be laid.

The *Fragments* affair is worth pondering, then, because it shows how the ghosts keep returning. A haunted society is not so much one that has ghosts, the way a house might have mice, as one whose ghosts do not submit to being laid. The fact that *Fragments* has proved so unwelcome a visitant among us may have less to do, therefore, with the matters overtly discussed (the fungibility of identity, the ethics of authorship), which are the epiphenomena of hauntedness, than with the fact that the story of Dössekker's hauntedness as a writer asks questions about our own Wilkomirskis, the Binjamins who haunt us all. After all, the most unequivocally genuine of Holocaust testimonies themselves frequently bear witness to their own utter inadequacy as testimonial. That is, they cannot report the full enormity of the Holocaust in such a way that this enormity might be, once and for all, recognized and put to rest, because there are Binjamins whose fate they cannot account for. Their testimony is haunting enough but it is itself also haunted; it testifies that there is no end to the business of laying our ghosts. Specters, as Derrida has said, are always plural; one reason for that is that they have specters of their own.

The Binjamins who haunt authentic Holocaust testimonial are those for whom it knows it does not and cannot speak, but who insist on their right to "live," that is, on the injustice of their death. These are the shades of all those who, undergoing extermination, did not get a chance to testify, a category of people that was, so to speak, already recognized in the camps and came to be identified later, in the argot, with the fatalists or *Muselmänner* (cf. Levi's "sommersi" as opposed to the "salvati," and see Agamben).[4] In order to testify one must first survive—or one's story must survive. The nonsurvivors who haunt survivor testimony do so precisely because it is both surviving testimony and the testimony of survivors. It is the memory of the nonsurvivors that so-called survivor guilt acknowledges. And it is the category of the nonsurvivors that is poignantly figured in *Fragments* by the symbolic figure of the child—*in-fans,* not speaking—and represented in Dössekker's text as Binjamin Wilkomirski. A dubious figure who will not go away—a figure neither historical nor yet fictional, neither real nor imaginary, but symbolic—Binjamin stands for all the ghosts that inhabit a haunting testimonial text but do not, cannot speak, with their own voice, within it. The ghosts who, a fortiori, therefore haunt also all who survive in the aftermath of the camps.

(In AIDS writing, too, there is a corresponding category, although it is much less frequently acknowledged than in Holocaust writing. It is that of the countless millions of anonymous infected people who have died and continue to die in inner-city ghettoes and some rural areas of the West, and in the many underdeveloped regions of the world where life-prolonging therapy is unavailable. If they haunt the testimony of middle-class Western writers, they mainly do so without so much as being named. As AIDS itself becomes more mentionable, more manageable, and even more culturally acceptable in the West, these Wilkomirskis have rarely found the Dössekker able—whether in deluded fashion or no—to perform the act of agencing that might presence *them* in Western consciousness. Jamaica Kincaid has symbolized them in *My Brother,* though [as I will suggest briefly in chapter 8]; and I'll try to hint at the end of this chapter that John Greyson's impertinent film *Zero Patience* offers a niche for their haunting presence under the ghostly identity of "Patient Zero.")

My thesis, then, is that there are Wilkomirskis, or orphaned memories, who haunt the collective consciousness but *need a Dössekker*—a "host"—if they are to achieve some sort of "vividness," some degree of discursive status within culture, and force our acknowledgment that they do indeed haunt us—an acknowledgment that takes the form, partly of the laying of ghosts, but also of anxiety over symptoms of their haunting: a "borrowed" identity, a generic conundrum, lapses in a journalist's hasty prose. When *Fragments* was still understood to be an authentic text of Holocaust witness, the very implausibility of a small, unprotected, Jewish child's surviving the conditions of the extermination camps was sometimes cited as paradoxical evidence of the text's authenticity, or at least as evidence that did not disprove its authenticity. After all, the Holocaust itself was so improbable, and the most unlikely things were known to have happened! But now the same implausibility, along with some smaller historical and other inaccuracies, is held to prove the text's inauthenticity and, as an apparently unexamined consequence, its inability "therefore" to embody any form of truth: *Fragments,* that is, is "no more than a vivid fantasy." I submit rather that a "vivid fantasy" has truth as a cultural symptom, its very vividness testifying to its slightly uncanny quality, and that, in this case, its testimonial truth is quite directly conditioned on the very implausibility in historical terms of a child's having survived Auschwitz to tell the story of that survival. It is only through an anomaly of this kind—the anomaly of the symbolic or figural as that which is neither historically true nor yet a fiction—that what haunts our hauntedness can return, and in doing so, gain some sort of recognition of that hauntedness itself.

Inauthentic as *Fragments* doubtless is as an actual representation of a child's experience of Nazi persecution and the camps, it does force us, for example, to try to imagine what that experience must have been like for children; and in doing so it requires us, when more authentic survivor testimonies remind us, explicitly or not, that they too are haunted by orphaned memories—by the silenced voices of those who died—to realize with some anxiety that we can't so much as imagine the experience of all those whose very names—even the numbers—have not come down to us; to realize, that is, that we have therefore not adequately mourned them, and perhaps cannot do so. The more dead they are, as Brett says, the more uncomfortably alive they are capable of becoming, to us. Quite paradoxically, then, it is the sense in which *Fragments* is an unlikely and problematic text of Holocaust testimonial that gives the book, nevertheless, its agencing and presencing function—one that more genuine, more straightforwardly truthful, testimonies are precluded from subserving by virtue of their very honesty and authenticity. Their eyewitness scrupulousness is extremely valuable, but it sets limits to the range of their testimony, limits that can be gotten around only through the possibility of less literal, symbolic, or figural praxes—including a parapraxis such as Dössekker's felicitous blunder *(Fehlleistung).* For parapraxes, too, are an *art de faire.* Those who did not survive cannot give survivor testimony. Or they can, but only through language's unruly capacity to say more than we think it can, more than we may want it to do, more than we believe it ought to be allowed to do. Its capacity, that is, to foster the orphaned.

Orphaned Memory, Foster Writing

A central topos of Holocaust writing is its thematics of violent separation: the extermination of huge populations, the destruction of a culture, the brutal breakup of couples and family groups. Orphanages and foster care have little place in the story such writing tells; their prominence in *Fragments* is therefore noteworthy. It points to a thematics of continuity and survival—survival of violent separation, but survival in a mode significantly different from the already painful survival described by those witnesses (e.g., Wiesel, Levi, or Delbo) who emerged from the camps as young adults. It's not just that Wilkomirski survives as a young child, though. It's also that a survival that is institutionally marked as palliative, continuing to bear the traces of interruption, is a more dubious and troubled form of survival, more *assisted,* than that of others, deeply traumatized as they too may be. Such a survival is survival by relay, a highly mediated mode of discontinuous continuity that implies dependence on the intervention of another (or of others). Like the identity of Wilkomirski and Dössekker, claimed by Dössekker but now contested, it's a *fostered* survival, and one that therefore seems both fragile and artificial, even suspect.

There's a striking symmetry in *Fragments* between two orphanages, one in Cracow and one in Switzerland; the connecting train journey with Frau Grosz figures their relay. It's evident also that orphanages and foster care are the point of junction where the fragmentary narrative of Wilkomirski, as told in the book, grafts onto the biography of Dössekker, as it is now known from research. Elena Lappin cautiously suggests that Bruno Dössekker's early experiences of separation from his mother and subsequent life in the strict and probably unloving conditions of Swiss orphanages in the 1940s account for this grafting; they are the common ground on which Dössekker's deluded self-identification with Binjamin Wilkomirski, Holocaust survivor, actually rests. This seems a plausible hypothesis. Learning at school the history of the Holocaust, as he recounts in *Fragments,* Bruno Dössekker would have reinterpreted his personal experience of pain, by back-formation or *Nachträglichkeit* (another form of relay), as Holocaust memory. Assuming this psychological hypothesis, I want to suggest in turn that a further dynamics of relay is at work in the actual writing of *Fragments.* I mean that in experiencing Wilkomirski's pain as his own, Dössekker the man transforms his personal sense of orphanhood into the experience of a "phantom" pain; and that his writing then functions as a mode of transmission for the painful Wilkomirski memories that derive from the collective memory but that he takes as his own, in such a way that they become phantom pain in the minds of his book's readers. This is to understand writing as itself the agent of a relay in the sense that it both records the evidence of a break, the damage done by the Holocaust, and produces a continuity, which is the survival, despite that break, of an orphaned memory, or the set of orphaned memories named Wilkomirski, in the form of a phantom pain experienced by readers. The agencing of that survival is the work of relay performed by Dössekker's writing as a fostering of the orphaned.

Foster writing, then, fosters in the double sense of that word.[5] It's a surrogate, offering a form of hospitality or pseudohome to that which is culturally homeless and agencing a phantom cultural existence for it. But thus it fosters, that is, encourages, the entry of the culturally homeless into culture, albeit in the uncanny form it owes to the highly mediated act of its presencing. Where once it was culturally ignored, like a waif, the haunt is recognized, in the form of pain. These, a reading of *Fragments* suggests, are the inevitable conditions of survival, contingent on the relay of writing, for a memory that culture would rather forget. So it is worth pointing out that the German title, *Bruchstücke,* "broken pieces," is considerably more concrete than its translation as *Fragments* can convey; and that *Stücke,* or items, was part of the Nazi administrative lingo, referring to the human victims of the extermination machine. The word *symbol* (throwing together) refers, for its part, to an ancient practice for identifying people long separated, each of whom held a fragment of an object—say a ring—broken into two or more parts. Phantom pain, the readerly effect of foster writing, can be thought of, therefore, in a quite specific sense, as a bringing together of broken pieces: the symbolic re-membering of dis-membered identities. What Dössekker understands, deludedly, as remembering in the literal sense is arguably true, I am suggesting—but in just such a symbolic sense, as a phantasmatically imagined re-membering.

The reason an orphaned memory haunts is that such a memory is both detached, like all memories, from its there-and-then context in the past and—more unusually—seemingly without attachment also in the here-and-now context of its present remembering. In discursive terms, the connection between the reference of the memory's statement and the circumstances of its utterance has been interrupted, except for the very fact of its being uttered (remembered), a fact that seems to imply a connection per se. Thus the memory is received by the remembering subject, but as a kind of visitation. Phantom pain, properly speaking, refers to the neurophysiological phenomenon whereby people who have lost a limb experience a sensation of physical pain in the amputated extremity; but I use it here, by an extension of the metaphor, as a name for a certain capacity of moral hospitality—a capacity that Bruno Dössekker appears to have exercised in unusual measure. This is the capacity to experience the pain of another, or of others, as wholly or partly indistinguishable from a "remembered" pain of one's own.

Each phenomenon—orphaned memory and phantom pain—is a phenomenon of memory, then. But the effect of phantom pain is the converse of that of orphaned memory. Where orphaned memory is disconnected, except for the thread of its being remembered by the remembering subject, phantom pain is equally uncanny because it makes for a strong sense of connection and continuity, but of an unexpected kind, a connection between subjects—the subject of the remembered pain (say Wilkomirski) and the subject of the remembering (say Dössekker)—that are thought to be separate, because other. Memory-statement and memory-utterance are in this case continuous with each other; they have the same object, but each has a different subject—a phenomenon that might be compared with vivid identificatory reading. In each case, there is thus the experience of an anomalous copresence of different contexts or categories that in normal circumstances (including normal memory) are not thought capable of coinciding: the there-and-then and the here-and-now in orphaned memory, in phantom pain I and not-I, self and other.

Gilles Deleuze would refer to each of these anomalous occurrences of dedifferentiation as a stammer and describe it as a case of "disjunctive synthesis" (see chapter 3). I would add that they are disruptive of the workings of genre, whose seduction (Lyotard's word) consists in part of blinding us to the implications of, and aberrant possibilities inherent in, the split between statement and utterance that is constitutive of the discursive and characteristic, inter alia, of memory (in chapter 3 I described reporting in terms of this split, as the nexus of reference and address). In the case of autobiography, for example, or when I give legal testimony, it is assumed that I am *not* my other (unlike the evidence of phantom pain) and that (unlike the case of orphaned memory) there is an equivalence between the content of my memory and my remembering of it, such that (roughly speaking) my statements about the then and there can be trusted in the here and now. Generic conformity, in short, tends to exclude, or at least to diminish, the possibility of haunting (as an orphaned memory haunts) and of hauntedness (as in phantom pain). Thus it is the book's failure to conform to the conventions of genres such as these, as a consequence of its participation in the phenomena of orphaned memory and phantom pain, that has made *Fragments* an aberrant text, a ghost to be laid.

My argument that foster writing is the relay that transforms the orphaned memory experienced by the writing subject into a readerly experience of phantom pain—that is, a hauntedness into a haunting—proposes then (and to put it technically) that *Fragments* is readable, first, as a mimesis of orphaned memory, but second, as a mimesis that works rhetorically as a device or agencing capable of making readerly subjectivity hospitable to phantom pain, a device, that is, of reader involvement. I'll argue more specifically that asyndeton, in the form of a fragmented narrative, and hypotyposis (or vividness) are the key tropes that, in combination, produce such an outcome. Narrative fragmentation as the mimesis of orphaned memory merges first, as the narrative develops, with a mimesis of phantom pain in the form of an experience of hypotyposis—the experience of the child Binjamin in the orphanage, where Auschwitz is still more real than his actual surroundings. But by virtue of the reader-involving power of asyndeton, this latter mimesis also involves the reader, so that the experience it describes, as Binjamin's phantom pain, becomes an effect of hypotyposis—that is, phantom pain—experienced by the reader. The *model* of the narrated experience becomes an *effect* of narration. The relay produced by this assemblage of figural means consists of a rhetorical shift that turns the mimesis of orphaned memory into an effect of address designed to make vividly copresent, to a readerly imagination nourished by its own personal memories of pain, the here and now of reading and the there and then of the pain named, inadequately, by the word *Holocaust.* In that way the mimesis of a haunted subjectivity becomes a text that itself haunts: not just "about" pain, it also *hurts.*

The "paradox" of language is sometimes described (e.g., by Becker, 5, citing Ortega y Gasset) in terms of simultaneous deficit and excess: language does less than we want and more than we intend. That is, language as statement is deficient with respect to reference, while as utterance it lends itself to effects of readability that appear unlimited because subject to infinite semiosis. Of course, here too genres intervene to restrict these effects, limiting the range of interpretability of utterances and thus producing their statement-referentiality as adequate in the way that genres like legal testimony and autobiography restrict the unreliability, the fantastic quality of memory. It's only when genre breaks down—a misunderstanding or differend arises, or genre conventions are flouted by being turned to unexpected or unwanted purposes, as is commonly the case in the practice of testimonial—that language users become uncomfortably aware of "aboutness" as lack and of readability as embarrassingly plethoric. My point, of course, will be that foster writing, as a generic solecism, turns these linguistic embarrassments to a certain rhetorical advantage, in ways that recall the dedifferentiating effects both of orphaned memory and of phantom pain.

As orphaned memory exacerbates the statement/utterance or remembered/remembering split, so foster writing works to produce a simultaneous sense of severe referential inadequacy (the effect of fragmentation) and of hyperreadability (the effect of hypotyposis). But it does so—and this is the crucial point—in such a way as to align, in the mind of a reader, the object of referential lack and the object of interpretive excess—a combination that might be regarded as an exact definition of phantom pain. In foster writing, then, questions like "What is this statement *about?*" and "What does this act of utterance *mean?*" begin to converge; they become nearly the same question.[6] As a result the referential does not become less elusive, but even more so because of its status as an (unstated) object of an act of phrasing (the status that, theoretically, it always has); and the outcome is that it thus comes to enjoy a kind of hallucinatory or hyper reality, the effect of the "phantom." In orphaned memory the split between the there and then of reference and the here and now of utterance is uncanny because, as I've explained, memory brings together in an individual's psychic experience that which is known to be other; in phantom pain as it is produced through foster writing the effect of strangeness arises because the disjoined—that is, the referential pain of the other in the there and then and the object of my reading in the here and now—becomes the same, the same pain, although now it is the difference between subjects (my reading, the other's experience) that persists. Relaying orphaned memory as phantom pain by means of the figural assemblage I'm about to describe, foster writing combines the effects of both. Because the (orphaned) referential object and the (phantom) object of my reading are dedifferentiated—the same object but not the same as each other—the distant referent (say Auschwitz, the Lager) and the immediate circumstances in which I read (say Ann Arbor, Michigan, in the year 2000), which I *know* to be vastly different, are crammed into a stammer. Reality becomes oddly dual.

With respect to a Swiss orphanage in the immediate postwar period, that experience of dedifferentiation or disjunctive synthesis is what, in *Fragments,* Dössekker describes as having been Binjamin Wilkomirski's experience. And the trope that structures this account of Wilkomirski's phantom pain is the trope of vividness that is known technically as hypotyposis. If asyndeton is etymologically the trope of lack of binding together, hypotyposis is the trope of vivid particularity that produces a hallucinatory effect of copresence: copresence of the here and now (of reading) and the there and then (of the read), and thus of subject and object of an experience of perception that is nevertheless known to be mediated by distance in time and space. Of course, all the memories reported in *Fragments* are elusive, amputated, fragmented. It is those associated with Switzerland, that is, with orphanhood and foster care, that are also shot through, in the first instance for the young Binjamin, with hauntedness, copresence, and hypotyposis. In the narrative logic of the book, it's obviously necessary for the child to leave the camp in Poland for that experience to subsist, hauntingly, in Switzerland. So the train journey, as I've mentioned, furnishes the relay between the two; and the two orphanages, one in Cracow, the other in Switzerland, underscore the symmetry, suggesting indeed that the whole book can be read as a meditation on transportation and transportability as that which connects the disconnected.

But the crucial and determining moment of break in the narrative is not, therefore—as in most Holocaust narratives—the entry into the camp but rather the child's exit from the camp, when he quits his only reality and enters an outside world that for him is devoid of reality because it does not exist, so that he is able to imagine his release from the Lager only in strictly Lager terms: it is "what the older children call 'the death walk'" (111). One can only leave the camp in order to die. Logically, therefore, his emergence from the camp coincides with his becoming a ghost, someone who lives—or seems to live—although really dead. Already in Poland he confides to his Cracow friend Mila: "Both of us were living among the living. Yet we didn't really belong with them—we were actually dead, on stolen leave, accidental survivors who got left behind in life" (82). This sense of his spectrality in the world outside the camp—the ghostliness that makes him an embodiment of orphaned memory—coincides absolutely, then, with his own hauntedness: his consciousness that there is a reality of pain that lies behind in Auschwitz and has not been abolished by, but is more real than, the new, unfamiliar, not really credible, and therefore doubly frightening world into which he has emerged. The two coexist, and their coexistence—for the young survivor of the camps—is the meaning of aftermath.

In Switzerland, then, it's not the long trip from Poland but a simple rail trip from the orphanage to his foster home that instantly calls up a piece of camp knowledge: to be put on a transport is to disappear, never to return. "'No, no transport, no—I won't go on any transport,' I screamed despairingly" (120). Food becomes an ordeal of anxiety *because* it is scarily abundant and varied. The garden is surrounded, like a camp, by a high fence that it is forbidden to climb. The cellar is a nightmare; it contains racks for storing fruit that resemble the stacked bunks in the barracks, and more frighteningly still, a furnace (German *Ofen*). "The oven door is smaller than usual, but it's big enough for children. I know, I've seen, they use children for heating too" (125). At school, a lesson about Wilhelm Tell—Swiss national hero—resonates with the phrase "heroes of the Third Reich": the teacher metamorphoses into a block warden, and the image of Tell shooting the apple from his son's head becomes an SS man aiming at a child—bizarrely, however, since bullets are too precious to waste on children (132). On an excursion, a ski lift becomes a "death machine," or rather *the* death machine itself, to which children are hooked and carried up the mountain, only to disappear, the hooks returning empty for more children (142). In short, "the camp's still here. Everything's still here" (125). And it's the camp that's real, everything else is deceit and trickery. And so later, on watching a documentary on the liberation of the camps: "Liberation—it's not true! . . . Nobody ever told me the war was over. Nobody told me that the camp was over. Finally, definitively over" (148–49).

This derealization of the actual, the Swiss here and now, in favor of a much more real there and then, is, of course, what motivates Dössekker's firm belief that his identity is that of Wilkomirski, not the ghostly identity now named Dössekker. It is also, for readers, a powerful ironizing device, vividly demonstrating the actual proximity of allegedly civilized existence to the barbaric, and denouncing civilization, therefore, as a pretense. But finally it is a device of hypotyposis that ultimately presences the world of the Lager, both in Switzerland and in the world in which one reads. Before it does this, however, it is only the *description* of a hypotyposis, that is, of an illusion—a form of flashback—that afflicts the traumatized consciousness of the young Wilkomirski. The illusion can be of interest to us, as readers, but we don't necessarily have to participate in it. What is it, then, that shifts the mimesis of Wilkomirski's phantom pain so that the description becomes a vehicle of phantom pain for readers?

This outcome arises, I propose, from the fact that the figure of hypotyposis in these passages is grafted onto the figure that informs the writing as a whole, which is that of fragmentation, a form of asyndeton. Fragmentation and hypotyposis have in common their concentration on detached details. Fragmented discourse obviously functions in this way as a mimesis of amputated, orphaned, free-floating memories, bereft of context; the text strings together these bits of memory in short chapters, following more an associative than a chronological order. Fragmented narrative thus allies itself readily with the feature of hypotyposis that consists of focusing on a detail (a fruit rack, a furnace, an image of Tell) that is amputated from its derealized context (that of peaceful Switzerland) and becomes what the fragments of memory have been all along, for the reader: metonyms of the *univers concentrationnaire* (barrack bunks, a crematorium oven, an SS man anomalously wasting a bullet on a child), that is, of the *real.* In this way, the effect of hypotyposis described as Binjamin's experience merges into the response to fragmentation the reader has developed throughout the whole narrative, which is itself a response of involvement.

Asyndeton is a privileged figure of Holocaust witnessing, but it is also crucial to the genres of AIDS testimonial that I call dual autobiography and collective autobiography (or the farewell symphony). It's a figure that can take different forms. It is classically described as arising when syntactic connectives are strategically omitted (e.g., in the phrase "here today, gone tomorrow"): a certain disconnectedness is mimed, but a continuity of sense is left to the audience to supply, and the audience does so. A similar compensatory response underlies the effectiveness of "suspended" sentences ("Do that again and I'll . . .") in which the meaning is interrupted on the assumption that it does not *have* to be spelled out. Similarly, the kind of narrative fragmentation that occurs in texts like *Fragments* that mime orphaned memory compels interpretive amplification on the part of readers; a "symbolic" reading supplies the missing pieces that form a context—here the context of the Holocaust—for the mere *Bruchstücke,* the broken bits, that are all the text is able to furnish, a little as when, in conversation, someone says: "You know what I'm saying?" By synecdoche, a "whole" is extrapolated from its scattered parts, from whose nature that of the whole (which does not have to be stated) is deduced. To do this, I need not have "known" the Holocaust in the sense of having been there, or in the way that a historian might know it; I need only to recognize its reality and *relate it to myself,* which presumably I do on the basis of personal experiences of pain that I remember. My response, to something that is phrased in this way for me to read but not said, is one of anagnorisis—recognition as remembering, remembering as the negation of my previously supposed ignorance. It's an acknowledgment that I did not need for this thing to be spelled out, although I did need to be re-minded of it, for it to become real to me, real as it is to Binjamin Wilkomirski, hauntingly so. In the supposedly strange (that which, for me, is devoid of context) I recognize something deeply familiar (its context is mine). My identificatory reading, in response to textual asyndeton as the mimesis of orphaned memory, has brought me close to an experience of hypotyposis like that of Binjamin in Switzerland, an experience of the phantom.

Reading *Fragments,* then, and compensating in this way for its gaps, we draw on the cultural memory we've always had of the Holocaust, but in order to recognize now, thanks to our own memory of personal pain, the horror of the Holocaust that we had forgotten, denied, or ignored. We always knew, somehow, about the children, did we not? But now we remember them; and their pain is *realized,* by us, in the form of a phantom pain of our own. I intend both senses of the word *realized,* for this is not only like young Binjamin's inability to forget Auschwitz in Switzerland; it's also not so different from what happens when Bruno Dössekker, a Swiss musician and instrument-maker, draws on collective memory and offers the hospitality of an identity to the probably imagined Binjamin Wilkomirski, orphaned like so many others in the Holocaust but whom Dössekker *recognizes* and takes in, recognizes as "himself." Few readers, I take it, will go so far as actually to exchange identities as Dössekker has done. But reading, for us, is like memory for him in that it mobilizes our capacity to foster the orphaned, and to give it the reality—the haunting reality—of a phantom pain of our own. As in the cruel ditty with which his schoolfellows taunt young Binjamin:

> Der Bettelbub, der Bettelbub,
> Er hat noch immer
> Nicht genug,

there's always a beggar child in culture, whose demand goes unsatisfied ("er hat *noch immer* nicht genug") and whose haunting, therefore, can't be plumbed. It's an endlessly plural specter that can't be laid, but whom, at least, we can acknowledge and to whom we can respond, in the form of our anxiety and phantom pain.[7] Aftermath texts like *Fragments*—or *Auschwitz and After* or *Zero Patience*—are the agencing vehicles through which that response of recognition is solicited for culture's *Bettelbub.*

Given its legacy of trauma, such writing can't be literal, then. Relaying a severely deficient referentiality of representation (the hauntedness of orphaned memory) by plethorically interpretive readability (the haunting quality of a phrasing of the unstatable productive of phantom pain), its mode is inevitably that of the symbolic. Its truth is neither the verifiable truth of the historical (which attempts to deal with the real) nor the unverifiable, if believable, truth of the fictional (which deals in the imaginary)—nor yet the combination of the two that would make it a historical fiction—but the recognizable truth that arises from the readability of the figural. In the thinking of young Binjamin Wilkomirski, "[A]ll mothers have to die once they've had children" (85), and orphanhood, therefore, is both universal and exactly synonymous with survival. Our inheritance from the dead is the very fact of their death, itself the consequence of our being born; and the question, therefore, is to understand the nature of this fatal orphanhood. *Fragments* furnishes at least three allegories of the crucial event that is the death of the mother and the birth of the orphan. One is the gaunt female cadaver, lying on a pile of cadavers in the camp, whose belly moves and "gives birth"—to a rat, which has been gnawing her insides.

> Other rats run startled out of the confusion of bodies, heading for open ground.
> I saw it! I saw it! The dead women are giving birth to rats!
> Rats!—they're the deadly enemies of the little children in the camp. (86)

In this nightmare vision, orphanhood is nothing but disconnection, interruption, break: "Nothing connects to anything else any more" (87). The death of the mother is the death of the child; the vision is a figuration of the Real of the camps (the impossible in Lacan's lapidary definition).[8] But then, there is also Frau Grosz's disappearance as the train from Poland arrives in Switzerland, leaving the child in a "waiting room" that is the exact point of conjunction between the Wilkomirski narrative and the story of Bruno Dössekker (*né* Grosjean). Surely this is a figuration of the Lacanian Imaginary, an illusory solution whereby in orphanhood there is *no* break, but only identity—not an identity with the mother, however, but an identity constructed, somewhat desperately, out of abandonment, as absolute continuity between the Polish orphan and the Swiss orphan. It's as if, ultimately, *all* our orphanhoods were the *same* orphanhood, so that Binjamin's plaintive question: "Why am I always the one who's left behind?" (18) means that the one left behind is always *I,* the one with whom "I" identifies.

Orphaned Memories, Phantom Pain

The third figuration of survival as inheritance is the episode in which Binjamin is surreptitiously taken through the camp to see his dying mother, who hands him a strange gift:

> "What's this?" I asked the gray uniform as we reached my barracks.
>
> "That's bread," she said, and "You have to soften it in water, then you can eat it." Then she went away. (50)

The piece of dry, stale bread—a *Bruchstück* or fragment—is a figure of orphaned memory, but also, as a fragment that joins the child to his mother even as it marks their separation, a symbol of the Symbolic, that is, of the register in which I've attempted to read *Fragments* and the category to which the representations of the Real and the Imaginary in the text themselves belong. Young Wilkomirski draws surprising sustenance from this, his sole inheritance from the lost mother, even as it shrinks to virtually nothing:

> I spent a long time chewing on the softened bread and then dunking it again into the little ration of water in my mug, and chewing again, over and over again, until the water was all used up and the crust had shrunk to a tiny little ball.
>
> Finally, all that remained was the indescribably delicious smell of bread on my fingers as I held them to my nose again and again. (50–51)

What we survivors have inherited from the dead is the order of the Symbolic; its signs are the inevitability of mediation, transportation, relay; all the evidence of aftermath that is hauntedness and haunting; copresences that do not coincide, the "again and again" of the *Bettelbub* who never gets enough, orphaned memories and phantom pain. Perhaps that isn't much; but like the bread whose smell never quite leaves the fingers, it isn't quite nothing at all.

Roll Call, or Carrying the Dead

If aftermath writing is symbolic and relays a hauntedness (a severe referential lack) by—or more accurately as—a haunting (a compensatory interpretive readability), a deficiency of statement by/as a phrasing of the unstated that hypostasizes its status as utterance, one of its symbolic practices is to deploy symbolic objects, such as Binjamin's bread, and symbolic places like the orphanage, which become the topoi of aftermath. Such objects and places are symbols in that they refer to disconnectedness as an effect of trauma but do so by figuring it, metaphorically or metonymically, in such a way as to make the disconnectedness itself readable as an index of pain, and hence produce some sort of reconnection. It is this relay that they perform that produces the effect of "reporting" I described in chapter 3. (We can say, then, in retrospect, that the hospital in *Regeneration* is a symbolic place, where the poetry of Sassoon and Owen transforms the rifles' stutter into a stammering text—and we'll see in chapters 6 and 8 other hospitals that function similarly as symbolic sites and places of relay.) In *None of Us Will Return,* the first volume of Charlotte Delbo's *Auschwitz and After* trilogy, there is both a memorable symbolic object, Alice's leg, and an unforgettable symbolic place, to which the narrative returns again and again like Binjamin making his bitter-delicious bread last. This place is the *Appellplatz* where the twice-daily ordeal of roll call occurs.

After Alice died, and left Block 25 for the crematorium, her artificial leg, having somehow "detached itself" from her body, was—as Wilkomirski might say—left behind, orphaned. We readers have not previously met Alice; we know of her only her abandoned leg.

> Lying in the snow, Alice's leg is alive and sentient. It must have detached itself from the dead Alice. . . .
>
> . . . Alice had been dead for weeks yet her artificial leg was still resting in the snow. Then it snowed again. The leg was covered over. It reappeared in the mud. This leg in the mud. Alice's leg—severed alive—in the mud. (41)

The leg is a *Bruchstück,* an abandoned, orphaned memory—and it returns, again and again, as a sign of reconnection and for Alice's friends a bearer of phantom pain. A figure of aftermath, it is also, as a prosthetic device, an emblem for writing as relay. For the trilogy's title, *Auschwitz and After,* tells us that Delbo's writing is itself conceived both as an exploration of aftermath (not just Auschwitz but also Auschwitz's after) and, as something left behind, a potential mode of reconnection following a brutal interruption—that is, as both a study of and an intervention in the problematics of survival.

Less evidently, the title also hints at a temporal problematics tied to the phenomenon of return, that is, to the relation of a "math" or disaster (Anglo-Saxon *maeth,* a mowing of grass) and its aftermath (originally a second mowing in the same season). For math and aftermath are conjoined in such a way that before and after cannot be disentangled: Auschwitz remains present in after-Auschwitz (when Auschwitz is supposedly over), but conversely Auschwitz's aftermath was already anticipated in Auschwitz, as if aftermath were part of its nature as math. (Alice's leg, for example, which returns as the aftermath of Alice's death, also demonstrates the sense in which aftermath is already part of the math called Auschwitz.) As a result of this tangle, the time of aftermath is chronological or "measured"—there is Auschwitz and after-Auschwitz—but simultaneously unmeasured and achronological, because "after" does not signify that the math is over; Auschwitz returns in, and as, its own aftermath. This out-of-jointness of time—a symptom of hauntedness (*Hamlet* again)—will be a major topic, indeed to my mind the major topic, of the trilogy. It might be described, like the limp to which one imagines Alice in life was subject—a limp both produced and palliated by her device—as a dehiscence; and it makes relay at best a clumsy business. My difficulty with prepositions is a sign of this clumsiness. Does the symbolic relay the hauntedness of representation as referential deficiency *by* (substituting for it) the hauntingness of interpretive readability, or *as* (in the form of) such a haunt? Does Auschwitz return *in,* or *as,* its aftermath? These impossible both/ands are figured in Alice's leg, on which she limped out the (un)measure of her days in the camp and which now returns, and returns—spectrally—as the aftermath of her having been mowed down.

Each of the titles of the trilogy's three volumes—which, like the trilogy's own title, map out a chronological narrative of deportation, internment, and return—also alludes, like the leg and the main title, to the problematics of (after)math. *None of Us Will Return (Aucun de nous ne reviendra)* sounds the key verb, *return* (or in French *revenir,* whose connotations include that of ghostliness, cf. *revenant*). It does so in the future tense, putting us, so to speak, on Auschwitz time; for this is the despairing perspective of the prisoners in the camp. It becomes ironic, though, in the perspective of our reading, since the existence of Delbo's text is evidence of her having, in some sense, returned: she has survived Auschwitz in order to write *None of Us Will Return,* with its now inappropriate—but *therefore* still valid—negative future tense. In recognition of which the final sentence of the volume repeats the titular phrase, but rephrases it as "None of us was meant to return" (114). This translation is deceptively clarifying, though, for the French reads "Aucun de nous n'aurait dû revenir" (not *ne devait revenir*). The sentence can certainly be interpreted, logically, in the way that Rosette Lamont's translation suggests; but it also means, more enigmatically, none of us *should* have returned. It's as if, even though the return has taken place, there is something problematic or wrong with it: Auschwitz is the place, it seems, from which to return may well be a mistake, for—as will eventually become clear—aftermath cannot be discounted (as the English translation discounts it), and surviving may not signal the cessation of pain but rather the return of that pain.

Similarly, the second volume, *Useless Knowledge,* mediates narratively between Auschwitz and after-Auschwitz according to conventional before-and-after chronology. This title, however, turns out to amplify and clarify, and thus to repeat, the sense of "Aucun de nous n'aurait dû revenir," for the text makes it clear that, although the knowledge acquired in Auschwitz persists when the prisoners return, such knowledge is without currency in France. Its persistence serves only to dissociate their painful survival from the blithe survivorhood of those who regard Auschwitz knowledge as irrelevant to their lives. Although it haunts the living, through the very presence of the survivors among them, it does so without their being aware of it and its force and significance go unrecognized; while its bearers, the handful of Auschwitz survivors, find that they have, therefore, not really returned at all and are still, as it were, confined to their camp. As in Auschwitz they were beasts of burden, they now carry the burden, equally absurdly, of their Auschwitz knowledge, which has the form of their remembrance of the dead. Their return *from* Auschwitz is rendered a non-return by the return *of* Auschwitz in their very survival: a double experience of untimeliness. So finally the third title, *The Measure of Our Days (Mesure de nos jours),* is taken from a line of verse that was quoted by Delbo in the camp but is now recalled in aftermath by another survivor, Mado, because of its peculiar aptness to their situation as survivors burdened with useless knowledge. The line, to which I'll return in some detail, captures the temporal disjunction that separates "we," the survivors who in aftermath are still on Auschwitz time, from the measured time of the living ("measured" in all senses) who do not know what it is to live: "The time you measure is not the measure of our days" (257). And if one recalls that mensuration (including the metrical measurement of verse) was once performed by pacing, this line also refers us back to Alice's leg, and the unsteady gait it implies. If, in *Fragments,* the disjunctive synthesis that is the relation of (after)math takes the form of uncanny copresence (orphaned memory, phantom pain), it arises in Delbo's trilogy rather as a problem of disjunction within time itself: a dehiscence between time that is measurable, having a before and after, and a time that is without measure—the time of Auschwitz, and of death—that nevertheless co-occurs with the first, like a temporal stammer.

The rhetorical problem of relay that is thus posed for the text will be how to cause the unmeasured time of Auschwitz and death to return in the measured time of narrative, as it returns in the survival of the survivors—how, that is, to mime time's out-of-jointedness—but in such a way that time without measure becomes readable for those of the living whose state of survivorhood, confining them to measured time, precludes them from awareness of unmeasure. If this could be done, the return of Auschwitz in the text would make possible the full return of the survivors, which is otherwise made impossible by the returning of Auschwitz that distinguishes their survival from the survivorhood of the living. And the full return of the survivors would coincide with a new awareness, on the part of the living, of their own hauntedness, that is, of their connection not only to the survivors who haunt them, but also to the dead of Auschwitz by whom the survivors are themselves haunted. By its haunting effect on the survivors in the camp, Alice's leg prefigures such a successful return, while the leg's prosthetic character also suggests an understanding of writing as a similar device of prosthesis, one that would make walking with a limp a model for writing capable of relaying time without measure and time that's measured—writing that would thus palliate, if not heal, the effects of amputation, of the separation (of the dead from the living, of the inmates of the camp from the world, of the survivors from the living) that constitutes the initial trauma.

So it's notable that the detached limb can be thought an emblem of the choppy, fragmented style of Delbo's asyndetic writing, severely shorn, as it is, of connectives. Delbo's sentences are short and paratactically disconnected. The whole text is segmented into fragments of narrative or description, interspersed with short bursts of more meditative but similarly choppy, asyndetic verse. I cite one example only, a (complete) prose fragment in two sections:

> Roll call lasted till the searchlights illuminated the barbed wire, till night.
> Throughout the roll call, we never looked at them.
> A corpse. The left eye devoured by a rat. The other open with its fringe of lashes.
>
> Try to look. Just try and see. [Essayez de regarder. Essayez pour voir.] (84)

Moreover, as the focus here on graphic detail and the emphasis on the concluding injunction indicate, Delbo's terse writing seeks the effect of hypotyposis, and on occasion even mimes the vividness of flashback, the sense of a haunting copresence of there and then (Auschwitz) and here and now (Paris). A truck unloading window dresser's dummies in an urban street/a pile of stiff corpses in the snow. The "thirst" in a café that means "I'd like a drink"/the unbearable thirst of the camp. A train station where arrivals and departures are separate/the selection ramp where "those who arrive are those who are leaving" (3). Similar figures of aftermath as a combination of asyndeton and hypotyposis we encountered in *Fragments;* here too they bespeak a dismemberment painfully re-membered.

But remembering writing like this is survival writing, visited by the return of Auschwitz; what it mimes is the condition of a return that is a nonreturn. To begin to see how it might make an appeal and engage the commitment of readers absorbed in their survivorhood, and thus become the vehicle of a true return of the survivors—not only haunted but also haunting—we need to look at the model proposed by the symbolic place with which Alice's leg is also associated, the *Appellplatz.* A common topos of Holocaust writing, roll call in the camp is a subject to which, in *None of Us,* Delbo reverts as to an obsession, as if for her roll call is the ordeal that best captures the nature of the whole Ordeal, its crucial synecdoche. The reduction of individuals to a gray mass of anonymous figures; the gratuitous cruelty of forcing starved, thinly clad, physically exhausted and psychologically demoralized people to stand for hours motionless in the snow; the selections for the gas and for medical experiments; the sight of the dead en route to the ovens, but also (as we've seen) the mandatory presence, alongside the still living, of the corpses of those who have died overnight or during the day; all this on top of endless deprivation, unbearable fatigue, daily beatings—this ordeal figures the nature of the camps itself: their inhuman cruelty, meticulously organized in conception, random in execution. "Who can endure roll call?" (22; translation modified).

But where Alice's leg figures detachment and the possibility/impossibility of return, roll call figures a situation of extremity that is at the opposite pole from return—the very threshold of death. At the same time, however—something that surprises Delbo—it is a twice-daily manifestation of a will to survive, and of tacit agreement among the women prisoners that the only way to endure is through collective solidarity and mutual support.[9] Its meaning, then, is that detachment from the community itself spells death. Integration into a group doesn't make one invulnerable, but it does provide a degree of protection, warmth, companionship; for the worst form of invulnerability is to be separated from the group. So the women huddle together:

> Shoulders hunched and chests drawn in, each woman places her hands under the arms of the one in front. Those in the front row can't do this, we rotate [*on se relaie,* "we relay one another"]. Backs to chests, we stand pressed against one another, and even as we establish a single circulatory system we are still frozen by the cold. Feet, isolated extremities that remain outside the system, cease to exist. (63; translation modified)

This dual character of roll call—an unendurable ordeal bordering on death, an occasion for solidarity—is dramatized in her own person by Delbo's narrator, who mainly says "we," not "I" (as indeed she does here), and dramatizes herself only rarely. But at roll call, she tells us in this passage, there is a regular occurrence. Charlotte is tempted to slip away from the group; yielding to the desire for release in death, she allows herself to faint. That is, she momentarily becomes "I," and in so doing emulates the feet that, outside the system of circulation, cease to exist (the reference to Alice's leg is perhaps unconscious, but not accidental). Fortunately Viva is at her side, Viva rightly so named, who calls her back, slapping her cheeks and calling her name ("it is my mother's voice I hear" [65]). "Viva is strong. She does not faint at roll call. I do" (65). And so, "I return"—"je reviens à l'appel"; that is, I respond to Viva's call, but also I return to roll call.

Roll call, then—French *appel,* German *Appell*—is the occasion of a double *appeal:* the tug of death, the call back to life, albeit a life that, but for group solidarity, would itself be death. And the presence of the dead among the living (the barely surviving) at roll call is the sign, therefore, of roll call's liminal status, between death and life, and, by extrapolation from the metaphor, of a similar inbetweenness of the camp itself, as a place where death and life are likewise not separate but so closely joined that those who are "alive" not only live on intimate terms with the dead but themselves feel as if they inhabit, already, the space of death. The *Appellplatz,* in short, is a space for ghosts: a place of conflicting appeals, where the power of death and the power of life are locked in combat, the odds heavily in favor of death; a space not of life itself but one whence those who inhabit it, so close to the dead, might conceivably return, as ghosts do, to haunt the living. But to die, then, as Alice does and as Charlotte is daily tempted to do, is no longer to be at that intersection, neither to call nor to respond to calls, and to be lost, therefore, not really to the possibility of returning, but rather to collective solidarity—unable to return among those who are themselves ghosts except as an amputated figure, like a frozen foot or Alice's detached leg.

Thus the leg left behind by Alice's death is indissociable, for the group of survivors, from an image of Alice herself as, at the end, she already was in life, that is, of Alice dying in the snow, "Alice dying alone, not calling anyone" [Alice qui mourait solitaire et n'appelait personne] (41). As her ghost, returning from the dead like an orphaned memory, it has its place among those who, symmetrically, are ghostly because, although far from life they are not quite dead; it responds, as it were, to the survivors' call for Alice and returns, as Charlotte comes back in response to Viva's call. But it does not itself call, as Alice in her death called to no one; its return is an only partial and incomplete return of Alice herself. And it is in this incomplete return that the leg foreshadows (by flashforward, as it were) the later fate of the survivors who, like Charlotte and a sad few of her friends, will eventually themselves return from the camps—metaphorically from the dead—to live among the living. For they too will return only incompletely because they return as a partial fragment of the initial group, its detached remnants; and they remain closer to one another and to Auschwitz, therefore, closer also to their dead, than to life in France, and so attached to their old ritual of roll call, their cry unheard by the living and therefore as if they did not call at all, useless as their knowledge is useless. Like Charlotte returning "à l'appel" in the camp, and like Alice's leg, they can return, but only to an *Appellplatz.* That is the sense in which, for them, math continues into aftermath.

Yet it's in keeping with the dual nature of roll call (an ordeal, an occasion of solidarity) that there be, already in Auschwitz, two kinds of roll call: the camp's twice-daily ordeal, and a survivors' roll call, a counter-roll call that signifies a will to endure, like Viva's call to Charlotte. The roll call of math and the roll call of aftermath, that takes stock of the damage and seeks, somehow, to keep going. That it is this second roll call that, like Viva's call to Charlotte, calls to the dead and restores something of the lost continuity between them and the group of survivors is what the story of Alice's leg suggests. On the day in question, a prolonged roll call on the *Appellplatz* was further prolonged by a whole long day spent by fifteen thousand women, who stood under close guard in the frozen air of an icy plain, during which the only event was the passing of a convoy of trucks loaded with corpses but also carrying some howling, protesting women being taken from Block 25 to the gas. When, finally, the assembled women are marched back to the camp, already frozen and exhausted, they are subjected to a gauntlet of SS and guards armed with clubs and whips, which they must run. To stumble and fall is to be beaten some more and hauled off to Block 25 to await death without food, water, or care, or alternatively transport to the gas, whichever comes first. The whole daylong event, in short, has been a selection procedure, a deliberately devised ordeal to sort the weakest from those with greater endurance, and in that sense a kind of exacerbation of Auschwitz's normal roll calls. It was in the panic of the gauntlet that Alice fell and was left behind; with her clumsy leg she had no chance. If she did not call, no one called to her; the failure of solidarity was mutual. "I held on to her as long as I could," reports Hélène remorsefully (39).

Death is described, in *Auschwitz and After,* then, as the sanction of a *general* failure of solidarity, of call and countercall, a failure that occurs under the pressure of extremity and ordeal (i.e., of the Lager, with the *Appellplatz* as its epitome). As a result, the second roll call—the counter–roll call of aftermath, held by the survivors—has two functions. One is to assess the damage and measure what survives: here the question "Who's there?" becomes synonymous with the question "What survives?" The other is to restore the relation of call and countercall that has been interrupted by death and to reassert a measure of sociality and solidarity: the question who's there becomes a call: is anyone there? and awaits a response; the roll call as summation (French *sommer,* to add up) becomes a summons (French *sommer,* to call upon). So the important difference between roll call on the *Appellplatz,* essentially a counting of heads in which it is required only that the numbers add up, and the counter-roll call held as a ritual of survival in the aftermath of disaster will be that the latter is a calling of names. As the rank of five (a counting device for the convenience of the SS) is rewritten throughout the trilogy as the group of five friends (Charlotte, Viva, Mado, Lulu, Carmen), so the régime of the *Appellplatz* is relayed now, by or as another kind of appeal.

> "Viva, is your whole group here?"
> "Yes, all eight of us."
> "What about the next square? Are you all there?"
> "No, Madame Brabander is missing."
> "Who else is missing?"

> "Madame Van der Lee."
>
> "And what about Grandma Yvonne?"
>
> We inquire about the aged, the sick, the weak.
>
> "Here I am," answers the almost imperceptible voice of Grandma Yvonne. We make another count. Fourteen are missing. (38; translation modified)

If Grandma Yvonne responds to the appeal, fourteen do not; they include Alice, "the one who took the longest time to die," as it is later learned (40); Alice alone in the snow, not calling.

When her leg returns, then, it's as if, like Charlotte responding to Viva's call, it returns to *this* appeal, returns to roll call in response to the calling of names. "One morning *before roll call,* little Simone, who had gone to the latrine behind block 25, returned all shaken up. 'Alice's leg is over there. Come see'" (41; emphasis added). Moreover, the response of Alice's leg calls forth, on the part of the survivors, a response to the response, as Simone's "Venez voir" makes clear, so that the reciprocity of calling that was broken by Alice's death is now restored, albeit in a new, spectral form. But I need to back up a bit in order to explain what I mean by this spectrality. In the passage I quoted earlier, the injunction "Essayez de regarder. Essayez pour voir" (84), which recurs twice more in a sequence of three such vivid fragments (84–86), has a double address: self-addressed by the "we" of the group—Delbo's collective subject—it addresses the same injunction (force yourselves to look, don't look away, in order to see) to readers of the text, to whom it means: try to respond to the hypotyposis with vision. Moreover, what the translation "Try to look. Just try and see" tends to obscure is the very careful distinction being made between looking (the means) and seeing (the end), a distinction whose force is clarified, moreover, by the context of Simone's "Venez voir" on the occasion of the return of Alice's leg. "Voir" is a collective response to a *revenir,* a spectral return, the response that, as it were, *validates the return,* and does so by offering the specter the kind of recognition implied in French by the word *voyance* (from *voir*), the form of vision that sees beyond the visible.[10] This, then, is the response accorded to Alice's leg by her surviving friends in the camp, following its return in response to the call of their roll call: they look at the leg and see Alice. But it is the response denied the straggle of survivors who return from Auschwitz to France at war's end, leaving them stranded and unable really to return, still huddled together, despite their release, as they formerly huddled on the *Appellplatz:*

> [The crowd] falls into ranks of five in a bedlam of shrieks and blows. It takes a long time for all these shadows to line up, as they lose their footing on the ice, in the mud and the snow, all these shadows looking for one another, huddling to reduce their exposure to the icy wind. (63; translation modified)

And the question, then, is whether readers of Delbo's text, a collective text emblematized by its recurrent "we," will be able to look at the group of *shadows* it presents, "toutes ces ombres" huddled together and looking for one another, and see them as *shades,* spectral figures returning, whose haunt will otherwise go unrecognized. (The French word "ombres" has both senses.) Will readers offer them the hospitality of a reading that *sees,* the reading requested three times on pages 84–86, or deny that hospitality as, in Delbo's account, it was largely denied the returnees of 1945?[11]

Since the survivors are struggling with their own guilt, their own failure of solidarity with respect to their dead ("I held on to her as long as I could"), they have every reason to assume, if not to expect, that their own returning appeal will go without response. For forgetting the dead, among the survivors, that is, letting them go by failing to call them, is an abandonment of them exactly equivalent to the failure of hospitality, the inability to "see" the returning specters, that the living display; and Hélène's holding on to Alice as long as she could before letting go exemplifies this problem of forgetting as the eventual abandonment of the dead by those who outlive them. It's just a matter of time in each case. The difference, though, is that, whereas the failure of solidarity of the living toward both the survivors and their dead is quite unconscious and guilt-free, forgetting for the survivors is more like an intensely poignant problem, one might say the crucial or defining problem of their survival, like Hélène's guilt over not having held on to Alice long enough. The survivors know themselves to be haunted; the living do not. As a result, the *calling* function of the counter-roll call performed by the survivors in the camp, but repeated and epitomized in the text of *Auschwitz and After* as a narrative of survival, is itself doubled by a function of *recall,* as a counter to forgetting.

But the function of recall will be not only to recall the dead, in the sense of calling them back, but also, finally, to *recall the dead to the living,* in the sense of reminding the living—calling upon them—to remember the dead. And the function of recall in this latter sense has to be understood as compensatory, since recruiting the living to the task of remembrance is the only way to ensure, by relaying the survivors' hauntedness from their personal memory to the collective memory, that forgetfulness (and hence Auschwitz) do not eventually prevail. For the survivors will themselves eventually die—they will abandon their dead in the course of time—and only those who outlive the survivors can inherit their duty of fidelity, the task of reaffirming sociality against death by recalling/calling to the dead. Whence the urgency of the returning survivors truly to return, that is, to convey to the living their own hauntedness—their memory of the dead—by having them hear, and respond to, their call.

As one reads *None of Us,* then *Useless Knowledge* and *The Measure of Our Days,* the roll call motif comes therefore to refer less and less to the *Appellplatz,* which virtually disappears in the later volumes, and to develop instead into scenes of ritual remembering. Calling the names now coincides with an act of deliberate memorization, not a memorializing (which would be an alibi for forgetting), but an active re-membering conceived as a deliberate disciplining of the memory, understood to be subject to forgetting by virtue of the very fact of survival. That is, calling the names, as an act of memorization, works a counterdiscipline to the punitive pseudo-discipline of the *Appellplatz* and of Auschwitz, opposing forgetting—the denial of the dead that prevents their return—in the way the huddling at roll call opposes the cold and the whips, reaffirming solidarity. But roll call as summation (remembering) must also work as summons, and as summons it must call, not only *to* the dead but also—in a way I want to try to understand—*upon* the living, with an implied reminder not to forget the dead. The symbolic structure of calling the names, relaying summation by/as a summons, has as its rhetorical function the duty of making remembering an act of reminding.

But if forgetting is the given of surviving ("to go on breathing is to forget, and to continue remembering is also to forget," as Delbo puts it in a prominent passage concerning her executed husband Georges, 207), if forgetting is just a matter of time, then, it is most specifically associated with the conditions of Auschwitz in that forgetfulness is aided and abetted by the measureless time of Auschwitz, whose victory is marked and confirmed whenever one of the dead is forgotten. In the monotony of the days and nights, for those who live the life of the as-good-as dead, chronology all but disappears, the endless sameness being broken only by exceptional ordeals, special penalties and unusually punitive roll calls (52)—which thereby, however, become precious mnemonic aids. For this purgatorial time of the camp, out of joint with the measured time of the living, makes it very easy to lose track of the deaths and thus to forget the dead. And as a mnemonic device, roll call as the calling of the names—the names both of the dead and of the survivors—is first and foremost a way of combatting this deadly effect of Auschwitz time by reintroducing into it some degree of recall in the form of time-measurement, keeping track. In the same way, Delbo describes herself exercising her memory by recalling telephone numbers, Metro lines and, most crucially, poems—fifty-seven of them. For measure aids memory, and metrical verse is the epitome of time that is measured and hence an essential key to battling Auschwitz. "I was so afraid that they might escape my mind that I recited them to myself every day, all of them, one after the other, during roll call" (188).

In their later survival, which is purgatorial and Auschwitz-like by virtue of the returnees' inability to return, Delbo and her friends continue, therefore, to apply themselves to the same mnemonic exercise of recalling the names. Indeed, the problem of forgetting and remembering, as what is common to survival in the camp and to postcamp survival, is central in particular to *Useless Knowledge,* the mediating volume of the Auschwitz/after-Auschwitz trilogy, as if their failure to resolve this key problem is what actually constitutes the uselessness of the knowledge acquired in Auschwitz and hence the inability of the survivors to return. In one crucial passage of this volume Delbo is attempting, then, as an exercise of memory, to recall, some years "after Auschwitz," a particular day when she was able to bathe briefly in a stream. When exactly was it? All the details except the stream and her bath have gone; in her attempt to reconstitute them, she calls the names.

> Since it was the beginning of April—a fact I know by performing a simple calculation: it was sixty-seven days after our arrival on January 27—seventy members of our group [of 230] were still alive. I have a reliable memory of having kept a tally of these figures at the time. But there weren't seventy of us at the stream, because among the survivors many were confined to the *Rewier* with typhus. Yvonne Picard had died already, Yvonne Blech also, Vera not yet; she died only in July. I was therefore with my small group: Viva, Carmen, Lulu, Mado. They entered the *Rewier* later, after coming down with typhus. (148; translation modified)

Her after-Auschwitz calculation thus reproduces, and repeats, the calculations that the group had already regarded it as their duty to perform in the camp:

> We had taken the trouble to count the days since our arrival . . . in order to keep track of the dates. What dates? Why did it matter whether it was Friday or Saturday, this or that anniversary? The dates we had to remember were those of Yvonne's or Suzanne's death, the death of Rosette or Marcelle. We wanted to be able to say, "So and so died on . . ." when they'd ask us after we returned. That's why we kept a scrupulous count. There were long discussions among us when we did not agree on the count. But it seems to me that we kept accurate records. We'd keep checking all the time. "No, the dogs, that was two days ago not yesterday." On Sundays, the columns did not leave the camp. That provided a point of reference and allowed us to reestablish a correct count when we lost track of the days. (149; translation modified)

Calling the names, then, like keeping a tally of the dates and seasons, reciting poetry or learning Molière's *Le Misanthrope* by heart from a copy bought at the exorbitant price of one day's ration of bread, is part of a struggle against camp time that continues, unabated, in postcamp survival. It continues because the inability of the living to hear the survivors calling, and to see what they are given to look at, retains the returnees in "Auschwitz," and because the survivors' own inability accurately to recall the dead (in all senses of the word recall) makes their calling of the names an insufficient reminder to the living of their hauntedness.

There are two figures of this insufficiency. One is Charlotte's husband Georges, executed in the prison of La Santé before her deportation. Delbo recalls their final meeting as the crucial moment of separation after which survival, as the dilemma of forgetting and remembering, the limp of measured time and measureless time, began. She is like Ondine in Giraudoux's play, condemned ("called") to forget her human lover:

> The third time [the guard] called [*Au troisième appel*], I had to go, just like . . . Ondine whom the King of the Sylphs had to call thrice while she was bidding farewell to the Chevalier who was about to die. After the third call, Ondine would forget . . . [for] to go on breathing is to forget. . . . (207).

The moment when math merges into aftermath is the moment when forgetting begins. But the other figure of memory's insufficiency is all those in the camp whom the "we" of the small group of French women political prisoners excludes, as an anonymous "they" whose names cannot be called. Of these, Jewish women are emblematic. Delbo records an early encounter with an anonymous girl who has given up hope. "Smoke sweeps across the camp weighing upon us and enveloping us in the odor of burning flesh" (32; translation modified). Later, in *Useless Knowledge,* it is "Esther," who has a name but whose fate signifies the failure of comradeship (139). Frequently Delbo records herself observing with anxiety the conditions, so much worse than those she and her friends endured, under which the Jewish women who had escaped selection at the ramp labored and struggled. But there is also the teddy bear that Charlotte is given at the Christmas party of 1943, an even more general symbol, perhaps, for those not included in her calling of the names because, like Alice's leg, it surfaces specifically as a ghostly residue or returnee, a remnant, but of someone Delbo never knew. "This is how a doll, a teddy-bear, arrived in Auschwitz. In the arms of a little girl who would leave her plaything, with her clothing carefully folded, at the entrance to 'the showers'" (166; translation modified). If calling the names is necessary, then, it cannot be sufficient as an exercise of recall, summation and summonsing, because the list is not exhausted by the names one knows and can call. The hauntedness that such an act of memorization enacts is seriously disabled, as an instrument of anti-Auschwitz reminding (i.e., witness), because that hauntedness is itself haunted by those of the dead whom it "forgets."

Yet, if calling the names cannot recall the dead from death, it does remain a necessary act; and that is because it responds to a moral obligation. Faithfulness to the dead requires that, if they cannot be reclaimed (called back) from death, they be at least reclaimed from the possession of the camp. And this can be done if the survivors assume, as a responsibility, what is imposed by the camp—by virtue of the rules of roll call on the *Appellplatz*—as a back-breaking task. For the dead must be present at roll call, which means they must be carried by the survivors. Carrying loads in general, in Delbo's account, sums up the camp's punitive discipline, whether it be working in the marshes or on demolition sites, or carrying soil under a hail of blows for purposes of "gardening." She pays careful attention, therefore, to the ubiquitous if rudimentary carrying devices that seem to define the prisoners' lives: what she calls the "tragues," or hods (German *Tragen,* from *tragen* to carry) and, for the corpses, the "civières," or stretchers. And the portability of the dead thus becomes crucial to her thinking about the battle for significance (death against solidarity) and the conflicting calls (the call of death, the survivors' countercall) that define the *Appellplatz* and make it a synecdoche for the camp. The ease with which the dead can slip from being a person to becoming a load is counterbalanced by the sense in which they can be shouldered, as an act of moral defiance, and brought back into the company of the survivors through memory and the calling of names. So, after the meditations in *Useless Knowledge* on the duty of memory and the fatality of forgetting, it is this issue of the portability of the dead and the task of carrying them that surfaces most urgently in *The Measure of Our Days,* where the question arises of making the survivors' calling of the names into an instrument—the *trague* or the *civière*—that not only brings the dead back from Auschwitz in their company, but also extends their portability, beyond the company of the survivors who are their haunted bearers but will themselves die one day, into the world of the living, where they will be more permanently and securely reclaimed from the possession of the camp. Can the survivors' calling of the names, inadequate and deficient as it is, function as an *agencement,* an instrument of relay and reclamation, capable of reintroducing the dead into the collectivity of the living that ignores them, causing them to be "seen" and their haunt to be recognized?

But the stakes of carrying the dead were in fact defined as early as the text entitled "Evening" in *None of Us.* One day, as the group works in the hellish conditions of the marshes, two of their number, Berthe and Anne Marie, succumb and fall dead under the guards' shrieks and blows. They were counted out at morning roll call, they must be present in the evening. So four prisoners, including Charlotte, are told to haul off the bodies many kilometers back to the camp. There are no stretchers; their friends must be their bearers, although the bodies sag heavily in their awkward grasp. "At first, we are carrying Berthe and Anne-Marie. Soon they are nothing but heavy loads that slip out of our grasp with each step" (81); the camp is winning. But then a turning point is reached. The main column is moving too fast and the struggling bearers begin to fall behind; in turn the rearguard escort slows down and relaxes; a young guard reminds Charlotte of her brother and she is emboldened to ask, unthinkingly, if a passing truck might not take the bodies to the camp—an absurd request that is met, of course, by loud laughter and a blow. Discipline is immediately tightened and the stakes again become clear. Lugging their unbearable loads now with dogs straining at their legs, their eyes filled with tears of exhaustion and helplessness, the bearers reach the camp and march past the gate carrying "their" dead with heads held high (according to their motto, "head high or feet first"). Evening roll call with Berthe and Anne-Marie present seems short, although it lasts as long as usual. "Our hearts filled our chests and were beating strongly" (82). Having reclaimed their dead in this way, the survivors are able to weep, not only for Berthe and Anne-Marie but also for the Jewish women who, like them—but as *they* do every day—have brought two bodies back to camp. And thus a kind of victory has been won, a victory for solidarity and survival over the annihilation to which the camp is dedicated; and it's this victory that holds the key, I suggest, to the rhetorical structure of the trilogy as summation and summons, calling up and calling back the dead and calling upon the living.

The only difference between such a manifestation of survivor pride in response to the humiliations of the camp and the significance with which calling the names/carrying the dead is endowed when the survivors (fail to) return to France has to do with the new implied addressee of the act—no longer, in France, those responsible for the Lager but the ordinary folks, enclosed in their self-absorbed survivorhood, whom Delbo calls the living. Fidelity to the dead, as the act of "carrying" them with head held high, now entails a different act of refusal, the rhetorical act of withholding explanation when explanation is demanded as the condition of the hospitality that would enable the survivors, the ghosts who are themselves haunted, truly to return. It isn't just that the survival of the survivors *can't* be explained (as Delbo puts it, if their account of the Lager is true, they should not be there to give it). It's also that, whatever the degree of guilt each survivor may feel for having survived where others unjustly died, explanation would amount to self-disculpation, which would imply acceptance of shame—the same shame against which it was necessary to struggle, on behalf of the dead, in the camp. And finally, too, withholding explanation is in itself an act of fidelity toward the dead in that explanation, supposing it to be possible, in explaining away what is inexplicable in survival, would deprive the dead of their power to haunt, since the hauntedness of the survivors is exactly that which defines the difference between those who bear the memory of the dead and the blithe survivorhood of the living. It would lay the ghosts. Rather, the living must be led to acknowledge the dead by recognizing their own hauntedness, inexplicable as it too may be, in that of the survivors.

At the very end of *Useless Knowledge,* Delbo therefore offers this ironic advice to the living: "After all / better not to believe / these ghostly tales / for if you do / you'll never sleep again / if you believe / these ghostly phantoms / revenants returning / yet unable to tell / how [*ces revenants / qui reviennent / sans pouvoir même / expliquer comment*]" (230–31). This does not mean she would like to explain what does not bear explanation. Rather, in *The Measure of Our Days,* she will substitute for the inexplicable the interpretable, by making the inexplicability of survival the very occasion of a calling of the names. "You don't believe what we say / because / if what we say were true / we wouldn't be here to say it. / We'd have to explain the inexplicable / why Vera who was so strong / died / and I did not / why Mounette . . . / why Yvonne / . . . and not Lulu, why Rosie / . . . and not Lucie, why Mariette / and not Poupette / . . . why Madeleine / and not Hélène / who slept by her side" (276). In this way, the very solidarity of the dead and the survivors that these lines enact, even as they describe the hauntedness of the latter, becomes a challenge to read, that is to "see," by virtue of what amounts to a kind of flaunting of the inexplicable: its display in the absence of any attempt to explain it. The flaunt becomes the vehicle of a relay that makes calling the names, a statement of hauntedness, a way of calling upon that summons the response of reading, that is, an act of haunting. Reference and address—here a deficient reference and a desperate act of address—are once more (see chapter 3) in solidarity, forming an act of relay, a *trague* or a *civière,* that makes the portability of the dead a matter of reporting.

If *The Measure of Our Days* is one long roll call of the survivors, then, it is also, in the first place—like the calling of names that followed the day of the gauntlet and of Alice's death—a remembering of the dead on the part of those who are themselves like ghosts. There is a calling of the names of the survivors—Charlotte, Gilberte, Mado, Poupette, Marie-Louise, Ida, Loulou, Poupette again, Germain, Jacques, Denise, Gaby, Louise, Marceline, Françoise—who each respond with a narrative of return that is always different but essentially concordant with that of the others, concerning the difficulty of returning, the remembrance of the dead, the impossibility of explaining. Mado: "We wanted this struggle, these deaths, not to have been in vain. . . . Our return must therefore assume some meaning. That is why I keep explaining what it was like, around me" (26—note that to explain "what it was like" is exactly the opposite of explaining one's survival). These first-person narratives are orchestrated through Charlotte's writing into a collective "we," which gives the plural narrative the force of a chorus (a technique that foreshadows the "collective autobiographies" of AIDS that I will look at in chapter 7). The specter is plural in this sense, then, as well as in the sense of its being itself haunted. But this chorus reproduces, as a rhetorical phenomenon, the huddling and regrouping, the old rituals of survival—calling the names, recalling the dead—that were developed in the camp, rituals that closely identify the ghostlike survivors with their remembered dead. Gilberte: "I could have shed endless tears after Dédée's death. After the death of Viva, of Grandma Yvonne, of all our companions from Bordeaux. . . . And for Berthe, whose body you carried. . . . Lulu, Carmen, Viva and you" (247). Mado: "Since all are dead, it seems impossible I shouldn't be also. All dead. Mounette, Viva, Sylviane, Rosie, all the others" (257).

And so, everything repeats. The death of Germaine, a survivor, recalls that of Sylviane in the camp; for Charlotte it is a hallucinatory experience of flashback and copresence (312). Germaine's funeral reunites a group who take mutual stock and revive their old habit of obsessive remembering, keeping track, tallying (the incident of the tomatoes: when did it happen? why doesn't Charlotte remember it since, if everything tallies, she must have been there?). "It's us," Delbo says simply. "Among us, it's us" (342; translation modified): "Entre nous, nous sommes nous." "Only when I'm with you all do I remember," adds another, "or perhaps I ought to say recognize your own remembrances." Among "us," there is no problem of communication and no real problem of solidarity with the dead. The problem of communication and solidarity arises elsewhere, in relations between "us" and the living, whose life is lived to a different chronology, one in which Auschwitz does not endlessly repeat, a "measured" time different from the Auschwitz time the survivors share with their remembered dead. And thus Mado *repeats* to Charlotte the verse that Charlotte used to *repeat* back there, *là-bas.* "'The time that you measure is not the measure of our days.' Over there it was. This came from a poem you used to recite. I still remember it" (257). Mado quotes this line in order to correct it, in its reference to Auschwitz: her "Là-bas, si" [Over there it was] means that measured time *was* the measure of the prisoners' days because they engaged in such feverish tallying and keeping count, *against* the measurelessness of Auschwitz time. But the patent sense of the line remains clear: back then, and still now, the measured time of the living is incompatible with the unmeasured days the survivors knew in Auschwitz, and after Auschwitz continue to know, having failed to return among the living.

And yet . . . What the line states is not what it enacts when it is read as verse, that is, in terms of a measured time which is that of the living but in which (as Mado recalls) the survivors too have an important stake since they clung to it so desperately in the unmeasure of Auschwitz. It is not surprising that, of all the poetry Charlotte recited in the camp, it is this verse (whose source I've not been able to identify) that sticks in Mado's mind: for it's a haunting line, already in English prose but much more so in French, and it haunts because it enacts an intimacy of measured and unmeasured time that the statement, with its emphatic negative ("n'est point" in French) denies. True, as Mado gives it—and presumably therefore, as Delbo recalled and recited it in the camp—it forms a sentence that does not readily scan; its unmetricality identifies it with the measureless days of Auschwitz and after. However, its metrical structure is readable, and can be shown as follows:

Le temps que l'on mesure
N'est point mesure de nos jours

(which might be more strictly translated as "Time that is measured / is no measure of our days"). The phenomenon of enjambment, a form of relay, is key to this relation of measured verse to unmeasured sentence: an interruption (the line break) is relayed by a continuity (the run-on sentence), the second hemistich of a classical (6/6) alexandrine being followed by an also perfectly regular (5/3) octosyllabic line. In verse, the statement of incompatibility enacts, rather, a sort of limping relation of dehiscence that joins the two, as an effect of poetic reading.

Notice too that the relation between the hemistich and the octosyllable is one of chiasmus: *Le temps—que l'on mesure—n'est point mesure—de nos jours,* although the symmetry is slightly out of balance, or dehiscent, because of the difference in syllabic length between the hemistich and the octosyllable. Similarly, in the chiasmus, "jours" repeats (but does not echo) "temps" and the three-syllable noun "mesure" of the octosyllable echoes (but does not repeat) the two-syllable verb "mesure" of the hemistich.[12] Alice walks here, on her artificial limb, in this enactment of copresence, that is, of the hauntedness of survivors living simultaneously in the time of the living and in days that approximate the time of the dead. But chiasmus, finally, is also a figure of reversibility, and hence of portability or (two-way) relay: one can't read the unmeasure in the measured verse without, in turn, bringing unmeasure into the time in which one reads; and one can't read the limp of dissociated copresence—the out-of-joint time of aftermath—without becoming aware of the sense in which one participates in it, and is haunted, therefore, as the survivors are haunted. So in the end what the line describes as dissociation is enacted as communication and community, the neutral pronoun "on" functioning, not as the sign of an act of address (as the translation "you" might suggest), but rather as an indicator of that imaginable community, one in which the living ("on"), in their measured time, would also have a place for "nous" and recognize the measurelessness of "our" days.

If the line haunts, then, it's because the complicated relay of statement and utterance works here, like "our" calling of the names, as a calling up of the dead in their measureless time, while calling also upon the living, like Alice's leg—calling upon them, not only to look, but also to see: to see our hauntedness and hence those who haunt us, becoming haunted in turn. Calling upon them, that is, to read, since Mado's line offers no explanation of the inexplicable but merely states the out-of-jointness of (after)math as the experience of the survivors. Since this haunting line also furnishes the title of the volume, one can extrapolate that the volume too, and by extension the trilogy as a whole, constitutes a statement of the inability of the Auschwitz survivors to return from Auschwitz, given the incompatibility of Auschwitz time with measured time, but a statement that in its utterance enacts, or intends to enact, the hauntingness of its readability—a readability whereby measured time bespeaks the measurelessness of Auschwitz and of death, and hence the return of that measurelessness in measured time itself. The prisoners' return among the living depends on the ability of a descriptive statement to be read as a haunting utterance by virtue of the semiotics of indexicality.

As a way of calling upon the living, the description of Auschwitz and after-Auschwitz as roll call in *Auschwitz and After* can finally be said, therefore, to work rhetorically, like Mado's line, as a form of declamation (Latin *clamare,* to cry out), where declamation is understood neither to explain, nor directly to address those who would require an explanation, but to present the inexplicable as a writerly performance requiring to be read. In this, it is like the counter-roll call practiced by the survivors in the ritual of calling the names, which calls up the dead but also functions implicitly as a way of calling upon the living. The declamatory presupposes an audience, but presents its performance—in this case a performance of hauntedness—as itself the object whose significance lies in its being read. That is, it seeks to function as an interpellation (Latin *interpellare,* to call upon or buttonhole), and thus to interrupt (another sense of *interpellare*), to insert itself into the ongoing, measured lives of the living—"measured," of course, in all senses of that word—in a way that disturbs and troubles that measured existence. Or switching to Greek, we might say that Delbo's writing is apodictic (demonstrative) in character. It aims, as my Webster's puts it, to "display, exhibit or explain" what its referential statement represents—the state of survival as (after)math—or more accurately, since in this case its subject matter is the inexplicable, to demonstrate that inexplicability, that is, to manifest it, in lieu of explaining it, and to do so, precisely, by abstaining from any attempt to explain it away. It aims, that is, to make hauntedness haunting, not to lay the ghosts.

To demonstrate or display without explanation is, as I've suggested, to flaunt, and Delbo's work enables us to say, finally, that it is the flaunting of hauntedness that makes hauntedness haunting. If it is true that there is no ontology without a hauntology, it seems to be also the case that there can be no hauntology without a flauntology, since flaunting names the apodictic gesture, the act of relay, that, in causing hauntedness to be *seen,* makes it haunting. Flaunting is, par excellence, the gesture of visibility that requires reading, and the mediation therefore whereby the lacking object of representational or mimetic referentiality can be figurally presenced as an interpretive, that is, recognizable object—the object that haunts. And if haunting is a mode of cultural infiltration, the vehicle by means of which it infiltrates is inevitably, to some degree and always relatively speaking, spectacular and confrontational, therefore, because it is necessarily the performance of a state of im-pertinence (see chapter 2): of the lack of pertinence that characterizes the inexplicable as well as the supposedly irrelevant and makes it an untimely manifestation when, unexpectedly, it shows itself to be relevant.

Giorgio Agamben has recently argued that the aftermath of Auschwitz is shame, that what remains, *quel che resta,* of the camps, their aftermath, is the shame of witness. Shame is the knowledge that the human can be outlived by the inhuman, as in the camps the existence of the *Muselmann* testified. The witness testifies, conversely, to the possibility of the human's surviving the inhuman, but does so only as the bearer of that shameful knowledge, for the true subject of witnessing is the *Muselmann,* while the witness's task is to function as *auctor* or authorizing agent, since the *Muselmann*'s anomic status can become sayable only through the witness's access to the conventional norms of speech. This argument, largely grounded in a reading of Primo Levi, is powerful and highly germane, except that it is skewed and partial because, on the one hand, it identifies the phenomenon of survivor guilt with shame or humiliation *(vergogna),* as opposed to dissociation and im-pertinence, and because on the other, it understands witnessing exclusively as a task of mimetic representation or description, ignoring the phenomenon of reading and readability, that is, of figuration, and hence the possibility of indexical agencing on which my own argument for the witness as a haunted haunter rests. Flaunting, including the flaunting of one's sense of guilt, but also of one's im-pertinence, is exactly the display of not-shame, like carrying one's dead past the gate of Auschwitz with head held high, but in the rhetorical form of a self-affirmation that withholds explanation. It tends therefore to favor semantically empty definitions like the phrase that might be the trilogy's motto: "Entre nous, nous sommes nous." But such tautologies are in turn apodictic because their statement is also a performance that exhibits something—and that something is a haunt. In this respect, Bruno Dössekker's near-tautology, "I am Binjamin Wilkomirski," is exemplary of the agencing function that defines the witness's identity as that of a haunted subject whose hauntedness is made haunting in the act of its affirmation.

The legacy of historical trauma, then, what survives "after Auschwitz," is not just shame, I argue, but also the figure or the symbol, the relay through which language's hauntedness, its inability adequately to represent, becomes haunting language, whose testimonial power—the power of the figural to summon the response of reading—is difficult to ignore because it is a shameless enactment of anomaly, of im-pertinence. The visible transparency of the witness-ghost as flaunter of a haunt, the carrier of the dead, is the sign of the power of figurality to disturb. Like Binjamin's bit of bread, I've said, the symbolic is not much, but it's not nothing. As the flaunt of a haunt, its transparent visibility, one might say, is a way of exercising the powers of the not-nothing that's called zero.

Flaunting the Haunt, or How to Survive in an Epidemic

In 1982, early in the history of the AIDS epidemic, the Centers for Disease Control carried out a "cluster study" designed to confirm what was already suspected, that "GRID" was sexually transmitted by a single infectious agent. In 1987, Randy Shilts published a widely read history of this period, *And the Band Played On,* in which he wrote: "At the center of this cluster diagram was Gaetan Dugas, marked on the chart as Patient Zero *of the GRID epidemic*" (147; emphasis added), a leap of logic that he proceeded to aggravate by identifying Dugas as "the Québécois version of Typhoid Mary" (157). But even when he is more cautious, Shilts continues to finger the hapless flight attendant as "the person who brought AIDS to North America":

> Whether Gaetan Dugas was the person who brought AIDS to North America remains a question of debate and is ultimately unanswerable. The fact that the first cases in New York City and Los Angeles could be linked to Gaetan, who was himself one of the first half-dozen or so patients on the continent, gives weight to the theory. Gaetan traveled frequently to France, the western nation where the disease was most widespread before 1980. . . . (439)

Of course the mass media were even less cautious than Shilts, and soon Dugas was a reviled figure. But then, AIDS had given rise to an epidemic of finger-pointing from the start: first gay men, then Haitians, then African green monkeys were declared the source of infection and became, not unfortunate hosts to a virus whose presence in the bloodstream proved almost always fatal, but dangerous "carriers" to be shunned and avoided. Dugas was but one among many scapegoats.

Scapegoating, a phenomenon that has been influentially studied by René Girard, functions, in circumstances of fear and uncertainty, so as to manufacture some sort of reassuring certainty for an "unaffected majority." More particularly, it seeks to lay the ghost of shared guilt by pinning responsibility for a problem onto a target or targets not randomly, but nevertheless irresponsibly, chosen. The real guilt of a community is deflected and "disacknowledged," disowned by a simple trick. An individual or group is designated as the bearer of the collective guilt and driven out, in a gesture of disconnection that functions as a symbolic act of purification—one, however, that has the most unjust real consequences. The issue on which John Greyson's 1993 film, *Zero Patience,* turns is therefore that of how the victims can respond to what is, in the case in question, a double epidemic: one biomedical, called AIDS, the other a social pathology, an epidemic of blame that functions to deny collective responsibility. And it offers two responses, telling the story of Patient Zero's return among the living as a ghost in search of vindication, the return of the specter (of the collective guilt) that scapegoating sought to lay, but embedding that story in a performance of storytelling that relays Zero's unsuccessful haunt, and turns it, I'll propose, into a successful haunting by substituting a flaunt of its own for Zero's attempted self-disculpation.

Since Zero returns to "tell the story" and "clear [his] name," we can say that the film links the issue of surviving the double epidemic with that of narrative, and asks what story to tell and how to tell it. And since also, like the promiscuous slut he allegedly is, Zero returns in hopes of "getting laid,"—only to get laid, instead, in the sense in which ghosts get laid—it seems that the question that exercises the film (how to respond to an epidemic of blame) reprises the famous title of the pamphlet in which, almost as early in the epidemic as the cluster study, two gay men enunciated the principles of safe(r) sex: "How to Have Sex in an Epidemic." In an atmosphere in which the only alternative to dying gay men were offered by the establishment was—unrealistically, homophobically, and therefore unjustly—the option of giving up sex for the duration, Michael Callen and Richard Berkowitz proposed a thoughtful alternative solution to the problem of surviving; and in the same way *Zero Patience* enacts an alternative, neither-nor solution to the dilemma of blaming or self-disculpation (which, of course, assumes the inculpation it seeks to counter). This is the solution I'll call flaunting the haunt: the questions of how to tell the story, and how to have sex, resolve into the issue of how to haunt without getting laid.

"How can I get laid," wails Zero at a crucial moment, "if nobody can see me?" The issue for him is not the fact of being a ghost, which is a given; ghosts are the normal and necessary product of scapegoating. It is rather how to parlay his invisible or zero-degree haunt into presence and substantiality among the living. But being seen, for him, is the equivalent of telling the true and authentic story of who he is and what he was in life. When he discovers that all representations are deficient—that scapegoating is, in that sense, the type of all representation—his only alternative will be to accept being laid as a ghost, as opposed to getting laid as a living person, and to go back to limbo whence he came. In a way reminiscent of the survivors in *Auschwitz and After,* his return among the living will have been a failed return. He ought rather, the film proposes, to have taken a leaf from Scheherazade's book, for Scheherazade, in *Zero Patience,* is the figure of the consummate survivor. Under the daily renewed sentence of death that is her lot, she survives (and gets sex as well) by telling stories—but crucially *not* the kind of story that Zero wishes to tell. Scheherazade does not survive by telling King Shahriyar the true story of her life (which would be the story of her submission to his cruel whims) but entertains and intrigues him with beguiling fictions. And it is Greyson's film that imitates Scheherazade: it makes no attempt to tell the true story of Gaetan Dugas (whatever that would be), but instead spins an entertaining fiction about the adventures of Patient Zero when he seeks, as a ghost, to return among the living.

But it departs also from Scheherazade's model, in two ways. One is that the film is educational—indeed didactic—in exactly the way Scheherazade's story would be if she were to tell the king the story of her own life, that is, of her persecution by him. The other is that where she is of course discreet about her ingenious solution to the problem of surviving, which consists of gulling her lord and master, the film is entirely up-front about its own alliance with the seductions of representation (which are, of course, those against which Zero himself struggles so ineffectually). That is, it shamelessly flaunts its fictionality, but also—and it is here that its pedagogical character is apparent—its figurality and readability: the fiction is a fable. Where Zero wishes, impossibly, to cease to be a ghost (whether by returning to life or by returning to limbo), the film instead allies itself in this way with his ineffectual haunt, the specter being as we've seen, the figure of figurality and the symbolic. But it does so with a view to making Zero's zero degree haunt more efficacious, that is, truly haunting, amplifying it by passing it through the relay of its own flaunt and giving it, in this way, the visibility that Zero fails to achieve. Its generic models, therefore, are those of campy performance, where camp is understood to imply maximal self-consciousness, and hence affirmation, with respect to artifice. Genres like the satiric review and the Broadway or Hollywood musical are gayified, but so too are the Voltairean philosophical fable and the Brechtean theatrical parable. With Leonard Bernstein's oeuvre in mind, one could say that *Zero Patience* combines *Candide* and *West Side Story*—the tale of star-cross'd lovers and the tale of the innocent abroad (Zero being exactly that camp icon, the ingenue as slut)—and, by blatantly (and indeed shamelessly) camping them up, updates them to the era of epidemic.[13]

This combination of teacherly purpose and love story under the auspices of an art of display brings us to the museum, which is the film's principal symbolic place. As an educational institution, a function it shares in the film with the schoolroom, the museum is the equivalent of the *Appellplatz* in *Auschwitz and After:* it is a microcosmic world of, in this case, scapegoating representations, inhabited (literally) by an arch-scapegoater, Richard Burton. This is Burton the nineteenth-century traveler, translator of the *Thousand and One Nights,* and inventor of the "sotadic zone," who has survived, like the Victorian values he embodies, into the late twentieth century and is employed as a taxidermist in a natural history museum. His current big project is the Hall of Contagion, where dioramas are displayed in which "carriers" of epidemics like plague, typhus, syphilis, and AIDS (the Marseilles plague ship, Typhoid Mary, the black sharecroppers of Tuskeegee, an African green monkey) are represented as the actual causes and origins of these public health disasters. Burton's dusty dioramas with their stiff figures strongly suggest that the museum's perverse understanding of its teaching mission makes it a place that, through scapegoating representation, inflicts death on the living. And the love story that enlivens this therefore spooky place ensues, significantly enough, when Zero the ghost encounters Burton the scapegoater, who traps and imprisons him, planning to make "the person who brought AIDS to North America" (in Burton's eyes a serial killer) the centerpiece of a new display.

As predicted by the fact that Burton is the only person able to see Zero the ghost, love does blossom between scapegoat and victim; and simultaneously Zero's visitation brings the dreary dioramas to life, as they fight back against the confining representations in which they are imprisoned. He represents the zero degree of interpretability that survives scapegoating's fatally reductive mode of referentiality. But, at the same time, and as he learns from the diorama figures, Zero himself begins to *see*—to see, that is, the grounds of his affinity with Burton, which is their shared faith in description as a mode of representation (incriminating in one case, self-disculpatory in the other). But all such representation lies, he now understands, because it produces referentiality as constitutively deficient. Burton can view Zero either as "the person who brought AIDS to North America" or, from a different angle, as "the slut who inspired safer sex"; one representation is (somewhat) more flattering than the other, but each is equally reductive. It's the fact of descriptive representation itself, then, or rather its hypostasization in scapegoating and self-vindication, that comes between the lovers, and Zero opts, therefore, to return whence he came, to death. The museum can only misrepresent; it has no power to restore Zero to life, because its attempt (in this case successful) is always to lay the ghost that haunts it, the "zero" that its representations can't capture.

But since Zero can't be made visible as a living man, there *is* a possibility that remains unexplored, which is that of making him visible, but *as a ghost,* actualizing his potential to haunt instead of diminishing or inhibiting it. A middle way between his getting laid as a human and his getting laid as a ghost, in the way that safe sex is a middle way between sex that brings death and no sex at all, this is the possibility that the film both clarifies, as an option, and enacts rhetorically through the flaunt that is its own performance of im-pertinence. There is, in short, an other way, the film's way, of inhabiting the museum of scapegoating representations, which is to haunt it more visibly than Zero does; and the museum's appropriability in this respect is indicated through Burton's advice to his boss, Dr. Placebo, that it should borrow the techniques of music video, "hi-tech image bombardment," advice that Placebo dismisses as too expensive but that *Zero Patience* follows, and then some—albeit in an engagingly campy, low-tech, homemade (and inexpensive) kind of way. I take this to mean that the deficiency of representation, exemplified by Burton and deplored by Zero, is not inevitably fatal; and that it can be compensated by a relay—the image bombardment, or the flaunt—that produces interpretability, relaying the regime of the descriptive representation by that of the figural, the symbolic, an act of agencing.

The relay that is a flaunt might well be described, indeed, as exactly a *placebo effect,* not in the sense that a placebo is an inadequate gesture falsely presented as an adequate measure (which would describe scapegoating), but in the sense that "placebo effects" can compensate for deficient medications, and share with phantom pain the not insignificant character of demonstrating the power of the figural. That is, the figural effect of the symbolic can be produced through the giving of pleasure (placebo, "I will please") as it can through the production of anxiety, the problem being only, as it always is in the case of performances of im-pertinence, to find an etiquette to make the pill go down. But then the giving of narrative pleasure was exactly Scheherazade's trick: "If she could tell a story that would please the king," a child translates in the classroom scene that precedes the credits, "her life would be saved." Then he corrects himself; her life would be "spared, until the next night." The placebo, in other words, is no cure for death, but a device of survival, like safe sex, in the midst of epidemic, and in aftermath, a way in which the ghosts can return. Thus flaunting Zero's haunt will be *Zero Patience*'s placebo effect against the regime of unjust representations that is the museum, where scapegoating is offered as a placebo to a society that prefers false certainties to justice.

I don't mean to imply, in saying this, that the film is not confrontational, uncompromising, and deliberately outrageous. My undergraduate students often complain that it is *outré* and are sometimes offended, in particular by its broad sexual humor: the "boner in the shower" trio, with its flaunting message ("if you pop a boner in the shower / don't blush, be proud, display"), for example, or the assholes' duo and accompanying ballet. Flaunting is inevitably confrontational, where haunting is infiltrational, because it implies a rejection of the values according to which the flaunter is judged (those of tidiness in the case of Eric Michaels, or those of Victorian morality and the scapegoating "culture of certainty" in the present instance). Outrageousness, in other words, is a readable manifestation of *outrage,* and flaunting who one is performs a victimized identity as a gesture of refusal; that is, indeed, why flaunting can function as an amplifier of the sense of injustice that's figured by the haunting of ghosts. And in this respect *Zero Patience* has a good deal in common, on the rhetorical plane, with the politics of provocation that the ACT-UP movement cultivated in those years of the late eighties and early nineties, constituting a second historical act of (mainly) gay self-affirmation, following the invention of safe sex, in the face of the epidemic of death and the epidemic of blame. The film pursues a policy of shameless acting up in lieu of Zero's failed policy of self-disculpation, but it does so as a way of relaying Zero's ineffectual haunt, and the sense of outrage—that is, pain and anger—that it signifies.

But it is exactly in this witnessing function, and in its status as a form of aftermath writing, that it crucially differs from the activist politics of ACT-UP, a difference that it signals through the character George. Symmetrically with Zero, the haunting victim of scapegoating, George is the figure of the haunted survivor, while as an educator he contrasts with Burton, the scapegoater. George doesn't flaunt, and the schoolroom, with its language drills and paper airplanes, is his environment: no hi-tech image bombardment here. But he teaches his students French, Zero's native language, and adduces the model of Scheherazade. In the face of the culture of certainty, his is the voice of epistemological modesty, expressing a position against scapegoating, as a way of manufacturing false certainties by unjust means, that the film clearly subscribes to. "I know, I know that I don't know" is one of his drill exercises in class, and in the same spirit he is critical of the smugness and self-righteousness of his ACT-UP colleagues, their synchronized crossing and recrossing of legs as they demonstrate their own allegiance to the culture of certainty by participating in the epidemic of blame (demonizing the pharmaceutical companies, for example, on which PWAs nevertheless depend for such therapies as are available).

Even more crucially, though, George is distinguished by his sense of personal guilt, which centers on his having abandoned Zero as he lay dying. "He died lonely. Because we were all scared." Symbolically, therefore, he is one of those who will be unable to see Zero when he returns, and having pinned his hopes on ZPO—a drug that turns out to have been only an expensive placebo and is therefore nicknamed "zippo," another synonym for nought—he goes blind from CMV retinitis. If there are those who are "blinded by greed," like Gilbert-Sullivan, the pharmaceutical company, or blinded by scapegoating like Burton, George doesn't claim to be less blind, to see more clearly than these participants in the culture of certainty, who all form part of the epidemic that is killing him as it killed Zero. He embodies only a certain (guilty) faithfulness to the dead combined with rejection of the shame induced by the epidemic of blame, which, not coincidentally, are also the defining principles of *Zero Patience,* although the film's educational methods contrast markedly with George's reliance on the methods of the classroom, as the pleasurable contrasts with the disciplinary. George shows clearly that to reject the epidemic of blame does not imply exemption from blindness or guilt, but only a refusal of shame; and it is in that respect that he functions as a transitional figure, connecting Zero's trajectory (from a desire for disculpation that implies a sense of shame to a rejection of descriptive representation) with the film's own self-assured—and hence (in all senses of the word) shameless—deployment of a self-flaunting representation at the service of the specter of Zero that haunts it.

As opposed to his activist friends, George as the haunted survivor, witness and teacher has an element of the martyr in him (Greek *martys,* witness): that's perhaps the point of the episode in which he is tormented by a student who stages a lurid version of death by AIDS, but later visits George on his hospital bed. And in martyrdom there is already some idea of witnessing as an exemplary act of display. Nevertheless the closest models for *Zero Patience*'s flaunt are the mentors Zero meets in the course of his adventure in the museum, figures who, as scapegoats, have no truck with either martyrdom or self-disculpation, and prefer to any response that might suggest complicity with the epidemic of blame the tactics of debunking (debunking both scapegoating practices and the culture of certainty they subserve) and of self-flaunting. Like George, they are aware that, about AIDS, there is no certainty; one knows only that no one can know; incriminating charges may or may not be groundless, but should not cause shame. "Me the first?" scoffs the African green monkey, accused by Burton of responsibility for the "contagion." (She has come alive as a butch lesbian with a gravelly voice and a motorbike jacket.) "First scapegoat maybe!" And she adds: "Guilt? Moi? . . . Don't be ridic," going on to perform a dance to the rhyming refrain of "Contagious? Outrageous!" (where the interjection "Outrageous!" is readable both as a comment on the false idea that AIDS is contagious, and as a corrective self-description: I'm not contagious, I'm outrageous). AIDS being indeed infectious but not contagious, her response identifies "contagion" as the *essential* scapegoating move—the move that makes PWAs seem dangerous and thus underlies and supports all other scapegoating moves—at the same time as it performs the only appropriate response: that of contemptuous rejection.

Her lesson is confirmed when, examining a specimen of his blood under Burton's microscope, Zero finds himself engaged by none other than Ms. HIV herself (played in drag by Michael Callen, one of the inventors of safe sex). She drifts in his bloodstream in stately splendor, like Cleopatra on the Nile in a Liz Taylor (and Richard Burton) spectacular, and turns out to be a fervent proponent both of safe sex and of AIDS theories that attribute the syndrome's etiology to factors (or cofactors) other than viral. Indeed a few other antigens floating by clamor for their own cofactorial rights; none of them bother with either the question of guilt or that of shame but imperturbably perform their own identities, with flair and style. The education they dispense, then, is a lesson in how to be, not just "out" as oneself, but if possible defiantly and blatantly—that is, campily—so; it's a lesson in the form of heroism that, since Stonewall, has been thought both courageous and exemplary in gay liberation circles, the self-flaunting heroism of the flaming queen and the bull dyke. So it's not surprising that the moment when Zero becomes maximally seeable (so that even Burton's camera picks him up for a while) is the moment when he exults: "I'm not the first," but adds, with a broad grin, "I'm not the first, but I'm still the best!"

He has learned to flaunt. But perhaps he has not fully absorbed the teaching of his mentors, who made their flaunting an occasion, also, for an active refutation—more performed than argued, it's true—of the culture of certainty. Their self-assurance rests on an affirmation of identity but also on the promotion of a principle of uncertainty and interpretability. The symmetry of the superlatives in Zero's flaunt ("best" balancing and replacing "first") suggests that he is still at a transitional moment between self-disculpation and flaunting, but the semantic emptiness of his boast (the best at what? the best in what sense?) also suggests that he has understood flaunting's first principle, which—as we saw in the case of *Auschwitz and After*—is to withhold explanation. To the extent that flaunting as utterance makes a statement at all, it reduces all representational description to its zero degree, that of a tautology: I am who I am (cf. Dössekker's deluded "I am Binjamin Wilkomirski," and Delbo's "Entre nous, nous sommes nous"). Where scapegoating hypostasizes descriptive representation, then, and seeks to reduce interpretability to its zero degree—the zero degree that haunts it, for example in the figure of Zero—flaunting converts that zero degree of interpretability, which is supposed to eliminate all possibility of the statement's being interpreted *otherwise* than it intends, into a zero degree of both description and explanation, thus *inviting* interpretation by enacting the dynamics of the figural: maximal utterance, minimal statement.

But such a gesture functions initially as a refutation of the culture of certainty, since the utterance's first meaning is necessarily the implication: you know that you don't know. That is, you don't know *me,* you don't know "who I am." You think that you know me, but . . . I am who I am. The scapegoating statement is not necessarily refuted, but its certainty is; its foreclosure of interpretability is rejected. Such a challenge can obviously be received huffily and indignantly and dismissed out of hand. But alternatively flaunting's performance of unknowability can present itself as intriguing, and constitute an invitation, therefore, to consider the interpretive possibilities, instead of closing them off in the haste for certainty that is satisfied by scapegoating. Exactly reversing the discursive structure of scapegoating and self-disculpation, as the hypostasization of descriptive and/or explanatory representation and the reduction of interpretability to zero, flaunting substitutes in this way a potential object of interpretation for the erstwhile object of mimesis, its zero degree of referential statement implying a hypostasization of readability, and prominently displays that object's readability. As a reminder, then, that there is no statement that isn't also an interpretable utterance, it offers both a performed refutation of the culture of certainty, and—potentially—an invitation to read.

And it is here that the issue of pleasing the king—that is of the placebo effect that responds to the kinds of placebos administered (in both senses) by Burton's boss in the museum—enters the picture. For a flaunt capable of pleasing, that is, entertaining the flauntee goes beyond the performed refutation of the culture of certainty by disposing the flauntee actually to enter into, to get involved in, the world of interpretability that flaunting proposes as an alternative to the culture of certainty. I would argue that the crucial component of *Zero Patience*'s flaunt, the element that simultaneously pleases the king, performs an identity, and destabilizes certainty, is the quality that can be named wit. Like what Eric Michaels calls style in *Unbecoming* (chapter 2), wit constitutes the etiquette that makes palatable, and hence readable, the performance of im-pertinence that responds outrageously to the culture that makes AIDS an epidemic of blame. But sharp-tongued, outrageous, and impertinent wit is also a marker of the queenly and the campy, that is, of gayness in its flaunting mode. And at the same time wit exerts the power, often associated with the queer and the deconstructive, to challenge complacent certainties by demonstrating a readability of things that *outwits* the deliberate reductiveness of scapegoating. Perceiving and drawing attention to unexpected relations and equivalences and making surprising comparisons, it fosters the view that there is nothing, however accepted and conventional, that cannot be read otherwise, nothing therefore that speaks for itself. By uncovering the relevance of unexpected contexts, it reinterprets what had seemed self-evident, cutting the ground of unproblematic reference from scapegoating practices whose authority depends on their ability to make statements stick by severely limiting their interpretability. Glaxo-Wellcome, the pharmaceutical company, has as one of its possible contexts the world of Gilbert and Sullivan; HIV is, inter alia, the Cleopatra of the bloodstream; and since they have the Nile in common, Richard Burton the Victorian traveler turns out, therefore, not to be wholly distinct from Richard Burton the actor. Witty flaunting dehypostasizes scapegoating's reliance on invidious representation by demonstrating the interpretability of absolutely everything; it treats nothing as sacrosanct.

One or two further examples of *Zero Patience*'s endless bombardment of witticisms will have to suffice. If the culture of certainty has a museum that is a Hall of Contagion as its microcosm, then obviously its "sotadic zone" will be a gay steam-bath. So Burton ventures intrepidly into the baths as a hero of knowledge, just as in 1845 he investigated "the male brothels of Karachi." But contrariwise, when Zero drops from the swimming pool that is limbo and comes up in the hot tub at the baths, *his* first thought is that he is in paradise (although his T-shirt motto says TOO DARN HOT). A running joke about synchronized swimming also starts in limbo (represented by languorous underwater images of synchronized swimmers), connects to Zero's hot tub, and then to the hopelessly *un*synchronized swimmers in his bloodstream, whose unruliness in turn teaches a lesson in acting up to ACT-UP itself (whose members engage, as we know, in synchronized leg-crossing). The recurrent image of the optometrist's chart links the problematics of blindness to a figure of readability that defines wit as anagrammatic in character: the chart yields messages like BLINDED BY GREED (ACT-UP's characterization of pharmaceutical companies), and Zero's changing T-shirt slogans ring changes on familiar clichés that turn out to have unexpected applicability (LOVE IS BLIND, THE EYE OF THE STORM, etc.). There is a parody here of the acronymitis spawned by the AIDS epidemic (the "alphabet soup" of abbreviations like AIDS itself, PWA, CMV, AZT, HAART, and the rest)—but the parody, in addition to being entertaining, just might lead one to reflect on the desirability and necessity of making meaning, so to speak anagrammatically, out of the whole phenomenon that is AIDS, rather than turning it, say, into an epidemic of blame. That is, AIDS might better be thought of as an occasion demanding the exercise of our wit(s)—as in their different ways the invention of safe sex and the intervention of ACT-UP demonstrated—than as requiring bluster and blame in defense of nonexistent certainties.

The specific affinity of Greyson's wit and de Duve's punning (see chapter 4) is evident. But wit is a good name too for the rhetorical skill or agencing we've seen at work in each of the three texts discussed in this chapter, the art of recontextualization I've called relay but might well have called metaphorization (transport, carrying over). Orphanhood is relayed by/as fostering, roll call by/as the calling of names that has the force of an interpellation, the haunted museum by/as the museum that teaches flaunting—in short, a representation of traumatized hauntedness becomes, in each case, the means of communication of that hauntedness, an act of haunting that, to a degree, palliates the trauma by making it recognizable. But another, more general name, for this form of wit, therefore, is figuration, which can be understood as a way of mobilizing the haunted character of language, its failures of representation, so that language can become haunting. Language is haunted by virtue of its inadequacy to represent the reality of history, an inadequacy that is associated with the effects of trauma (orphanhood, the ordeal of roll call, the scapegoating museum) because it becomes particularly evident in circumstances such as those of (after)math that challenge or put stress on the power of genres to seduce. Figuration is what, in compensating for this mimetic deficiency, realizes the potential of language's hauntedness to become haunting, through making readable what language cannot say. It is the etiquette without which the unstatable would remain unutterable. Through being troped into indexicality, the hauntedness comes to haunt, because it is now recognized. If the ghost is the figure of the figural, figuration is the means through which, in the form of readability, the specter—by virtue of being flaunted—becomes seeable.[14]

It's such a recognition of hauntedness that's honored in *Zero Patience,* I think, by the anonymity that shrouds Patient Zero and makes him a general symbol. This character is not a descriptive representation of a certain airline steward named Gaetan Dugas—the representation of Dugas is ostentatiously inadequate—but, precisely a *figure:* one in whom all the sufferers ("patients") from AIDS, whether biomedical AIDS or social pathology AIDS, and unknown as they may be, can potentially be recognized, one, that is, *through* which that world of unfathomable because depthless suffering can be read. For, like a ghost, figuration as the flaunt of a haunt—the wit in witnessing—enjoys a certain visibility but simultaneously presents a certain inexhaustible transparency: it draws attention, in order to be seen *through,* for as far as the seeing eye can read. Such is its indexical character and function. Not surprisingly, Robert Kaplan says something strikingly similar of the cypher zero, "the nothing that is": "If you look at zero, you see nothing; but look through it and you will see the world" (1). To see the world, in the sense both of "to see" and of "the world" that aftermath writing promotes, that is, to see the historical world's inexhaustible hauntedness and hence to experience it as haunting, is *not* what many desire. But it *is* the outcome that both the writing of extremity and aftermath writing, in their ultimately convergent ways, try to foster. So, in response, let's try to look, as Delbo asks, in order to see. *Essayons pour voir.* What we might glimpse is the phantom of pain.

6. Suspended Sentences: Aftermath Writing and the Dual Autobiography

. . . quelque chose d'impossible, un lien sublime et secret . . .

[. . . something impossible, a bond sublime and secret . . .]
—René Duquénelle *L'Aztèque*

Connection(s)

When Harold Brodkey (see chapter 1) writes: "The trouble with death-at-your-doorstep is that it is happening to you" (68), it is clear that his main concern is not with surviving the death of someone close to you, but with handling your own death. Nevertheless, he goes on in a way that implicitly describes the responsibilities of surviving, even though his remark is explicitly phrased as a complaint about his own dispossession as a dying man: "Also, that you are no longer the hero of your story, no longer even the narrator. Barry was the hero of my story, and Ellen the narrator. The tale was of my death amid others' lives—like a rock in the garden." Brodkey anticipates here, as if it was already actual, a postmortem situation in which other people (Barry his physician and Ellen his wife) both live and narrate the story of his dying, his own role being reduced to the mute residuality, the inertia of a rock in the garden. In this chapter I want to ask what it means for a Barry or an Ellen to have inherited the responsibility of living (as hero) or telling (as narrator) the story of another's death, when that other has been dispossessed by death of all personal agency so that only an act of *agencement*—assemblage and agencing—can make that story available.

What is the bond, Duquénelle's "lien," that causes responsibility for the story (lived or narrated) to be passed on in this way? What does it mean to receive such a responsibility and to act upon it? Barry and Ellen are likely to be possessed by a sense of anxiety, and even of guilt, proportionate to their awareness of the dispossession of the other that is the condition of their own agency. How is it possible to discharge the responsibility entailed in the contradictory task of telling, as one's own, another's story? Is such a project not at best an illusion, and at worst a sham? The thoughts of Barry and Ellen are likely to dwell upon the nature of the link that binds them to the deceased person whose story rights, privileges, and obligations they have inherited, but also on the radical disconnection that has been produced by death, one that seems thoroughly to invalidate any claim to the continuity between other and self that their project implies. These are the issues—of connectedness and disconnection—that plague and energize the genre I will call dual autobiography, which—following an early spate of AIDS diaries (Chambers 1999)—became perhaps the major vehicle of AIDS witnessing in at least the three national cultures with which this book is concerned, and for which I will take two texts as paradigmatic: Duquénelle's *L'Aztèque* and Amy Hoffman's *Hospital Time.*[1]

There is a sentence in Duquénelle that corresponds to Brodkey's death-at-your-doorstep pronouncement: it is one in which relationality among "Aztecs," that is, people who take AZT, is likewise described in terms of dying and surviving. "When two Aztecs are friends, the first to die is the winner; the one who remains witnesses his own death, lucid and powerless, in that of the other. When you have lived one Aztec's dying [*agonie*], you don't want to start over" (103). Here the perspective and emphasis have visibly shifted to the side of surviving and of the survivor, who has a double burden: that of witnessing the dying of the now deceased Aztec while living an identical dying of his or her own. The perspective is that of a sharing of agonic experience, which does alleviate the responsibility entailed in living/telling another's death (for in this case the bond between survivor and deceased approaches identity), but simultaneously aggravates the survivor's situation by virtue of a cumulative effect—a worsening—that is attributed to repetition. To have to live one dying is bad enough, to have to live it over again is doubly burdensome. These, in their simplest and most intense form, are the conditions of aftermath in which all survivors (all of us who are still alive) live. Aftermath is the experience of a continuing "friendship," of the dead and the surviving, and of a double burden: that of the "math" and that of the after-math.

But if all of us survivors must follow those who have already died to the grave sometime, the concept of aftermath has particular relevance, therefore, to a community visited by a lethal epidemic. Barry and Ellen are presumed HIV-negative; they can assume (but not count on) a "normal" life span; Duquénelle, though, was writing/living the story of his lover's demise in the situation of a survivor who was himself within a few months of death, and thus in expectation of a rapid repetition of that demise. All survivors are under suspended sentence, then, but some more than others, which is why I continue in this chapter to distinguish between survival and mere survivorhood. And here too I will define aftermath writing, in consequence—writing of which I take the AIDS dual autobiography to be paradigmatic—as writing that betrays a consciousness of this difference, regardless of the HIV status of the survivor who writes. From this definition it follows that in such aftermath writing there are actually two differences to be negotiated (where the word *difference* implies both continuity and a break—more accurately, therefore, a split). There is the difference between the dying who have died and the dying who survive them, and then there is the difference between those among the survivors who are conscious of the conditions and implications of aftermath and those who may be in varying degrees oblivious of them, and blinded by their survivorhood to their affinity with both the dead and the friends who survive the dead. And there are two bonds of connection to be invented, therefore, if the dual autobiography, as aftermath writing, wishes to remember the dead but to address those who, in this latter sense, survive.

The dilemma of surviving AIDS witnesses has much in common therefore with that of Holocaust survivor-witnesses and that of the witness survivors of trench warfare. It is the dilemma of having only a story of surviving to tell, when the story to be told would rightly be that of those who did not survive, and of having to tell that story of surviving for an audience one step further removed by virtue of a survivorhood that blinds them to the hauntedness of the situation of survival. A conviction emerges that the second problem is more difficult than the first, but that it might itself evaporate if only the first could be adequately solved. And the problem of writing becomes, therefore, that of how to tell the only story that survivors can legitimately and authentically tell, the story of having survived the death(s) of another (or of others), in such a way that this story can do duty for—that is, become readable figurally as—the story that necessarily goes untold, a story significantly different from the story of living on. This is the problem of agencing. It does not entail speaking for (on behalf of) the dead, or lending a voice to the mute (as in the figure of prosopopoeia), but it is a matter of using one's own voice to make the tellable story, of surviving, readable as referring to, because haunted by, the story that cannot otherwise be told. One residual figure, the survivor who lives on, must give a kind of life to those who have only the kind of residuality represented by a rock in the garden, a project that entails gaining the engaged attention of readers assumed to be absorbed in the obliviousness of their own survivorhood. Writing, then, as the act of agencing that would forge a link where no connection appears to exist—between oblivious survivors and the dead—and do so by finding the appropriate phrasing of the story of a survivor's survival, holds the key to resolving the problem of aftermath that is the survivor's lot. This would be the "bond, sublime and secret" of which Duquénelle speaks, having already defined it, however as "quelque chose d'impossible." It is impossible because the two sets of links on which this supreme bond depends, between the survivor and the dead, and between the survivor and the narrative's putative readers, are both—but especially the second—severely damaged. They have been interrupted by disaster (by war, by the Holocaust, by AIDS).

Thinking of a word employed by Mark Doty in his poem "Rope," to which I will shortly return, we might say that such links are severely "frayed." The disconnection is not complete in either case, but the continuity is severely stressed. The sublime bond must be forged in the context of continuities so severely damaged as to make the task of agencing, always problematic, impossible. But of the two frayed links, it is the second (the social gulf defined by the difference between survivorhood and survival) that is regularly assessed in survivor writing, and notably in the two cases I want to consider more carefully here, as the more damaged and difficult to counter. Indeed the problem posed by the dead to their close survivors tends to be less that of a break than that of the continuity—productive of the community of "Aztecs," for example—that arises from their restlessness and refusal to lie down and be dead, and the consequent inability of the survivors to mourn them successfully, to lay them to rest, as the saying goes. "Totsein ist mühsam," as the phrase from the first of Rilke's *Duineser Elegien* has it, being dead is laborious and painful (notably when their death is understood to have been unjust), or in the translation that furnishes Olivier de Vleeschouwer's title, "la vie des morts est épuisante," being alive is an exhausting business for the dead. So it is precisely the solidarity among the restless dead and their troubled survivors that distinguishes a community that is marginalized—this will be most particularly Amy Hoffman's theme—by a society at large that is inattentive, unconcerned, and indeed indifferent. Whence the conviction among survivor witnesses that telling the story of surviving right—thanks to the community among those who are haunted and those who haunt—holds the key to finding readers among a survivorhood-oriented society oblivious to its links with the dead *and* with their survivors—oblivious, that is, to its own hauntedness—and consequently lacking in a sense of community with them.

Nevertheless that solidarity is itself traversed by a sense of ineradicable separation: the rope holds, but it is frayed. For a Hervé Guibert, who writes of the death of his friend Muzil (a fictionalization of Michel Foucault) that "it wasn't so much my friend's last agony I was describing as it was my own, which was waiting for me and would be just like his" and who refers to the bond that joins them as "un sort thanatologique commun" (*A l'ami,* 106–7; *To the Friend,* 91), there is a René de Ceccatty (to whom I will return in chapter 8) who, having accepted the responsibility of writing the death of his friend—himself a writer conscious, like Brodkey, of the impossibility of writing his own death struggle—broods over the impossibility of carrying out that task with integrity: "I shall strive not to abuse the trust that has been placed in me, although writing in his place is already a sham" (11–12). The survivor is *not* the other, and has another life; yet the survivor's responsibility—to continue the other's life by telling the story of the other's death—is of a kind that, out of solidarity, cannot be refused, especially when one both survives the other and is conscious of sharing the other's fate, "un sort thanatologique commun." That is what makes the difference between the solidarity of a distressed community, and the much more alienated relation of that community to the oblivious and the indifferent.

Perhaps the concept of relay, which has already arisen in other contexts (see chapters 3 and 5), captures something of the frayed continuity that governs both the narrative structure and the rhetorical address—the relation to the dead and the relation to the living—of many dual autobiographies. But it also clarifies the difference between the community solidarity of AIDS people (surviving and dead) and the markedly more fragile bond between that community and a neglectful society, for a relay can be smoothly continuous or awkwardly discontinuous. In both English and French, the verb *to relay* (French *relayer*) is from Latin *laxare,* meaning to quit or leave behind; but semantically *relayer* in French is closer to *relever,* to pick up again (Latin *levare*), as in the phrase *prendre la relève,* to pick up where someone has left off, than it is to *laisser,* to leave. This emphasis on cooperation is operative where community is affirmed, the implication of distance where solidarity is neglected or denied. Yet the principle of relay is nevertheless always the possibility of passing a baton, an act of coordination that should ideally be achieved in such a way that the smoothness of continuity compensates for the discontinuity produced by the fact that someone has left off (running, for example, or living) and been replaced by another. And in rhetoric there is a trope of relay, that we have also already encountered (chapter 5) and will encounter again (chapter 7). It is known as asyndeton (etymologically a lack of binding together, from Greek *syndein,* to tie together). In asyndeton, a lack of grammatical or structural binding—a gap—is counterbalanced and compensated for by a continuity of thought that seems stronger than the (elided, interrupted) grammar. Hence a certain effect of fatality, or at least of inevitability, frequently attaches to the figure, and is evidenced, for example in Julius Caesar's famous dictum *veni vidi vici* or in stock phrases like "day in day out" or French *bon gré mal gré.* Gaps in the statement are compensated for as an effect of utterance. Asyndeton of this kind is the key trope that governs the narrative smoothness, or lack of smoothness, with which dual autobiographies pass, or attempt to pass, from the narrative of a dying to a narrative of surviving that dying, by negotiating the break wrought by death.

But there is also a rhetorical, not grammatical, form of asyndeton, which arises when a sentence is suspended, that is, interrupted by an ellipsis and allowed to hang, because the speaker is confident that the hearer is capable of picking up the relay of thought: "When the cat's away . . ."; "Tommy, if you don't stop bothering me . . ."; "See ya . . ." It is on asyndeton of this kind, involving the cooperation of the reader in an act of relayed thought, that AIDS dual autobiographies often rely when, having narrated the passing of the baton of responsibility from the dying, now dead, hero to the surviving writer (the trope developed for example, in Paul Monette's *Borrowed Time*), they then tend to peter out uncertainly in the midst of their account of the problem of surviving, *as if* to pass further responsibility to the reader. I say as if, though, for what is lacking in this case—as opposed to the inevitability implied by the passage in the narrative from the story of dying to the story of surviving—is precisely the assurance that the suspended narration *will* be adequately picked up by its reader. This lack of confidence constitutes the difference between the community-affirming asyndeton in the narrative structure, and the sense of social disjunction implied by the narrative's also asyndetic rhetorical relation to a readership in its act of narration.

But as I've said, it is also often implied in dual autobiographies that the narrative would inevitably be adequately picked up by its reader if only it were itself truly adequate to its assigned narrative task, that is, the production of smooth continuity between the story of a dying and the story of a surviving, a continuity that is denied, on the face of it, by the brutal fact that the other is now dead. Agencing, I have said often enough in this book, is governed by a semiotics, not of (supposedly direct) representation but of (indirect) indexicality, and can only point to an object that it is for a reader to recognize. How, then, to convey to detached and perhaps indifferent others the full horror and injustice of a dying and death that one is oneself, by virtue of the plain fact of being a survivor, inadequate to express, and can only indicate—that is, gesture toward? This cruel sense that a story of surviving should, but cannot, be an immediate representation of the other's story of dying is the form of survivor guilt most characteristic of writer survivors in dual autobiography.

As a result, to the desired but never fully achieved smoothness of relay is always added in this genre the component of awkwardness or syncopation inherent in the idea of enjambment (etymologically stepping over an obstacle). An enjambed line of verse derives its expressivity and significance expressly and precisely from its enactment of a break that is only imperfectly transcended. The interruption remains active even as it is, to some degree, repaired; the tension between continuity and discontinuity does not achieve a resolution but becomes itself the point of the writing, I mean the source of its poignancy as well as of its pointedness. If aftermath writing in general, and dual autobiography in particular, has asyndeton at its heart, as the figure that governs its attempted relay of a hauntedness (the neither discontinuous nor completely continuous relation of survivors to the restless dead) as a haunting (the neither continuous nor yet completely discontinuous relation of this haunted writing to its readership), it is because both grammatical or structural and rhetorical asyndeton—asyndeton in the narrative and asyndeton in the narration—admit this dynamic of enjambment as the sign of the narratives' failure to sublate—to *relever* or *prendre la relève,* to pick up (German *aufheben,* whence *Aufhebung*)—what death has broken, even as life continues, and dying too. There is thus no resolution, no outcome—only a kind of dwelling on the suspended moment of irresolution in which the discontinuity of death does not destroy all continuity but that deficient continuity cannot overcome discontinuity in the form of a social break. This irresolution describes the moment of survival, and of aftermath, as that which is neither death nor yet living, as those who survive in the blithe but deluded mode of survivorhood know life.

Thus something irreparable resolves into something interminable as a consequence of writing's failure to achieve something impossible: a bond secret and sublime. As the figure of aftermath, asyndeton might be said, therefore, to substitute the gracelessness, as well as the interminability, of melancholia—a long, unresolved, suspension—for the closure allegedly achieved (at least in classic psychoanalytic accounts) by the process of mourning. And in such writing it is the ungainliness of suspended enjambment, the gracelessness of failed mourning, that itself indexes anger and pain. In short, what a dual autobiography regularly enacts is a prolonged inability on the survivor's part to "turn the page" and move out of the limbo of survival into a regained survivorhood, to bring about an *outcome* in more senses than one—an inability that becomes the very definition of the experience of aftermath as, also in two senses, a suspended sentence. Such a survivor is too connected to the dead not to be disconnected from the living, as the survivor's inability to mourn demonstrates; but not so disconnected from the living as to be genuinely bonded with the dead, as the persistent awkwardness of relay in survivor writing betrays. Listen to the anger in these persistently enjambed lines with their asyndetic syntax from Paul Monette's collection *Love Alone,* the dual autobiography in verse (or in Jahan Ramazani's sense the "modern elegy," cf. chapter 3) that preceded his prose narrative, *Borrowed Time:*

> the wrongest of the wrong things said that day
> as I stepped from the chapel an idiot cousin
> once-removed jiggled my shoulder *time to turn*
> *the page* he intoned like it's all been so appalling
> we must hasten now to the land of brunch
> . . .
> BUT THIS *IS* MY PAGE IT CANNOT BE TURNED
> ("The Very Same," 20)

There are only wrong things to say, the syntactic pieces don't quite fit, and cousins are of course idiot and once-removed (asyndeton governs the rhetorical relation). That is why the wrongest of the wrong things to say is "turn the page." For turning the page implies consolation, and aftermath is unconsoled. The page, therefore, is suspended because there is no way of writing it that would make it turnable. Is there an *idiom,* the poem asks, that might release us from this condition of *idiocy*—of irrevocable wrongness—that circumstances of aftermath impose?

Suspension(s)

There are, however, two forms of this agonized state of seemingly endless suspension, according as death is viewed in anticipation, as something announced and awaited or alternatively seen in retrospect, by a survivor or group of survivors living on in aftermath. The anticipatory suspension is usually narrated retrospectively in dual autobiography; but the aftermath perspective can be and often is prospective as well as retrospective, when the sentence of suspension that hangs over the survivor in the form of an inability to mourn and to turn the page is also a suspended sentence: the long drawn out anticipation of the survivor's own dying and death. This last is the situation of a survivor whose friend or lover has died from the effects of AIDS and who is also seropositive or symptomatic, like Paul Monette or Bertrand Duquénelle: it is the situation described by Duquénelle as a "sempiternel sursis," an everlasting deferment in which the anticipatory suspension of his friend's dying and death is retrospectively recalled and described, from the even more agonizing situation of the survivor's own everlasting dying and anticipated death. But even Amy Hoffman, whose own death is not imminent and whose aftermath perspective is therefore wholly retrospective although it seems never-ending, describes that experience as an extension of "hospital time," in which "time ticks by differently" and "there's no comfortable place to sit" (3). These narrative perspectives are ways of making palpable a certain experience of untimeliness, aftermath writing's eternal subject, since they produce death as no longer an event that divides before and after. Or rather, it does divide before and after, but it also and simultaneously confounds the categories of past, present, and future by making its presence heavily felt in the after as well as the before, thus producing after and before as uncannily similar, although different, because each is a matter of living on in a state of suspension.

In narrative terms, then, dual autobiography consists of an alignment, or rather a would-be alignment, of these two similar forms of suspension, anticipatory and retrospective(-prospective), as if their identity, if it could be achieved through memory and in writing, might cancel the hiatus of death itself, as the fact responsible for the torment of aftermath. But death, we know, is irreparable, and the smooth alignment the narrative longs for becomes instead a dehiscence, a relay both necessary and impossible, with the further consequence that the end remains inconclusive. Death, as the signifier of trauma, thus names the inescapable and unrepresentable fact on which the structure and character of dual narrative turns, its textual presence making itself felt only in the two (mis)aligned suspensions of dying and surviving that become the index of its presence. If I am correct in thinking that dual autobiography had become by the mid-1990s the major genre of AIDS writing—others being the diary (Chambers 1999) and other individual autobiographical forms, and the form I call community auto/biography (chapter 7)—this is perhaps because such an asyndetic narrative structure, joining and failing to bind an anticipatory suspension and a retrospective suspension, accurately mimes something that was, and still largely is, definitional in the collective experience of AIDS as it has been known in Western countries: an experience of waiting, an experience of deferment (notably the deferment of mourning), an experience of community born of a shared proximity to death, and finally an experience of that community's isolation.

AIDS is defined in this genre, then, as an epidemic of suspended sentences, in the form first of all of waiting for the blow (the blow of HIV positivity, the blow of the onset of symptoms, the final blow of death) to fall; and also in the form, among survivors, of the inability and/or unwillingness to turn the page: a failure of mourning, whether through anxiety, anger, guilt, or a sense of prior urgencies, and hence a deferment of closure. The epidemic is described too as being a lived experience of disruption and untimeliness, the syncopation of the narrative patterns and rhythms of life by a form of death that is felt to strike at the wrong time and in a way incompatible with the order of things—an epidemic, that is, of wrongness, as Monette ("the wrongest of the wrong things that were said that day") might say, to which conventional responses—geared to a world of rightness—are patently inappropriate and inadequate. With its syncopated narrative structure, dual autobiography not only describes but itself mimes that experience of wrongness as the failure of normative patterns. (Syncope, etymologically a cutting together, is akin to asyndeton: in music it refers to a missed beat, in medicine to a fainting fit, a gap in the continuity of consciousness.) At the same time, by exploring the bond of community that forms among "AIDS people" around the shock of death, and simultaneously by addressing the corresponding gap—or failure of consciousness—that separates this group from society "at large," a gap that confirms its existence as a community (and not a society in its own right), the genre responds—through the rhetorical suspension of its sentences, the problematics of their address to an audience that is to all intents and purposes missing—to what was perhaps the wrongest and most grievous, because avoidable, consequence of all the epidemic's consequences, which was the emergence of a new form of social division, and often a consequent denial of support and solidarity to people enduring a cruel ordeal. Thus it reproduces wrongness in one form, while seeking to mitigate it in another of its forms, the form in which a community, as a site of phantom pain, may also—in *bearing* that pain—relay its haunt. (Community, that is, is the name of the specter when it is a haunted/haunting spectrality.)

In the aftermath of what, in 1948, was not yet known as the Holocaust, Maurice Blanchot wrote *L'Arrêt de mort,* whose punning title refers to a state of metaphysical wrongness—death *(la mort)* is at once, and for all mortals, decreed *(arrêté)* and deferred (*arrêté* in the sense of halted). This difficult text has rightly become the text of reference and locus classicus for any understanding of the untimeliness of aftermath. The pun in my own title, "Suspended Sentences," pays homage to Blanchot and refers to the same existential dilemma, then. But because the writing I am reading here has a more immediate social relevance and an urgent sense of parasocial purpose, my pun should be read also as having a more pointed reference, focusing more particularly on the specific conditions of the AIDS epidemic as the texts in question do, what it is like to be sentenced to AIDS, and intending only a secondary allusion to the general dilemma entailed in being mortal.

For that reason, though, I begin this chapter's series of readings with a poem, Mark Doty's "Rope" (from *Atlantis*), which itself straddles an, in this case implied, particularity of reference to AIDS and an overt treatment of certain supposedly universal laws of life and art in its articulation of the anticipatory suspendedness of the sentence of death. But "Rope" does not have the character of a dual autobiography, and I want also, therefore, in imitation of the narrative texts by Duquénelle and Hoffman to which I'll eventually turn, to bring "Rope's" exploration of anticipatory suspension into, of course dehiscent, alignment with another poem, Paul Monette's "Current Status 1/22/87" (from *Love Alone*), which, as a postmortem poem of retrospective, and simultaneously anticipatory, suspension, brings us closer to the problematics of aftermath writing, and of dual autobiography. As an artifice of criticism, I thus imitate the structure of dual autobiographies that turn on, and elide, the crucial moment of death.

"Rope" is about decrepitude as a state of anticipatory suspension; and it is about anticipation as that moment when one is suspended, at the bend of a path or on the brink of a gulf, looking forward to what lies beyond; finally, it is about suspension in the sense of support—the support provided by the solidarity that joins (as by a frayed rope) those whose lives are similarly precarious, and hence the solidarity of community, but also the support furnished by art when it is capable of suspending life itself, and notably life at its most precarious, in a semblance of endless existence. The context of the collection, and also of Doty's own dual autobiography, *Heaven's Coast,* indicates that the setting is Provincetown, Massachusetts, in the era of AIDS: a town three-quarters surrounded by the Atlantic at the tip of the promontory of Cape Cod, and suspended as it were, between a narrow strip of land and the vast sea.

But the central passage of the poem concerns two variously decrepit creatures whose symbolic reference is more pointed, although it remains unspecified. Antony, an old man (figurative of the youthful-become-prematurely-ancient, which is a common trope for the effects of AIDS), walks his even more ancient dog, Charley, who sets a pace so slow that he is like a porcelain figure walking—a suspended pace, then, that is matched by Antony "as if together they were / one thing (something submerged / adapted to the pressure of great depths)," and mimed by the gait of the poem, ceaselessly suspended by enjambments. Moreover, this central section is itself suspended, as it were, between shorter introductory and concluding sections from which it is separated, at beginning and end, by the three dots of an ellipsis (called in French *points de suspension*). It hangs in this way in a supportive poetic structure that corresponds, in the form of the poem itself, to the supportive rope harness that Antony has fashioned to support Charley's failing steps:

> a sort of rope harness
> which the good soldier of ongoingness
> wears, and when he falls
> . . .
> Antony can lift him
> up again,
> even hold him suspended
> a while, so that Charley
> can move his failing legs
> and feel that he has been
> for a walk.

The poem thus supports Antony and Charley in its apparatus of suspension as Antony supports Charley in his frayed rope harness. The enjambed lines mime both the impeded walking of the old man and the old dog, creeping toward harbor in "the fragility of their old age," and the effect of continuity across a break—of asyndeton—that is produced also by the suspension points, or ellipses, that connect the larger segments of the poem. That the pair are creeping toward the symbolic "shore" where they will "soak up moonshine" gives poignancy and point to the restrictive adverbial phrase, emphasized by enjambment, in "suspended / a while." If Charley, and Antony and Charley, are suspended in time, their suspense is nevertheless only a deferment, the deferment of something that is simultaneously imminent.

So there is a general tension in the poem between the sense of suspension as seemingly endless and a sense of it as, in reality, anticipatory. Charley's vague monologues, "which do not have endings—lucid, / interesting even, but listening's a commitment of uncertain, / considerable length"—notice here the combination of metrical enjambment with choppy, asyndetic syntax in the alignment of phrases—are one figure for the form of apparent suspension the poem achieves: a stasis, also of "uncertain, / considerable length." But each of the two suspensive ellipses that support the account of Antony and Charley is also clearly anticipatory and almost portentous; and each marks the limit between what one can say (and art can achieve) and, something unstated but implied that is left for us to think, because it refers to what lies inevitably beyond the stasis. They are thus suspensive in a second sense: not only do they, between them, suspend the central passage of the poem like Charley's harness, but they also leave a sentence hanging in the air, the better of course to involve us, the poem's readers, in completing it. And these suspensions can be completed only by supplying the thought that the whole poem fails to state, but likewise everywhere implies. At the end of the description of the contraption in which Antony is able to suspend Charley, we learn this:

> and the neighbors say,
> when that dog goes . . .

The neighbors' ellipsis (a rhetorical asyndeton) is like the ellipsis in "When the cat's away . . ."; it is not difficult to complete it.

As for the opening stanzas, which take us on a walk down to the harbor that parallels and foreshadows Antony and Charley's suspended walking to the shore, they are framed by a quotation:

> *Art,* William Avery wrote,
> *is turning a corner, you don't know*
> *what's around the bend*
>
> *till you get there.*

(Again the sentence structure is asyndetic, and an expressive enjambment cuts across the stanza break.) "Our curve," the poem goes on, "surprises with harbor glitter," a scene of boats

> idly going about
> whatever their business is . . .

The equivalence between the two ellipses, this one introducing the account of Antony and Charley, the other concluding it, implies that the business of the boats on the harbor and the death the neighbors invoke (but do not name) are the same destination. There is an end point, one that art—suspending life on the curve, like Charley in his harness, before the end comes into view—can indirectly indicate, but cannot counter, or even make us forget. For art wields suspension only, it seems, as an instrument of comforting illusion: Charley in his harness "can move his failing legs / and feel that he has been / for a walk," but the reality is otherwise.

So it is significant that in its final section the poem draws back from the implications of the neighbors' comment ("when that dog goes . . .") as if to deny its validity and preserve the illusion. It is unthinkable that "Charley has lived long enough" or that the bond between master and dog, frayed though it be, should be broken. Art is strong, and "love's gravity" counterbalances the droop of Charley's head toward the ground:

> Art is this strong
> exactly: love's gravity,
> the weight of Charley's body,
> in his rope harness, suspended
> from his master's hand.

In this way the relation between the opening and the closing sections of this poem—the latter insisting on art's power of suspensive stasis but the former implying a beyond of that stasis and an inevitable turning of the corner toward the harbor and the business of the boats—reproduces the tension in the central section between the symbolic implication of Antony and Charley's slow, painfully slow, walk to the shore and the signification given to the supportive harness that binds them both into "one living thing" seemingly capable of resisting the pressures of the deep, "the rope / that holds them both / in the world." And even the confident statement of art's power in the final lines is undermined, it seems to me, in two ways. First, it is undermined by the enjambment after "suspended" at the last line, which repeats the previous enjambment of "suspended / a while," making the duration of Charley's suspension conditional on the (dubious) firmness of "his master's hand." And second, it is undermined by the grammatical asyndeton of the sentence, which promises an exact demonstration of love's strength, then lapses instead into simple appositions, whose loose conceptual links are not grammatically indicated. Art is this strong: love's gravity, the weight of Charley's body.

But how strong, exactly, is that? . . .

. . . Where suspension in "Rope" is anticipatory, then, and placed under the sign of a deferment of death, in Paul Monette's "Current Status 1/22/87" a death has occurred (the death of Roger), and the perspective is therefore that of aftermath. Of aftermath in the strict etymological sense, in which a second math (the dying and death of the poet, Paul) is expected to follow the dying and death of the hero, Roger. Indeed, Paul's death is already announced although it has not yet occurred; so that his desire and hope, given the temporal proximity of math and aftermath, is for his dying and death actually to identify him with the heroic agony of Roger, which is evoked in some detail in the poem as a model to be followed (and is recounted also in *Borrowed Time*).[2]

But the sense of aftermath as a mere living on following an irreparable event is also active: the situation of the survivor is in fact *not* identical to that of Roger's dying and death, if only because that first event has made the survivor's outlook bleaker. A devastation has occurred, the repetition cannot be the same as what it repeats. When Roger was alive, all the couple's effort went into defeating the disease—"we never talked about dying because we were fighting so hard to stay alive" (*Borrowed Time,* 75)—whereas now . . . The disease has won; the expectation is that it will win again, and rather than its being a question of Paul's fighting to stay alive, there is a new sense of death's inevitability arising from the fact that the expectation of death has become, for Paul, a source of hope as well as of apprehension, because it will put an end to the long period of suspension and separation that follows the break in their union caused by Roger's death, and permit Paul to become identical with his lover once more. "We are the same person," Roger had said in surprise toward the end of his life, "when did that happen?" But if death is inevitable in this sense, then the medicine on which the couple formerly relied must become, now that Paul is alone, a vain pursuit, referred to in "Current Status" as "all / the useless measures." And the word "measures" of course embraces also the writing of poetry like the "elegies for Rog" that are the love poems of *Love Alone,* which—implying the uselessness also of these "measures"—precludes Paul from matching in his verse the heroic resistance that Roger had displayed until the moment of his succumbing.

For in light of Paul's Pindaric sense of the interdependence of the hero and the poet (a line from Pindar, "Unsung the noblest deed will die," is the epigraph to *Borrowed Time*), such an admission of defeat, made necessary as it is by Paul's desire to repair the break in the relationship of the lovers by dying as Roger has died, has devastating consequences. It means not only that Roger's noble deeds must die with him, but also that, failing to match Roger's heroic struggle, Paul's death cannot reproduce Roger's and the identity of the couple must remain, forever, broken. "Current Status" is a meditation on the perverse logic of survival that confirms in this way the irreparability of death rather than resisting its power. Because, as Kierkegaard saw, a repetition cannot be the same as what it repeats, Paul is caught in a trap of futile imitation that "Current Status" explores in some detail.

Already during Roger's illness, Monette had searched for a way of resisting AIDS—AIDS as socially enforced shame and secrecy—by writing about it. The idea came to him, he explains in *Borrowed Time* (150), of writing "conspiracy" poems, to be secretly exchanged with his friend Carol, also a poet and these poems' sole audience. Conspiracy implies a kind of covert community, as opposed to solitude. The poems of *Love Alone* are conspiracy poems too, but as elegies "for Rog" (as the subtitle specifies) they are in conspiracy not with Carol but with Roger, who is addressed in "Current Status" as "you," "my friend," and urged by Paul to "stay at my side" through the ordeal of his survival. And their potential audience is greatly expanded by the fact of publication. As readers of these published poems we might want to reflect, therefore, on what it means to make public in this way a conspiracy, and what it means to overhear, as it were, rather than to participate in, an intimate if no longer secret conversation, which is thus conspiratorial, but not in the sense of what is called a conspiracy of silence.

Rather the conspiracy, as already in the poems shared with Carol but more daringly so, is conspiracy *against* being silenced, since through publication the conspiratorial relation is made to signify, and to signify not conspiracy as such, but the fact of silencing that makes conspiracy necessary; and since, in so doing, publication seeks to overcome this silencing in the very act of creating a community by making it readable.

One might say that in this way the long-standing convention by which the reader of lyric verse overhears the thoughts of a solitary speaker becomes a means of *implicating* the reader in the tenor of those conspiratorial thoughts, so that, in the way that dual autobiography breaches the conventions of autobiography by substituting the dual subjectivity of aftermath, a "haunted" self, for the supposedly self-sufficient personal self of the genre's tradition, the traditional convention of lyric verse is being observed in Monette's elegies, but observed in the breach, since the distance of overhearing is supplanted, for the reader, by conspiratorial involvement. There is thus a kind of "breakthrough" here, a word to which we shall return. For in this way the poems are an occasion, not only to write about AIDS within the context of strong social pressure to observe secrecy (the date, one must remember, is 1987 at the latest)—the pressure that is figured in *Borrowed Time* through the figure of Roger's brother, Sheldon, the representative of family—but also to index the writing's uncomfortable social position in the face of an audience presumed hostile and thus to break through the confinement of secrecy. That, in a nutshell, is *their* claim to a heroism comparable with Roger's resistance to AIDS as a biomedical manifestation.

It follows that publishing conspiracy poems is a way of overcoming, more accurately of seeking to overcome, not one but two different gaps. Restoring the interrupted bond with Roger—affirming it through poetic conspiracy, confirming it through the heroism entailed in publishing the conspiracy—it also infiltrates the defenses of an audience accustomed to lyric conventions of overhearing but unwilling to know about AIDS, and anxious for the epidemic's depredations to be kept decorously secret, making that audience part of what will have become a "public conspiracy." This attempted closing of the gap(s) can be seen, I've suggested, as communitarian in character: the conspiracy of the couple across and in spite of the break of death creates a microcosm of the band of brothers that is the AIDS community, "a community of the stricken who will not lie down and die" (*Borrowed Time,* 103), while publication both displays and enacts, for the benefit of those who read (potential members—or at least honorary members—of the stricken community), the conspiratorial practice that is forced, by social squeamishness, on the community of AIDSers. Thus, publishing conspiratorial poetry is a way of refusing to lie down and die, socially, that corresponds to the refusal to lie down and die that Roger displayed in his battle with the disease. As such, it constitutes Paul's ticket, if I may put it that way, to a community membership of his own; it is a kind of qualification—another word to which we shall return. For it is on "breakthrough" in a number of senses, but starting with the generic breakthrough that might break through the wall of secrecy and silence that isolates the stricken community of AIDS people, that *his* qualification depends.

"Conspiracy: literally, breathing together" (*Borrowed Time,* 151—understand "literally" to mean etymologically, of course). Breathing together with Roger has the function of keeping Roger alive, despite his death, and conversely of manifesting Paul's oneness with his lover. The problem, though, is that the two agonic experiences that are supposed to breathe together—Roger's dying, Paul's surviving—have been *staggered* by the irreparable event of Roger's death: struck, that is, and made to stagger, but also separated in time, as an event and its (thereby imperfect because nonidentical) repetition. The desired coincidence of breathing that would signify the ideal identity of the dead lover and the surviving lover has, instead, been made subject to a deferment that calls its possibility into question. And thus the poem that ought to be an enactment of shared breathing with the other ("you," "my friend") becomes, instead, a report (cf. French *reporter,* "to defer," and see chapter 3). A report "for" the other (both addressed to, and undertaken on behalf of, the other), and dated, like a medical bulletin or a lab report, on the survivor's "Current Status": the situation of deferment or suspension in which he continues to live on, *above* the equator *below* which the other has already sunk. Whence the appeal to Roger—the other who has gone before—for support and assistance in the effort to make surviving worthy of, and adequate to, the other's example:

> stay with me will you
> so I don't do anything vain or cease to honor
> you and all the brothers below the Equator

The fact of re-porting signifies a failure to con-spire—to breathe together—and betrays a sense on Paul's part of the possible vanity of his efforts, given the impossibility of resynchronizing them on the example of

Roger's heroism. And so does the *facture* of his verse, with its choppy, asyndetic syntax, and its obsessive practice of metrical enjambment, miming the poet's failure—in the state of syncopated existence, marked by a missed beat, that is his state of survival—to breathe in perfect measure with his friend, and exemplifying "all / the useless measures" of which it speaks.

For Paul is not only above the equator, he is above another even higher tropic. The equator signifies the "rift" of death, marking the separation of the dead from those who survive:

> David E who just got back from the Rift
> Valley where man began says if you flush
> a toilet five feet south of the Equator
> the spiral flows clockwise five feet north
> flows counterclock . . .

But Paul is hovering above another dividing line altogether, that of his T-cell count, which, at around 500, heralds a breakthrough that seems imminent but has yet to occur—his breakthrough into symptomatic AIDS:

> marginal no change T-4 four-sixty-five
> as of 12/8 but the labs are notoriously
> inexact nerdy white-coat sits eyeballing
> his microscope counts the squiggles in a cubic
> inch racks them up on his abacus and writes
> his apt # on the lab slip thus I'm fifteen
> less than August thirty-five more than June
> this is not statistically meaningful nor am I
> the walking wounded do not count the counting
> begins at breakthrough

So not only is breakthrough—all the breakthroughs on which Paul is "counting," and which are mimed by the breakthrough from verse to verse that is enjambment—still deferred, although imminent, but also breakthrough is itself only a qualifying ordeal, where the counting "begins." To be "not statistically meaningful" is to be at a very great distance from enjoying the heroic status Paul needs to achieve in order to be worthy of Roger and reaffirm the couple's identity. It is, literally—but of course literally means figuratively—*not to count,* to fail to "measure" up, to be out of conspiratorial synchrony—in the untimeliness of suspended survival—

with the dead hero whose deeds are, therefore, inadequately, inappropriately sung, and in that sense fatally unsung.

Perhaps we can extrapolate that where publishing conspiratorial verse would qualify as breakthrough, the beginning of heroism, this qualifying ordeal must be confirmed by the kind of heroism required by symptomatic AIDS if Paul is, eventually, to measure up. But instead he is, in his ongoing, seemingly unending "current status," just a neophyte who must qualify for admittance to the community of brothers below the equator in the knowledge that his performance takes place in the circumstances of imitation and repetition that make him an epigone: one who does not take the lead but comes after, a follower therefore who is unlikely to match the achievement of his predecessors and, in a sense—precisely because they *were* the predecessors—is precluded from doing so. Yet an inadequate performance on his part would imply the impossibility of his ever achieving the parity that would be rewarded by perfect breathing together, a true conspiracy with Roger.

> Rog I am still in the anteroom of all
> the useless measures leafing old *Peoples*
> reading diplomas . . .
>   clinically healthy why
> does that sound like a qualification

Paul's qualification, then, is moot: his only "clinical" health qualifies him at the start of his ordeal; that is, it legitimates him as potentially heroic, while his relative healthiness qualifies that qualification (moderates it, calls it into question):

>   why
> does that sound like a qualification is this
> how being a hero starts or just dying
> Ypres and Verdun men have lain down in certain
> fields with all their unspent years but meanwhile
> there is the fighting before that the target
> practice I'm learning to hold a sword
> but there is no telling what I will do when I get there

Being a hero? or just dying? What is it that is about to start? And getting there, too, is ambiguous, for "there" is *probably* just the equivalent of reaching the front lines in the trench warfare of Ypres and Verdun, but it *might* also refer, beyond that, to achieving Paul's ultimate goal of reunion and perfect conspiration with Roger. From Paul's "present" situation, "learning to hold a sword," each seems equally remote, which is why the poem goes on to end on the lines I have already quoted: "stay at my side will you / so I don't do anything vain. . . ." That publishing a poem like "Current Status" may well prove to be such a vain act—not so much an act of vanity, I think, as one that is a useless measure and has an inglorious outcome—is the point that, in contradistinction to Roger's self-evident heroism, necessarily remains moot, and with it—but at an even further remove—the question of Paul's likely heroism in his own dying and death, which understandably he doubts.

To align "Rope" and "Current Status" across the hiatus of death, as I have attempted to do here in imitation of the structure of dual autobiographies, depends, then, on constructing an analogy between "all / the useless measures" to which Monette refers and Doty's apologia for art as a mode of suspension, a frayed rope, that illusorily holds death at bay, "a while." Each poem thinks in terms of writing (and community) as a measure—illusory or useless, to be sure—against AIDS and against death. Each also enlists love as the force that strengthens human bonds against the interruption, threatened in one case, already actual in the other, that death produces. However, whereas "love's gravity" is a counterforce to the tug of death in Doty's poem, love in Monette's (modern) elegy does not really counter death at all; it can only provide support, perhaps, to face it in its inevitability. The ultimate inadequacy of "measures"—medicine, poetry, love—is thus the theme that links the two poems across the anticipatory-retrospective divide that itself figures death. But the narrative I have constructed on the basis of this thematic continuity is a story that, like the relation of Paul's survivorhood to Roger's dying and death, tells a tale of *increasing* inadequacy and aggravated wrongness, so that death intervenes between the two poems I have attempted to align as that which irreparably condemns Paul to the ingloriousness of coming after, to the impossibility of mending what is broken, that haunts his will to heroism and disables it. And so my narrative in turn stumbles, staggers, enjambs only clumsily at the point of relay where the death, anticipated in Doty, remembered in Monette, disables my critical enterprise of creating, as it were, a fellowship or community of the two poems and the two poets.

But the two prose narratives to which I am about to turn, each of which is similarly structured as a prospective wrongness that gets worse in the retrospective situation of survival, differ from the poems in that they do not even consider writing as a measure, however useless, against death. It is not simply that writing fails in these narratives to mitigate death's effects, although that is true of them; but writing has itself become one of the effects of disaster, bearing its trace. Not a sword against AIDS or a supportive harness, it is presented as a profoundly uncomfortable symptom of the epidemic of wrongness that is AIDS, a social equivalent, as it were, of corporeal afflictions like incontinence or, its opposite, constipation. If Monette's sense of the heroism entailed in publishing verse that is of necessity conspiratorial can be read as an index of his awareness of generic misfit and social im-pertinence, the indexing of that discomfort in *L'Aztèque* and *Hospital Time* becomes something more like an exhibition of abjection, an exhibition undertaken not only uselessly but, as it were, involuntarily and against one's better judgment (if not quite against one's will). That is, the genre discomfort is such that writing itself becomes infected here with the sense of wrongness that is aftermath's most salient characteristic. Where "Rope" and "Current Status" are brilliantly realized poems whose subject is the inadequacy of "measures" against disaster, the writing of Duquénelle and Hoffman is itself the site of a debacle, and it is that debacle—the debacle of the "conspiracy" in which Monette continues to believe—that is given to us, or more accurately thrust disgustedly at us, to be read. Writing can only say too much or too little; whether excessive or retentive it is constitutively wrong. Yet, oddly, it still wants to be read.

The Irreparable

In *L'Aztèque,* there is a red lamp that falls and is smashed to smithereens. Painstakingly, the narrator Bertrand pieces it together again, and is quite pleased with the result: "from a distance you would be deceived" (77). But a hole remains, unrepaired because unrepairable: "doubtless the point of impact when it fell." The red lamp is an object symbolic of survival and illustrating the law of aftermath, which is that of the irreparable. Any *present* break is beyond efforts to mend it because it is the product of a previous disaster, a disruption or interruption—like the fall of the lamp—that has made its *impact* in the past and can't be overcome. The break has a prior cause, an earlier break, that escapes present efforts at repair. And whereas both "Rope" and "Present Status" emphasize the closeness of the bonds of love even as they acknowledge their fragility or inadequacy in the face of death, *L'Aztèque* and *Hospital Time* agree in identifying the crucial breakage, the disaster that the death of the other sanctions, as a premortem failure—a failure of love or of generosity, amounting to a kind of betrayal, on the part of the survivor. Thus disaster seems always to be prior to itself. A first division, moral or physical, separating the dying man (Jean-François or Mike) from the caregiver (Bertrand or Amy) during the former's life foretells the henceforth irreparable distance that will intervene, after death, between survivor and deceased, a distance produced by the interruption of death but aggravated by the survivor's awareness of the irreparability of his or her initial failure. And this distance in turn foretells yet another rift: that between the survivor's writing, attempting vainly to repair the two initial breaks, and the readership that might make such writing worthwhile.

So the law of aftermath—the priority of an irreparable break—becomes also a law of aggravation or degradation, as the conviction of the disaster's irreparability grows. Premortem division is repeated in the postmortem state of survival, but aggravated by the failure of the survivor to repair it. And because writing is both the means whereby the survivor attempts to repair the initial disaster(s) and the phenomenon in which the irreparability of the damage is measured, since responsibility for repair now rests on a very hypothetical reader and is out of the writer-survivor's control, writing becomes the defining activity of survival. It signifies both the character of survival as degraded repetition, and the failure of repetition to mend the impact of the previous fall(s). Like the red lamp, writing is thus permanently damaged, marked by the impact of the traumatic: dented and holed. For Hoffman it becomes, therefore, a painful effort to squeeze out a few honest sentences from an overwhelming sense of blockage and powerlessness; for Duquénelle, a hypocritical self-indulgence and self-display—the sin of *impudeur,* "impudicity" (in bourgeois France a shameful lapse, like losing control of one's sphincter in public). What reader, this writing asks, could be expected to take an interest in, let alone be moved by, Hoffman's always deficient phrasing, or Duquénelle's shameless excess of words? But unless it is read, how can writing repair the failure of love that death has sanctioned? It is more probable that the failure of love will be reproduced in the writing's relation to a society of survivors unconscious in their survivorhood both of the burdens of survival and of any link between those so burdened and those who live on in blithe disregard of disaster.

But it is in this latter context of writing's social failure that it comes to be associated with, and to figure the mode of existence of, not solely a couple but a community, one that is defined, in contradistinction to the society at large, by its common experience of disaster. Such a community is composed both of those who have died and of those who survive and remember them, for if the death that divides the community and interrupts its narratives forms an irreparable disruption, it is the community's shared knowledge of death—its consciousness of disaster—that forms the bond holding it together.[3] Writing comes to be the figure of such a community's existence, as the emblematic activity of Duquénelle's tribe or of those who live in Hoffman's "hospital time"—the time of endless deferment (Duquénelle's "sempiternel sursis") as the clock ticks "differently"—to the extent that, like the red lamp, it bears the mark of death's impact in its apparent interminability, its inability to stop. That is, it is not only the site of the community's knowledge of death, but it is itself disabled by that knowledge, which is why, as a vehicle that might potentially restore a bond between the disaster-struck community and the oblivious society, thus healing the damage done by death, it is disqualified in advance by the wrongness—the excess of words, the insufficiency of its phrasing—that makes it so unlikely to be read. So writing is what defines and enacts the community's knowledge of death as a knowledge of the irreparable, of disaster: of that which divides in a way that cannot be repaired and so divides even the community itself between the dead and those who survive.

"The telephone rings. It's over" (*L'Aztèque,* 50). Of course, it's not over, that is the point, but the break in the narrative at Jean-François's death is clearly marked in *L'Aztèque.* So is the relay that makes Bertrand both the protagonist and the writer of the continuation/repetition of Jean-François's story, the story of his own dying of AIDS. "My. Turn. Now." he thinks (49), contemplating the skin allergy that has just appeared on his face, a reminder of his own infection. The periods that punctuate the phrase are signs of emphasis, markers of inevitability, reminders of interruption—they make an asyndeton of a statement that implies smooth transition. And there is a kind of fumble in the narrative relay, too, since the allergy appears while Jean-François is still living, albeit comatose. And these discontinuities themselves record and confirm the fact that distance has been present between Jean-François and Bertrand, as the law of aftermath requires, almost from the beginning of the narrative. Their love affair is evoked in the early pages, but it is over and Jean-François has returned to Bertrand, for support and friendship, only on becoming ill. In the course of Jean-François's agony, their disconnection is not repaired but becomes worse: just as the illness frightens off Jean-François's other friends and ex-lovers, so it comes between him and Bertrand, who comments: "Even when

I am with him, he is alone" (24); "He is already dead. For everyone he is dead. Past. For me too, even though I resist the idea" (29). Finally a physical separation intervenes: Jean-François retreats to Compiègne, outside of Paris, where his family lives: Bertrand's visits are now restricted by train schedules and the panicky rules of a provincial hospital unaccustomed (it is the year 1986) to AIDS patients. As the agony wears on interminably, Bertrand daydreams of a *radical* disconnection that would permit him, he imagines, to turn the page: he would take the train, sneak into the hospital in disguise, "slip into the deserted ward, then into Jean-François's room, surreptitiously disconnect the equipment, and wait" (48)—the sentence hangs incomplete without a final period, thus countermanding the desired disconnection and replacing it with a suspension, in accord with the implications and connotations, in the context of AIDS, of the word "wait." So, of course, he does not in fact pull the plug on his friend, and the drawn-out agony of Jean-François's dying—"I don't know what I'm doing there," Bertrand had written earlier; "All I know is that it will turn out badly and it will take forever" (24)—is thus described as a function of Bertrand's inability either fully to disconnect or to connect completely in his relation with his former lover, the impossibility, that is, of ever fully turning the page.

The geographic difference between them stands, therefore, for a more important psychological tension, which is reflected in the text by the contrast between the external perspective of Bertrand's narrative concerning Jean-François, always referred to in the third person (as "il"), and the internal focus of his own first-person ("je") musings. (Thus Jean-François, unlike say Monette's Roger, has a speaking part of his own only in the letters quoted from the time, in 1982–83, when the pair were a couple.) Bertrand, who understands Jean-François to be cutting himself off from everyone and everything in preparation for death, responds by simultaneously identifying with Jean-François's embrace of death, his failure to resist, and feeling alienated and rejected by it. "I let myself die with him and hate him for it" (31). The miscommunication produces an inescapable game of hide-and-go-seek ("cache-cache") in which each seeks and fails to find the other: "Our thoughts cross without meeting. Him, me, him, him, him" (35). And significantly, this psychological misconnection is enacted most crucially in relation to issues of writing and reading. Jean-François has written a manuscript that foreshadows Bertrand's own future text; asked to read it, Bertrand (mis)understands its style—all ellipses and absent punctuation, as *L'Aztèque* will also be—as an attempt on Jean-

François's part to "use literature to give legitimacy to his having given up" (37). "The effect of the book," he tells the writer, "is to close off your life as an inexorable, logical trajectory toward illness" and death; it is just "a way to destroy yourself" (36–37), and the stylistic fragmentation and obscurity are a device to deprive the reader of freedom. The implied address to the reader is "You have to get your feet wet. You have to come onto my terrain where I am protected by subtleties and hermetic phrasing from overhasty judgment" (37). Bertrand fails to see, that is, that another game of hide-and-go-seek is being played and that Jean-François's hiding in hermeticism is more like an invitation to the reader to come seek him out than a device to restrict the reader's freedom (which, as Bertrand's own reaction unfortunately shows, the reader will exercise in any case). So it becomes a game of "cache-cache" in the sense that each of the friends is concealed from the other.

This reaction, of course, foreshadows the sense of his own readership that Bertrand will have when, following Jean-François's death and as his own dying agonizingly proceeds, he too turns to a mode of writing that he himself imagines as supremely off-putting. Bertrand's own readers, then, should note that in retrospect he understands his response to Jean-François's uncompromising writing—in reality the dying man's attempt to make his tormented private world available to Bertrand's reading—as a fatal and indeed lethal error. "In talking to him about his book I have killed him. How can I have been so unconsciously cruel? Suddenly he is remote from me. Inaccessible." (38). And so "mutual disappointment submerges us." "I disappoint him by not having found something impossible, a bond, sublime and secret, that would illumine his end. He disappoints me by allowing himself to die in this way, paralyzed by panic" (39). This is the standoff that is still in force when Jean-François dies, his death thus sanctioning the fatal failure of connection, and driving home to the reader the lesson that *L'Aztèque*'s own idiosyncrasies and inadequacies of communicative writing should not be similarly misinterpreted, that an effort of "symbolic" reading of those failings is required, at the same time as it is predicted, of course, that Bertrand's writing *will* be so misunderstood and rejected, given that we are being invited (?) to read a book that judges itself to be so much unreadable "pus" (110). For Jean-François's death also makes the misconnection irreparable, according to the lesson of the red lamp, so that it now hangs over the ensuing account of Bertrand's survival, both confirming his sense of survival as separation and distance and ensuring that it be experienced by Bertrand as an absurd and purposeless extension of his own life and of Jean-François's memory—a second never-ending agony in aggravated repetition of the first.

But of course, things get worse. If the premortem failure of communication foreshadows and determines the sense of futility and guilt that attaches to Bertrand's survival and makes the failure of writing its emblem, the error of his reading of Jean-François's text hanging now over his own writing and depriving it of conviction as concerns both the possibility of repairing the original failure and that of reaching an appropriate readership in its own right, there is also a new element that simultaneously prolongs Bertrand's everlasting survival and aggravates his sense of guilt. That element is "the new treatment, AZT" (58), which along with the absurdity of writing now becomes a second emblem of the new period into which the narrative moves at Jean-François's death. AZT confirms the separation with Jean-François (who did not have access to the drug) and—as the first AIDS treatment to be at all effective—extends Bertrand's survival into an indeterminate future. Thus the task he had initially defined as trying "to survive in order to die correctly" (62) comes to be redefined as another mode of absurdity: "to hold out. . . , to hold out until the next treatment, which will make it possible to await another treatment, which will make it possible to last out as long as I have to" (76), so that the mood initially defined by the question "Why should I survive?" shifts to "What shall I survive for?" (75), without the underlying sense of living a useless deferment—"le temps qu'il faudra," as Bertrand vaguely puts it, "as long as I have to"—having in any way changed.

Becoming an Aztec—a taker of AZT—does not affect Bertrand's sense that everything is already played out, then, so that only waiting (and writing) remain; indeed it confirms and aggravates his sense of futility, absurdity, and interminability. But it does also introduce another novelty with respect to Jean-François's solitary dying in that it gives him a sense of belonging to a community, a difference from Jean-François that also defines a difference in relation to the general population of Paris, the non-Aztecs. One key diary entry brings together the two sensations, of absurd survival and of community:

> *October 26, 1987.* Aztec! I'm another man. A man of a new tribe. How many of us are there? Maybe a hundred in Paris. By virtue of a white capsule with a thin, blue band, AZT, I've become a kind of Aztec, an Aztec initiated into a terrible secret rite; it consists of swallowing a capsule every four hours washed down with a tall glass of water, under pain of imminent death.

> With his eternal Mona Lisa smile, Dr R. types at the keyboard of his new computer. "How long will it help me to hold out?"
>
> "Don't ask me questions I can't answer." (74)

And so the text also contains a brilliantly sardonic "ethnography" of the Aztec, described on the one hand as a community of survivors, subject to a paradoxical law of simultaneous diminution and increase:

> So the Aztec is not the representative of a vanished civilization of the Americas even though he is himself a disappearing species; indeed his deepest nature is to be subject to rapid disappearance. Nevertheless Aztecs are on the increase.
>
> The Aztec is a survivor. By all rights he should be already dead. (101)

On the other, however, these survivors are also described in terms of their problematic relation as a community to the society of non-Aztecs whose existence the Aztec disturbs or "complicates" (101), so that non-Aztecs do not know how best to deny the threat an Aztec poses:

> Among non-Aztecs, there are those who consider themselves sufficiently removed from the Aztec to drop him;
>
> those who try to persuade the Aztec that he isn't going to die, that it's impossible, and imagine that in this way they are working to cheer him up;
>
> those who . . . [etc.] (102)

The list of ways the non-Aztec, in denying the Aztec's reality, lets him know that he is a problem is quite a long one, since it extends both to forms of communication (postcards, phone calls, visits) and to acts of non-communication like not calling, not writing, not visiting. Noncommunication is of course not an absence of communication but a form of interrupted communication having the interruption as its message—but so too, in this case, is communication itself, which always signifies that the Aztec is being held at a distance from the non-Aztec.

So it is the community of Aztecs that links the thematics of surviving, as a useless deferment, with a problematics of communication under conditions of social interruption, the "secret rite" of AZT-taking defining the particularity of the group as survivors whose survival is not only lived as a useless deferment but also experienced socially as unwelcome and unwanted. And if writing, the survivor's other defining occupation, signifies the uselessness of the deferment, it too is crucially bound up with the problematics of Aztec/non-Aztec communication. For writing entails reading: in addition to, and as a corollary of, the question, "What is the point of my surviving?" it asks: "For whom do I imagine I am writing?" And perhaps the most remarkable sign of the general disaster that sets in following Jean-François's death is the disintegration in Bertrand's writing that starts from the moment of relay ("My. Turn. Now.") that makes him Jean-François's survivor. Throughout the book, the writing is fragmented, consisting of short passages that often end in suspension, without a final period, and are (dis)connected by signs of ellipsis *(points de suspension).* Despite the many gaps, however, a semblance of continuous narration is maintained through the story of the love affair and then that of Jean-François's illness, decline, seemingly interminable agony, and death. It is only from that point on that the very possibility of narrative coherence disappears; as Bertrand's survival resolves into everlasting deferment, story structure dissolves. And it is in the context of this disintegration of narrative that, soon, the issues of writing and reading will begin to emerge as topics of Bertrand's reflection. Although it has death as its inevitable end point, survival in itself has no telos; writing both confirms this pointlessness, since Bertrand fails to say what needs to be said, and itself becomes, therefore, a meaningless activity, a form of useless self-indulgence in which the writer nevertheless engages in the way that he is willy-nilly engaged in survival (*embarqué,* as one would say in French, with a nod to Pascal, or in Heidegger's German, *geworfen,* thrown). As such, then, writing is unworthy of an audience, whose anticipated rejection—the rejection of the Aztec by a society of non-Aztecs—in turn confirms and aggravates the sense of pointlessness.

So the writing of *L'Aztèque* now becomes episodic and diary-like, a loose collection of snippets, thoughts, observations, reports of dreams, accounts of medical consultation with Dr R(ozenbaum), treatments and hospitalizations, personal betrayals and subjective responses to the "impasse" Bertrand is in. Responses of anger—"I bear everyone and everything a grudge"—lapse immediately into resignation: "Never mind, I was really at a dead end, and still am" (95). Responses of resignation combine lucidity with a kind of bafflement:

> The diagnosis is repetitive but not monotonous: I am dying. Like everyone. Without knowing how much longer I have to live, like everyone. The difference is that I am no longer able to ignore it; I can't live without thinking

> of it. I could once imagine slowing down time by inhabiting it with greater and greater intensity until the final second. Maybe I didn't believe enough in that. In any case it turns out not to be happening; my life is gradually fading in a state of incompleteness and weakness. (98)

It is only toward the end, though, that among these thoughts disabused commentary on writing itself, and eventually on reading, becomes prominent. This emerging theme is readable, therefore, as a function of increasing frustration, as Bertrand's death approaches but does not come. For there is really only one state to write about—"All I have left to narrate is my everlasting deferment" (106)—yet it is exactly that state that deprives writing, like everything else, of structure and point.

> What is more bathetic [*dérisoire*] than a book that can't manage to say what it has to say, always supposing there is something to say, but how to know this in advance without lapsing into defeatism? At the start, a person with AIDS who is experiencing an exceptional event imagines it to be an ideal topic and thinks himself a writer (109)

(The thought is left hanging, unpunctuated, for the reader to complete.)

And the urge to write nevertheless persists absurdly, precisely as death approaches, because approaching death stimulates what Bertrand calls the "Proust syndrome" (telling word), the desire to leave a "work" worthy of the reader's attention. "Conscious of his imminent end, Proust's narrator tells himself at the end of *La Recherche,* that it is time to get started and to write at last the work of his life and to fuse himself with it." That, however, is exactly what, for Bertrand, has become impossible.

> Isn't that the syndrome that affects us all? In extremis, don't we all write the same book: the same wretched book, literary so as not to come off as morbid, immodest [*impudique*] so as to come off as sincere, elliptical so as not to seem to be complaining, ferocious to persuade ourselves that we exist, a book full of cruel anecdotes, physicians' slipups, cowardices and betrayals, leaks, lapses into Paris-speak, twisted devices to get ourselves off the hook, different forms of masochism, confessions, poses, sighs . . . To be sure the reader did not deserve to have to swallow such a load of pus. But also, when push comes to shove, out it comes, as best it may. Not everyone can be Proust. (110)

In the era of AIDS, the Proust syndrome does not and cannot give rise to a "work" like *A la recherche du temps perdu,* but becomes instead this meaningless combination of the urge to write with knowledge that writing is both worthless and an imposition on its reader. As a judgment on the readability of Duquénelle's book, this relentless analysis of the fake rhetoricity of all such "last writes" is undoubtedly harsh; but to the extent that it pinpoints the writing's lack of conviction and correlates its "worklessness" or *désoeuvrement* (the word and the pun are Blanchot's) with, on the one hand, aftermath experience and, on the other, the reader's assumed indifference and disgust—the non-Aztec's avoidance and denial of Aztecs—it requires our careful reflection and interpretation. For this is not just a meditation on the failure of "measures" (medical or artistic *techne*) in the face of death; the anger is fueled by something that is of a social order rather than purely metaphysical, the failure of readerly love that was predicted by Bertrand's own inability to *read past* the impediments of Jean-François's awful prose.

Which is why it centers finally on the problem of *impudeur,* the social sin par excellence of bourgeois France (as Hervé Guibert also understood; see Chambers 1998b). Duquénelle is clearly conscious of the impudicity entailed in forcing on the reader a load of pus; that is, he understands the writing-reading relation to be governed in part by the writer's contradictory urge to write and publish in the absence of belief in the writing's value (a form of self-indulgence), but in part, also by the dynamics of aversion, the turning away from abjection, that non-Aztecs display in all their social dealings with Aztecs. In his list of the forms this aversion takes, he significantly notes "those who think the Aztec is not sufficiently discreet concerning his imminent demise and advise him not to be so provocative, pathetic, or overemphatic [*pesant*]" (102). On the face of it, such impudicity is the opposite of the hermeticism that he held against Jean-François—it is not a way of retreating prematurely into death so much as of failing to go gently, and of shoving one's dying down the throats of people who do not wish to know about it. But it too does look suspiciously like a counsel of despair, an attempt to "use literature to give legitimacy to the writer's having given up" (37) and hence—the very misinterpretation that sealed the breach between the lovers and made it irrevocable—a way of sanctioning the rupture between the writer as *moriturus* and his audience among the living. The impudicity that the writing of *L'Aztèque* displays could be read as a deliberate turnoff to the non-Aztec reader, whose response of indignation and rejection it courts. We know, though, from the earlier episode, that such a reading would be a fatal and indeed lethal one, in that it confirms the very breach (of death) that the writer, despite all odds and contrary to appearances, is desperately attempting to bridge. And it is important therefore that a few pages later Duquénelle suggests another interpretation—one that might go some way toward mending, rather than inflaming, the break—when he writes, "Impudicity is just a symptom of the disease, like wasting or fatigue, a symptom that is closer to incontinence than it is to provocation" (109).

In this understanding AIDS writing is subject to wasting, fatigue, and impudicity because wasting, fatigue, and incontinence are common effects of AIDS, symptoms that together form a "syndrome" comparable—but at the opposite extreme of the work-worklessness continuum—with the "Proust syndrome." If writing fails, in other words, and it does, its very failure has semiotic value—the value of an indexical sign—because it is a product, hence a symptom, of the conditions of epidemic, conditions that include a desire on the part of Aztecs to display their pus *and* the attitudes of denial on the part of non-Aztecs that lead to accusations of impudicity and a refusal to read, the incompatible coexistence of these two conditions encapsulating the problematics of disaster and its aftermath. The writing of aftermath is necessarily failed writing in this sense; it is strictly unreadable because enmeshed in that incompatibility. But that condition of unreadability *might* itself become readable, therefore, as—to echo Blanchot—the "writing of disaster," the very sign of disaster's presence among us, provided only that there be a reader whose revulsion from the pus would not be so great as to provoke immediate rejection, the form of denial that is the refusal to read, and who would be capable, therefore, of realizing the writing's semiotic potential. The only question is: can there be such a reader?

In such an analysis, some distinction is implied between two areas of the disaster's impact. One such area is that of *techne:* the "measures," like medical treatments and writing but also including love, that fail in the face of death and disaster, because they are without sufficient strength. This we saw is Monette's concern. But in the area of ethics, failure is viewed more as a matter of human deficiencies than of technical insufficiency; and such deficiencies are understood to be of such a kind that they might ideally be overcome. Failures of love, of generosity, and of empathy, such as the ungenerous misreading of Jean-François's writing for which Bertrand feels not so much incapable or even inadequate as guilty, certainly do make of such love a useless measure. Ethical failings, that is, form part of the disaster, as an epidemic of generalized wrongness; AIDS is an epidemic of social alienation as much as of untimely death; and such alienations aggravate, as we have seen, what are already the intolerable burdens of living on amid disaster, repeating and confirming its patterns of division, disruption, and failure. But as Bertrand's remorse concerning his misreading of Jean-François's writing suggests, failures of love and generosity are not to be understood *solely* as a given, in the way that the inadequacy of the medical armamentarium, or even of artistic practice, is a given; rather they result from poor choices, which are made, inevitably enough, in the midst of panic and an urgency to deny, and then turn out to have irreparable consequences. Guilt arises, then, from an ethical consciousness that another, more responsible choice was conceivable—that Bertrand, for example, might against the odds not have misread Jean-François's writing. And such a not-misreading would have consisted of understanding that writing *both* as an abject and off-putting display of pus, *and* as the symptom—the sign of a disaster both existential and social, personal and collective, affecting culture as *techne* and culture as ethics, and disabling both—that it is. (I do not say a "right" or "correct" reading: that would presuppose an ability, not only to read pus as a symptom, but also to know without denial the real nature of the "disease" indicated by the symptom, an ability incompatible—if my analysis is correct—with the state of being a survivor.)

So it should be noted that there *is* a category of non-Aztecs, mentioned in Duquénelle's catalog just before those who take umbrage at the Aztecs' supposed impudicity: "those who are so disoriented that they are unhappier than the Aztec himself, who regrets having taken them into so painful a confidence" (102). Such non-Aztecs are unlikely to be capable of resolving the problem of the general interruption of communication that has been brought about by the disaster of AIDS; indeed, in making the Aztec feel guilty for having made them unhappy they might well be accused of aggravating and deepening the Aztec/non-Aztec divide. But rather than, say, blaming the Aztec for *impudeur* or otherwise failing to comprehend the import of the Aztec's brazen self-display, they have allowed themselves to be, in an important sense successfully, taken into a painful confidence. They have made another, ethically preferable, choice. These disoriented, unhappy non-Aztecs, we can say, have at least become conscious, as Aztecs are, of the conditions of aftermath that their fellow non-Aztecs are so anxious to deny but in which these particular non-Aztecs now share (and which they reproduce and confirm). Given that these conditions have the status of a fatality, implied by the word *aftermath* and by the law of irreparability according to which the break is always prior, such a response of unhappiness, which signifies membership in the same unhappy community as those who ritually take pills and compulsively write, does not repair those conditions, which remain in force. The relay has expanded consciousness of them, but it does not and cannot abolish, for example, Bertrand's failures of relay in relation to Jean-François, or his guilt over those failures. The ethically superior response is only the least bad of all the wrong responses that one might imagine. The best response would be for love never to have failed at all—but that response (which would make love a successful measure against disaster) is exactly the impossibility that defines the disaster.

Certainly the response of these unhappy non-Aztecs is at the opposite pole from the advice to turn the page that Monette declared "the wrongest of all the wrong things" one can say. But in acknowledging the unhappiness of knowing that the page cannot be blithely turned, it recognizes (as well as enacts) the second law of irreparability, a corollary of the first, the law decreeing that since the break is always prior and cannot be repaired, the situation of aftermath can only get worse, through successive relays and repetitions. Thus to acknowledge the conditions of aftermath—here called unhappiness and guilt—while it is a preferable response, affirming community, does not abolish the prior disaster; rather it confirms disaster's irreparability in repeating and extending its effects. Disaster is that which is both irretrievably in the past because beyond repair, and never over because the dent made by its impact not only does not go away, but even deepens. Always over, but never over; never over because always already over.

Heavy Ashes

Amy Hoffman's subject is also wrongness and the impossibility of moving on. Hoffman does not herself write, like Duquénelle, under threat of imminent death, yet she too describes surviving as an absurd living on without closure, a suspended sentence of her own. Freed by her presumed HIV-negative status from the sense of inevitable imitation and repetition that is so strong in survivors who are themselves infected (Monette or Duquénelle, for example), she identifies the defining feature of survival even more explicitly than they as the inability to mourn, which has as its corollary the necessity and the impossibility of writing. The lack of agreed conventions for writing the agony of aftermath matches the inadequacy, in Amy's eyes, of conventional social practices like those of mourning in the face of a disaster like AIDS.

As members of the collective producing the pioneering Boston newspaper *Gay Community News* in the late seventies, she and Mike Riegle had become friends; but she did not expect him to ask her, years later, to become his "health care proxy" in the last stages of his illness. In pained and angry, often self-reproachful prose, she tells of what she describes as her inability to be of real assistance to him in his painful dying, and then of the ensuing agony of being unable, after his death, either to forget his ordeal or to repair the deficiencies of caring she charges herself with. In this second part of the narrative, that is, a continuing sense of responsibility for Mike combines with continued powerlessness to discharge that responsibility, and so resolves into further anger, resentment, and guilt, with the result that neither she nor he can rest. "I give him no peace, dragging him around like this" (146). And concomitantly she writes of her inability to write, which becomes a second agony of suspension commensurate with her failure to mourn, as she fails to find the form of words that might release her, and him, by miraculously repairing the damage done by AIDS—that is, by adequately expressing that damage to others who are bent on denying it. So the intense discomfort of "hospital time" that she experiences at Mike's bedside, "where there is no comfortable place to sit" (3), does not end, as caregivers might hope, at the patient's death. Once one has entered it, hospital time, which "ticks by differently" (3), becomes interminable. And from its perspective the world that denies the existence and reality of hospital time comes to seem itself unreal and irrelevant, absurd. "It's utterly frivolous, the world and its other times. Here in the hospital is the real thing. Eternity" (5).

Yet hospital time is, by definition, time interrupted by death. Even more emphatically than in *L'Aztèque,* that wrenching disjuncture that destroys time's normal continuity and progression is dramatized here by the phone call from the hospital. "I'd been at the hospital all afternoon, and Roberta and I were going out to dinner. Our coats were on. One of us had her hand upon the doorknob, about to turn it, and the phone rang" (77). And once again, with that interruption, the narrative, composed from the beginning of short bursts of prose separated by generous blanks, begins to lose the relative coherence and directionality furnished by the story of a dying and becomes a considerably more dispersed set of stories and musings, the plotless account of survival. But the dispersal corresponds also to a broadening of focus from the story of two individuals to a concern with community, which in this case is not that of "Aztecs" alone but a broader one of AIDS people,[4] including the ill, the dying, and the dead but also those who give them care and afterward deal with the responsibilities of aftermath, "calling the names" at commemorative gatherings (91), receiving the inheritances, material and moral, remembering and attempting to mourn, feeling the solitude for which, too, "there is no cure" (138). Here it is Mike's ashes, received by Amy as another heavy burden of painful responsibility, "one more never-ending thing" (86), but scattered by his friends in the reedy marshes of the Fenway, that mark the fatal disjunction and continuity between the dead and those who survive. The ashes become the figure for continuing responsibility, including narrative responsibility, and simultaneously for the dispersal and pluralization the narrative undergoes as it too becomes scattered and directionless, albeit obsessed, while opening out to explore the nature of the AIDS community. Or perhaps memory, in the end, is the crucial culprit, like the ashes a factor of continuity that inhibits the work of mourning (which ultimately is forgetting), but like them too a phenomenon of discontinuity and dispersal. "You carry the person with you, and thus he lives, as part of you and yours. Too bad my memory is full of holes" (104).

During the period of his illness and death, Mike—as described by Amy—was one of the most difficult of difficult patients, exasperating in his personal habits and his insistence on maintaining his independence when others had to care for him in every way, unwilling to compromise his strict radical principles even under conditions of extreme personal urgency, and uncooperative when it came to making important decisions (whether to sign the Do Not Resuscitate order, whether to move from the hospital into a hospice), which he left to Amy even though conscious, rational, and capable of making them for himself. "I want to live" was all he would say, expressing the desire—more accurately the demand—that makes caregivers feel guilty, powerless, and exasperated, since it is definitionally impossible to satisfy. Amy had not hesitated to respond to his request for help. "With the virus, you make a choice. When someone gets sick you're either in or out. That's it. No middle ground" (15). Her commitment entailed no hesitation, but of course the categorical imperative to be "in" rather than "out" does not guarantee that one enjoys the experience or require that one approach it in a spirit of saintly self-abnegation. Rather her feelings, in this circumstance, are first of helplessness and inadequacy, then of resentment—at being put in the insoluble double bind of receiving an appeal ("I want to live") that can be neither rejected nor satisfied—and finally of anger, anger against Mike substituting for a deeper anger against AIDS, the disaster that makes the nearly unbearable commitment to Mike necessary while ensuring that it be discharged under conditions of frustration and resentment that amount to a failure of generosity and love. She wants mainly to be let off the hook: after a description of the many irritations of accompanying Mike on shopping excursions, she reports, "I would kiss him goodnight and run down the stairs. Running felt good" (25). And grateful as she is for the break when Mike announces an ill-judged plan to visit a friend in Texas, she quickly regrets not having discouraged his departure (he collapses en route, and Amy must fly guiltily to Memphis to take responsibility for him again). In retrospect, then, she writes:

> I wish every day that I had been more genuinely kind, more open and loving and freely generous. Although if it happened again, someone I know having AIDS—and it has, it will—I'd do it again and feel the same, because that is what AIDS does, the fucker. (22)

AIDS is that which requires an absolute commitment, while withholding all possibility of deriving from one's commitment any sense of personal achievement or emotional satisfaction, so that the quality of one's commitment inevitably falters and guilt ensues. As in *L'Aztèque* the break that death sanctions is prior to that death; it takes the form of a failure of love—but the *name* of that always prior disaster, Amy specifies here, is AIDS.

Following Mike's death, then, to the burden of continued responsibility and of continued anger is added that of remorse, the knowledge not only of the failure of one's generosity under the test of AIDS but also that the damage done (Mike's death, Amy's despair) cannot be repaired or forgotten—the page cannot be turned because the pain persists. "I cry because I miss him, because I love him, because I feel so mean, because his death was so terrible, hard and early, and I didn't treat him tenderly" (97). And because the effects of AIDS are such that the disaster cannot be overcome, mourning—supposedly a transitional period whose telos is a return to so-called normalcy (i.e., obliviousness of death)—becomes impossible. It resolves instead into everything that Mike's ashes symbolize ("one more never-ending thing"), as memory simultaneously refuses to fade yet disintegrates into dispersal, becoming "full of holes." While Amy's friends recall Mike's idiosyncrasies with affection, she herself remains irritated, as when he was still alive, by what she cannot regard as harmless quirks. When they report signs that his spirit is now free—the sighting of a blue heron (87) or in the case of another AIDS death, a tree in the forest that suddenly sheds its leaves (104)—she cannot share the illusory comfort: "I wish more than anything I believed that" (87); "If it comforts you, okay, I told her" (104). These staples of the conventional mourning process have no purchase on her pain and grief; she continues therefore to carry her unbearable burden of heavy memory and undischarged responsibility, giving Mike no rest and enjoying none herself. "No rest for the weary. That was Mike's motto. . . . He is ashes, but his body persists in memory: weary, wicked, wandering" (146). He has, in other words, become spectral, "Mike the Ghost" as she jokes at another point (112); and his spectrality signifies, of course, her own hauntedness—her inability either to repair or to forget the disaster that his dying and death have come to figure for her, the disaster of AIDS that has interrupted her life. To be haunted, we know, is the sign of one's inability to mourn.

But the words that describe Mike's spectrality, "weary, wicked, wandering" (I've omitted two more—"bent, delicious"—that have his dick as primary referent) apply equally to Amy's writing, haunted by him and spectral, therefore, in imitation of his own ghostlike state: writing that is itself in a state of interruptedness and suspension, unable to achieve the coherence of narrative grammaticality, lacking the substance that telos and the possibility of closure would confer, weary, wicked, and wandering. Her caring for Mike originally interrupted a novel on which she was engaged; the novel is now shelved permanently and has been relayed by the writing of *Hospital Time,* on which she finds it desperately hard to make progress. Where Carrie is able to use writing to "work through" her feelings about Mike, Amy finds herself, by contrast—having in desperation taken a two-week vacation (as she had already fruitlessly done when working on the novel)—sharing a house in the country with a group of confident writers ("they all produce quantities of words" [95]), listening to one of them tap away steadily on a manual typewriter "like an all-day rainstorm" while she herself sits at her desk, remembering, reproaching herself, failing to work through and unable to turn out a sentence. "It's silently snowing, shrouding the view. Leaning over the silent keys on my computer, I stare out the window. A skier moves across the field, and a squirrel skitters up a tree" (95). So there is an equation here: her aridity as a writer—her frozen snowboundness—is to the quantities of words produced around her—the fertility of soaking rain—as her inability to mourn to the ease with which friends like Loie or Carrie are able to take comfort. It is the same blockage, evidence of the same hauntedness.

That this blockage, however, has at least as much to do with the phenomenon of AIDS as a public disaster as it does with the specific deficiencies of Amy's relation to Mike is made manifest by the fact that now, in the period of aftermath, Mike's name becomes associated with the whole AIDS community as Amy knows it, that is, with both her women friends and lovers—Roberta, Loie, Carrie—and her gay male friends, dead and surviving: Bob and Steve, Gregory and Harry, Walta and Bronski, Richard. Derrida's dictum that the specter is plural is confirmed here: Mike the ghost has become the symbolic center—but a center that, crucially, has been lost—of a spectrum of figures who form the haunted and potentially haunting community of those who know the disaster that is AIDS:

> We're a group of people who were trapped in a terrible storm. Mike was the big tree that sheltered us. When the rain stopped and the wind died down, we dispersed through the woods and fields. (117)

This unexpectedly sentimental characterization of Mike as the "big tree that sheltered us" seems designed less as a tribute to his actual centrality in the group (about which we hear no more) than it is a way of emphasizing their dispersal as an AIDS community subject to the epidemic's dire effects: death and loss, math and aftermath. Dispersal, then—the symbolic scattering of Mike's ashes, the failure of Amy's writing to "come together," the group itself scattered and to an extent divided in its very solidarity—is something like a general name for the conditions of existence of those whose lives, having been interrupted by the storm, are now endured in the unresolved, suspended state Amy calls hospital time. A name, that is, for a plural spectrality, joining in the experience of their phantom pain—the pain of surviving—both the dead who haunt and the haunted survivors, become haunters in their turn. But whom do these survivors haunt? To whom might their pain be transmitted?

For just as there are those who, like Amy, are unable to mourn and those, even within the community, who take easy comfort, and those who, again like Amy, stare out the window at the snow while others tap away confidently and produce quantities of words, so too there is this dispersed community of the disaster-stricken and there is those whose existence has not undergone interruption or become subject to suspension. That is, there are those who, as Amy puts it, know the AIDS language and others who, like the straight Yoga teacher, do not recognize a word like *neuropathy* or grasp its implications—those, that is, for whom such a word is not an indexical, a clue. "It was obvious that she didn't speak our language, mine and Mike's. She had never heard its nouns: *neuropathy, cytomegalovirus, mycobacterial avium intercellulare, Hickman catheter*" (27–28). Similarly, some "call the names," but others do not carry such lists in their heads. "I'm not talking anymore," Amy says, "to anyone who doesn't have a list, who hasn't been ticking off the names of people they know" (113–14). The first group consists of a kind of substitute family—"I have the paperwork to prove it: the healthcare proxy, the power of attorney, that's what these are about" (109)—while biological family members like Amy's father tell her, "I can't accept your lifestyle." To Amy the inevitability of her parents' death, even though they form the older generation, "seems more theoretical than real" (108–9), by comparison with the proximity to death that conditions existence among her friends. And so, finally, there are Mike and his friends (the big tree and those exposed, like the tree, to the storm), and there is Mike's brother Chuck, who sends a scarf when Mike is no longer capable of going out into the cold, and attends the memorial service because, he says, he wants to "understand why Mike had become so alienated" from the family that cut him off when he came out (111). Chuck stands dutifully, discreetly—a mite condescendingly, perhaps?—at the back of "our small group of mourners" (the object of everyone's attention nevertheless) before departing again as he had come. "The real family," Amy comments angrily, "doesn't have to do anything, they have merely to exist in their majesty and righteousness, and they are a bulwark to all who gaze upon them. With AIDS, nine times out of ten, it's the fake family who clean up the shit" (112).

Like the splits internal to the AIDS community, between its dead and its survivors, between survivors able to mourn and survivors who cannot, none of the social divisions that Amy is conscious of—between those able to write and those whose sentences are suspended, between the strange visitants from another world like Chuck and the fake family of AIDS people—amounts to a clean break, although the divisions are certainly, albeit paradoxically, deeper than those between the survivors and the dead. Amy's relation to her family is typical in this respect, because it is simultaneously affectionate and resentful, if not alienated. But when it comes to the division between those who know AIDS and those distant mortals who do not know the words or tick off lists and seem to have washed their hands of the whole business, it is to Amy a different matter from her sometimes strained relation with her parents and her friends or even that between her and her facile and confident fellow writers. She becomes vehement, and adamant in her insistence on signaling a rupture, a breakdown of relations, between herself and these distant mortals. "I'm not talking anymore to anyone who hasn't been ticking off the names of people they know like the *malach hamaves,* the Angel of Death, who flies around with His list. . . . *Fuck* everyone who, at the mention of AIDS, wants to tell me about it because they saw it on TV or sobbed openly at the story of the gallant death of some acquaintance's second cousin" (114).

And what is odd here is that, unless the author is writing (imposing upon herself the intense pain of squeezing out her difficult sentences) exclusively for herself, or to explain the nature of hospital time to those who already, at least to some extent, know, understand, and suffer it—like Roberta, or Loie, or Bronski, or Richard—this is Hoffman's own implied audience as a writer that Amy is refusing to communicate with, the very purpose of writing a book like *Hospital Time* that she is *writing off.* Her rejection seems more absolute, more radical, and (perhaps not coincidentally more Mike-like) than Duquénelle's own intensely troubled lucidity, for example, about the fraught relations between Aztecs and non-Aztecs, which never quite comes to the point of standoff. It is like her refusal to say Kaddish because it is a "prayer of reconciliation" and her rejection of the Named One, "who in His Wisdom named for us AIDS" (149). For the very vehemence of such a rejection on her part is telltale. It is more an expression of anger and a refusal to reconcile, perhaps (to reconcile either with AIDS itself or with those willing to "accept this suffering, and the order that encompasses it" [149]), than it intends an actual rupture of relations with those who are already so remote. For to whom can this declaration of rupture be *addressed,* if not to those whose rejection it states? It seems an ultimate appeal to them as much as a breaking off of relations.

In the way that Amy's bitterness toward Mike coexists with love for him, one might assume, then, that a considerable degree of ambivalence is at work also, both in her relation to the Named One and in her stance toward those who do not have close experience of AIDS and shun the community of the dead, the dying and the survivors who do. I mean that it is possible to understand Amy's rejection of the book's putative audience as being in the nature of a preemptive strike: a way of assuming responsibility herself for a communicative breakdown in preference to having its preexistent reality in the form of AIDS phobia and homophobic prejudice brought home to her in the way that it is so painfully brought home, for example, by Chuck's polite indifference at Mike's funeral or her father's words of rejection. She may be refusing to communicate with those whose refusal of love it is better not to have to acknowledge, even as she wants them to know that she is refusing them. And if that is the case, perhaps the "failure" of Amy's writing, which she describes as her failure to write, has something to do, likewise, with such an anticipated rejection, not unlike the similar prediction in Duquénelle but here taking the form not of the offering of a load of pus but of a *preemptive withholding* and thus amounting to an apparent self-deprivation of audience? An anticipated rejection and an actual self-deprivation that, in turn, cannot be unrelated, however, to her insuperable guilt over the disaster of Mike's dying and the painful charade of her caregiving relation with him—the disaster, that is, of being a survivor of the disaster that is AIDS.

For of course the text of *Hospital Time*—tied up as it is in costiveness, a sort of involuntary retention, in the way that *L'Aztèque* suffers from incontinence—is not in fact failed writing; nor is it the product of a failure to write. It is rather a writing that tropes failure as an act of retention and in so doing tropes itself as failed. It recalls Paul Monette's paradoxical publishing of conspiracy, in that the author has not followed through on Amy's announced refusal to talk with those who aren't of her community but has published her supposedly withheld text so that I am able to read it. Possibly the final clue to the address structure of this "unsettling memoir," as Urvashi Vaid calls it in her foreword (ix), lies then in some information Vaid gives us about the fierce pretense of independence that Mike Riegle put up to the very end of his life. Vaid points out that Mike's assertions of independence and rejections of help provided an alibi that permitted "some of his best gay male friends" to turn away and distance themselves from his dying, like so many non-Aztecs in Duquénelle's description. It was Mike's lesbian friends like Amy Hoffman, and others of his male friends, who, refusing to be taken in by his leave-me-alone signals (or to interpret them self-deceptively), "showed up" when he needed them (ix). I'm arguing, then, that there is a case of repetition here, just as there is in Paul's writerly repetition of Roger's heroism in "Present Status" and in Bertrand's writerly repetition of Jean-François's writing in *L'Aztèque.* Amy is more like Mike in a certain rhetorical respect than she acknowledges, and *Hospital Time*'s staging of her rejection of audience is not incompatible, therefore, with the book's having been written in deep distress, and out of a sense of solitude, indeed abandonment, not unlike Mike's, but written nevertheless (and published) to see who, if anyone, among those who do not have lists, will take advantage of the alibi it offers them to shun it and who will nevertheless "show up" for it and become its readers. Written, that is (and published), as a kind of test. Those readers able to perceive the book's anger and its rejection, like the retention apparent in its terse, sparse, and uncompromising style, not as an actual refusal of audience but as a symptom—and a symptom, moreover, of the whole pathology Amy calls "AIDS, the fucker"—would in the end be somewhat like Amy herself, angrily putting up with Mike's self-contradictory and perversely distancing behavior. They do not have to like what they are faced with, but only to do the necessary by showing up and being there.

Indeed, I am not sure one cannot read in Amy's preemptive rejection of Hoffman's readership something akin to the religious respect that is still detectable, irony being the tricky rhetorical mode that it is, in her rejection of the Named One, with its capital letters and its avoidance of pronouncing God's name that suggest her continued belief in the One who is being refused. I mean that her rejection betrays an authorial hope, perhaps, even a conviction, that there *will,* against all the odds, be someone to show up for the text just as Amy herself showed up, however resentfully, begrudgingly, jealously, angrily and in the end guiltily, for Mike. Recall the categorical imperative to choose that, in Amy's maxim, AIDS imposes on all. "With the virus, you make a choice. When someone gets sick, you're either in or out" (15). Mutatis mutandis, that dictum should apply also to the readership of a text like *Hospital Time* that brings word of the virus—of disaster and its disastrous aftermath—by virtue of its being one of the virus's symptomatic manifestations. As Amy opted "in" for her friend, so might *some* readers—resentfully, anxiously, guiltily, or otherwise—opt to attend *seriously* to Hoffman's text: to read it thoughtfully, that is, symptomatically, instead of congratulating themselves on knowing AIDS from having watched TV.

They will not, of course, claim as a result to know AIDS, as the TV watchers do. Clearly, the nature and extent of the disaster are not knowable in any simple sense, even to those closest to it, like Mike and Amy who themselves only "know the language" and "call the names." But in the way that physicians *recognize* something called AIDS in a syndrome of so-called opportunistic disorders that thus function as diagnostic indicators, so readers who in Hoffman's text as in Duquénelle's recognize as indexicals (or in another vocabulary symbols) the concurrence of disorders of all kinds that are constitutive of aftermath—the anger, the despair, the guilt, the irreparable sense of brokenness, the evidence of writing self-described as inept and abject (and, as such, testimony to a whole epidemic of wrongness)—will have recognized and so, in this necessarily indirect way, *acknowledged* the disaster itself. By attending to the residua of the disaster's depredations not as something irrelevant to be ignored but rather as a manifestation of significance, such readers will in a real sense have taken up the relay—the relay whose own repetitive structure, like the disorders to which it responds, also constitutes one of aftermath's realities.

A Rhetoric of Wrongness

Because it is simultaneously confrontational and—lacking the self-confidence that might make its frankness more acceptable—insecure, and uncomfortable with itself, writing like Duquénelle's and Hoffman's is rhetorically more precarious than any other writing considered in this book. I've argued heretofore that the norm of testimonial writing lies in its adoption of a kind of etiquette (Michaels's word) or a metaetiquette (chapter 1) that parlays solecism into a certain form of readability; but this writing stands self-accused as lacking in such a saving grace. Not coincidentally, perhaps, *L'Aztèque* has been out of print for years, and *Hospital Time* is published semiconfidentially by a university press.

Yet it is in that very precariousness, the uncomfortableness of the position it describes itself as occupying—the state of wrongness this writing both describes and enacts—that its significance as a rhetorical intervention lies. Duquénelle's and Hoffman's writing has something of the straightforwardness and gaucherie attached to the gesture of the people in Paley's story "Three Days and a Question" (chapter 1) who, unable to explain or describe what is wrong, are reduced to baring an arm so as to exhibit a sign of that wrongness: a tattooed serial number, Kaposi's lesions, pigmented skin. There is something similarly *naked,* as well as persistent and brave ("heroic," as Monette might say), in the way this writing exhibits itself as symptomatic evidence of a state of wrongness—one in which the writing inevitably participates, which it cannot correct and that it perhaps aggravates by reproducing it.

No flair, then; no fluency and especially no flaunt. If flaunting (chapter 5) is a way of rejecting, not guilt per se, but culpabilization, as in Delbo's "Head high or feet first!" this writing, one might say, is all fault and very little flaunt—its sense of wrongness, including guilt, precludes the flaunting of its hauntedness. It is not that it does not acknowledge and deplore the social isolation of AIDS people. But it reads social prejudice, squeamishness, indifference, and ignorance as a version of the same ethical failure of which Bertrand and Amy accuse themselves, in relation to Jean-François or Mike, the betrayal that it attempts hopelessly to repair through narration while knowing that, as one of the manifestations of disaster, it is irreparable. There is, then, so to speak, nothing to flaunt, which leaves only self-accusation on the one hand and the flouting of conventional expectations on the other—itself a consequence of the writing's generic misfit—as its own indicators of hauntedness: of its proximity to the dead and the thrall it is under to death and disaster.

So in lieu of the stylishness that Michaels (chapter 2) identified as the precondition for texts that perform acts of im-pertinence to achieve readability, these texts emphasize their own ineptness and even abjection. Their lack of investment in *captatio benevolentiae* gives them an uncompromising tone. They don't deploy the wit displayed by Michaels (chapter 2) or Greyson (chapter 5), or the figural devices of reader involvement that are active elsewhere: the stammer as report (or the report as stammer), for instance (chapter 3), or the trick of turning away that involves an audience in one's address (chapter 4). Asyndeton itself, which functions in *Fragments* (chapter 5) as an invitation for reading to convert orphaned memory into phantom pain, is more like a merely mimetic figure here, drawing attention to incompleteness, discontinuity, and fumbled relay. In this respect, the writing is closest, perhaps, to the apodictic mode of *Auschwitz and After* (chapter 5), displaying the baffling unintelligibility of the state of survival, but like Paley's characters exhibiting it, as it were, involuntarily—perhaps compulsively—and for lack of alternative rather than assertively, as Delbo does. Yet displaying it nevertheless, like her, and like Paley's characters, by way of making an interpellation—as if displaying it constituted in itself a sort of mute call.

So a figural structure does govern this rhetoric of wrongness. It is just that, combining functions that Peirce would name iconic and indexical, the writing mimes in order to symbolize, and it does so in phrasing—a phrasing of wrongness—that seems more likely to flout readerly expectation and even to offend than it is designed to capture benevolent attention and encourage involvement. For what it does is to symbolize *disaster* by miming the state of *aftermath,* and by producing that latter state of residuality or left-overness, in all its wrongness, as a symptom, indeed one of the major symptoms, of the syndrome of wrongnesses that is the disaster of AIDS. Thus the wrongness of the writing—its inability to come out right, the way it falls short of appropriateness and hence fails simultaneously to achieve closure and to appeal to a readership—is crucial, since such ineptness, such everlasting discomfort with itself, performs both of these functions—the mimetic and the symbolic—at once. It makes the writing mimetic of survival (aftermath) as a state of unresolvable and intolerable tension and suspension, doing so by an extension of the principle of onomatopoeia, or name-making, from the mimetic word to text-length narrative. And simultaneously, since a symptom is definitionally a manifestation of something amiss or awry, its wrongness gives this writing the indexical character of a symptom, requiring diagnostic interpretation. It is indicative of a disaster (or "math") that is itself, by definition, excluded from the knowledge of those who have survived/are surviving it—except precisely, to the extent that, *through* its aftermath, of which the writing presents itself as a token, it becomes readable.

Obviously, if wrongness, in this way, is of the essence in producing the signification of these texts—the key both to their "onomatopoeic" miming of aftermath as a state of wrongness and to the anomalous, cluelike character of the writing of aftermath as an indicator of disaster—such texts cannot afford to engage in rhetorical practices that, in capturing readerly benevolence, would make the writing itself seem somehow suitable—appropriate, that is, in its very wrongness—by bringing it under the aegis of a (meta)etiquette of solecism. They have to get themselves read, but without compromising their wrongness, the means by which they signify, which is what would occur if they made themselves too readily readable. Thus even their readability, in the end, must be somehow wrong. Whence their rhetorical precariousness: it is as if such aftermath writing cannot succeed, as testimony, without failing as writing, because successful writing would deprive it of its rhetorical point and, hence, make it ineffective as testimony.

So it flouts, nakedly. And although it flouts, it does not really flaunt. To capture something of the precariousness—but also the delicacy—of such a rhetorical enterprise, let me invent a suitably ungainly and unattractive neologism. This writing "flounts" us, as its readers. It does so by flouting our expectations in order to (not-)flaunt—to exhibit without flaunting—the haunt that is the state of aftermath, thereby gaining our perhaps unwilling or repelled attention for the signs of wrongness that indicate an unstatable, if not unutterable, disaster. The relay thus performed is perilous, more perilous perhaps than all the difficult relays we have examined in previous chapters. But it *is,* still, a relay—a rickety and unreliable contraption or assemblage, an agencing or *agencement* that finds the means to gain attention, however unwilling or repelled, and thus to presence and make recognizable, for any reader who may respond to the flount, what readers of course know but most characteristically shirk acknowledging, the culturally obscene, whose name in this case is AIDS.

7. Farewell Symphonies: AIDS Writing as Community Auto/Biography

Asyndeton Again

In the summer of 1772, at Esterház, Josef Haydn had an orchestra of sixteen musicians, a good size for the period: it consisted of nine string players and seven winds (four horns, two oboes, and a bassoon). Complaining of noise and overcrowding, Prince Esterházy had banished wives and children from the castle, and as summer wore on with no sign of the household's returning to Eisenstadt (now Budapest) emotional and sexual deprivation took its toll on the musicians, who appealed to Haydn to intercede. The *Kapellmeister*'s response was to compose and perform an unconventional symphony (now cataloged as no. 45 in F-sharp Minor). Apart from the slightly unexpected key, the symphony proceeds fairly normally (but the slow movement has muted violins throughout) until the end of the development section of the final presto. Here there is a portentous pause following repeated chords on the dominant, a strong signal to expect a return to the opening subject and a rapid conclusion. Instead there's a change of key, tempo and mood; and an adagio of 106 measures follows presenting entirely new musical material. It is in the course of this unexpected and as it were digressive section that the musicians, one after the other, begin to stop playing and leave their desks. At the end only two violins are left playing, *con sordino;* they bring the music to an extremely subdued (pianissimo) close. As Haydn prepared to make his own silent exit, we are told, Esterházy stopped him and said: "I see what you are up to [*Ich habe Ihre Absicht wohl durchschaut*] . . . Very well, tomorrow we pack up."

So the story goes.[1] My interest here is in the refraction of these events in a certain genre of contemporary testimonial writing about AIDS. But let us first glance at the score to see how carefully Haydn worked his rhetorical effect. He maximizes both the number of departures and their potential to be noticed. His violins are divided into four parts instead of the normal two; bass instruments that share a single line are split a few measures before each departs, and the first to go (the contrabass) is given several measures (55–67) of exposed and unusually athletic music before departing; the harmonic wind instruments (oboes and horns) depart in groups (one oboe and two horns at measure 31, the rest at measure 54); from measure 85, when only two violins and a viola remain, the violins are muted. Haydn appears to have decided against ending with a solo violin, perhaps because he could not imagine ending a symphony on a single, harmonically unsupported line, even for a few measures—or perhaps, more cannily, because, despite the conventional closural effect of the final tonic chords, he wanted to end on a hint of suspension, by allowing for one more potential departure right up to the piece's conclusion.

This rhetorical care is evidence that Haydn was conscious of more than the formal innovation entailed by his invention of a kind of ungrammatical narrative form—or really two anomalous forms (one the symphony that pursues a conventional path until it suddenly digresses into new material at its end; the other the adagio itself, whose music undergoes a kind of epidemic of disappearance as it nevertheless continues to its end). But the forms are interesting in themselves, structured as both are by versions of the rhetorical trope of asyndeton. Asyndeton, as we have seen in previous chapters (5 and 6), implies interrupted continuity, as in Julius Caesar's famous *veni vidi vici* or expressions like "day in day out": the thought continues, despite the break—the lack of grammatical or syntactic binding—that interrupts it, but it also remains *marked* by the break, as is shown by the digressiveness and diminution in Haydn's drawn-out coda; the continuity is only partial. Similarly, dual autobiography (chapter 6) lapses, after the break of death, into dispersal and suspension. In the community AIDS writing to which I turn here, the asyndetic principle as Haydnesque change of pace and mood, or last-minute digression, is exemplified by Edmund White's *The Farewell Symphony,* a title that explicitly acknowledges a debt to Haydn's precedent. Norman René's well-known film *Longtime Companion,* on the other hand—which makes no specific reference to Haydn—has a narrative structured by serial disappearance, like the *Farewell* Symphony's final adagio. In each case the asyndetic narrative serves to make a statement about the effects on a close-knit community of the interruption to its culture brought about by the incursion of AIDS. As for Guillaume Dustan's first two novels, *Dans ma chambre* and *Je sors ce soir,* which likewise do not refer specifically to the *Farewell* Symphony, they relate rather to the social revolt—the symbolic walkout of the musicians—and to the form of communication across a social gap to which the orchestra's concerted flouting of convention and the prince's surprised response ("I see what you are up to") refer.

In chapter 6, I referred to this asyndetic relation of aftermath writing to its hypothetical readership as rhetorical asyndeton. That is, it makes of the statement that mimes in its form the effects of disaster a way of making also a symbolic point, one through which (in the best-case scenario) an audience assumed to be oblivious, like Esterházy, is drawn into readership, and hence an acknowledgment of unstatable disaster. For asyndeton functions as a powerful and suggestive device of audience involvement—powerful because completion of an interrupted structural pattern (in this case a pattern of interruption) becomes reflexive and irresistible, suggestive, however, because continuity is (re)established only at the price of acknowledging the break—the gap or the interruption—that required it to be restored and continues to require that the communication be indirect and symbolic. Esterházy was oblivious to the problems of his servants, the musicians, until he was led by the ungrammaticality of Haydn's music to bridge a social gap by making an effort of interpretation. Yes, I see, the musicians are homesick ("Die Musiker sehnen sich nach Hause")—this is what had not previously occurred to him. Thus the ungrammatical narrative interrupted by asyndeton becomes a rhetorical troping that has social consequences; and in order for this effect of troping and these consequences to be achieved under conditions of social difference and inequality, it was necessary for Haydn and his musicians to resort to quite unconventional means. They had to commit a kind of "error" that would nevertheless be perceived as not an error at all but a mode of utterance marked with the emphasis of its ungrammaticality. One more symphony off Haydn's assembly line would not have done the trick. It takes wit to make an impact.

So we might also notice that what is formally an infraction of narrative rules in the *Farewell* symphony, a first generic breach by eighteenth-century standards, is emphasized by a second infraction, that of the performance rules of symphonic music, that helps to interpret the first. Introducing an asyndeton into the ordinarily seamless musical narrative we now call the classical symphony, Haydn compounds the "error" by having his musicians depart when their part ends. In this way he tropes, and thus gives significance to, actions (those of a musician taking his music and instrument, extinguishing his candle, and leaving the performance space) that are in one way perfectly normal but are not usually regarded as part of the musical performance. By moving the musicians' departure back into the performance time of the symphony, so that some musicians are still playing while others are pushing back their chairs, gathering their sometimes cumbersome things, and brushing past their still performing colleagues, Haydn adds to the narrative effect of asyndeton in the music a troping of departure itself as a significant element in the performance. And because departure, becoming a metaphor of itself in this way, can be read in two ways—briefly as signifying both a metaphysical phenomenon (death) and a social act (the walkout)—this staging of interruption proposes two further senses of the musical asyndeton, to neither of which the prince adverts (content with his psychological reading: the musicians are homesick), although he undoubtedly was sensitive to them. And these are senses that will be highly active in later deployments of the farewell symphony trope of the kind that interest me in AIDS writing, although such writing—which does not enjoy the same performative potential as musical performance—is required to thematize what is suggested here by enactment.

By their departure the musicians are troping death, as the symbolism of blowing out candles, always mentioned in versions of this anecdote, clearly suggests; and death can perhaps stand for all the forms of syncope that might literally, and so understandably or legitimately, "cut short" a performance. A musician who is taken ill might well, normally, leave the orchestra in midperformance. The AIDS epidemic, in this sense, is the syncope or interruption—the missed beat or the untimely departure—that, in the early eighties when it seemed to be a largely gay disease, bade fair to extinguish the life of gay communities in the West and forced them to invent or reinvent their continuity asyndetically, catching up as it were on the missed beat, the sudden gapping of their existence. But as a social act, the act of departure—particularly when it gives every evidence of being a product of concertation, and one that is, so to speak, written into the very score of the "symphony" (sounding together)—begins to suggest the sort of collective action for which neither Haydn and his musicians nor their noble employer would have had a word in 1772, but which we might now call a strike, or a threat of strike—a symbolic, simulated, or metaphorical strike.

In that case the infraction that occurs in the *Farewell* symphony is not only narrative (the asyndetic narrative of an epidemic of disappearance), and not only performative (the introduction of the musicians' departure into the performance) but also, finally, social in the sense in which one speaks now of "social" problems and "social" action. Esterházy is enjoined to imagine what life would be like in the country if the musicians departed in reality instead of symbolically, what it would be like *if music died.* It is in this context of departure that the gradual diminishment of musical substance and power as the musicians depart becomes suggestive, as does the diminuendo, the fading, in the music itself, ending as it does with just two muted strings. But this diminishment also evokes the effects on persons, but also on communities, of what might now be called a hunger strike (the strike of moral protest), and hunger striking is in turn a metaphor that suggests itself to AIDS writers conscious, on the one hand, of the physical wasting that AIDS often causes and, on the other, of the social intent of writing that seeks to draw attention to the plight of those affected by the syndrome.

I noted in chapter 4 the black pun by means of which, in *Cargo vie* (13), Pascal de Duve frames the writing and publication of his journal as at once a hunger strike ("grève de la faim") and an ending strike ("grève de la fin"), a strike performed by the manner of his dying. But much AIDS writing, to the extent that it deliberately represents as socially meaningful the various forms of diminishment that overtake the lives of people (and of communities) with AIDS, can be thought of as executing, like the *Farewell* Symphony, a metaphoric "grève de la fin." All such texts turn the troping of death—the introduction of death into the performance—into an act of social self-assertion designed to penetrate the obliviousness of those who, like Prince Esterházy, might otherwise remain confined within the limitations of their mental (cultural or ideological) horizons. Among them, though, we can distinguish, on the one hand, those in which such self-assertion is largely understood as a somewhat lonely act, as it is in the diaries of Eric Michaels (chapter 2) and Pascal de Duve (chapter 4) that I considered in part I under the rubric of "discourses of extremity." This writing is at best only secondarily and as it were accidentally concerned with AIDS as a visitation both destructive and productive of a community of *grévistes de la fin* or farewell symphonists; whereas, on the other hand, there is a small body of writing in the mode of "phantom pain," the writing with which I am concerned in this chapter, that explores the problematics of testimonial autobiography in relation to the dynamics of a group—a group that is simultaneously isolated socially and brought together, bonded by the experience of death, into a community of *those who depart.* I consider dual autobiographies (chapter 6) to occupy an intermediary position in this taxonomy.

Farewell Symphonies

Like dual autobiographies, then, farewell symphonies challenge the primacy and autonomy of individual subjectivity in a genre—the autobiography—that assumes and privileges the personal subject. But, more radically than is possible in dual autobiographies, and so even more paradoxically, the farewell symphony challenges the individual voice's legitimacy by developing a vision of community as a spectral plurality—a spectrum of similarly haunted/haunting subjects in which individuality has relatively little place except as the agent of writing that Deleuze would term deterritorialized or minor and I am describing as asyndetic in character and parasocial in effect. A hunger strike, it seems, may be either individual or collective; each makes of diminishment its mode of rhetorical action, a mode of haunting. But *pace* de Duve, it seems that an end strike, or *grève de la fin,* derives its most forceful rhetorical character from a combination of the phenomenon of diminishment with a principle of collectivity, as exemplified by Haydn's *Farewell* symphony. Community thus becomes a band of ghosts, both haunted and haunting, but—gayness oblige—of ghosts with *attitude,* who make of their collective diminishment, subject as they are to an epidemic of disappearance(s), their means of affirming a certain kind of social presence even as they depart. Disappearance becomes apparitional; but the effect depends on the transformation of a series of individual departures, as each symphonist disappears and thins the group (a little as asyndeton thins a sentence), into a presencing of the collectivity as spectral, exercising a power to haunt that would not be theirs were the group to be either undiminished (i.e., unmarked by death) or, alternatively, reduced to a single, individual subject (i.e., no longer capable of exercising a plural presence).

Of this strange effect of rhetorical less-is-more that endows a group undergoing asyndetic diminishment with a power that would be unavailable to the undiminished group, Haydn appears to have been intuitively aware when he chose to end the F-sharp Minor Symphony on the spectral harmony of two violins, as opposed both to the undiminished strength of the sixteen-musician ensemble (the way symphonies normally end) and to the "other" pathos—haunting but nonspectral—of a solitary melodic line. That being so, we must attend to the way a certain myth of the final solo surfaces in exactly the two instances of the farewell symphony AIDS genre that refer explicitly to the anecdote that gave the *Farewell* symphony its name. These are Edmund White's *The Farewell Symphony,* already mentioned, and Hervé Guibert's earlier *A l'ami qui ne m'a pas sauvé la vie* (To the friend who did not save my life), from which most probably White took the anecdote.[2] For it is as if the AIDS genre of the farewell symphony is split between texts like these that emphasize the *autos* in what is nevertheless still a community autobiography and make the author a privileged survivor-witness of collective disaster, and those that inflect the autobiographical genre even more radically by deprivileging this individual voice, and—somewhat in the manner of Delbo's "we" (chapter 5)—emphasizing the pluralized experience of a community undergoing diminishment, as itself the true subjective source of the writing and the agency of its haunting effect, of which the writer is only the agencer.

The key difference is one of outlook. The AIDS farewell symphony adopts a retrospective perspective on an epidemic of disappearance(s) that, at the time of narration, is still under way; it suggests the probability of further disappearances, but it is prospective in outlook only to the extent that there is a narrator who, explicitly or implicitly, foresees such disappearances, including his (always his) own. In performative narratives such as the Haydn symphony or the Norman René film *Longtime Companion,* in which the narrated disappearances occur in the real time of the narration and retrospectivity and prospectivity can arise only in the mind of the audience, there being no identifiable narrator whose perspective might be reflected in the narrative, no opportunity arises for a difference of outlook between narrator and the other members of the community that is undergoing diminishment. But in writing like Guibert's and White's, the fact of writing is explicitly understood to confer a special privilege, which is not necessarily the privilege of a survival extending far into the future, but amounts to the kind of uniqueness that arises from being the last in a series. And it is these writers who refer explicitly to the example of the *Farewell* symphony while imagining a final violin solo that is not in Haydn's score. Which means that in these cases lastness is imagined as conferring also a rhetorical and even aesthetic distinction, one that implies a stronger degree of autonomous agency than mere *agencement.* If it is the spectral plural of a community undergoing an epidemic of disappearance(s) that haunts, its apparitional effect is understood in texts such as these to owe something not negligible to the intervention of a "last write" whose agent—the site of a prospective project—is the autobiographical *autos.*

There is thus a version of what Duquénelle would call the "Proust syndrome" (chapter 6) at work in these texts, which in that respect do therefore resemble the dual autobiography (and it may be remembered that in note 1 of chapter 6 I felt able to classify *To the Friend* as dual autobiography, so mitigated is its symphonic character). I will refer to this form of farewell symphony, then, as community autobiography, and introduce a slash (community auto/biography) as a way of pointing to the greater commonality of writing self and collective subjectivity in the work on which I intend to concentrate: Dustan's first two novels and René's film, in which the Proust syndrome is either not apparent or only barely so, and the, of course real, agency exercised by the writer or filmmaker is de-emphasized to the profit of collective, plural haunting. Dustan's narrator, it is true, is distinguished from his fellow ghetto survivors by a distance that is figured by his ability to travel, itself a function of the proclivity to think that he cannot completely shake off. But he enjoys no aesthetic distinction or privilege of lastness, no exemption, that is, from the rule of one-by-one diminishment from which the community derives its spectrality and power of haunting and which, it is implied, will continue in an extended and apparently endless holding pattern into the future. (*Longtime Companion,* by contrast—the product of a particularly gloomy historical moment when a show of optimism must have seemed mandatory, projects a futurity in which there will be a cure, the epidemic of serial disappearance[s] will come to an end, and the community of the dead and the surviving will reunite. In this, it differs from Guibert and White as well as from Dustan.) This refusal to exempt the witness from the general pattern of ongoing diminishment might well, in honor of the two violins that are still playing at the end of the *Farewell* Symphony, be named the "Haydn syndrome," by contrast with the Proust syndrome in Guibert and White. I do not do so, however, for the reason that a reference to classical music would be somewhat misleading: one reason why the Haydn reference is missing from René's film and Dustan's novel may well be that their generic starting point lies rather in models of what I will call seriality that derive from popular culture: the soap opera in one case, the porn flick in the other.

"I was silently horrified," White writes of a dying friend, "that things had gone so far and that, in the few weeks since I'd stopped phoning, Joshua had become blissed out and diapered, and that his preference for freesias was now referred to in the past tense. I kept thinking of Haydn's *Farewell Symphony.* In the last movement more and more of the musicians get up and leave the stage, blowing out their candles as they go. In the end just one violinist is playing" (405). This brief reference (given weight in the text by its being taken up in the title) is clearly both retrospective (as regards Joshua) and prospective (in respect of the narrator). It occurs near the end of the narrative of a series of deaths occurring among a group of friends: the narrator is guilty at being unable—because of distance—to look after Ned, who tells him of Fox's death and memorial service and is himself too ill to care for Joshua, who is also failing. More particularly, where Joshua is described (prospectively-)retrospectively as being already (as good as) dead, since he is blissed out and diapered and referred to in the past tense, the passage itself moves from this retrospective view of Joshua, via the allusion to the symphony, to a figure for the writer himself, the last remaining violinist, whose own death is thus anticipated but also suspended.

The novel as a whole is a stunning orchestration of a huge cast of friends, lovers, cruising companions, and tricks of the narrator's, but this detail (particularly to the degree that it is historically inaccurate) tends to put emphasis on its autobiographical character and to give prominence to the role and the responsibility of the writer, as if in his role as chronicler of the life and death of a community he must somehow outlast all others. (White is known to have been HIV-positive for many years and to be in the category of "long-term survivor.") Not unexpectedly the novel ends, therefore, only a few pages further on, after a brief account of Joshua's death and then of the death, ten years later, of Brice (the narrator's lover), with the words, relating to some nondescript objects of Joshua's left behind in Venice: "Joshua's spirit was no more in these things than was our virus; his spirit was lodged in Eddie's pages, in his own, even, I hoped, in mine" (413). The narrator does not deny his own future death, but privileges his own and others' writing as the site of a survival that escapes death.

Guibert's account of the *Farewell* Symphony in *To the Friend* is more elaborate than White's and also more obviously prospective in its faith in the future of writing. This novel is more about betrayal than about death as such: an epidemic of personal betrayals—those of Bill, the eponymous friend, and of the actress Marine—allegorizes a larger betrayal, that of a society unwilling or unable to rescue the community of people with HIV disease, here represented in a somewhat minimalist fashion by the "Club of Five" (the narrator, his lover Jules, Jules's wife and two children). At a low point in her career, Marine abandons Hervé, from whom she had promised to commission a film scenario, and takes refuge in Hollywood. Muzil, Hervé's dying friend (widely acknowledged to be a fictionalization of Michel Foucault, while Marine similarly fictionalizes Isabelle Adjani), tells Hervé the story of the *Farewell* Symphony, and advises him to relate it in turn to Marine in a letter. In other words, the story is intended to function as a reproach to Marine concerning her departure and the sense of abandonment Hervé is experiencing, and this letter to Marine is thus a *mise en abyme* of the narrative itself, addressed to an audience presumed to be likewise self-centered and uncaring:

> The symphony began in full splendor, using every instrument in the orchestra, whose members then slowly left, one by one and in full view of the audience, since Haydn had written the score with the successive elimination of all the instruments, up to the very last solo, even including in the music the breath of the musicians as they blew out the candles on their music stands, and the sound of their footsteps tiptoeing away, making the gleaming parquet floor of the concert hall creak as they went. I had to admit it was a lovely idea. (82–83)

What Hervé calls Muzil's "embroidery" on the story (but some or all of it may be his own) clearly functions, however, to make it not only a reproach to Marine but also a prospective account of Muzil's own disappearance—he likes this story, Hervé says, because it is "concomitante à la fois du crépuscule de Muzil et de l'évanouissement de Marine" (97) [fitting in with Muzil's twilight and Marine's disappearance] (83). That is, Marine's departure—her *évanouissement* or syncope—figures Muzil's impending death, of which Hervé later says that it foreshadows his own.[3] And that is why Haydn's middle-period work becomes "his last symphony" (82), and it is described as an act of resistance and a "manifesto" against Esterházy, who (as an "esthète tyrannique" [96]) becomes a figure of social injustice. Furthermore, it is not enough that the score record what the French text calls the "extinction successive" (97) of all the instruments; even the musicians' breath as they blow out the candles and the creaking parquetry as they withdraw must be written into the piece. It is as if Guibert is fantasizing here a mode of writing that would fuse into a supreme figuration of death the formal device of "successive elimination" in the score and the performative effect of the musicians' departure, the fusion being in part produced through the word "extinction" applied to the instruments as well as the candles. In short, the symphony is imagined as a great creator's supreme work, in which death itself (including the creator's own) is incorporated, in the form of musicians' breath and creaking floorboards, into the very substance of the composition. This is Guibert's way of projecting what Hervé would like *To the Friend*—in reality a very different work—to be: a "last solo" in the form of a supreme masterpiece, and a reproach of such aesthetic splendor that society at large would be unable to ignore its impact. But in the end Marine doesn't even respond to the letter—Guibert the ironist wins out over Hervé the Romantic genius.

Although both writers are careful to undercut the self-aggrandizement implicit in their "last solo" fantasy, then, there does nevertheless seem to be some correlation in their writing between referencing the Haydn anecdote and distorting the story in a way that distinguishes the writer from those with whom he shares the ordeal of the epidemic and bestows a certain privilege on the act of writing itself. I don't detect anything similar in René's film or Dustan's narratives. In *Longtime Companion* the focal subjectivity is that of Willie, who works in a gym, and not, as one might expect, Sean the writer. Apart from the differences I've already mentioned and the fact that he keeps a kind of diary that he calls his "erotic autobiography" (*Dans ma chambre,* 63), there is little to distinguish Dustan's first-person narrator, Guillaume, from his nonwriting friends; and this is because (rather than in spite) of the fact that he practices a highly self-conscious form of narcissism. These texts are more like *community* auto/biographies than they are community *autobiographies.* That is why I now turn to reading them in a little more detail, with an interest in two things: first, how they represent as spectral the community of survivors the AIDS epidemic has created, and second, how they represent, but also enact, as a haunt, the discursive relation of this marginalized community to an audience assumed to be oblivious to the disaster it is undergoing. How, that is, they both represent and seek to spread the sensation of phantom pain as the marker of a spectral community subject to effects of aftermath that seem indistinguishable from disaster itself.

An Epidemic of Disappearance(s)

Thus far I've been using the word *disappearance,* as in the phrase "epidemic of disappearance," a bit disingenuously, as a rough synonym for departure, on the one hand (what Haydn's musicians do), and for death on the other. But disappearance is not strictly the same as either departure or death; we use the word of these events most particularly when they occur in circumstances that make them in some way anomalous, and to be precise when they are experienced in the mode of syncope or asyndeton: a break having irreparable consequences (chapter 6). There are a number of reasons why AIDS was experienced—especially in the early years—as just such an unjust and even unnatural visitation. It seemed to attack particularly the young, in societies no longer accustomed to the idea that it is possible to die young. It seemed actually to target specific segments of the population that were already subject to various forms of social inequality, neglect, and hostility. Attitudes prevalent in government, public health systems, and the media nourished the strong suspicion that people with AIDS were being allowed to die. The cultural attitude of dismissal—part phobia, part denial, part sheer indifference—to which AIDS and AIDS people were and still are subject produced a sense of stigma and pariahhood while it motivated writers, artists, and ordinary sufferers to attempt to force the supposedly unaffected into some sort of acknowledgment and understanding of both the pain and the anger entailed in being subject simultaneously to the terror of a seemingly arbitrary epidemic and to the consequences of social ostracism.

But in Argentina, during the years 1976–83, the period of the so-called Proceso, also known as the dirty war, the phrase "epidemic of disappearance" had an even grimmer resonance, since the population was then undergoing a form of state terrorism: the abduction (often carried out in public), detention, torture, and secret killing (often through being thrown, drugged but alive, from a plane) of an unknown number (amounting to at least thirty thousand) of men, women, and children who were suspected, mostly without evidence, of "subversive" actions, intentions, or just thoughts. Meticulous records were kept of this operation but were spirited out of the country when the regime collapsed and have themselves disappeared.

In Avery Gordon's analysis of these events, disappearance, in the transitive sense of the verb that became current ("to disappear someone"), was a carefully crafted technique, inspired by the 1942 Nazi *Nacht und Nebel* (night and fog) order in Western Europe,[4] and designed to haunt the whole population into submission by producing ghosts—figures who, although they could not be known with certainty to be dead, were nevertheless physically absent, their half-life as objects of thought and memory a function of their absence. The political skill of the oppositional group known as the Mothers (las Madres de Plaza de Mayo) consisted in *accepting* and even insisting on this liminal status of the *desaparecidos,* neither living nor dead, such that they came in turn to haunt the regime itself, as an ineradicable reminder of its injustice. For there is, Gordon suggests, something *apparitional* inherent in disappearance (the two words are cognate), because disappearance is the product of an active repression—I would say that it actually "stage-manages" departure and/or death, turning these events into performances of themselves as evidence of state power—and is hence subject to the rule of the return, in transformed guise, of the repressed. Specters, as Derrida (1993) also has reminded us, are not only figures of return (called *revenants* in French) but also signifiers of an injustice that is denied (unrecognized and hence unrepaired). And, in part for that reason—but *specter* is in any case cognate with *spectrum*—the specter is always plural: as we've seen in previous chapters (3, 5, 6), specters are communitarian, and those that return have ghosts of their own. Their uncanniness is evidence of a society haunted by its unacknowledged acts of social injustice, and the two spectral texts I now turn to—each in its own way the representation of a liminal group haunted by death as disappearance—are texts that make manifest such a spectral relation to the site of social power. But where *Longtime Companion* can properly be described as an apparitional text, in Dustan's two linked novels it is appearance, and the spectrality of simulacrum, that respond to the conditions of disappearance. Spectrality becomes a matter of *striking attitudes*—and simultaneously of *giving attitude*—in relation to the larger society.

Although there is a slightly uncanny chronological overlap between the two events, I am not claiming any real equivalence between Argentina's metaphoric "epidemic" of quite literal disappearance(s) and the literal epidemic of metaphoric "disappearance(s)" that is called AIDS, an epidemic that first drew medical attention in 1981. But the serial deaths that AIDS causes and continues to cause, initially in urban gay male communities in the West, *were* experienced as "disappearances," so anomalous did they appear from the start (young, apparently healthy people being taken gravely ill and, in those early years, disappearing within months of the onset of symptoms), and so unjust did they rapidly come to be judged, as it became clear, first that there would be no rapid, efficacious, government-backed scientific research response (of the kind with which the then recent outbreak of Legionnaires' disease had been met), and then that there would not even be a well-judged and properly funded public health campaign aimed at preventing the syndrome's spread. The uncanniness inherent in an epidemic that appeared to pick off its victims and disappear them indiscriminately, while nevertheless life continued as if normally, is well captured, I am arguing, in narratives that are themselves subjected, anomalously, to a rule of grammatical asyndeton, of (in this case serial) apparitional disappearance(s); but the apparitional character of such anomalous disappearance(s) in turn makes such narratives haunting in respect of their audience, so that the gap produced by the social marginalization of a community subject to diminishment—the denial of AIDS or the phobia of homosexuality—is bridged. It is bridged, however, by an action that simultaneously enacts that gap (what I will call infiltration in the case of *Longtime Companion*), or alternatively the gap is enacted in the very act of bridging it (which I will call attitude when I come to describe the rhetorical status of Dustan's writing). And in both cases, these rhetorical asyndeta produce an aesthetic of *estrangement,* because they entail the defamiliarization of generic arrangements that are conventional and familiar. This making strange has its distant model in Haydn's appropriation of classical symphonic form for new significations and in ways that made it darker and more disturbing, getting the attention of his noble employer through what was in effect a semiotic practice of indexicality in the form of a subtle—or perhaps not so subtle—hint.

The most obvious precedent for telling the AIDS story as a series of disappearances is the type of detective story in which the mystery to be solved consists of multiple, apparently related, but mysterious deaths. Umberto Eco's *Il nome della rosa* (The name of the rose) borrows this plot, for example—and relevantly enough uses it to allegorize the disintegration of a culture (that of the high Middle Ages). But in these cases, there is always a rational story that counterbalances the disintegrative effect of the first, anomalous, narrative, and restores a sense of order; this is the story of the detective's attempts to find an explanation of the mystery. In *Longtime Companion,* though, it is precisely such explanation that is missing, and the anomaly of a story whose agents keep disappearing is never cleared up; order is not restored. The genre to which the film refers is not the detective novel, then, but one in which, more uncannily, disappearance is itself habitual and treated as part of the order of things. Recall the scene in which the characters come together as a "family" to celebrate the peak of Sean's career as a scriptwriter of TV soap operas: he has succeeded in incorporating into afternoon television a kiss between two young men (itself an act of generic appropriation). Clearly *Longtime Companion* is distinguishing its own relatively realistic representation of gay mens' lives in New York in the 1980s from the prudery and homophobia of the soaps; but it is also reflecting here on the way in which the unmentionable may nevertheless infiltrate ordinary culture, bridging a gap that it simultaneously points up, by making catachrestic use of a genre that appeared to exclude it. And in the process it is also designating the target of its own act of generic appropriation. The soap-opera genre is the film's own catachrestic vehicle for performing such an infiltration on behalf of the ordeal of disappearance to which, ignored by most of America, the community it represents is subject.[5]

We can read *Longtime Companion,* then, as a defamiliarization or estrangement of soap opera, a gayification and especially an AIDSification of the genre, with which the film shares a number of features: its episodic narrative form, the legibility of its characterization and dialogue, the frequency of hospital scenes (particularly emergency room and intensive care), its focus on moments of intense emotion around major issues of living and dying—and last but not least a certain practice of the disappearing character, which arises in the soaps when an actress or actor assigned to a particular role is laid off or becomes unavailable. It is as if the effects of the AIDS epidemic on New York's gay community, the particular form of terror it injects into supposedly ordinary life, were being described as a sudden incursion into the everyday lives of ordinary gay men (working, cruising, sharing domesticity, summering or weekending on Fire Island), of the norms—the quite extraordinary norms—that characterize the world of the soaps. What makes the description uncanny, then, is our recognition of a certain unexpected aptness of the appropriation: the familiarity of the soaps turns out to have always already harbored knowledge of the dire reality of AIDS, although we could not see it . . .

In soap opera, the disappearance of characters is an ordinary event that sometimes passes without comment or remark. If the disappearing character is a major figure, the disappearance tends to be motivated and stage-managed with some care, in particular so as to allow maximum freedom for future plot developments (including the possibility of the character's ghostlike return, whether played by the same or another actor). Frequently a disappeared character will enjoy a spectral half-life for a time, surviving in the dialogue of other characters without being seen on camera. In *Unbecoming* (chapter 2), another connoisseur of TV, Eric Michaels, displays considerable interest, only a short while before his death, in how the death of Pam is staged in *Dallas* with a view to her possible return (121, 124); he is clearly calculating an analogous postmortem survival or "cultural future" for himself, through the stage management of his death that he wants his diary to accomplish. It seems that the makers of *Longtime Companion* have been similarly struck by the strangeness of soap-opera disappearances—by their apparitional quality—and that they intend their film to produce an intensification of that effect, which they obtain by multiplying the deaths so that the pattern of disappearance, in becoming serial, becomes inescapable and acquires a wholly new significance. Who knew that soap opera was about life, and life in its darkest dimension, subject to disaster?

Whereas the relation of soap opera to life is developed in the film partly through Sean's profession as a scriptwriter, partly through the career of the TV actor Howard (gay at home, straight on screen; the hero of Sean's on-screen kiss; shunned and reviled as a consequence, the victim of entertainment industry homophobia; and finally fully out as an "actor with AIDS"), and partly through Fuzzy's sister, Lisa, who claims that the soaps, not school, educated her about life, it is the character of John, Willie's inseparable friend (people think they are lovers) who launches the pattern of repeated disappearances. Few spectators notice the brief moment, soon after the credits and before we have learned the characters or their names, when Sean notices a "bruise" on John's neck; it passes as a stupid joke because it coincides with David's reading of the *New York Times*'s description of Kaposi's sarcoma lesions as bruiselike. But it is actually a dramatic irony. In the course of the day John engineers a meeting between Willie and Fuzzy, whose love affair will provide the main thread of continuity in the film, then discreetly *slips away,* leaving the couple to discover each other. This moment will come to appear retrospectively as the film's defining instant, when soon the action moves to an emergency room in a poorly equipped public hospital—John is "between jobs" and has no health insurance—where he must wait twenty-five hours, suffering from acute pneumonia and without a blanket, for an intensive care bed: we last see him, eerily lit and photographed from above, looking flat and spectral amid a clutter of life-support equipment. He returns only at the end of the film, among the spirits of the dead who materialize on the beach; and since his disappearance will by then have been followed by three more (Paul's, Sean's, and David's), so that we have had time to "forget" him, his reappearance is marked for spectators, as it is enacted by Willie and John, as a moment of uncanny recognition, an apparition.

Associated with the practice of disappearance is another major characteristic of soap-opera aesthetics, which is the randomness and simultaneously the relentlessness of its plotting, a combination exemplified by the film's deployment of effects of dramatic irony. Soon after John melts away,

Willie and Fuzzy walk, then sit, on the moonlit beach; it is their getting-to-know-you moment, and as Willie leans closer to Fuzzy's face for the anticipated kiss, he remarks: "You got something, here on your lip." Fade; end of scene. Since, like Sean's mention of John's bruise, this is happening on the very day the *Times* makes the first public announcement of the epidemic of Kaposi's and pneumocystis among gay men, and since this time the comment is not slipped unobtrusively into bantering dialogue but culminates a scene, the moment seems portentous. In the event, however, it turns out to have been totally insignificant; no dire consequences, indeed no consequences of any kind, follow. The something on Fuzzy's lip is never again mentioned, and the couple will survive the epidemic unscathed to the end of the film. Their function in the plot is to represent continuity in the asyndetic world of disappearances that surrounds them; they will have time, therefore, for their relationship to develop and for each of them to overcome AIDS phobia and take up community work, Fuzzy volunteering at Gay Men's Health Crisis and Willie becoming a "buddy." By contrast with John's story, Fuzzy's demonstrates the soap-opera habit of laying clues for future plotting that may or may not be taken up, depending on future script decisions, but it resignifies that arbitrariness by making it one of the scarier characteristics of the AIDS epidemic.

Sean's case contrasts again, with John's obliviousness on the one hand and with the nonevent involving Fuzzy on the other. On the very day of his triumph as a scriptwriter (the day of the gay kiss), he too discovers a lesion on his neck. The development of his character leads us to interpret his anxious reaction as a case of AIDS hysteria, the opposite of John's insouciance. But very soon it becomes evident that his anxiety is justified, and the film now relentlessly chronicles the downward path of his health through stages of increasingly ignominious decline that are mitigated only by the devotion of his lover David. But then David's own disappearance, when it occurs, having been foreshadowed for the viewer only by his concern when John falls ill, now takes place in a rapid narrative ellipsis, the exact opposite of Sean's attentively chronicled decline. It is signaled only by the telescoping of his memorial service with Sean's. Our surprise contrasts, then, with the drawn-out agony of Sean's story, underlining another form of unpredictability in the film's representation of the epidemic.

The upshot of all this for the viewer is a strong sense of narrative arbitrariness. Obvious signals *may* be significant. Or they may equally turn out to be insignificant. Momentous events affecting central characters take place without preparation and by allusion alone. An apparently major character (like John) may disappear less than one-third into the film, while a supposedly second-rank character (like Sean) may be given a starring role for a considerable period before disappearing in turn. Imitating soap-opera aesthetics, this arbitrariness deprives the spectator of the comfort and sense of security that derive from ordinary narrative grammaticality, and thus creates a narrative experience of powerlessness and bewilderment that is analogous to the loss of control over their lives, the sense of absurdity, of precariousness and of threat, in short the particular form of terror (not dissimilar, despite the political differences, from that in which a whole population existed in Argentina during the Proceso) in which the characters live in the grip of the epidemic.

And if the effect of this narrative ungrammaticality is slightly uncanny for the spectator, the characters in turn are shown by the film to be haunted by the epidemic of disappearance(s) that assails them. Ghostly imagery occurs throughout the film: a group of white-clad revelers on the moonlit beach haunts Willie and Fuzzy's first walk together, anticipating the noisy, animated crowd of daytime ghosts who fill the screen at the end, a partying crowd that is itself symmetrical with the tea dance at the beginning, and so retrospectively forces us to reinterpret this initial happy scene as having been already (prospectively) haunted by the epidemic its participants were so cheerfully ignorant of. In similar fashion, if more explicitly, a lonely and bereft "man with KS" spooks a cheery and oblivious Fire Island breakfast group. Not only does John look ghostly in our last glimpse of him, but in other hospital scenes gowned and masked figures—more frequently visitors than medical personnel—surround the patient. In these ways, the film insists from the start on the continuity between those who haunt, the ghosts, and those who are haunted, the still living, a continuity that is celebrated in the final scene of revelry and reunion, which—since the figment is that they have lived to celebrate together the end of the epidemic—joins the officially living (Willie, Fuzzy, and Lisa) and the officially dead (John, Sean, David, and all the rest) under the sign of their common survival more than of their shared relation to death. The dead and the living are two kinds of survivors—the dead by their refusal to be forgotten, the living by their increasing power to resist the terror of the epidemic, both groups by a certain refusal, then, to just lie down and die. This alliance of the living and the dead, celebrated by their joyful fraternizing in the final scene, has actually been thematic in all the concluding episodes of the film, notably the memorial service and the scenes that show the new community involvement of living survivors like Fuzzy, Willie, and

Howard. But—a little as in *Hospital Time* (chapter 6)—the alliance of the living and the dead does not extend beyond the group whose solidarity arises in the context of death, arbitrariness, and serial disappearance—those whose lives are led under the conventions of soap opera.

So it is important to recall that, as Avery Gordon points out with reference to the Mothers, those who are haunted have the power to haunt in their turn, since it is this ability to transmit the hauntedness that *Longtime Companion* is claiming for itself as a film. The final scene is one that has been much criticized: it is viewed as sentimental, idealizing, and overoptimistic, and indeed such criticisms are just if the scene is taken in isolation, as a kind of trumped-up, superadded, feel-good end. But that is to ignore the thematics of survival developed throughout the film and the increasing emphasis on resistance to the epidemic as the surviving characters mature and develop. One form of resistance, one way of contributing to everyone's survival, is for those who are haunted by the epidemic of disappearance to become haunters in their turn, in alliance with the (also surviving) dead, passing on their sense of a world become spooky to those the film addresses as its audience, who assume themselves to be unaffected by the epidemic, and not to lead lives governed by the conventions of the soaps. One must consider the significance of the beach, on which the final party occurs, as a liminal space between sea and land, at the edge of the continent, simultaneously proximate to and remote from New York (walking in the dunes on the way to a tea dance, one can encounter a deer). This liminal space is inhabited by a fringe community, that on which the epidemic of disappearance has fallen with its full weight of terror, a community diminished in the sense that it is made up of survivors who are both living and dead. It borders in one direction on a space of death, but in the other it is peripheral to a society that shuns it. What mode of communication is most readily available to such a community, most appropriate for getting through to those who seem ignorant of its very existence, and oblivious to its fate?

The gay kiss Sean engineers onto afternoon TV tells us that cultural infiltration, brought about through generic appropriation—in this case through appropriation of the aesthetics of the soaps—is the way the fringe community can make itself known to those who might prefer to ignore it. But the recognition-effect entailed, for the audience, by such an act of generic appropriation, is like the recognition-effect when, at the end, we see in the crowd of ghosts a curiously familiar face, and say to ourselves: "Yes, Willie had this close friend, what was his name? Oh yes, John. I forgot about him, but he has *returned.*" It is slightly uncanny. One forgets that, as Lisa knows, soap opera is about the nature of life, until the knowledge returns to haunt us in the form of an epidemic of disappearance. So the final scene of the two sets of survivors partying together on the beach is the vehicle, representative of the whole film (a *mise en abyme*), through which *Longtime Companion* seeks to produce its own equivalent of the gay-kiss-on-TV effect as an infiltration that has the effect of haunting. The AIDS community, itself subject to the hauntedness of disappearance, becomes that which, *per medium* of the film, haunts the larger society on whose margins it exists. The ghostly revelers troop onto the beach from the dunes like a spectral image coming to meet the film's own audience, which is itself about to troop out of the theater. The image, by implication, is that of the audience itself, rejoining "life" after a sojourn in the haunted darkness of a cinema in which they will have shared, at least for a moment, in the experience of spectral surviving that is the lot of those who are subject, chronically, to the norms of soap opera in the mode of an epidemic of disappearance(s). So the rhetorical dynamics is asyndetic: a social gap is closed, but only in a moment that, by enacting it, requires its recognition.

Attitude

One might begin to capture the rhetorical and political differences between *Longtime Companion* and Guillaume Dustan's two autobiographical novels by saying that whereas in the film Fire Island and the Village are populated almost exclusively by boys-next-door who happen to be gay (even the queenly David gets called "Dave" on occasion), the men of Dustan's Marais—the gay neighborhood of Paris, inhabited by another fringe community—lead lives governed by looks, look, and attitude; appearance is their defense against disappearance. Straight-looking, straight-acting types like Willie and Fuzzy are part of the film's foot-in-the-door politics of accommodation, appropriation, and infiltration; the willed self-isolation of Dustan's gay "ghetto" dwellers,[6] who associate with the general culture only when they go to work or visit their families, suggests the policy (and politics) of disdain—the striking of attitudes for oneself and the giving of attitude for others—for which the word *attitude* (as in "attitude queen") was invented. Cultivating one's look, one's looks, and one's sense of fashion, giving oneself over to posing and self-contemplation, engaging in sexual practices cultivated erotically, that is, as forms of pleasure regulated and calculated in terms of positions and scenes (French *plans*)—these are ways of holding death at bay indefinitely, substituting, as it were, style for a substance that is full of threat. A sculpted body and the right clothes function fetishistically, so that, immediately after noting, "For four years now I've thought I would die next year," Dustan's narrator Guillaume adds: "But I think myself beautiful all the same" (*Chambre,* 40). And disdain for death doubles with a similar disdain for an equally ignored straight world, the world of substance without style.

It is not that this community that has renounced infiltration in favor of attitude is not haunted, or that it does not have a spectral quality of its own. But rather there is an important historical difference between *Longtime Companion,* which was finished in 1990 and chronicles the AIDS years from 1981 through 1988 or so—years of terror, panic, and (in the English-speaking world) the organization of community resistance—and *Dans ma chambre* and *Je sors ce soir,* which were published in 1996 and 1997 respectively and relate therefore to the midnineties, the transition years when in France a quite new gay community had begun to emerge, while the long medical stalemate of the AZT era was displaced by what was to become a new holding pattern, with the advent of protease inhibitors and the invention of combination therapies. The conditions of survival have begun to change markedly, so that in Dustan's writing there is a veteran's sense of weariness and fatigue, along with a survivor's sense of interminability and inevitability, that contrasts markedly with the energy of the earlier film.

It is not exactly that disappearance has ceased, or that the characters are not haunted by death. They expect to die "next year," and remember dead friends. *Je sors ce soir* is dedicated to such a dead friend, Alain, whose "fetish T-shirt" (i.e., the "lucky" garment he went dancing/cruising in) the narrator fetishistically wears throughout the evening, in part as an act of both memory and identification with a man whose death, for him, has the unreality of a disappearance ("I can't believe it's possible for him to be dead" [14]). Alain thus survives in Guillaume, who himself acquires the characteristics of a specter. But the T-shirt is talismanic also because Guillaume's disbelief derives, again, from his fetishistic faith in the power of attitude to ward off death. Alain was, for him, something of an icon of Marais style, in that "each of his attitudes was a perfect image" (14), and at the same time a figure of Marais denial. "I didn't know he was HIV-positive. Perhaps he was unaware of it himself. He was the type who wouldn't know" (14). In short, AIDS and the threat of disappearance, in this world, are stored in as remote a corner of the mind as can be managed, like the life outside the ghetto that goes barely mentioned, as if both were being denied—grudgingly acknowledged, perhaps, but mainly subjected to an active not-knowing. Between the two unthinkable eventualities that are straight life on the one hand and death from AIDS on the other, there is a liminal area that—unlike the threatened liminality of *Longtime Companion*—feels *safe* because life in it is dedicated to style and to desire, and to the relation between them: the right look, the right looks, the right boyfriend, the right dope, the right way of dancing to the right music, the right sexual scenario and the most accomplished sexual performance. That is, to perfect images that function like Alain's T-shirt as talismans. Attitude is primarily a fetish in the sense of a security blanket, even though it is also a sign of hauntedness and a mode of haunting.

Such a life necessarily has two characteristics: it is suspended, a life of waiting (somewhat as in the dual autobiographies of chapter 6), and (unlike them) it is very largely affectless. Given the continued reality of disappearance, no one can afford to recognize their deepest emotions or to "think" (54), under pain of "freaking out" (which nevertheless happens once in a while, and is affectlessly recorded: "During dinner Stéphane learned that a guy he knew from the S/M group died. It freaked him out [*Ça l'a flippé*], but he didn't mention it until next day" [67]). What substitutes for emotion is the depthless but exciting world of erotic desire that is stimulated by fashion, games, equipment, fetishes, looks, and appearance(s), a Baudrillard-like world of simulacrum, from which everything that might constitute substance or reality and function as a reminder of straightness or death is willfully expelled. The advantage of such a world is that it can be both exactly calculated and meticulously controlled. The supreme questions become how to sculpt one's body, what to wear, what music to listen to, what "scene" to play out with which partner(s), using which apparatus and what toys, adopting which positions in what sequence, while high from which drugs, ingested when and in what quantity. The best sexual positions can be figured out mathematically and described, as if by an engineer, in terms of angles of insertion and camber (51); like Guillaume's rationally ordered toys closet (71–72), its central shrine, such a world is a kind of paradise, albeit a paradise of denial: "Je trouve bien toute cette invention," as Guillaume puts it (71), "The whole invention is fun."

Like the world of the eighteenth-century *libertins,* that of Dustan's modern gay voluptuaries requires a great deal of savoir faire, combined with a kind of narcissistic self-detachment, the ability to watch oneself perform and to enjoy it as spectacle: "I look back and in the mirror I catch sight of a world-class image [*un truc de classe internationale*]; it pleasures me, reassures me, and flatters me" (31). But because everyone's performance is simulacral in this way, more important as image than as reality, and so an imitation that is measured against everyone else's (also imitative) performance, everyone eventually winds up resembling everyone else: "I fuck him exactly the way Quentin used to fuck me" (50); "He's like me when I discovered my ass with Quentin five years ago" (53); "I live in a fabulous world [*un monde merveilleux*] in which everyone has slept with everyone" (70)—and also "Now everyone is HIV-positive; I don't know anyone who's negative" (47). This mimetic world of serialized copies without an original does have a model or an ideal type, however, which is not the eighteenth-century *libertin* (as it might be) but the contemporary American porn star, viewed of course on video. "I jerked off watching Eric Manchester doing his thing, the stuff he knows how to do, stuff I know how to do too" (38); "I fuck him. . . . I come like a geyser and it's like a supergood porn flick and straight after I start thinking again" (54); "I tell him that of the thousand guys I've fucked with there are only four or five, OK about ten, who know how to do what he did to me. There's also Chad Douglas, but he's only on video. Remote control. I just hope that in real life he isn't dead" (28).

But as these last quotations and the comment about universal HIV-positivity show there is a flaw in this paradise world—denying is not the same as not knowing. One name for this flaw is HIV, another is thought, a third is time. The universe of remote control feels safe but is actually precarious: if the porn star on video is reassuring, endlessly going through the motions that constitute perfect images, it is also entirely possible that "en vrai" he may be dead, and that he is therefore a ghost; and if so, those who imitate him in real life are survivors headed for the same fate, and thus already in a sense ghosts themselves. Ghetto existence, the life of simulacrum, is haunted in this way but also suspended: suspended between the alien world of the city on which it turns its back and the abyss it borders on that no one wants to think about; but suspended too in the sense that in this liminal place time—the enemy of perfect images and of attitude—seems unnaturally *stretched,* a bit like the fermata in Haydn that prolongs the symphony oddly by leading into a superadded adagio, or (in the terms of *Dans ma chambre*) like a very slowly measured countdown of diminishment, "le compte-à-rebours de la fin" (23), of which the adagio itself, with its diminuendo of successive disappearances, is a model. There is respite, but in the end it is temporary. In his room Guillaume is writing *Dans ma chambre* to the background, not of Haydn but of Depeche Mode playing "In your room," a perfect image of self-sameness and identity; but in his room he is thinking also of the slow countdown of the years: "For four years I've thought I would die next year. I think myself beautiful just the same. I'm listening to Depeche Mode, in your room" (40). Thinking oneself beautiful in one's room is not a sure defense—but equally, in *Je sors ce soir* he recognizes that going out is likewise only another way of living out, while denying, the same interminable countdown of suspended time. "All the queens I know," he had already commented in *Dans ma chambre* (74), "they're nearly all HIV-positive. It's amazing how long-lasting they are [*C'est fou ce qu'ils durent*]. They're still going out. They're still fucking." (The Energizer bunny comes to mind.)

The thought of such durability isn't necessarily unpleasant, of course: in fact, in both cases I've just quoted Guillaume is reassuring himself, with his "I think myself beautiful" or his "They're still going out. They're still fucking." But the reassurance can itself sound very thin:

> They're still going out. They're still fucking. Lots of them get things, meningitis, diarrhea, shingles, Kaposi's, pneumocystis. And then they're OK. Some are just a bit thinner. Those who get CMV or other scarier stuff, generally speaking they haven't been around for a bit now. No one mentions them. . . . They say AIDS is evolving into a thing more like diabetes. They say as long as *la Sécu* has dough they'll treat us for whatever comes up. No need to worry. (74)

Guillaume's way of reassuring himself is transparently just another way of worrying, much as staying in one's room and going out—each being subject to the intrusion of thought—are variants of each other. Consequently the true marker of suspended time appears in the end to be a certain rhythm of absurd alternation: alternation, that is, between differences (like staying indoors and going out, worrying and reassuring oneself—or also being conscious of time and blotting it out with sex and drugs, having sex with Stéphane or having sex with Terrier, taking ecstasy or coke) that don't make a real difference. Everything finally becomes habit for this reason, somewhat like Guillaume's health-maintenance routine ("AZT, teeth, warts, maybe I'll jerk off again" [38]), or like his mechanical lingo, slangy, Americanized, repetitive, the hyped-up but mindless language of the Marais, full of words like *cool, look, stone(d), super* this and *hyper* that, with a bit of *verlan* (reverse slang) here and there, and a few stray bits of AIDS-speak. And habit, in turn, is a mask for depression, which at the same time, as is the way of masks, it reveals.

In this respect Terrier, who makes three suicide attempts in two weeks, is the central figure in the life of the Marais. But Guillaume, in turn, is so accustomed to Terrier's and others' attempts that he refers to them, in an offhand abbreviation that inevitably recalls the alphabetic ciphers of AIDS-speak (notably *KS*), as *ts (tentatives de suicide).* Terrier's habitual, failed suicide attempts, his *ts*'s, make an extremely suggestive metaphor, then, for the kind of suspended survival, neither really living nor really dying, that characterizes the liminality of existence in the ghetto. Guillaume shrugs them off as "ts bidon" (114); that is, they're phoney, *staged* suicide attempts, and at the same time transparently (and so poorly) staged, that is, *stagy,* and consequently unsuccessful both as suicide attempts and as staged suicide attempts. So they might also be a metaphor for Dustan's own writing of the life of the ghetto. For Dustan's writing, like Guillaume's dancing, tends to go to the brink, "au bord de la barrière de sécurité" (24–25), only to recoil from it, preferring always the reassurance of simulacral, fetishized spectral ghetto life to the exploration of what might lie beyond the brink, the content of the thought that, at the same time, in the figure of Guillaume, he can never quite shake off or distance himself from. As a result, his attitudinizing, too, has a stagy quality. If it has a message (as say an expression of pain or despair, even a call for help), the text thus predicts that, like the implied message of Terrier's suicide attempts that no one heeds, it will be ignored, dismissed, or shrugged off as *bidon,* fake. So it is proffered, but—again like Terrier's performances—without conviction and as it were involuntarily, as a matter of habit.

But to persist Terrier-like in activity that is self-defeating, and consciously so, and yet somehow necessary, as a marker of identity, a sign of "who we are," is ultimately *what the Marais does,* its defining mode of life. Each of these two novels concerns a period of suspended time that is devoted to a consciously self-defeating form of activity that functions as *deliberately* wasted time: time wasted, not in a Proustian sense (in order to be redeemed) but more as a way of metaphorically going on strike, making the waste of one's time significant precisely because it is a waste. Thus, in *Dans ma chambre,* Guillaume's "autobiographie érotique" takes the form of an account of his relation with Stéphane, which he knows to be an error from the start. Each is on the rebound (from the violent Quentin and the violent Jean-Marc respectively); Guillaume can't resist the pleasure he gets from the knowledge of being loved by Stéphane ("c'était tellement bon qu'il m'aime. C'était bon" [155]), and attempts therefore to make Stéphane over into his ideal sexual partner, a matter both of erotic education and of changing his "look" (13). In this he has considerable success, but there is no gainsaying the dilemma of alternation that defines what, in the other novel, will be called the impossibility of love, and in which here Guillaume knows himself to be caught. As he lucidly explains to his doctor, either you go with a "normal" type (i.e., Stéphane) and you're bored or you go with a "crazy" type (i.e., Quentin) "and he wants to throw acid in your face and everyone has a lot of fun" (62). It's like going out or staying at home. And as Guillaume and Stéphane's short affair comes to its inevitable end, Guillaume also decides it is time to break with the Marais and to travel. Can this be a crucial moment of decision, a way of breaking out of the differences without a difference that constitute his suspended existence?

> If I stay here I'll die. I'll end up putting sperm in everyone's ass and having the same done to me. The truth is that's all I feel like doing. In fact it's already well on the way to being the case. [If I leave,] I'll wait to fall ill. It surely won't take long. Then I'll be so disgusted with myself that at last it will be time to kill myself. I told myself all I had to do was leave. (152)

No, the terms of the alternative posed here—to die of boredom ("mourir" in the ghetto, a fake suicide), versus *real* suicide ("me tuer") outside—are unconvincing; they suggest another dilemma of alternation more than any real alternative offering the possibility of a clean break. Can one escape the ghetto by leaving it, or is that too a false alternative, a difference that doesn't make any difference?

Sure enough, in *Je sors ce soir,* Guillaume is in Paris, if not strictly in the Marais, after a two-year absence. Back on a weekend visit only, however; so the question of whether he has shaken free of the ghetto remains unresolved (certainly he has not fallen ill and killed himself, as "planned"). This time, suspended time will be a single evening, and on into the night, spent at the, of course prolonged, Sunday "gay tea-dance" at the Loco in Montmartre. But everyone is there; the Marais people are still going out, still cruising and fucking. And that is where the self-defeating aspect of Guillaume's participation comes in: he is more alienated than before, he is wearing the wrong clothes (his "look" is wrong, something in which he takes perverse pleasure, however), he dances, he cruises, but halfheartedly. Again the dynamic is that of the conscious error deliberately chosen, *as* an error. On the one hand, "It's cool to be back with my ghetto brothers," among whom he feels safe. "Paradise" (18). On the other, "It's very easy to be bored shitless in clubs" (16). Haunted by the death of Alain and wearing the famous "fetish" T-shirt, Guillaume in turn haunts the dance floors, the bars, and the johns, a ghostly presence among the partying. The new alternation, then, is between the present and the past, between Guillaume's present disaffected mood and the way things were, of which memories are constantly stirred as he runs into old friends and acquaintances and after desultory conversation drifts away, or is left, with a casual "Later!" ("A plus!"). He does get blissfully high. Then he goes home alone and masturbates, but only so as not to waste the last of the ecstasy effect—a pitiful contrast, he thinks, with the intense "scenes" of *Dans ma chambre.* "I've moved on from sex" [Je me suis éloigné du sexe] (80). But does moving on from sex really make a difference? And is masturbating—a figure, perhaps, for the solipsistic ghetto writing of attitude—really a way of moving on from sex, or is it another way of "doing" sex, especially when the sex was *always* attitudinizing and narcissistic, and always, so to speak, solo?

These questions are legitimate because he has *not* moved on from the impulse to substitute ghetto-style life for the thought that haunts it. That impulse is what—spurred by Alain's death—brought him to the Loco in the first place. And the cessation of thought (or a tantalizing approximation thereof) is what he achieves, finally, at the height of his ecstasy trip. Blissed out on a couch, he thinks:

> I'm not thinking.
> I'm not thinking of Alain.
> I'm not thinking of Terrier.
> I'm not thinking of Stéphane.
> I'm not thinking of Quentin.
> I'm not thinking of Vincent with whom the condom broke last year, there was blood and three months later he was positive.
> I'm not thinking of Marcelo, I'm not thinking I'm afraid of his being ill. I'm not thinking that I can't bring him to France because he's not a woman.
> I'm not thinking that for seven years I've been expecting to die. I'm not thinking that love is impossible. (88–89)[7]

Thinking one is not thinking is simultaneously a sign of one's distance from the ghetto's apparently successful pursuit of mindlessness, and the very epitome of the ghetto's meaning, as it is explored in both novels, the simultaneous possibility and impossibility of escape from thought (from time, from HIV, from death). Guillaume has moved on, and at the same time he is back at square one.

However, it is not just that Guillaume is self-absorbed here, plunged into the "ecstasy" *(ek-stasis)* of thinking (to himself) that he is not thinking, amid the partying crowd. It is also that Guillaume is writing (Guillaume Dustan has written) of Guillaume's thinking, to himself, that he is not thinking; and I am reading the text in which his self-absorption is thus made available, as an *attitude* of self-absorption mimed in writing, and addressed to readers. By the conventions of autobiography, and more specifically of an autobiography written in the present tense, a single—but not undivided—subject is writing that he is plunged into an ecstasy of self-absorption, thinking that he is not thinking; but he is doing so, then, in order to give the subject's self-absorption significance as an object open to reading. The paradox inherent in communicating, as an utterance, one's self-absorbed lack of interest in communicating, as the statement the utterance entails, that is, of making the absolute autonomy of one's identity into a social signal, is a version of what we have encountered (in chapter 5) as flaunting and (in chapter 6) as "flounting." It is the version that consists, as I have been emphasizing here, of the "giving" of attitude, where the word giving can be taken to imply both gratuitousness and generosity. If "striking" attitudes, in the ghetto, is a way of thinking (i.e., convincing oneself illusorily) that one is not thinking, "giving" attitude corresponds, not only to thinking (i.e., realizing) that one is not thinking but also to writing that one is not thinking for the benefit of an at least imaginable audience. If flounting, then, is what happens to flaunting under the conditions of wrongness that define aftermath as melancholic—the mode of survival that is marked by guilt—giving attitude is flaunting when, in the mode of disdain, it adopts the affectless mark of the ghetto style known as "cool"—which we have seen to be a complex dynamics of denial (thinking one is not thinking) and self-affirmation (asserting that one is still here)—and redirects it at an audience the ghetto affects to ignore. Thus it turns "striking" attitudes, as a mode of denial, into a (paradoxical) mode of address to others, the "giving" of attitude, an address that has the potential to counter *their* self-absorbed denial by advertising the hauntedness of ghetto denial.

And since Dustan's two novels are not simply personal autobiographies but also constitute community auto/biographies, we might conclude by noticing that the (non)difference between thinking one is not thinking as the very definition of ghetto life (a matter of denial) and thinking one is not thinking as what distinguishes Guillaume from his fellow ghetto-dwellers (a matter of writing) is the (non)difference of the collective and the personal that grounds the genre with which this chapter has been concerned (and grounds it in both of its two forms, depending on the extent to which the [non]difference is manifested as difference or nondifference). If so, then writing like Dustan's can be conceived as the act of agencing that makes readable, as a "giving" of attitude, the collective conditions of aftermath as survival—here denial as "striking" attitudes, elsewhere the panic of serial disappearance as in *Longtime Companion* or Guibert's sense of betrayal, and in dual autobiography the burden of guilt—that define the nature of community as disaster-struck and a site of phantom pain, thereby presenting the autobiography of community as a readable index of the disaster that would otherwise go ignored. It is, in other words, another version of flaunting the haunt (see chapter 5), where haunt refers to the hauntedness of the state of aftermath and flaunting to the operation that, in making it readable, makes the hauntedness haunting.

So let me now attempt to draw together some threads and venture to formulate the upshot of the long argument that has been pursued in part II. I'll do so by referring to the seminar on phantom pain—the clinical phenomenon—that the psychoanalyst Nicolas Abraham gave in Paris in 1974, the notes of which were published recently (Rand, 68–69). Interestingly, Abraham understood phantom pain as both a symptom of denial (the pain in the lost limb guarantees that the limb is not lost) and a manifestation of counterdenial: the "incorporation" of pain, such that successful mourning of the lost limb is blocked, as if the pain were being experienced, as Abraham puts it, in the stump. Phantom pain as denial describes what we have just seen to be Dustan's portrayal of life in the Marais, while the melancholic writing of failed mourning we saw in the dual autobiographies of Duquénelle and Hoffman (chapter 6) illustrates phantom pain as incorporation. And Abraham's analysis clarifies also why *Longtime Companion* is difficult to classify in relation to these categories; it is because in René's film the emergence of community in the circumstances of trauma is associated with a cure (the cure of AIDS that would simultaneously assuage the trauma). For Abraham presents community-formation as a third "possibility" in relation to the experience of phantom pain. Imagine, he says, a group of amputees who get together to form a "sect," and whose members "commune" through a set of "ritual, magical, or technical social acts" (think of AZT-taking in *L'Aztèque*) that center on the lost limb so that it acquires a compensatory "symbolic existence" as something like the emblem or marker of the group, whose group-belongingness it signifies.

Now Abraham's clinical orientation leads him to present community as the therapeutic, healing option, and by contrast to describe denial and incorporation as failed attempts to re-member, through "regression" (denial) and "melancholia" (incorporation), what has undergone dismemberment. But the evidence of aftermath writing, as I have described it, is rather that community formation is itself bound up with—indeed, inseparable from—the phenomena of denial and counterdenial, which are in turn inextricably associated with each other, phantom pain being in Abraham's analysis symptomatic of both. So community would be something like the very site of a phantom pain from the significance of which (as denial *and* counterdenial) it derives, however, its communitarian character, by contrast with a larger society so absorbed in denial that phantom pain, in the eyes of that society, has no significance whatsoever (it has the significance of being insignificant). And if writing, as we have seen (especially in chapter 6), is the characteristic activity of aftermath, and hence another of those "ritual, magical, or technical social acts" that define community, it seems that the writing of phantom pain in testimonial mode—that of a haunting hauntedness—is a communitarian pursuit also in the sense that it seeks to extend to the larger society a sense of its own participation in phantom pain. A sense, that is, of what that society defines itself by denying.

But writing in the mode of haunting hauntedness (flaunting or flounting the haunt, "giving" attitude) defines, as we have also seen, the figural, or symbolic, mode as the form of discursivity, characteristic of discourses of extremity and/or the writing of phantom pain in aftermath, that by favoring readability—the readability of what is known but not acknowledged, the cultural obscene—promotes in parasocial fashion, or more accurately agences, an ethics of community. Such an ethics is grounded in acknowledgment of culture's constitutive difference from itself, and consequently in an understanding of phantom pain as a manifestation of the mutual *relevance,* the pertinence one to the other of culture and the cultural obscene, civilization and disaster. Figuration actualizes that relevance in the form of rhetorical manifestations that, as interventions of the im-pertinent and the untimely (the untime-ly and the un-timely), function as reminders of such pertinence. And conversely, the untimely and the im-pertinent now turn out to be describable as names for the existential manner of being, within aftermath culture, of the communitarian ethos, its haunting parasocial presence.

On the side of the social, therefore, as opposed to the parasocial or the communitarian as what haunts the social, what is called for by an ethics of community would be the development of a corresponding ethics of hospitality in the form of practices of reading attuned to the (potential) readability of figural manifestations of untimeliness and im-pertinence, the harbingers of the obscene and of disaster. I turn now, then, in a final chapter that extends part II while, not exactly concluding, but perhaps suspending (in all senses) the argument developed in this book as a whole, to the issue of the role played in aftermath culture by social gatekeeping institutions. More specifically I turn to the role of literary pedagogy and the teaching of reading in educational institutions, in relation to testimonial writing—including discourses of extremity—understood as a vehicle of phantom pain and, hence, of a communitarian ethos requiring acknowledgment of disaster and of the culturally obscene. Can a gatekeeping institution be appropriated as a site where hospitality is taught and learned, and thus become more like a cultural threshold and less like a barrier? And what might be the pedagogical conditions of such a *détournement*? In search of answers, we will find ourselves revisiting, one more time, the hospital.

8. Hospitals, Families, Classrooms: Teaching the Untimely

As much as it terrfied me I found that I was also struck by a sense of awe when I found that I could look at the situation, gauge my fear, and then go ahead. . . . To this day, staring down that fear is the most empowering thing I have ever done in my life. I don't mean anything heroic about this. It wasn't heroism. Something compelling can't be termed heroic. I walked into those sweaty godforsaken deathbed rooms because I was doing it for me. It was my best defense against my enemy AIDS.

—Mark Senak, *A Fragile Circle*

Si l'avenir n'est vraiment que de se protéger, alors mon but à moi sera de contaminer la terre entière. Mais pas de la manière dont vous le redoutez.

[If the future truly lies only in self-protection, then my personal goal will be to contaminate the whole world. But not in the way you fear.]

—Thierry Mingot, *Felicità. Chronique d'un amour en exil*

Teaching Hospital Knowledge

It is 1984. Mark Senak is a young, activist, gay lawyer doing pro bono work preparing wills for men dying of AIDS, an epidemic not yet understood. There is no antibody test, and the mode of transmission is still so uncertain that hospital staff and visitors suit up from head to toe (caps, gloves, masks) before entering a patient's room. More than five thousand people, all of them gay men as far as anyone knows, have been mysteriously struck down and carried off. It takes guts to do what Senak is doing, but the story, he says, is not about heroism.

On one occasion—for him a turning point—he is forced to climb into bed with a man too weak to sign his name unaided:

> It meant . . . that I would have to hoist my body up next to him, half lying in his bed with him. I put my arm around him and my masked face next to his, and through my gloved hand I held his hand, which in turn held the pen. Together very slowly we wrote his name. (42)

Going to the bathroom afterward to disrobe, Senak discovers that his gloves have left an odor on his hands that won't scrub off: "To me it smelled exactly like a decaying body" (43). His contact with the dying man, their joint signing of a name, have had the meaning for him of an identification: "I could very clearly see myself sitting there in that bed, dying. . . . Inside, I could feel myself even now dying. I didn't know if I was infected. But I thought surely I would be dying here too" (41). So the odor that clings to his hands is the odor of death—of death in general ("it smelled exactly like a decaying body"), but of his own death in particular.

Something tells him to get out of the hospital, the place where he has encountered his own death and his own AIDS. But "when I got to the door to the street, I found I was terrified to go outside" (43). The very thought of taking the subway turns his stomach. "The stark contrast between the world out there and the world in this hospital was more than a door could separate. The people out there had no idea what was going on in here" (44). That is, there are those who *know* (who know AIDS, who know death), and those who don't. As one who now knows and is identified with death, with AIDS, he will be going out among the innocent—at what risk? The risk of contaminating them (with AIDS, with death, with knowledge)? Or of being himself contaminated, with AIDS ("I didn't know if I was infected")? He has the wits to call a helper on the Gay Men's Health Crisis hotline, who eventually persuades him he can take a taxi. The New York cabbie's seen-it-all attitude, as Senak sobs in the back seat, is also a help. "[T]he next day I did two deathbed wills" (45).

A bit oddly, Senak presents this story of crisis and turning point as a tribute to "good therapy." But his particular fear of the crowded subway, where no one knows what is going on in the hospital, seems a crucial detail. For while stripping his cumbersome protective garments in the hospital bathroom, he had reflected on "the ridiculous waste of money" represented by this clothing. "They make us wear this while [the PWA] is in hospital and if he were discharged he'd take a cab home or ride the subway, and no one would be wearing a cap or gown. It was all so stupid. I decided I wasn't going to wear them anymore" (42–43). This insight has to do with the futility in certain circumstances of protection—and more particularly of individual self-protection. If the PWA isn't contagious in the subway, why wear protective clothing in the hospital? But the insight is immediately followed in the narrative by Senak's discovery of the odor of death on his hands, which overdetermines his fear of taking the subway. He has been contaminated by death in spite of (and indeed in a sense because of) the gloves and other apparatus. So, like the PWA he imagines discharged from the hospital, *he* will be going out into the world of taxis and subways, where no one is taking precautions because they are innocent of hospital knowledge, as a kind of contagious agent in his own right. He is a carrier of the contagion that might be called hospital knowledge.

In 1984, neither Senak nor anyone else could be sure there was no risk of actual AIDS contamination in the subway; hence his concern about the PWA returning home from the hospital, even as he uses the disparity of hospital and subway as evidence in favor of rejecting protection in the hospital. But the point of his story has obviously more to do, in the long run, with metaphoric contagiousness—the sort of contamination to which Thierry Mingot also refers when he describes his goal, as a writer of AIDS testimonial, as being "to contaminate the whole world. But not in the way you fear." For self-protection is useless, indeed derisory—it is irrational and hysterical—in the face of *death*'s ability to get through to us whether, like Senak in the hospital, we protect ourselves obsessively, or like those in the subway, we are oblivious to its danger. Senak will go among the oblivious as the bearer of the knowledge that there is no protection against death.

Borrowing a word from Maurice Blanchot (1980), we can say that he has encountered disaster; his paralysis at the hospital door, unable either to stay in the hospital and face death or go out into the world that is innocently oblivious of it, is like the moment of *arrêt de mort*—the suspended sentence whereby one is condemned, but still has a life to live. But with the help of the GMHC volunteer, Senak converts disaster into commitment, a commitment to community in the face of disaster, getting on with the useful work of helping dying men write their wills: the experience, in the end, has "galvanized" him (45). For the reason self-protection is useless in the face of disaster is that disaster is only the discovery, traumatic as that discovery may be, of *what is the case.* What is the case is that the personal self can never be self-sufficient, or completely protected, to the extent that it is open to an impersonal otherness, here—as often—described as death. The self is, if one will, definitionally an exposed self. However—and this is the point of the turning-point story in the context of Senak's whole book—that openness of the self is also the foundation of community. What enables him to get on with useful work is a wisdom derived from the knowledge acquired in the hospital: not just the knowledge of death and disaster that he momentarily shrinks from communicating to the oblivious, not only the understanding that in a world subject to disaster reliance on self-protection is irrational and illusory, but also the insight that since we are exposed, self-protection should yield to community solidarity, which can at least mitigate the disaster. So no more cap, gown, and gloves: "I decided I wasn't going to wear them anymore" (43). But work on behalf of the dying continues: "[T]he next day I did two deathbed wills" (45).[1]

Perhaps it is not coincidental, then, that when one is a pro bono lawyer helping dying gay men with their wills, the work of community frequently entails keeping families at bay. So it is, precisely, in the episode in question:

> Suddenly there was a commotion at the door. His family had shown up and were trying to get into the room. They were seemingly hostile to the will and everyone else. I got up and asked them to leave. (39)

Homophobic families do not wish to see their son's gay lover inherit property they believe should come to them: in this respect, the family is community's natural rival. As in Amy Hoffman's *Hospital Time* (chapter 6), the antinomian character of relations between a gay community, or more broadly an AIDS community, which Hoffman calls the "fake" family, and the "real" family is patent, then, in this scene of intrusion. And what I want to explore in this chapter is something of the complexity that underlies the topos of family, especially in relation to community, as it persistently arises, most particularly in United States AIDS writing. I have a further goal, however, which is to draw out some of the implications of the antinomy of family and hospital (community) for my own practice as a classroom teacher of AIDS and other testimonial texts, a practice that in moments of hubris I think of as having affinities—like Mark Senak venturing onto the subway as a bearer of disaster—with the act of witnessing itself. "If my family is to take major responsibility for my care," wrote Eric Michaels on January 5, 1988, "we will have to invent that family" (*Unbecoming,* 38). But it's actually not so much the invention, or even the reinvention, of family as its defamiliarization—by which I mean both a strangifying and a de-family-ing of family—that constitutes the critical contribution of much U.S. AIDS writing. And I think the defamiliarizing of family has to be a preoccupation also of the teacher of witnessing texts in this country, where family is so pervasively imagined as a site of protection from disaster.

My hypothesis, then, is that, especially in the United States, community is to disaster (and the hospital) as family is to (self-)protection and the home. The contested status of safe(r) sex, which has protection as its principle and was, perhaps not coincidentally, invented in the United States, can perhaps illustrate something of the complexity that arises from such an equation—a complexity that hinges in this precise case on a sort of dual allegiance of the idea of protection itself, which can be recruited for community or alternatively seen as self-protection. For safe sex was invented not just in the United States but more particularly in San Francisco, and it was invented as a response of community to disaster: "how to have sex in an epidemic"—for which reason it was abominated by the family-oriented proponents of chastity and abstinence, who correctly see that sex and sexuality are major signifiers of gay community. With time, though, safe sex became increasingly understood, less as a communitarian means to combat an epidemic than as a device of individual self-protection—so it is taught, for example, in most high school sex education classes. And consequently—as it were in response to this appropriation—"barebacking" (unprotected penetrative sex) came more recently to be regarded among younger gay men (and much to the horror of many veterans of the epidemic's earlier years), as a *new* way of demonstrating the community values of solidarity and commitment that were formerly attached to safe sex—a new way, that is, to "have sex in an epidemic." An embrace of danger now replaced the earlier emphasis on safety, which had once seemed dangerous enough. What emerges from this complex history, which I have only outlined, is then that compromise positions—the position known as "harm reduction," for example—seem never to get much of a hearing in United States debate, much touted as they may be elsewhere. The underlying rivalry of family and community seems to require that antinomian positions that permit assertions of principle and declarations of doctrinal certainty be culturally preferred.

Of course, the knowledge that one is *exposed,* willy-nilly—and ultimately exposed to death, despite all efforts, rational or irrational, to protect oneself—is knowledge that people everywhere tend to shun. As I've argued in this book, such knowledge—the knowledge of disaster that survivors of traumatic events bear witness to—is the very knowledge that culture exists to keep at bay and consequently classes as obscene. But where white settler Australia, for example, puts its trust in good housekeeping to tidy the alien out of sight or exclude it from the national premises (see chapter 2), middle-class American culture, which has a not dissimilar history of settler expansion and immigration but has never—or, at least, not to the same extent—enjoyed the privileges (and the curse) of geographic isolation, seems much more conscious of threat and fearful of exposure. It relies rather more, therefore, on rituals of protection intended, not only to keep otherness (and others) out but also to ward off danger. There is little place in either Australia or the United States for an understanding of the kind of *entraînement* or intoxication that was celebrated in France by AIDS writers of the early nineties like Guibert, Collard, and de Duve (see chapter 4), the deliberate courting of exposure that Bataille saw as a way to "sovereignty." Australians, therefore, build fences. Americans too build fences—the border fence with Mexico being an egregious example—but when they are rich, they like to live in "gated" (i.e., guarded) communities, like medieval walled towns (so "community" is a misnomer); and if they are middle class enough, they subscribe to the view that the family is, or at least ought to be, a safe haven. Protection is more important, it seems, than keeping a distance.

Certainly I should have known, therefore, that the undergraduates who signed up, in the fall of 1996, for the first Comparative Literature course on AIDS writing I ever taught, would feel exposed, and seek protection (as, of course, sex ed had taught them) when I confronted them with texts by Michaels, Guibert, Monette, Wojnarowicz, Joslin, and others. As it happened, they were not the more or less committed and even activist group I had lazily expected; mostly they were students who needed a literature course to meet requirements or wanted a break from the demands of economics or biochemistry; and they had thought it would be a good idea to "learn about" AIDS, college students having been declared a risk group that year by some well-meaning agency. They expected, I think, to learn some facts and figures, perhaps to hear about the new treatment options, and probably to listen to safe sex-lectures—that sort of thing. Instead, they were affronted by written and filmic texts that, for them—so unexpected was the encounter—functioned as "direct representations" of a reality they had never previously even begun to imagine, an encounter with disaster. What were they to do?

They called home, of course. And in class, they astonished me by their ability to mobilize lit crit attitudes picked up in other classes (sometimes feminist and postcolonial in inspiration) to provide an alibi for dismissing texts that nevertheless clearly troubled them. Michaels's *Unbecoming*? Too intellectual (AIDS writers should not be thoughtful). Monette's *Borrowed Time*? Come on! A rich, white, middle-class, professional man, living in the Hollywood Hills? What was I thinking? And where were the women, the people of color, the third-worlders? Marlon Riggs's video, *Tongues Untied*? They were troubled that he had a white boyfriend, wasn't that a cop-out? Paul Rudnick's *Jeffrey,* for a change of pace? Yes, but AIDS is far too serious to be joked about. *Silverlake Life* (Tom Joslin)? They called home. My conscientious explanations (witnessing writing is definitionally unrepresentative; who knew, in 1985, that women were infected, or that "another epidemic" was raging, unrecognized, in Africa?) sounded like lame rationalizations and were received in stony silence. A pattern was set; there was nothing I could do.

Of course, as I later came to see, I had unwittingly performed a generic catachresis. But I had done it unannounced, unstylishly, unartfully, without attending to the necessity of *captatio benevolentiae,* and they were unwilling to forgive me; indeed some seemed quite anxious to punish me. Understanding the classroom as a safe haven, remote from life and its dangers—and everything about the institution, beginning with its geographical location in a small college town, abetted that understanding—they had signed up to "learn about" AIDS. I had violated that contract, and done the equivalent of inviting them to get into bed with an AIDS patient near death, and to sign the man's name as if it was their own. They had expected the classroom to be like an extension of their (imagined) family; they found an annex of the AIDS ward in a hospital. They felt tricked, betrayed, and bullied; and they fought back. I don't blame them in the least—but I sometimes wonder whether they didn't get a better educational bargain than they thought. The experience of being disturbed can be a precious one; I regretted only that what I had blindly and clumsily unleashed often seemed more like panic, a clearly unproductive experience.

As for me, I can report that the standoff was, in the end, extremely educational. It would be interesting to know how many scholarly books derive, as this one does, from aftermath meditations on pedagogical disasters (the term, in this case, can be used advisedly). I will not narrate here how I learned the rudiments of an art of *captatio* in later courses, but merely some of the trains of thought the initial experience set in motion.[2] Generic catachresis, I soon realized, was the name, not only of the blunder I had committed but also of the defining rhetorical move made by the testimonial texts themselves: what, then, was the relation, if any, between my blunder and these textual performances? But also, was it not my task to teach a manner of reading that would be hospitable to texts that, as vehicles of disaster, seemed to trigger in my students an automatic "protect yourself" response? Is there such a thing as a communitarian reading mode that would be more exposed—more like the (protected) openness of safe(r) sex, for example, as a response to the disaster of epidemic—than the self-protective panic I had witnessed? And if so, how might one teach such hospitable reading?

In *Facing It,* which I finished writing the same year, I had already, and I now think a bit prematurely, tackled such problems as I had myself experienced them, in the form of personal anxiety, as a reader of AIDS writing in the early nineties. But now my teaching experience led me to a third train of thought, this time concerning cultural issues raised by witnessing and particularly the gatekeeping responsibilities of institutions of cultural reproduction: schools, churches, the media, and so on. Which culture was I, as a teacher, supposed to reproduce? The self-protective culture that wishes to ignore disaster? Such is the comfortable option that America seems mostly to enjoin on its teachers. Or the culture open to disaster of which testimonial writing is a harbinger, and of which I had personally become increasingly aware? Should classroom culture be more like the imagined family that my students seemed, from their institutional experience, to have learned to expect and desire? Or should it be more like a hospital culture, as for example Mark Senak encountered that culture in 1984, and as my 1996 classroom had unexpectedly turned out to be? Over these questions it doesn't really seem possible to hesitate, and once I had formulated them in such terms, it was evident to me that the hospital option is the only one worth considering. But . . .

How to make it a reality? How to make a classroom hospitable to the knowledge of disaster, in an institution that does seem overwhelmingly devoted, except on the rarest of occasions, to the more comfortable option, providing a protected environment in which to "learn about" life, life "out there" in a world made safely remote? That's the tough question that I continue to ponder, and that writing this book has scarcely helped me to clarify. Except inasmuch as I now understand that a teacher of testimonial must be a kind of witness, a "moderator of pain," as a student once wrote.[3] Or—like so many of the testimonial authors I have read, and like Jamaica

Kincaid, to whom I am about to turn—an agencer, one who mediates a mode of reading the object of which is not the subjectivity of the author so much as that which haunts that subjectivity, and turns out, always, to have also haunted the subjectivity of the reader. Or else, as René de Ceccatty's *L'Accompagnement* will suggest, a conductor of souls, a psychopomp: one who is interpellated by the dead to guide the living toward accompanying them.

Defamiliarizing the Family

No one, as far as I know, has carefully surveyed the topos of family as it arises in North American AIDS writing; and such is not my own immediate purpose here. David Caron, borrowing a line from Tolstoy in a 1998 article ("Intrusions"), offers a point of departure. He points out that in AIDS writing also there are "happy" families and "unhappy" ones. Happy families remain impervious to disaster; even a case of AIDS in the family fails to disturb the family's equanimity or penetrate its protective shell. These families inhabit the kind of texts that, in search of a neutral term, I would call nontestimonial: frequently such texts are fictions, but mass-audience news reporting and of course much political discourse also often comforts the ideological belief in family as a bulwark against AIDS. "Mainstream" texts have the reassuring function of denying disaster by asserting the safety and protectedness of family. Caron, whose interest is in films, cites inter alia early made-for-TV movies like *An Early Frost,* and devotes his main attention to Jonathan Demme's more complex, but made-for-Hollywood, film *Philadelphia.*

Unhappy families, on the other hand, are those that respond to the "intrusion" of AIDS by discovering in themselves a new openness: a kind of flexibility, a willingness to improvise and to change that signals their acknowledgment of exposure to disaster. These families are, in that sense, more like communities. Caron's sole example is a documentary film by Paule Muxel and Bertrand de Solliers, *Sida: Paroles de familles,* in which members of various families visited by AIDS bear witness to the "deinstitutionalization" the family has undergone as a result of the disruptive incursion into their lives of "something fundamentally alien" (Caron, 68). But the problem is that it is hard to find further examples of AIDS writing in this category: authors of testimonial texts who are also spokespersons for family are rare to begin with, and they are even more rarely moved to acknowledge the precariousness of the family's supposed protectedness.

Joan Hurley's motherly testimony in *How Far Is It to London Bridge* (see chapter 2) resolves, for example, without apparent anxiety, into a celebration of her PWA daughter's courage and an assertion of the resilience displayed by the family in response to the threat. (One wonders, of course, what her clearly rebellious daughter might have written had she had a chance.)

What one does find, though, in much *gay* writing about AIDS in North America is a strong tendency to represent the family as homophobic (i.e., part of the problem that is AIDS, not a site of protection from it), and to figure through that representation the witnessing subject's audience. Examples would be Monette's *Borrowed Time,* Joslin's video film *Silverlake Life,* or Laurie Lynd's short film *RSVP* (on the latter two, see Chambers 1999). In these cases, part of the narrative tends to present either a coming-out on the part of the PWA (as in Monette, where this coming-out from the AIDS closet is equivalent to the act of bearing witness) and/or—as in all three of my examples—a kind of conversion on the part of the family, from its homophobic ignorance to a more sympathetic understanding—even, in the case of *Silverlake Life,* a degree of participation in the "fake" family (Amy Hoffman's word) that is community.

By virtue of their sense of family's problematic character and its convertibility to an acknowledgment of disaster, these accounts of family are not unrelated to what, however, is the much bleaker and more pointedly critical writing that I classify under the rubric of defamiliarizing the family. Conversion of the family is not presented here as easy or even likely. Rather it is a matter of strangifying the "familiar" (protected) family by showing that its supposed happiness is itself a precarious ideological construction, one that is made in the face of a danger and as a way of denying it, and is hence closely connected to disaster—to the hurt, the pain, the suffering, the atrocity that the very idea of family seems designed to keep at bay, to conceal or forget. Although one detects in such writing an edge of cruelty that surely derives from the hurt the authors have personally experienced in their own family, it can be looked on, I want to suggest, as proposing a pedagogical model that might be adapted, shorn of the cruelty, to the classroom, a method by which students might be weaned from their self-protective reading habits as a step toward acquiring a more exposed and hospitable practice of reading. I mean that it may be possible to address the family model of protectedness and security that students bring to class from a perspective that would first recognize the fragility of the model before going on to emphasize the reality of disaster that the model occludes. This fragility resides in family's own intimate, if largely unacknowledged, *acquaintance* with the danger it claims or seeks to hold at bay, the sense in which family happiness is haunted, albeit without necessarily knowing it is haunted. Haunted, that is, by "another family" with which the supposedly happy family is, when it comes to the point, not at all unfamiliar.

This intimacy is the common concern of the two otherwise dissimilar texts I want to discuss at greater length. In each case it is a sibling intimacy, figured by the death of a brother. I might have died where he did; we are joint inheritors of the family hurt; we could cosign the same name, like Mark Senak with the dying patient in the hospital—such are the implied and explicit acknowledgments, on the plane of the author's personal involvement in the narrative of the brother's death, that appear to guide the writing of texts like Clifford Chase's *The Hurry-Up Song* and Jamaica Kincaid's *My Brother.* They entail the further acknowledgment that family is not only not a place of protection but indeed the very site in which disaster occurs. And it is not hard to extrapolate an understanding that the ideology of family—supposedly the basic social unit—stands in, in texts like this, for an ideology of culture itself as the antidote, rather than the site, of disaster: the ideology of culture as coextensive with civilization.

In *The Hurry-Up Song,* the cosigned name of Cliff and Ken Chase might be spelled *precipitousness:* precipitousness in the sense of hurry, *and* in the sense of an abrupt drop. The author-narrator's name, Cliff Chase, translates, a friend tells him, as Precipitous Pursuit, and the eponymous "hurry-up song" is a wordless ditty of his brother Ken's invention. Both brothers are enamored of the world of animated cartoons, with their hectic, speeded-up narrative and plenty of chases and steep drops. Their childhood play with Muppet dolls, usually in savage parody of cartoons and TV shows and family life, is, says Cliff, "the height of a gay childhood" (6). But height, then, suggests here, as elsewhere, the imminence of danger—like cartoon characters, the gay brothers can drop off the family cliff at any moment and discover, like Bullwinkle in a famous episode of *Rocky and Bullwinkle,* that cartoon or not, it still *hurts.* So this sense of imminence is also an awareness of immanence: in the Chase family disaster lurks, a permanent presence as well as a threat.

The sense of danger and precipitousness coexists, however, with the family's denial, its careful maintenance of a facade of happiness, order, normalcy. "I don't see any danger," says mother Muppet in a cartoon as the

Muppetmobile approaches a meteor-swarm (151); and "Things aren't that bad" (201), she says to Cliff, in real life, when Ken is a few days from his death. Whence the anger that finds expression in the brothers' cartooning and Muppet play, and later in Cliff's autobiography; "dih! dih!" the cartoon Muppets groan through clenched teeth, in the patented ejaculation that signifies their rage and dismay. Not surprisingly, Normal Heights is the name, therefore, of the suburb of San Diego (presumably Hillcrest) in which Ken dies of AIDS; and not surprisingly again, his death catches the whole family by surprise, so steadfast has been their denial. Mother and father have returned to San Jose for a break from tending him; Cliff has ignored his brother's terse message ("Come soon") and trusted his mother's assurances that there is still time for him to come from New York.

But if precipitousness names the immanence/imminence of disaster in the household, the prevalence of conspiracy—in a sense exactly opposite to Paul Monette's deployment of the term (chapter 6)—is both the sign of the family's anticommunitarian character and the form taken by their collective cover-up. That is, it is their way of pretending to themselves that the family's unhappiness and disunity aren't the case, while simultaneously enacting that disunity and unhappiness. The mother colludes with the children against the father, whose bigotry embarrasses them all; different groups of siblings form alliances against the rest; as children, Ken and Cliff, alone in the back bedroom, bond as they engage in long sessions of vengeful cartoon and parody, but themselves compete in the family arena for their mother's attention and affection; Cliff and Ken share the secret of Ken's diagnosis, but Cliff feels betrayed when, learning the truth, the parents take over their son's care. In turn, he will betray his brother through his inability to "be there" for him (123), his failure to be "equal to the situation" (137) of his dying. It is because of these collusions and betrayals that anger is as endemic as self-deception in the household: the mother makes bitter jokes about her Christian Science upbringing (she was denied eyeglasses because her weak vision was ascribed to an inability on her part to "see the good in people"), but herself practices "positive thinking" and seems blind to the joylessness of her own marriage and the distress of her children.

The general denial of Ken's condition at the end, and Cliff's particular betrayal of his brother through his collusion in the family self-deception, are the source, and the object, of the book's own anger. With respect to Ken, Cliff both desires to escape the painful situation of accompanying his dying and fails to be truthful about his feelings (134); thus, the long-distance phone conversations between New York and San Diego, frequently reduced to the humming of the open phone-line as Ken sinks further into dementia and the autism of the dying, become symbolic, like the unheeded admonition to "come soon." There is no "final scene of reconciliation" as in the movies and the soaps; just a general breakdown of communication and a diffuse rage that is, itself, the disaster—Ken's AIDS being more like the occasion of its manifestation. It turns out, in short, and contrary to family belief, that love *can* hurt you.

"I lost him by the side of the road," Cliff laments, referring to his brother (16), much as before Cliff's birth, the family had nearly lost Ken on the shoulder of the road, through inadvertency, in the course of a happy family outing. It is this proneness to accident in the family that makes *The Hurry-Up Song,* as Wayne Koestenbaum says in his foreword, "extremely funny" (xiii). But the funniness is less in "Surrealist vein: North American absurdity" than it is in the *grinçant* manner of *humour noir,* surrealism's true proclivity and the specialty of the boys' cartooning. For what the proneness to accident signals is the proximity of family life to hurt, damage, and danger, the opposite of the protectedness ideologically ascribed to it. The book, as Cliff puts it at one point, is about "the familiar smell of near tragedy. . . , the burden of impending disaster" that hangs over family life (in this precise case, the dinner table) "like burnt rubber" (76). What is most *familiar* about the family, then, is not its happiness but its proximity—as close as the side of a road or as a long-distance call between brothers who cannot say what ought to be said—to disaster.

Precipitousness, imminence, a premonitory smell of burning—these are forms of untimeliness. The future is not in the future, where it belongs, but already here and now, haunting the present with a sense of impending disaster. When the family absentmindedly nearly lost Ken, aged three, on the roadside, the accident foreshadowed his childhood fugues and his wandering as a PWA suffering from dementia, and thus finally his slipping away from the family into death while everyone's attention was diverted. In *My Brother,* there is a similar set of premonitory accidents. On the day following his birth, Devon, who is to die of AIDS as a young man, is attacked by red ants while his mother sleeps; and his half sister later repeats his mother's negligence, becoming absorbed in a book that signifies her future vocation as a writer and neglecting to change his diaper or even to notice that it needs changing, so that she will be cruelly punished by her mother. Her comment on the incident of the ants is eloquent: "I was only wondering if it had any meaning that some small red things had almost killed him from the outside shortly after he was born and that now some small things were killing him from the inside, I don't believe it has any meaning; this is only something a mind like mine would think about" (6). A "mind like [hers]" is a haunted mind, preoccupied by untimeliness, which is not so much meaningful as it is a challenge to "meaning."

But in *My Brother* the form of untimeliness that is most preoccupying is the haunting of the present by the past, the burden common to aftermath writing and constitutive, not of premonition or imminence, but of "phantom pain." (Of course, *The Hurry-Up Song* is aftermath writing too, in the final analysis.) But in *My Brother* the untimely presence of a hurtful and as it were doomed past in the comfortable life of a successful writer is also coextensive with the relation of "another family"—Kincaid's birth family in Antigua—to the contented and happy family life she lives in Vermont, with husband, children, home and garden. The Antigua family is one in which, had she not been expelled to the care of a foster family and thus been able to receive an education and become a writer, she would have shared an existence no less stunted and doomed than that of her (half) brother, now dying of AIDS, his life unfulfilled. "I only now understand," she writes, "why it is that people lie about their past, why they say they are one thing other than the thing they really are, why they invent a self that bears no resemblance to who they really are, why anyone would want to feel as if he or she belongs to nothing, comes from no one, just fell out of the sky, whole" (12–13). The identity we "invent" for ourselves bears no relation to disaster; "who we really are" is another story, one that haunts the lying version of ourselves in which we nevertheless become absorbed. If Devon's sister has had a life he could not have (a guilty thought), "his life," as she puts it, "is the one I did not have" (176), her real life—a thought even more profoundly unsettling. (See Brophy for an extended commentary on these and related issues.)

If the occasion and the topic of *My Brother* is Kincaid's (re)discovery and recognition of this "other" life, both shadowy and more real than the life of comfort the Vermont family enjoys, it is important also to see that she is therefore writing about something of which she is aware but that she does not, and cannot, claim to know. Like premonition in relation to the future, memory connects past and present, makes an indecipherable stammer of their relation. But the past's familiarity, its intimacy and relevance to "who we really are," does not necessarily make it any more available for description and identification than imminence can specify the disaster it foretells. Devon, for instance, Kincaid has known only for the first three and the last three years of his life. "Who is he?" she wonders. "How does he feel about himself, what has he ever wanted?" (69–70). And after his death, and the completely unexpected revelation of his homosexuality—he who had such a reputation as a ladies' man—she asks which of the various Devons she cannot piece together was *he,* "which one of his selves made him happiest? I cannot tell this and perhaps neither could he" (191). Furthermore, if Devon's truest reality lies in his AIDS, that is, in the fact of his having lived all of his life "in death" (88), it is significant that he himself could not name his illness, calling it "the stupidness" ("de chupidness") instead, in the way, perhaps, that he favored the uninterpretable inarticulacy of the *truups* sound, made by sucking air through pursed lips, that Kincaid thinks is characteristic of him. What she can give us of Devon is only these questions that haunt *her,* not the Devon whose life she did not have and is her "real" life.

Of Kincaid's mother, her "awfulness and bitterness" (62), her destructive way of loving her children—the mother who sent her daughter away in favor of the sons she had with Mr. Drew—something like what is said of Devon is also true. Although she has known her intimately, and all her life, "I know nothing of her," Kincaid says (93). And the mother in turn, like Devon, is associated with the island of Antigua itself; indeed she is something like its very embodiment. But of Antigua too, this now unknown place that she remembers as where she comes from, Kincaid recalls having decided, as a child, that it was a place of death. "I decided that only people in Antigua died, that people living in other places did not die and as soon as I could, I would move somewhere else, to those places where the people living there do not die" (26–27). Correspondingly, as an adult she sees Antigua as the place where people cannot love one another, while to Devon it is the place that has made "wutlessness" (worthlessness) of his life and inflicted on him the "chupidness" that is AIDS (29). It's true that tropical Antigua is a garden, fertile both in principle and in fact; but a colonial garden, it lies devastated in much the same way that the figure for a way of loving that produces devastation is the mother, whom Kincaid does not understand and with whom, when she first learns of Devon's illness, she is not even on speaking terms. So the symbolic space of disaster in this memoir is the place where the painful separation occurred—biographically the child Kincaid's expulsion from her birth family—that has split "family" from "other family," making family known but a lie, while Antigua, the place of the other family and identified with disaster, is remembered, but as something at once intimate to the author, both real and essential to who she is, and beyond her ken. Something that haunts her.

So Kincaid turned to writing, as she says, "out of desperation," and knowing instinctively that in order to understand her brother, "or to make an attempt at understanding his dying, and not to die with him, I would write about it" (196). Writing then, for her, is both the manifestation of the problem, since it is as a writer that Kincaid is alienated from her real, "other family," and a way of responding to the problem, a desperate measure. Desperate because, since she herself neither knows nor understands Devon (Devon's dying, the disaster that is Antigua), the point of her writing can lie only in its finding a reader whose reading might compensate for what her writing fails to do. This, she says, would be a perfect reader, and indeed she did once know such a perfect reader: William Shawn (her editor and father-in-law). But like Devon, about whom she writes, this perfect reader is now dead, which means that she must write "about the dead for the dead" (197). For, she adds, "I can sooner get used to never hearing from him—the perfect reader—than to not being able to write for him at all" (198).

If that last statement is the measure of Kincaid's desperation, it is also the measure of the anxiety to which we living readers, as inadequate substitutes for the perfect reader, are being "called." In intruding itself into our self-absorbed lives, our protected happiness, Kincaid's writing comes in the guise of an intrusion of the dead (for and about whom she writes, but who cannot read, although they might do so perfectly), an intrusion that the living can scarcely refuse or ignore, even though its purpose is one we definitionally cannot fulfill. *We* must be the perfect reader, able to read what the writing fails to say, and hence at one with the dead; yet we *cannot* be the perfect reader, who is with Devon, among the dead, whereas we are alive. All that we can do, it may be, is to open our reading to an acknowledgment of the otherness to which the writing seeks to give presence without itself having direct access to it, the irretrievable "other family" otherness that taunts and haunts us through Kincaid's writing, to the extent that we recognize it as what we do not know, in the way that the dialect of Antigua haunts Kincaid's own anxious but impeccable English prose. This would *not* be a perfect reading. But it would signal our acceptance of the impossible contract that is proposed to us, in the absence of any ability to carry out its terms. And anxiety would be the sign of the openness to otherness such an acceptance entails. In lieu of perfection, one might call this a hospitable reading, then.

More technically, one might say that the textual mode that defamiliarizes the family is that of allegory, and that it defines the position of the reader as an allegorical reading subject. Definitionally excluded from "solving" the allegory (the disaster that haunts the text might be called colonialism, or AIDS, or death, or the inability to love, or . . .) the reader is invoked by the text in another capacity, which falls short of such perfection: that of realizing (in both senses of the word) the allegorical structure of the text, that is, its readability, and of entering into the allegorical contract while recognizing that it is impossible to fulfill. On the side of the writer, meanwhile, the allegorical mode implies awareness of a corresponding inadequacy: the inability to know that which is nevertheless deeply and intimately familiar to her, and impels her to write. Allegorical writing in this sense radically redefines authorship, which renounces the control of meaning—since "what it means" is what the author does not know—in favor of agencing acts of reading that are as "desperate" in their way as is the writing itself.

There is a moment very early in *My Brother* that allegorizes, in a more conventional sense, such an act of agencing. It is the moment of the untimely, intrusive phone call from Antigua:

> That Thursday night when I heard about *My Brother* through the telephone, from a friend of my mother's because at that moment my mother and I were in a period of not speaking to each other. . . , I was in my house in Vermont, absorbed with the well-being of my children, absorbed with the well-being of my husband, absorbed with the well-being of myself. (6–7)

It is the friend, here, who is the author figure, performing the act of agencing (and not, the point is crucial, speaking "on behalf of" the mother). Kincaid herself is the figure of the reader, while the mother, with whom she is not on speaking terms and whom she is called to call back, is the object of reading. Yet, it is all about a kind of unknown: "my brother." The call finds Kincaid-as-reader plunged into self-absorption, "absorbed with the well-being of my children, absorbed with the well-being of my husband, absorbed with the well-being of myself," living exclusively, as it were, "in Vermont," with no thought of what is other to Vermont. (The hammered-out, somewhat obsessive sentence underscores the obsession and—not coincidentally—typifies the obsessive style of this text.) However, self-absorbed as she is, Kincaid also has foreknowledge of the message that wakens her from absorption:

> When I spoke to this friend of my mother's, she said that there was something wrong with my brother and that I should call my mother to find out

> what it was. I said, What is wrong? She said, Call your mother. I asked her, using those exact words, three times, and three times she replied the same way. And then I said, He has AIDS, and she said, Yes. (7)

The message from her mother, about her brother, that she is invited to read, because it is not delivered to her direct, is one that she can formulate ("He has AIDS") and receive confirmation of ("Yes"), because it is something she already knew but was oblivious of. She does not need now to call her mother, because this message is the reader's message, not that of the agencing friend (who never formulates it) nor of the mother (who presumably is unaware that the reader-agencer interaction is taking place at all). It is the reader's message but a message about the reader's other, which is why the call itself and the anxious, repetitive dialogue, "What is wrong?" "Call your mother"—are indispensable: without them, there would be no awakening from obliviousness. Both a reader's other-oriented attention, drawn by textual redundancy (as a mode of emphasis, the figure here of *agencement* in the sense of "device"), and a text's equally emphatic reticence—its circling anxiously around what it does not, cannot, say—are necessary for the agencing to result in an act of reading, and thus to produce responsiveness, in the reader, to the otherness of which the text is an (allegorical) vehicle.

This means, of course, that for a reader of *My Brother,* the message "Kincaid's brother Devon had AIDS and died of it"—a fair summary of the book's statement, its *énoncé*—is not the equivalent of the message "He has AIDS," but the equivalent of an act of enunciation, the utterance "Call your mother." What the book's phone call to us is about is something both more and other than its stated message, which suffices to wake us from our absorption and to inspire in us the question "What is wrong?" but does not answer that question, except obliquely. The answer depends on our having a foreknowledge of it, and on the foreknowledge that we have (some will respond: colonialism names what is wrong, others AIDS, or death, or the inability to love, or a combination of these and other things); but it is the questioning itself, perhaps ("What is wrong?"), that is primary. Kincaid as reader does not know her "other family," her mother and her half brother, close kin though they be; but she does know that any message about them, interrupting the self-absorption of her Vermont family, any reminder of family otherness, has the significance that something is wrong. A reminder is all it takes.

Whence the importance of the story of the red ants that attacked Devon on the day following his birth, while his mother slept. It is a story about untimeliness, in the form of the premonitory; but for the mother who slept and so has no wish to hear it, it comes, like the phone call to Kincaid from Antigua, as an untimely reminder. In this case, then, the agencer of an untimely intervention is Kincaid herself, who insists as we've seen that she doesn't know the meaning of the story she tells or even whether it has a meaning, it is only something that "a mind like mine"—the mind of an agencer—"would think about." If there is allegory and if the allegory signifies, that is for an interlocutor reader, in this case the mother, to determine.

> One day during his illness, when my mother and I were standing over him, looking at him—he was asleep and so didn't know we were doing so—I reminded my mother of the ants almost devouring him and she looked at me, her eyes narrowing in suspicion, and she said, "What a memory you have!"—perhaps the thing she most dislikes about me. (6)

The brother sleeps, as he did as a baby, but the mother who slept then is awakened, now, by the memory that functions for her as a reminder (for of course she has forgotten), awakened to "suspicion." She has become a reader, and an allegorical reading subject—but *she* is not a hospitable reader: she fends off the act of recognition and the anxiety that both accompanies and signals it, by turning it back on the agencer-author in the form of an implied accusation. Why are you stirring up those forgotten red ants again, when all I wanted was to be left in my protective "self-absorption"?

In this respect she reminds me more than a bit, need I say, of those students of mine, in the fall of 1996, who recognized something in their texts (or at least glimpsed it) that they didn't wish to acknowledge, and protected themselves by blaming the agencer, me. In a way they were the best students I ever had: the honesty of their defensive response, the tenacity with which they fought back, attested to the power of the texts and the sensitivity of their reading of them. But nothing in their culture, including the expensive education they were receiving at my institution, had prepared them to understand the sense in which good reading always entails a degree of hospitality to otherness and sometimes—as in the presence of the writing of disaster—demands a considerable effort of that kind. Everything they knew taught them, instead, to be self-protective; and in that respect—because I failed either to acknowledge their need to protect themselves or to help them overcome it—I failed them too.

Hospitality

To be the agencer of the defamiliarizing of family, then, is to risk drawing self-protective hostility on oneself, for such defamiliarizing is synonymous with the agencing of disaster. For agencing of this kind to work, special conditions must be observed, both on the side of the agencing and—the focus of my present concern—on that of its reception. There must be a certain "etiquette" or sense of style (chapter 2), an art of figuration on the side of the agencing, as we have seen at some length in this book. But also, on the side of reading, a certain openness is called for, some fissure in the armor of self-protection, and even willingness to risk self-exposure. Writers of witnessing texts regularly gamble on finding readers so disposed, as we have seen; and I've suggested that such a predisposition on the part of readers must be the sign of an unrecognized hauntedness, on their part, that an appropriately conceived act of agencing can cause them to acknowledge.

If such is the case, then, there must always be, in addition to the defensive and repressive response of hostility, another factor that is in play, however virtually, in the act of reading, a factor that might be called a disposition to hospitality. It is more than an accident of etymology (the closeness, in certain declined forms, of Latin *hospes,* a host or a guest, and *hostis,* an enemy or a stranger) that links hostility and hospitality. Hostility and hospitality are complementary ways of "noticing" what is culturally other, closing the door on it in one case, opening the door in the other. Kincaid's mother in the instance of the red ants, and my students in the class that so resisted AIDS writing, could be said, then, to have demonstrated a kind of initial "opening of the door" of recognition—a momentary hospitality—quickly followed by its slamming shut, in a hostile refusal of hospitality to the evidence of disasters. The task of the witness, and of the educator, then, is to find a way of fostering and strengthening the disposition to hospitality, so that—in Derrida's metaphor, itself derived from Klossowski (chapter 1)—the door, once opened even a crack, remains open. Hospitality is governed, as Derrida (1997) and others point out, by a blanket law, prescribing openness to the other in all its forms. But at the same time many restrictive laws, of more local application, supplement the primary law and limit its applicability by proposing criteria that distinguish between potential guests thought eligible to receive hospitality and those regarded as beyond the pale and hence legitimately excludable. It is these secondary laws that govern the hostility or the hospitality accorded to the recognition of disaster. Testimonial writers and teachers of testimonial seek therefore to maximize the applicability of the law of universal hospitality in favor of the alien, the obscene, the disastrous, *against* the apparently automatic and often inflexible application of local laws that define the object of their testimonial (say AIDS, the Holocaust, or trench warfare) as—precisely—disastrous, obscene, and alien, hence excludable. And the rhetorical techniques of agencing that I've identified in preceding chapters can be understood, then, as so many appeals, ways of "calling" to the disposition to hospitality that is latent whenever a *hostis* (a virtual *hospes*) is perceived. (Notice, then, that it is to the *recognition* of disaster that hostility or hospitality is extended, not to disaster per se.)

For hospitality is a two-way street, a cooperative enterprise—something that is indicated by the semantics of *hospes,* still alive in French *hôte* and other Romance derivatives that refer both to a host and a guest. The situation described as an act of hospitality is not simply a matter of tolerance and welcome on the part of the host. The situation of hospitality is not fully controlled by either the host or the guest because hospitality, with its famous laws, governs what counts as appropriate behavior, not only on the part of the host but also on the part of the guest. It is the regulation of an interaction—or to put it another way, it is the name of a genre. One could even be tempted to say that hospitality *epitomizes* the workings of genre, so clear is it that in the case of hospitality, the "seduction" (Lyotard's word) or the enchantment that genre exercises over the participants is the product of conditions of negotiability that make for instability and flexibility "on the terrain," however much it may seem in theory to be a matter of regulation and of laws. For in hospitality, it is global flexibility with respect to laws and conventions that is generically recommended, both to the host (who does not know the conventions, including those of hospitality, subscribed to by the guest) and to the guest (who, symmetrically, is definitionally unaware of the conventions, including those of hospitality, subscribed to by the host). Each is enjoined to make the situation "work," in the absence of strict specification of what that injunction entails, which in turn means that each needs to be sensitive to a semiotics of indexicality, entailing a disposition to read as meaningful signs that may appear unconventional or anomalous and to interpret them as otherness speaking in the absence of more conventionally appropriate means of expression.

But this observation itself makes it clear that hospitality, if it epitomizes genre, is a peculiar genre in one respect. Its laws begin to apply *only* in circumstances where there is some degree of doubt, distrust, or uncertainty concerning the equal availability to both participants—who thereby become "host" and "guest"—of an array of other genres, held in common, genres that might more conventionally subserve the purposes of social interaction. Stereotypically, such a situation arises when there is interaction between subjects of different culture on the home terrain of one of them. But hospitality can arise even between, say, two close, long-term friends who have a very large array of genres in common, when (for example) one is invited into the home of the other. This is because prototypically hospitality is a recognition of the phenomenon of "home turf," that is of the protected domain of the familiar, with the particular set of conventions, and more particularly of exclusions, that themselves define the "homely" as the area of the not-strange ("strange" being from *extraneus*) and simultaneously ensure its hauntedness, its unrecognized openness to the un-homely, the *unheimlich.* Hospitality arises, precisely, when an exception is made to the exclusionary rules that define the familiar, which means that *for both parties,* host and guest, it is necessarily a defamiliarizing phenomenon: the genre of special cases, peculiar circumstances, and the particular.

In this light, it becomes easy to see why hospitality is of "particular" relevance to testimonial, and to the agencing whereby testimonial writing seeks to gain a hearing for—to introduce, but without domesticating—that which is ideologically excluded from the definition of culture as civilization, that is, the obscene, the alien, the disastrous, all that is both obscured by the familiar and hauntingly present, like the "other family" in the family, within it. Hospitality is the genre that pertains to the negotiations that constitute acts of witnessing because it is the genre that recommends flexibility and adaptability—indeed a certain amount of improvisation and making do—when, in the presence of what is alien to them, familiar genres fail.

But here is where the difference between a witness and a teacher becomes plain. The witness is placed by the rules of hospitality in the position of a guest, who must demonstrate the flexibility prescribed to the stranger in the presence of a host. I've called that flexibility agencing, and identified figuration as the name of the etiquette it practices, an art of the particular. To be a teacher of witnessing texts, though, is not so much to be either a guest or a host as it is to mediate relations of hospitality between text and reader, primarily by teaching the responsibilities of hostliness to inexperienced or apprentice readers. Such readers are immature to the extent that, for them, the protectedness of family/the familiar is understood to exclude their participating in acts of hospitality, notably in the role of host—a role usually assigned to the head of the household and so naturally associated with adulthood. They thus define themselves as children, and teaching involves weaning them from such a self-protective and self-limiting definition of subjectivity to one of more hospitable openness that implies a recognition of maturity on their part. That is, they need to acquire a certain flexibility, a willingness to suspend conventional rules under particular circumstances—one of these being, of course, that they observe a corresponding guestly hospitality on the part of the texts. They need to learn how and when to take the risk of "exposing" the familiar—of exposing it, not to a fleeting glimpse but to an open-door recognition of its other. And I've suggested that the process of defamiliarizing the family, of uncovering the family's own strangeness to itself—a process for which models are furnished by texts like *The Hurry-Up Song* and *My Brother*—would be a valuable first step in this apprenticeship to openness, helping to convert student readers from defensively hostile positions to those of hospitality.

However, in reading generally and in reading witnessing writing in particular, one cannot stop at saying that the reader should act as a kind of host toward a guestlike text. Reading is better described as a practice that demonstrates the fungibility of the host and guest positions. As a practice of hospitality it produces a kind of unstable equivalence, a relation of mutual exchange, between a hostly reader, whose hospitality, however, takes the form of adapting, like a guest, to the text's conventions (as though *they,* in this case, formed the home ground on which the interaction occurs), and a guestly text whose acknowledged home-base status combined with its openness to reading makes it, in turn, a kind of host. To learn to extend hospitality to a text, as a host to a guest, is to learn the responsibilities of a guest, which are to accord the other—in this case the text—the respect due to a host. We might say, then, that if it is the existence of a threshold—a dividing line that joins—that separates, and so defines, host and guest (that is, the familiar and the alien, the conventional and the obscene), reading as a practice of hospitality seeks not to favor either side of the threshold but to take up extended residence on the threshold itself. (It's a bit like house cats who, while you *hold the door open,* prefer to linger on the threshold rather than go out into the cold.)

To linger is to dwell, a word that seems etymologically connected to ideas of duality, doubleness, and duplicity; to dwell on the threshold, whether in the sense of inhabiting it or in the sense of emphasizing it or expatiating on it, is to explore an experience of doubleness as one that combines dividedness or split—that, say, of the familiar and the unfamiliar—with relationality and continuity. We have seen in preceding chapters that such an effect of asyndeton is sought by numerous testimonial texts. In *Facing It,* using a vocabulary of mourning and of the death of the author, I described the reading of AIDS diaries as a marking of the difference between dying and surviving—a marking that is both a remarking or observing of it and a benchmarking of it, creating a relation of continuity between writerly inadequacy in the face of death and readerly anxiety at the evidence of disaster. Here I have spoken of a similar relay, in which survivor witnesses take up and carry the burden of the dead, the burden of their hauntedness, and transfer it, through reading, to those who had not, until then, recognized that their own lives were also haunted. Thus threshold experience, in the perspective of the reader, is the experience of recognizing one's hauntedness, and of holding open the door to the haunt. And the teacher's task in this respect is to help inexperienced readers learn, not only to *make* that act of recognition but also to *dwell* on the threshold, holding open the door.

The symbolic place of hospitable reading in this sense is thus the hospital, a place in which one dwells on the threshold that separates and joins, as in a stammer, life and death, the familiar and the disastrous. And if that is so, the question, as I've said, is how to make apprentice readers' classroom experience less like their imagined family, a place of protection, and more like a hospital, a place of dual hospitality that receives the living but is open to death. Etymologically, the adjectival form from *hospes, hospitalis,* seems to have become substantivized over time so as to refer to alternative homes or dwellings available to those without a roof. Thus the hostelry offers commercial hospitality to homeless travelers, while the hospice is a place of charitable hospitality for those without a home in which to die (that is, according to a venerable tradition, in which to play host to death while becoming, in turn, death's guest). Even modern hospitals, although they are no longer frequented solely by the indigent, have retained something of this threshold quality, facing toward life and facing toward death, that makes the distinction of host and guest somewhat moot. If they serve as gatekeeping institutions for civil society, keeping death at bay, it is at the price of becoming, like Craiglockhart in *Regeneration* (chapter 3) or the hospitals in *Hospital Time* (chapter 6), prominent sites of witness, where the living are confronted, not just occasionally and fleetingly, but daily and permanently, with the evidence of disaster. Death is not only at the door, but the door is also open. And before 1996 (in the West), this was nowhere more the case than in AIDS wards. (It is still the case, horrifyingly so, in much of the rest of the world.)

Hospitals, then, are places that seem uniquely suited to figuring hospitable reading as a relation of mutual openness, baffling the definitions of host and guest, between life, with the conventions that define it as protected from intrusion, and the permanent threat of disaster, in the awareness of which one dwells. As sites of witness, testifying to disaster, they are available also as places of initiation, where the living might encounter the signs of disaster and learn, not to dismiss them, but to read them. There seems to be no good word in English to describe hospitality in this sense of dual openness that is required by the recognition of disaster. In French, however, the verb *accompagner,* "to accompany," along with its derivatives *(accompagnement, accompagnateur)* has expanded its semantic range since the late 1980s, so as to express hospitable sentiments, on the part of those lucky enough to be not directly touched, toward victims of social extremity, such as the unemployed or the homeless, and others in dire circumstances, including PWAs. (Indeed, the pressure of the epidemic appears to have been in part responsible for this linguistic development.) It translates ideas like "helping out" (cf. "buddying" in the English-speaking HIV/AIDS world), "dealing with" problems or emergencies, or less actively, just "being there" for people, or even feeling a minimum of compassion for them and concern for their fate. At one end of this extended semantic spectrum, this currently (late nineties) popular buzzword functions as a hypocritical alibi for indifference (hence, perhaps, its popularity); but at the other end, it *might* almost be pressed into service to describe the sort of threshold-dwelling hospitality of reading I am trying to evoke. I say "almost," though, because in ordinary parlance, *accompagner* refers exclusively to relations between human subjects (not to phenomena like the relationality of reading and writing, familiarity and disaster, life and death in which I'm interested); and indeed *accompagnement* is normally extended in a top-down, not even a host-guest, way that, to an observer such as myself, seems condescending and often even insulting to its beneficiaries. Companionship, in English, is a more egalitarian and communitarian idea—and one interestingly linked to hospitality through the etymology of commensality or bread-sharing that it shares with *accompagner*—but it does not imply a context of extremity as *accompagner* does.

I wasn't therefore disposed to end this chapter, and the book it concludes, with a reading of René de Ceccatty's *L'Accompagnement,* planning instead more developed and detailed readings of *The Hurry-Up Song* and, more particularly, *My Brother.* As my 1998 article on accompaniment will attest, I had not really seen this book's relevance to my interest in teaching hospitable reading, that is, the fact that Ceccatty is actually extending in his book the already extended semantics of the verb *accompagner* in a way that makes it interestingly resonant with the problematics of hospitable reading, viewed from the perspective of the reader as a potentially initiatory experience. But then two things happened. The author wrote to me, pointing out that in my article I was misreading a key passage. And in the summer of 2000 I taught *L'Accompagnement* as part of another course on witnessing literature, one in which I found myself marveling at the smoothness I had acquired since 1996—my art of litotes, in its etymological sense—in introducing testimonial texts in the classroom context. Things had been going so well in this course that I was worried; the students seemed so open to the texts that I feared I had made hospitality too easy for them, to the detriment of everything that makes the texts troublesome and intrusive, untimely interventions. And maybe that is so; some of them actually thanked me for having included Delbo's *Auschwitz and After,* which they had read in Delbo's French and experienced as deeply troubling.

When it came to reading *L'Accompagnement,* these students immediately recognized that, whereas we had been reading "survival" narratives, this was a narrative of "survivorhood," one that enacted a kind of allegory of their own experience as apprentice readers of testimonial writing. (For the survival/survivorhood distinction, see chapters 5 and 6.) The narrator of *L'Accompagnement* responds to an unexpected appeal that involves him, willy-nilly, in the drama of hospital/ity, as the main "accompanying" witness to the death from AIDS of a friend; the appeal, Ceccatty says, is one that cannot be refused, yet it can't be accepted either without bad faith, since what is asked of him—to describe his friend's dying agony in the hospital—is what only the dying man could legitimately do. This, the typical dilemma of surviving witnesses who know that the true witnesses are those who have died, the students recognized as a version, also, of their own relation to witnessing texts of all kinds, bad faith very much included. They were asked to "accompany" a disaster as if it were their own. Their reading, then, I realized, was not untinged with anxiety. But also, it was clear to all that Ceccatty's style, which deploys euphemism, preterition, litotes, and other forms of "klassische Dämpfung"—Leo Spitzer's term for the discreet, muted style of French "classical" tragedy, so respectful of *bienséance* and the sensibilities of its audience (which by coincidence some of the students were studying in another class)—was analogous to the smoothness of my own teacherly style. In discussing this style—did it mute the pain? or did it intensify it?—we were able to address, indirectly, my teaching as the students had experienced it. And somewhat to my surprise, I found, again, that for a number of students the class counted as one that had "changed" them. It had been, they said, or more often implied, quite intense; it left them feeling "weird." Without quite realizing it, and by contrast with the disastrous class of 1996, I had been initiating these students into an attitude of hospitality that made them responsive to—not dismissive or afraid of—texts that bore witness to disaster. Because I had "accompanied" their apprenticeship with some care, they were readier to "accompany" Ceccatty's own difficult hospital apprenticeship into disaster.

So Ceccatty's strong implication, in *L'Accompagnement,* that the experience of hospital/ity is initiatory, a wandering in a labyrinthine threshold space, the hospital, that is the "architecture given to death," had immediate resonance for me, not least because it is also strongly implied that the initiate, in accepting the impossible contract imposed by his friend, had agreed to become an initiator in turn, by writing (of) the other's death. That is, his book, assembled like a labyrinth (hospital) and veiling its secrets the better to reveal them, was itself modeling the act of testimonial as an initiation, directed toward its readers. The relation of initiator and initiate, their mutual substitutability, was a version of the relation of mutual (host-guest) openness that hospitality becomes in the presence, through reading, of disaster. But it was one that had relevance, I realized, not solely to the text-reader relation I, as a teacher, was attempting to foster, but also to my own mediating position, between testimonial texts and apprentice readers. Very much an initiate in relation to the texts, I was an initiator in relation to the students.

In Greek, the candidate for initiation was called *mystes.* So the role of the teacher as initiate-initiator did not imply solely the defamiliarization of the familiar and the revelation of its inherent strangeness and hauntedness, that is, an act of de-myst-ification, or negative initiation. It implied also a corresponding positive initiation, a re-myst-ification, which could only be conceived as a familiarizing process, making accessible that which it was for my student readers to recognize, in this case the reality of disaster. Teaching apprentice readers the form of hospitality that made them open to testimonial texts meant learning from the texts something like their own art of hospitality, that is, the way they made themselves open, as initiators, to reading, their art of agencing as an act of hospitality. It was a matter of "giving" an architecture to death, constructing it as an alternative home, like a hospital, so as to make it a place of some familiarity, in which it is possible to dwell, so that students might enter without apprehension, as guests, and in becoming initiates prepare themselves to act, on other occasions, as initiators in their turn.

That I turn now to French texts, then, after exploring the defamiliarization of family in American writing, is not entirely coincidental. France in particular, and more generally the major countries of the European Union, have experienced the postcolonial era, both culturally and politically, as a crisis of hospitality, and a large body of writing has appeared in French in recent years around the issue of immigration, viewed as a question of hospitality.[4] Little of this writing, it is true, acknowledges the parallel issue of AIDS and people with AIDS, although there is a striking similarity between the inhospitality (not to say hostility) generated in France by immigration and that experienced by AIDS people, especially during the 1980s, at a time when there was little in the way of community support to mitigate, as in many English-speaking countries, the effects of governmental neglect and public fear. It is as if the emergence of a discourse of accompaniment in France in the late 1980s and early 1990s—with all the ambiguities inherent in the vast semantic range the term acquired—was a compensatory mechanism for the absence of a sense of hospital/ity, one that Ceccatty was able to inflect in his book in the direction of a certain kind of community, that of the initiated. That his conception of hospital/ity therefore entails the teaching of hospitality—and understands teaching in turn as a hospitable practice—makes a rather pointed comment on the absence of such teaching around him. But it also serves my own project in this chapter, of understanding the teaching of testimonial writing as an education in hospitality, and an education in hospitality as a demystification of the protectively familiar that entails a complementary remystification of the alien, as well as of the danger it supposedly represents.

An Architecture Given to Death

> Henceforth all I could do was see and describe. And wherever I went, whatever I did, I would be the bearer of this message of death.
>
> —René de Ceccatty, *L'Accompagnement*

Untimely Interventions

I've always been certain—otherwise I wouldn't write—that literature is not a screen to conceal reality, however dramatic the reality may be, however unsayable its horror. Literature reveals reality, and extends it. It is our only strength.

—René de Ceccatty, *L'Accompagnement*

Accueillir l'étranger, il faut bien que ce soit aussi éprouver son intrusion.

—Jean-Luc Nancy, *L'Intrus*

[Welcoming a stranger is also necessarily an experience of intrusion.]

In French farce, the genre perfected at the turn of the century by Georges Feydeau, there is regularly a large double bed at center stage in the second act: the plot revolves, almost literally, around the hospitality of this bed, that is, to whom its hospitality has been, is being, and will be extended. This, the comedy of adultery, is the essence of "domestic" comedy, the comedy of family, as the boulevard understands it. In Copi's *Une visite inopportune* (1988), though, what occupies center stage throughout the action is a narrow hospital bed.[5] For if this is a sex farce, which it is, its implications are metaphysical: Feydeau plus Copi (and a good dash of Molière, with more than a hint of Ionesco), the whole camped up with zany humor and queenly wit. Although it is about sex, it is also about AIDS and death, the archetypal unwelcome visitor of the title. And it is about hospitality—the hospitality to be extended to an untimely intruder.

Cyrille is celebrating his second anniversary—that of the onset of his symptoms—with a slap-up feast (roast beef and sorbet) for a motley group of guests that includes his nurse, his doctor, a long-term admirer (perhaps companion) named Hubert, and a cute but dumb young journalist come to interview him, with whom Cyrille intermittently flirts. The various ins and outs of the sex plot need not detain us: it is Feydeau speeded up into a racy romp. In the middle of the celebration, though, as so often in farce (a genre that thrives on untimely intrusions), an unexpected guest turns up. It is none other than Regina Morti, the famous diva—her name (neither good Italian nor good Latin, and deriving perhaps from Regina Coeli, the Roman prison) is readily translated by Cyrille as Queen of the Dead. Although she is uninvited, no one has trouble recognizing her, and the farce turns momentarily into its close cousin: grand opera. The effect is a little as if the Queen of the Night (from *Zauberflöte*) had turned up in the middle of the party scene in *Don Giovanni*—a scene of hospitality and sexuality to which producers like, however, to add a few premonitory thunderclaps on occasion. No wonder the newcomer wonders what theater she has turned up in.

Communicating largely in coloratura and libretto Italian, Regina M. proceeds to make a real nuisance of herself, alternately vamping the male characters (death, it seems, is heterosexual) and threatening the lives of all with a carving knife (shades of *Tosca*) snatched from the roast. They resort to various stratagems to "deal with" the intrusion (i.e., to "accompany" it in one of those extended senses of the verb *accompagner* that were becoming fashionable around the time of Copi's death). The surgeon tries a brain transfusion, and later invites her to accompany him on his research trip to Africa, showing up for the purpose in full White Hunter tropical rig. Hubert gallantly tries to seduce her into a shopping trip to pick up some sexy underwear in Pigalle. The nurse shoots her in a fit of jealous rage: not only is she going off with the doctor, with whom the nurse has had her own adventures, but Regina M. has a higher score of deaths than the nurse's, much higher. The Queen of the Dead survives all these attempts to get her offstage, back into the wings, where the obscene belongs.

For obviously it is for Cyrille that she has come, and their reconciliation—for Cyrille, he says, has heretofore "given women a wide berth"—is just around the corner. Each of them fakes death so that they can be alone together; then she and Cyrille die for good, in a campy *Liebestod,* after which they set off happily for the luxurious mausoleum Hubert has fitted out for Cyrille in Père-Lachaise ("right opposite Oscar Wilde and a step away from Montherlant"). It is exactly five in the afternoon, "las cinco al punto de la tarde," as Hubert (speaking Spanish so that we won't miss the allusion) points out. So the last guest at Cyrille's celebration, which is also Copi's textual party, is Lorca, who—with Wagner, perhaps—is also the most thematically cogent of them all. The "Lament for Ignacio Sánchez Mejías" is, of course, being spoofed here along with all the rest; but perhaps too it is being invoked in "deadly" earnest? Life's best defense against the unwanted guest? Copi knows that it doesn't lie in trying to get her offstage but in a certain kind of hospitality: an affirmation of the continuity of life and death, of the possibility even of their sexual connection. In Georges Bataille's famous definition, eroticism is the affirmation of life even unto death; for Cyrille, the equivalent turns out to be an affirmation of gayness even unto heterosexuality. For nothing is separate, nothing is protected. "To isolate death from life," Jean-Luc Nancy intones a bit too sententiously for the present context, "not to allow them to interweave closely each with the other, each intruding into the other's very heart—that's what one should never do" (*L'Intrus,* 23).

René de Ceccatty's vision is not essentially different from Copi's, Bataille's, or Nancy's, although his tone, in *L'Accompagnement,* is more solemn than Copi's and for him it is writing ("la littérature")—another form of hospitality—that is our "only strength," through which life reconciles itself with death. Literature, he writes, is seeing and describing, that is all we can do (40). Furthermore, it entails a strong dose of self-deception and "bad faith," it is a confidence trick (12). But it nevertheless reveals reality instead of veiling it, keeping it under wraps; it does not separate death from life but allows them to interweave (14). The story he tells in his memoir can be read, therefore, as the story of a coming to writing, as *what can be done:* how to manage, in the face of the untimely visitor Blanchot called disaster; how to deal with it or "accompany" it, what form of hospitality it can be offered.

The author-narrator's dying friend, also a writer—he is unnamed, but can be plausibly identified as Gilles Barbedette—invites René to see and describe what, as the friend points out, has never been described by anyone on their own behalf—the "final struggle against death in the hospital" (11). What can be done, in other words, is to bear witness by seeing and describing; that is, to write and hence to reveal. But witnessing itself is a matter of relay: "I knew that the place he assigned me was the one he had occupied beside his own dying friend" (85). So seeing and describing is also a way of leading others to see and describe, to bear witness in their turn. And as we've seen (chapter 6), the "dual autobiography," which supplements conventional autobiography's inability to incorporate the death of the autobiographer, is a model of this dynamics of relay, and hence of the hospitality through writing that is owed to death and disaster. So I am tempted to rewrite Ceccatty's axiom about literature and to say that our sole strength, *notre seule force,* is the ability of humans to relay one another in the witnessing of disaster.

Contrary to what is the case in most dual autobiographies, however (Amy Hoffman's *Hospital Time* being also something of an exception), the relay relation in this case does not derive from a close intimacy, already established between the one who dies and the one who writes; and accordingly the responsibility of relay is accepted by René with some reluctance and considerable misgiving. This is why so many of my students, in 2000, recognized themselves in him. By Hoffman's criterion—distinguishing those who know the "AIDS language" from those who don't—he is an outsider, confused and baffled by test results, opportunistic infections, drugs and treatments, everything that, by contrast, his friend is so conversant with. Although one may guess that he is probably, but not necessarily, homosexual, we have to assume, in the absence of explicit information about either his sexuality or his serum status, that he is HIV-negative; and indeed he speculates that his friend has chosen him, in part because he has a flexible schedule, but partly also because of his very lack of involvement in the event of his friend's death: "He was counting on my coldness and serenity, maybe even my indifference," he writes, adding only: "I was simultaneously less indifferent and less *disponible* (available) than he believed" (20). As an AIDS outsider, then, he worries, in the way that most witnesses do (but with more justification), about his bona fides as a witness: "I shall try not to abuse the confidence placed in me although to write in his stead strikes me as a first abuse in itself, and I know I'll have to be constantly exorcizing that feeling, whether or not it is justified" (12). Not for him, then, the quiet and relatively spontaneous assumption of relay responsibilities that one finds in, say, Paul Monette, who knows that he and Roger were and are one person. Rather he stands much closer to "us"—where "we" are assumedly readers not closely involved in or touched by the epidemic, reader-outsiders—than to the friend whose death, he knows, will not radically affect the course of his life. Yet he does shoulder the burden, misgivings and all. After all, as people say, and as he repeats (perhaps more than a little dubiously?) in his last sentence, is not "death the same for all"?

This final sentence, implying that he regards his narrative as allegorical, gives us the key, however, both to what ultimately grounds René's otherwise dubious exercise in witnessing, the kind of position he understands himself to occupy vis-à-vis his friend—and to the position implicitly assigned to his readers. He, René, has undergone an *initiation* in the hospital. As an outsider, he has been guided by his friend and others through the pathways of dying, "accompanied" by them as, in ancient belief, the souls of the dying were conducted into death by the "psychopomp" (one of the names of Hermes). In this way he has first learned, before setting out to describe. But having taken on the task of describing, the former initiate is now acting as an initiator in turn, so that for his readers, who become René's *mystes,* guided ("accompanied") by him as he had been guided by his dying friend, the narrative of his experience becomes an initiatory narration in its own right: the equivalent for us readers of his own transformative experience. In the role of writer, the former guest, having been taken into the initiatory space of the hospital, becomes a host in his turn. Which, by the logic of relay, implies that we readers too will eventually, despite our own misgivings, shoulder the responsibility of bearing witness, in our own way and with the means of seeing and describing available to us. Receiving the hospital's initiatory hospitality implies extending that hospitality in turn, because "death is the same for all, people say" (132). It is what we most have in common, as writing is our only strength.

This does not mean that, as an outsider become initiator, René can claim insider status. Rather he has become a kind of teacher, the teacher of a certain dubious, in-bad-faith, confidence-trick insiderness. And we who are his students are being inducted into what René, like the "ignorant schoolmaster" of whom Jacques Rancière has written, teaches without really knowing. But teaching without really knowing is not a bad definition of what the allegorist, the agencer does; it is what the teacher, the writer, and the witness have in common, the "bad faith" they share, even though most witnesses (writers) know disaster more intimately than most teachers. With respect to disaster, no one in a position to communicate—to see and describe—is in a position to see and describe from within. Some are closer, much closer, to that position than others, but all survivors are wrong-footed in this way by disaster which, it seems, *must* be borne witness to—but also can *only* be "borne witness to"—precisely because, to those who survive, it cannot be truly known. At best, we can only be conducted into its vicinity. Since however there are no outsiders who are not also in some sense survivors, there are none, also, who are not potentially open to being drawn, by the operation of hospitality, into the position of in-bad-faith insiderness that is the position of the initiate-witness in the way that René is drawn into it; open to being "contaminated," that is, in the sense Thierry Mingot has in mind when, as a PWA, he says his goal is "to contaminate the whole world. But not in the way you fear" (*Felicitá,* 106).

René has accompanied his friend to the hospital on three previous occasions, each of which he will describe in the central chapters of his narrative. But it is only on the occasion of his friend's fourth and final hospitalization, his account of which frames the inner chapters, that he begins to grasp the hospitality of the hospital in the sense of being drawn into its logic of host-guest relay, and becoming "contaminated." The hospital's AIDS clinic is open at night, so that consultations and treatments will not impinge too badly on the patients' daily lives, allowing them a certain sense of normalcy. On his arrival with his friend, René, who has not previously visited the clinic, discovers in it an atmosphere of cordiality, complicity, and clandestinity—that is, of myst-ery—that leads him to compare it with an underground Resistance cell during the Occupation (25). But the atmosphere is also that of a subdued party: a young woman offers the newcomers a crêpe; the doctor himself (on the evidence, for he too is unnamed, it is Dr. Willy Rozenbaum)[6] comes up to welcome them. "His tone was elegant and sociable [*mondain*]. I had to be introduced" (26). Since the friend regards the doctor as *his* valid interlocutor, that is, initiator, in his struggle with death, his *agonie,* this is a crucial moment, fraught with implications of relay. For René immediately grasps "the complexity of the relation" between his friend and the physician (27), while the doctor in turn sees that René is himself a candidate for initiation, and hence his future interlocutor when the friend will no longer be able to speak for himself, and René will replace him in the complex and intimate relation of the initiate to his own initiator's initiator.

Meanwhile, however, René is conscious of being relegated to a minor role as nurses and aides, like so many psychopomps, guide his friend and himself through the hallways and take charge of the admission process. It is the friend, not he, who has the leading role—one he will perform with all the vanity and susceptibility of a diva, and from René's secondary (or accompanying) vantage point, the life of the hospital seems unreal, a mere simulation. This has to do in particular with the fact that his friend's intimacy with the doctor—the only person with whom he knowledgeably discusses test results and treatment options—excludes René from anything like a "direct" relation to the experience of death his friend is living through ("direct relation" being in any case a contradiction in terms). For, ceasing to be a caregiver, the doctor is now already in the role of "death's messenger" (28) , while it is the friend who continues to be René's guide and mentor. Although René is "accompanying" his friend to the hospital, supporting him in the secondary role of an assistant, the friend, in other words—in the role of principal, closer to death because closer to the doctor than he—is also accompanying (guiding) him, "knowing the time had come to send me out as a scout, an interpreter, to build a bridge toward death" (28). Ultimately, then, "I was enthroned," René concludes (28), "to dialogue with death, through the doctor." But the moment for this "direct" dialogue has not yet come, for it seems that to approach death is to move through a chain of mediatory figures, each (including the doctor himself) in a guestlike relation to death but each able, also, to play host—in lieu of death itself—to those further down the chain. It is this chain of mediation and relay—of seeing and describing—that constitutes humans' best response to disaster, and "our only strength."

René's moment will come, then, many pages later, when the friend's condition has worsened to the point where he is so close to death itself—not death's "messengers"—that the space of dialogue with the principal messenger of death is freed and can be occupied by a new interlocutor. Encountering the doctor in a hallway, René reintroduces himself—unnecessarily, as it turns out (but in hospital, he says, everyone clings to their social identity, so manifestly is it threatened by death). The two agree to talk later the same day. "For the first time I was in direct relation with my friend's disease; he was no longer filtering it" (101). But the conversation, when it happens, turns out in fact not to be about disease, but about easing the friend's dying, indeed hastening his death. "I wanted to let him know," René reports, "that I was his interlocutor, in case there was a decision to make. The conversation revolved around this pious euphemism" [Il s'agissait de tourner autour de cette litote] (107). The conversation, that is, is periphrastic: it circles around something that goes unnamed, although there is no doubt about what it refers to. ("What had I done," René will ask a little later, "if not authorize the doctor in [my friend's] name to have recourse to euthanasia?" [109] .) To dialogue with death through the doctor is not to know death, then, in the sense in which the friend is coming to know it. Rather it is to learn that language refers to death only at a remove, and by virtue of pious phrasing and euphemistic "turns" around which speakers circle. It is to be initiated, but not so much into death, the ultimate unknown, as into the character—allusive, euphemistic, and semiclandestine—of the initiatory dialogue, a dialogue that refers to disaster, but only by circling around something that is euphemized (euthanasia) and itself stands in for something (death) that goes unsaid.

As if in confirmation of this lesson, a second conversation, again replete with euphemisms and understatements, takes place a little later, on the very day of the friend's death:

> Our friend [this is a third party, not the dying man] and I were left standing in the hallway, silent. The doctor came out and said: "It's the end. He's exhausted. He will die in a matter of hours." And I came up with this stupid question: "But what can be done? Can we help him?" . . . He looked at me with an imperceptible hesitation and said: "But we're already seeing to it" [Mais nous l'accompagnons déjà]. (124)

The question "What can be done?" is like the question "Who's there?" or "What's left?" These are the "stupid" questions that arise when one becomes aware of disaster, and thus they define aftermath. *L'Accompagnement* answers René's question in exactly the way it is answered here, a trifle impatiently, by the doctor: accompanying is what can be done. The passage is thus a crucial one, because it defines access to the initiatory dialogue (accompaniment) as *itself* the object of the initiatory quest, death and disaster forming rather the context in which the dialogue occurs and, in that sense only, its referent. We do not have to understand disaster in order to be responsive, as survivors, to its consequences for one another, we do not have to know death in order to be able to teach one another to die. So it is important that this is the passage I had misread, about which René de Ceccatty took the trouble to write to me. I had (mis)understood the words: "Mais nous l'accompagnons déjà," here translated as "But we're already seeing to it," as evidence that the doctor was washing his hands of responsibility, interpreting his slight hesitation as a sign of professional shame at medicine's defeat by death. Authors' opinions are not necessarily to be accorded automatic authority, of course; but in this case I was clearly wrong.

For the topic of this second conversation, like the first, is something that cannot be spoken of without bad faith: not, as superficially appears, "helping" a dying man by staving off his death, but by helping him to die. Euthanasia, a practice illegal in France although it exists, as in many other countries, in the disguised (euphemized?) form of administering a high-risk dose of morphine to patients dying in great pain, cannot be discussed openly, but—like the practice of initiation that it figures, which is another way of helping people into death—must be shrouded in mystery. One circulates around the litotes, or euphemizing understatement that refers to euthanasia—but euthanasia is itself a sort of litotes that softens the process of dying, as does initiation: something that the whole hospital "circulates" around, tiptoeing about an unmentionable secret at its heart. The conversation with the doctor, about euthanasia, *is* most certainly a conversation about death—death is its ultimate referent, but what the conversation enacts, as an interlocutory utterance, is the practice of initiation as the dialogue of "appeal" and "response," and as the shrouding of death in mystery that, like euthanasia, makes dying easier. The living cannot know death itself—even the doctor is only "death's messenger"—but they *can,* as ignorant schoolmasters, teach one another what it is to live in the environment of death, and so how to die.

I had missed the significance of this passage in two ways: first, by failing to understand the topic of the conversation, but second by failing to notice that like the comment, "II s'agissait de tourner autour de cette litote," referring to the earlier conversation about euthanasia, this conversation also indexes a practice of rhetorical veiling or litotes (etymologically "smoothness") as the mode of initiatory discourse that René is learning from the doctor, or more accurately, is learning from his being admitted to interlocutory status with the doctor—that is, from the situation in relation to disaster that Blanchot (1964) calls *entretien.* In allowing myself to be misled by the practice of litotes, I had defined myself as a poor *mystes,* missing not only the point around which the two conversations turn, but also the further point—the point of the point—that, because its mode is that of litotes, initiatory discourse requires *complicity* (what in French is called the ability to understand *à demi-mot*) on the part of the initiate, who is truly participating in an "entre-tien" that entails, as the only possible response to disaster, a dynamics of betweenness or sociality.

The doctor's response, "Mais nous l'accompagnons déjà," both designates *accompagnement* as the name for initiatory complicity, then, and exemplifies the practice of litotes as that which, at the heart of initiatory discourse, requires the complicity of initiator and initiated, who "turn" together, as in a labyrinth, around understatements of the type used by René ("in case there was a decision to make") and by the physician ("nous l'accompagnons déjà"). So René's initial impression of the nighttime AIDS clinic as a place of hospitality, but also of complicity and clandestinity that felt to him like "entering into contact with a Resistance network" (25), proves not to have been a random analogy. Monette, recall, referred to a conspiracy (chapter 6). In the context of the disaster of AIDS, Ceccatty is pointing to the most salient period in recent French history when disaster could be met (dealt with, managed, *accompagné*) only in the mode of mystery and initiation, under the condition of collusion, *entre-tien,* complicity, understatement, and *à demi-mot.* The reference to the Resistance underscores a historical analogy while foreshadowing René's complicitous conversations with the doctor, suggesting—as Mireille Rosello points out to me—that a name for the kind of hospitality represented by initiation might be "asylum."

And in the sentence, "Il s'agissait de tourner autour de cette litote," it becomes clear, then, that the slightly odd "turn" of phrase, "il s'agissait de . . ." must be given its full force. It means something like: "It was for us," having no other option under the circumstances of disaster, "to circle together around this litotes." Which in turn suggests that a reader of *L'Accompagnement* should look closely, and complicitously, at the implications in this text of its own acts both of "turning" (turning in circles, turning as the mode of figuration) and of "smoothing" (litotes as rhetorical smoothing, and as a figure for initiatory smoothing of the way, the kind of hospitality offered in hospitals to those who, as survivors of disaster, must learn to acknowledge death). If to enter the circle of initiates, as René does, is to have only indirect and removed access to the ultimate object of mystery, and to circle around speech that reveals only by not revealing, we can be attentive to the way his own practice as an initiatory writer—a teacher—conforms to this lesson in indirection and euphemism.

As discursive smoothness, litotes implies not only understatement but also de-emphasis: it is the opposite of hyperbole or exaggeration, but also of emphasis (etymologically inflation) in the sense of overinsistence. As underinsistence, it is a way of mentioning something crucial, but in such a way that it may well escape notice (as my misreading demonstrated), unless the interlocutor is alert to the signs. And if the litotes around which René and the doctor circle in their two conversations lies in words like *make a decision* in the first case, or *help* and *accompany* in the second, all referring to euthanasia and thus ultimately, the friend's death, what these conversations themselves enact for us, as their readers, is less a litotes per se than something more like a periphrasis (a way of phrasing that turns "around" something unnamed). And periphrasis, like litotes, shares with preterition (Latin *praeter-ire,* going in front) a de-emphasizing function that allows something to be mentioned without the appearance of its having been alluded to other than accidentally or in passing. The most frequent form of preterition consists of bypassing something by mentioning that one is not mentioning it, for example, "I'll not detain you today by discussing X, but move on immediately to Y." That is, by "going out of one's way" not to emphasize X, one de-emphasizes it in an "emphatic" (unnecessary, inflated) way, thus presencing what is supposed to be absent and acknowledging it as important through the very act of bypassing it. To bypass something in such a way is to acknowledge it.

So, along with the various figures discussed in earlier chapters, we might identify preterition, finally, as another of the key figural modes of testimonial writing. It too is an operation of agencing that recruits the attention of readers for something other and more than what the "I" of the text takes responsibility for saying. But it does so in a way less up-front and confrontational than, say prosopopoeia, the mask-making that permits the dead to speak, and more insinuating and infiltrational than Michaels's impudent syllepsis (chapter 2), or asyndetic rhetorical practices, which as we have seen (chapters 5, 6, 7) tend to function epidictically and to flaunt their hauntedness. What asyndetic writing "displays" (without explanation or argument), preterition acknowledges by "playing it down." It has an element of equivocation that makes it akin to de Duve's deployment of apostrophe (chapter 4).

If that is so, then the restrained style of Ceccatty's writing, its mutedness, is not simply an authorial quirk, although it may also be that. It is a vehicle of agencing that makes his book itself an act of preterition, grounded in figures like litotes and periphrasis. In particular, the text's odd chariness about naming people and things, its way of mentioning without particularizing the friend, the friend's disease, his doctor, various Parisian hospitals, and so forth (all of which can readily be identified)[7]—is an important index, pointing not simply to discretion on the narrator's part but to a textual device of initiation that itself indexes death. It is integral to a more general French-classical aesthetics of muting or strategic "vagueness" to which *L'Accompagnement* conforms, one that seeks to universalize by understating, de-emphasizing or downplaying the specific. This is a form of litotes that respects readerly queasiness while indicating, by the generality of reference, the relevance to the reader of what is invoked ("death is the same for all"). But as a practice of periphrasis (cf. "Until now I have made use of periphrases so as to avoid proper nouns" [73]), the policy of describing without naming is also of a piece with René's perception of the hospital as a labyrinth, the "architectural form," as he says (121), that is universally ascribed to death.

Guiding and/or being guided smoothly through the labyrinth is what it means in this text to "accompany" someone. On the evening when the friend makes his untimely call on René, who has planned a party (a phone call that is the first in a series of such *appels*), it is because traffic in Paris is blocked and the friend, unable to get a taxi, needs a ride to the hospital. To get to his friend's apartment, René must negotiate the littered and obstructed streets, shouting at other drivers and "zigzagging so fast that I was astonished when I looked at my watch" (21). On his arrival at the apartment, the problem of getting to the hospital arises. "I pointed out that we would be unable to cross the Place de la République, which normally was on our path to the hospital. . . . With his usual authority and realism in practical matters, he showed me a detour that allowed us to avoid the demonstrators" (22). Thus it is the friend who—in teacherly fashion—inculcates an art of bypassing, while guiding René away from the *domestic* hospitality in which he had planned to pass the evening (a dinner party), into and through an urban labyrinthine space, to the new hospitality of the *hospital,* which, of course, turns out itself to have the form of a maze: "I had frequently visited him in this labyrinth before" (24)—a space that opens, in turn, onto death and is inhabited, as we've seen, by welcoming and guiding figures. The doctor, having greeted the friend, passes them on to a "sort of orderly" charged with escorting them, "as on a battlefield, between two combat zones" (29), and the orderly is relayed by another psychopomp, Angelica, who in turn welcomes the friend joyfully and "conducts us through the hallways with the graciousness of a well-brought-up hostess" (29). Thus the labyrinth implies the necessity of *conduction*—but conduction is itself, of necessity, an art of the labyrinthine.

And now René's initiation starts in earnest, as he stands by his increasingly anguished and difficult friend, encountering as he does so two kinds of staff. There are those who, on the side of death, are abrupt, confrontational, homophobic, and otherwise lacking in empathy for either the friend or René himself: their rhetorical mode is the opposite of periphrastic, and litotes is not their forte. But fortunately there are also those who, like the just mentioned Angelica, are given the exceptional privilege of being named for their graciousness, good humor, and especially their supportive willingness to improvise, that is, to adapt to the conditions of disaster rather than aggravating or abetting them. These figures (Angelica, Annie, André) are psychopomps who smooth the path of entry into death as a way of affirming the continuing value of life, and if periphrasis consists of finding alternatives—alternatives to the harsh reality of naming names—then their flexibility is a periphrastic practice. And then, finally, comes René's direct meeting with the doctor, with the result that it is as an initiate become initiator—not one who knows death, but one who has learned the ways of initiation (into death)—that René will eventually have the duty of conducting his friend, as a psychopomp himself, through the labyrinth of his final hours. As a result both of the friend's close proximity to death and of René's new understanding of what it is to accompany, to initiate, to smooth the way, the initial relation, in which it was the friend who, teaching the art of bypassing, guided René through the labyrinth of the city, has now been reversed. For the friend is about to enter the other city, the city of the dead (called *necropolis* by the Greeks), to which the hospital, open on one side to the city of the living and on the other to death, gives access.

Oddly, on what proves to be the friend's last day of life, the doctor orders chemotherapy, responding to René's question with a long list of drugs whose names, René says, "meant nothing" to him (118). One can only assume that this alleged chemo is what the doctor is referring to when, later in the day, he hints obliquely at euthanasia, with the phrase, "Mais nous l'accompagnons déjà." But in order to receive the transfusion, the patient must be moved to another part of the hospital, passing through a maze of corridors beneath a parking lot. Trundled on a gurney, the friend believes René, who is behind him, has abandoned him, and once more—after the initial phone call, and after his appeal to René to write of his death agony ("C'était un appel" [11])—calls out ("il m'a appelé" [120]).

> "I'm here," I said. And I was thinking that we were in the hallways of death, that everyone imagined death in this architectural form: a mournful maze, in which you advance among strangers who guide you without speaking, without knowing who you are, and with no knowledge of where you come from or where you are going, who forbid you to turn back. (121)

Like the conversation with the doctor ("What can be done?"—"Mais nous l'accompagnons déjà"), this moment encapsulates the narrative as a whole, as its *mise en abyme.* It describes the narrative as a story of initiatory appeal *and* response, and as a narration that itself, in its understated way, makes an appeal, an appeal to its readers, and expects the response of accompaniment. One calls, the other responds: "I'm here."

To accompany those who are dying, then, is not at all to hold back their progress toward death; rather it is to provide that last shred of comforting living identity, the identity to which they cling. One does so by speaking to them, knowing who they are, having knowledge of where they come from and where they are going. For "in a hospital, we are all afraid of losing our identity" (100), so palpable there is the (absent) presence of death, which for the dying, is experienced exactly as the imperative loss, from which one cannot turn back, of that social identity. To initiate, to accompany, is thus to recognize the nature of death, and to aid the living in their dying, by affirming sociality as the value of life, even unto death. And this sociality is itself grounded in our common "apprehension about ceasing to exist," as Ceccatty puts it with a characteristic periphrasis (100); for in hospitals, "it is not only the ill who have this fear"; everyone fears the loss of identity that is implied by death's (absent) presence. If death is the same for everyone, as people say, it is, then, because death inflicts on all of us *the same loss,* so that to the dying the simple act of accompaniment, the simple response, "I'm here," suffices to smooth the way. So I was not wrong, perhaps, to interpret the doctor's response, "Mais nous l'accompagnons déjà," as meaning something like, "All we can do is hold his hand," but I was wrong to read it as a confession of defeat, when to the contrary the value that it has in Ceccatty's book is that of an affirmation. It affirms that initiating, accompanying, witnessing, teaching, in the context of disaster, are not wasted or derisory acts, to the extent that they assert, or reassert, against what destroys it, the existence of social bondedness in the form of an ethos of community, and do so by asserting the possibility of what is called communication.

The great care taken by Ceccatty's text to acknowledge and respect its readers' assumed apprehension about "ceasing to exist" is exemplary, then, in that it demonstrates the book's own participation in this dynamics of smooth initiation. Over and beyond local examples of litotes, periphrasis, or preterition, the great sign of this care is in the "architectural" design of the overall narrative, which incorporates a lengthy analepsis. Having introduced us into the hospital on the occasion of the friend's fourth and last hospitalization, the narrator breaks off, and goes back to trace the friend's earlier struggles with dire opportunistic infections and his three previous hospitalizations. It is as if the narrative, while not precisely labyrinthine, goes out of its way, deviating at some length from its forward course, to teach by underemphasis and smooth the path of its reader's initiation. Thus, it returns to the account of the friend's final days only when we have been prepared, as it were, to face the inevitability of his death in the course of this long, complexly layered, retrospective account.

Such a move produces a kind of thickening of time into achronicity that is an equivalent of the architectural labyrinth as well as of "hospital time" as a kind of untime. But by the same token it introduces a strategic delay or detour—a kind of bypass or preterition—into what would otherwise have been the narrative's frightening precipitousness, a rush to death. And since the early hospitalizations function as euphemized versions of the final one, the text can thus be said, quite explicitly to "turn," that is, to deviate, around the smoothness of a litotes, like René's conversation with the doctor. The difference is only that here the turning is one into which the book's readers are introduced and in which they participate, as opposed to merely reading about it. So we are brought in this way, by gentle stages, *not* to know death, but nevertheless to something like the acknowledgment of disaster (in lieu of its denial) that is the goal of any initiatory process.

Bearing in mind that in Cliff Chase's *The Hurry-Up Song* it is precipitousness that, simulating untime, is charged with defamiliarizing the family, we can conclude that, symmetrically and indeed in complementary fashion, the form of initiatory hospitality proposed in *L'Accompagnement* is one that takes its time, and goes out of its way, because its goal is not to dispel an illusion of protectedness but to conduct (Latin *cum-ducere,* to guide by accompanying), to lead us *gently* into the sphere where life encounters death. Demystification may well be a matter of shock tactics, but remystification is an art that entails indirection, patience, and care, a practice of understatement and underemphasis, of preterition. Such an art also simulates untime, but it does so by working *within time,* so as to give the untimely a "recognizable" form. It is "conducive," but less to shock than to a permanent acknowledgment of death, danger, and disaster, to dwelling on the threshold and holding open the door.

I argued earlier that a teacher of testimonial writing, seeking to hold open the classroom door to untimely interventions, needs to have some grasp, intuitive or theorized, of the art of defamiliarization, which may well be threatening to students accustomed to a sense of protectedness. But successful teaching, it can now be observed, also requires the teacher to be a practitioner of conduction or *accompagnement,* an art of patience and care that can lead, through an alliance with time, to acknowledgment and awareness of the untimely. The trick is obviously to know when, how, and with whom to "take off the gloves," and to conduct through a rhetoric of demystification, and when, how and with whom the gloves should go on again, as required by a rhetoric of remystification. For if classrooms can and should become more like hospitals and less like the family, as students tend to imagine it, a classroom is not a hospital—the two gatekeeping institutions have different social functions—and a teacher's charge is always that of a psychopomp, a gentle conductor of souls, even and perhaps especially when the pedagogical agenda entails defamiliarization. That is what, in my 1996 course, I did not understand.

With the obvious difference that testimonial writers do not know their audience as teachers do, and know disaster more intimately than is the experience of most teachers, something similar can be said of the art of witnessing, which oscillates, as this book demonstrates, between a pole of defamiliarizing confrontation or transgression, which, however, cannot be too extreme under penalty of rhetorical failure, and a pole of remystifying infiltration, which conversely risks assimilation and ineffectiveness. Taking off the gloves and putting them on are not opposed, as a supposedly nonrhetorical practice to a rhetorical one, but are complementary rhetorical practices between which one might hesitate, or alternate, as circumstances may seem to require. Which is why, returning briefly to *L'Accompagnement* for my pretext and recalling Mark Senak's dilemma over wearing gloves for (self-)protection, with which I began, I want to conclude this chapter, which concludes my book, with a brief reflection about the flexible substance from which hospital gloves, as well as condoms, the apparatus of safe(r) sex, are made. What can be learned, by teachers and others, concerning protection, adaptability, and conduction, from latex?

Learning from Latex

To say, as many do, that disaster, the obscene, the catastrophic is unsayable is to raise the question of what, in the context of the sublime, Lyotard (1988) has called the presentation of the unpresentable and I have defined in this book as the problematics of figuration as a way of uttering the unstatable. It is not because of any inherent deficiency of language, nor because of any essential characteristic of extreme events and experiences, but because of an inadequacy produced by discursive conventions—those that regulate how language may appropriately be used—that certain matters are relegated to the category of the "unspeakable." I have argued in this book that such an inadequacy, which takes the form of the unavailability of a genre that would accommodate the reality of disaster, is culturally functional in that it produces an ideology that identifies culture with that which is "civilized," producing in cultural subjects an inability, or an unwillingness, to recognize the nevertheless historical realities that haunt their consciousness.

But if the problem resides in the conventional character of the discursive apparatus that may be available at a given time, in a given place, in the circumstances of a given social interaction, then the presentation of the unpresentable does not pose an altogether insoluble dilemma. It merely requires that "presencing" take place through means other than conventional, or more specifically, through an adaptation of the available, conventional means to purposes other than those to which they are, again conventionally, dedicated. This is what I have described here as generic catachresis, a practice the anticonventional character of which implies that it necessarily be a matter of improvisation and making do—what Michel de Certeau calls an "art de faire," getting something done without necessarily being able to theorize what one is doing. And this improvisational art I have described in what precedes as a *captatio benevolentiae,* one that is performed through figuration and results in the phenomenon of readability to which I have given Deleuze's name of *agencement,* or agencing. If it is a general rule that disaster is what confounds convention, and that the only appropriate response to disaster lies, therefore, in the flexibility, the adaptability, the skill, and the wit of making do, then testimonial writing exemplifies that rule.

The metaphors we have encountered in the texts to refer to these practices of presencing what is conventionally unpresentable have mainly been metaphors of portability: reporting, transfer, relay. Testimonial writing "reports" news from the front, carries the dead, fosters adoption of the culturally orphaned, and moves, in general terms, from extremity to the familiar and domestic, negotiating as best it may the cultural gulf that divides them. Conduction, though—the metaphor that has surfaced in this chapter—changes the direction of the metaphorics of portability; and this is because it is most crucially concerned with the dynamics of *captatio,* bringing readers to the news rather than the news to the readers, and moving therefore from the familiar, the domestic, and the conventional in the direction of what, from that position of protectedness, inevitably appears alien and threatening. Of course, conduction (guiding and accompanying) and portability (bringing the news) are mutually interdependent, each the condition of the other's possibility, in the way that generic catachresis and *captatio* ultimately define, from different "ends" of the process, one and the same phenomenon (the "hijacked" genre). But conduction is the term that best describes what testimonial and teaching have in common, since it is the teacher's task to support the textual work of bringing the news by bringing to the texts readers more hospitably disposed to such news than they might otherwise be. And it is not irrelevant to observe, therefore, that conduction is described, notably in *L'Accompagnement,* as an art of rhetorical invention that requires the same kind of improvisational skill, inventiveness, etiquette, and ready adaptability that I have described as the rhetoric of portability. For the presencing of the unpresentable, the bringing of the unstatable to utterance, requires the same kind of skilled rusing with conventionality whether it be a matter of the witness's bringing of unwelcome testimony or of the teacher's attempt to induce readerly hospitality in those who cling to the protections of the familiar.

If, however, as I've argued, conduction therefore has as its complement—and indeed actually includes—the defamiliarization of the familiar, from which I have artificially separated it for purposes of exposition, its rhetorical resourcefulness nevertheless inevitably favors the pole of smoothing the way, as opposed to the pole of precipitousness, since its task is to bring about the remystification of disaster that complements the demystification of the familiar. The special relevance of latex as a model for teaching lies therefore in the fact that, in addition to the elasticity that provides a convenient symbol of adaptability and allows it to function as a vehicle of conduction—in this case the conduction of sensation—latex allies conduction with a protective function, in that it presents an impermeable barrier to microorganisms (whether spermatozoa or bacteria and viruses), whence its role in safe(r) sex as well as in clinical situations. For this reason, the metaphorics of latex defines conduction as affording a form of mediated contact that tact-fully—I mean both carefully and inventively—renegotiates protectedness-as-isolation (or self-protection) into a form of "aesthetic" *communication* (Greek *aisthesis,* sensation): a form of contact that remains "safe" precisely to the extent that it is not only mediated (as of course all communication is), but *experienced* as mediated. In that sense, latex is a figure for agencing, then, as a rhetorical practice that makes readable what convention does not allow to be said. So it is worth recalling here what was mentioned earlier in this chapter, that the invention of "safe(r) sex" in San Francisco in the early years of the AIDS emergency—an exemplary case of inventive improvisation in the context of disaster—was conceived as a way of parlaying protectedness into "how to have sex in an epidemic," that is, how to have community under circumstances of extreme danger. Not surprisingly, as we saw in chapter 5, this admirable invention figures in John Greyson's *Zero Patience* as both a model and an inspiration for the testimonial enterprise itself, pitting wit, just as witnessing does, against the effects of disaster and doing so in the interests of survival. In the interests, that is, of a manner of surviving that is informed, thoughtful and alert to danger, *not* the survivorhood that ignores disaster, the better to undergo its effects.

It is true that, in the character of George, Greyson's film identifies the relevance of teaching to witnessing while distancing its own more confrontational practice of flaunting the haunt from pedagogical purposes. By contrast, Ceccatty's caution in *L'Accompagnement* with respect to "protecting" his readership resembles the care displayed by writers like John Foster (by profession a teacher of German, including Holocaust, history) and even Pascal de Duve (also a teacher) (see chapters 2 and 4). That Ceccatty's cautious style is specifically teacherly, however, ultimately emerges only in his final chapter, in which two "scenes of learning" that are also scenes of teaching are presented.

In one of these, René returns to the hospital three weeks after his friend's death, having been commissioned as a journalist to write about what—piling a litotes on a periphrasis—he calls "books concerning the disease [my friend] had not survived" (13), that is, AIDS writing. His friend's doctor agrees to initiate him into the syndrome about which, throughout his friend's illness and death, he had remained steadfastly uninstructed, something that each recognizes will entail "cutting and tacking," or *louvoiement.* "Our conversation tacked between refined analyses and the simplifying summaries he was forced into by the deficiencies in my background information" (131). Tacking implies zigzagging and indirection: one makes headway but only by a roundabout route, adjusting to the prevailing wind. And not coincidentally we discover that it is from this teacherly doctor that René has learned the very term that gives his book its title: "It was he who liked to use the term 'accompaniment'" (131). But most strikingly, in the context of a reflection on teaching, on this occasion the doctor gives precedence to his teacherly task over the needs of a patient who is in a state of preoperative anxiety: "I was depriving some patient of the only visit that would have enabled him to get some sleep" (131).

The implication, then, is that in hospitals hospitality is split—split between addressing the needs of the ill and the dying (accompaniment in the form of caregiving) and addressing those of the living, whose need, as they enter the process of initiation, is for a teacherly form of conduction that may on occasion claim priority over the conduction that is caregiving. This is exactly the split that is enacted, though with the priority apparently reversed, in the other scene of René's learning, in which a nurse replaces the doctor in the role of informant and initiator. On the very evening of the friend's death, as René stands outside the hospital hoping for a taxi, a car pulls up and offers him a ride. Its driver is Annie, who has just washed and prepared his friend's body. Their conversation turns on the fact that both René and his friend are writers, "an occupation less useful than yours," says René gallantly (129). She does not disagree; indeed what can writing do, René adds by way of commentary, his hypothetical ("A quoi servirait d'écrire?") nevertheless foreshadowing the conclusion he will have reached on this matter by the time he announces his opinion at the beginning of his book that "seeing and describing"—writing as a mode of teaching—is "our only strength."

But for now the topic of conversation shifts to gloves, the latex gloves that, René has noticed, Annie and her colleagues rarely wear when tending AIDS patients. Annie points out that gloves don't prevent needle-sticks and, referring to her patients, goes on to say: "They need our skin on their skin. . . . Nothing can replace that sort of contact" (128). In the context of René's concerns, it is as if a distinction is being made between two modes of hospitality, two modes of conduction into death, the one real, the other symbolic. The hospital's hospitality to the dying (and to death itself as it enters the domain of the living), is one that requires gloves-off "contact," as opposed, therefore, to the "tact"—the wearing of rhetorical gloves, as in the expression *prendre des gants*—that is appropriate, as René's experience with the doctor has demonstrated, when the living are conducted into the sphere of death. Gloves off and gloves on are two different ways in which, according to circumstance, that form of life-affirming solidarity or complicity that amounts to a recognition of the other's identity—of con/tact—can be expressed in the context of disaster. And since initiators or psychopomps—caregivers—like Annie and more particularly the doctor, need to practice *both* kinds of hospitality (caring for the friend as he enters death, but also instructing René as he enters the initiatory sphere that is the hospital), we can see that the two modes, the two rhetorics of conduction, are being differentiated but ultimately equated. In given circumstances of hospital/ity, each is appropriate, because *in neither case is self-protection the issue.* What is at issue is the other's need, for gloves off in one case, for gloves on in the other.

Differentiated and equated, the two must also, in the case of Ceccatty's narrative but also of all testimonial writing of any integrity, be fused, for in testimonial one writes—sees and describes—for a readership whose sensitivities must be respected, but also in solidarity with those—the dead—who, like René's friend, cannot testify for themselves, those whose haunting presence one's writing seeks to make readable. And the same is true, I submit, of teaching, which must be as loyal as possible to testimonial texts, in their integrity, while simultaneously finding tactful ways of bringing readers to them. Gloves off in one respect, gloves on in the other. It is of course the duty of "withness" with respect to the dying and the dead, an alliance amounting to identification, that Mark Senak drew attention to in the episode of will signing (the signing of a testament if not a testimonial) with which I began this chapter. The signing is a cosigning, as Senak lies in bed with the patient and guides his hand. But it is perhaps not accidental, then, that Senak, who moments later (like Annie) will abjure the wearing of gloves (and of all the rest of the protective gear) in visiting patients, nevertheless (co)signs the text here "through" a glove: "through the glove I held his hand, which held the pen" (Senak, 42).

For the withness of his authorial gesture—a cosigning that offers a striking allegorization of what I have been calling agencing throughout this book—is exactly what readers like my students (notably in that 1996 class) fear and reject in testimonial texts. They deny the identification, or even the mere alliance, the simple gloves-off connection of survivors and the dead, or of ordinary life and disaster, which is what witnessing writing bears witness to and seeks to lead its readers to acknowledge. Without initiation, readers cannot be expected to understand the logic of Senak's comment: "I walked into those sweaty godforsaken deathbed rooms because I was doing it for me. It was my best defense against my enemy AIDS" (36). His image of writing *with* the dying but *through* the glove—the glove that readers require—thus conflates the two modes of hospital/ity, the two modes of address and of conduction (caring, and writing/teaching) that together define hospitals as places of initiatory agencing. And by implication writing that is hospitable in this dual sense—writing "with" and writing "for"—is defined as our "best defense" against disaster. The image chimes well with Ceccatty's view of writing—"seeing and describing"—as initiatory in a similarly dual sense, a conduction of the dying into death and of the living into the sphere of death that is "our only strength."

Ceccatty's understanding of writing, like Senak's, entails gloves-off "contact" with the dying (the simple rhetoric of "I'm here") and gloves-on "tact" or complicity—a labyrinthine rhetoric of understatement, underemphasis, and "going out of one's way" in order not to mention what one is thereby mentioning—in its address to living readers. Of teaching in its relation to testimonial texts and the writing of disaster on the one hand and to student readers on the other, something similar must be said. A teacher learns to teach testimonial texts by reading them in a spirit of open hospitality and by learning from them in this way something of their own rhetorical canniness and savoir faire, their flexibility, adaptability, and inventiveness, a latexlike rhetorical elasticity that is a requirement of hospitality in the relation between teacher and student reader. But the texts teach also that such teacherly hospitality toward those who are learning to read does not necessarily entail giving them the "kid-glove" treatment, in the way that a perhaps hasty reading of Ceccatty might suggest. Simple fidelity to the reality of disaster and what I have called withness with the dead may dictate on occasion a rhetoric of confrontation and a flaunting of the haunt, an Annie-like gloves-off directness capable of balancing and completing more cautious and tactful effects. So a thoughtful teacher of testimonial texts is likely to be engaged in something very like the confrontation-infiltration dialectic that we have seen played out in a number of texts of witness, with the sole but important proviso, perhaps, that the special circumstances of teaching, and in particular the fact that one is concerned with the cultural education of young people, may recommend favoring caution and the tactful end of the spectrum, in the knowledge that in the classroom "contact" itself, when and if it can be achieved, will remain metaphoric—a mediated and symbolic experience.

But this is to say in turn that, like testimonial writers, and like the nurses René de Ceccatty praises for their willingness to improvise, teachers too are condemned by the conditions of disaster to be agencers, not authors, and consequently to practice the arts of bricolage and perpetual invention that get something necessary done when theory is confounded and conventional attitudes look the other way. And it is to say, too, that like the writing of witness, teaching is therefore an art of the singular, since singularity (say an act of generic catachresis legitimated by inventive troping) is exactly that which convention does not expect and theory cannot explain. It is the ghost that haunts the use of language as the category of the obscene haunts culture. In the case of testimonial writing, there are two important aspects of its singular character that can be emphasized, and each is transferable, mutatis mutandis, to the practice of teaching testimonial texts. One is that such writing evolves and changes rapidly, under the impact of new and sometimes unexpected or unexpectedly extreme historical events that make new rhetorical demands (for disaster is itself always particular), but also because over time an effect of rhetorical familiarization or conventionalization sets in, so that devices that once were effective in mobilizing readerly attention and involvement lose their impact. When we encounter "Tommy talk" in poetry of the 1914–18 war, it strikes us much less forcefully than it once did, because that stylistic practice itself launched a modernist, and then postmodernist, colloquialization of high culture that is now a norm. Similarly, for Holocaust writing, Michael Rothberg has sketched an important stylistic history of such writing that identifies realist, modernist, and postmodern "stages" in its evolution.

The second aspect of this art of singularity, though, is the one I have emphasized in this book, which is the great diversity of individual solutions that arise, according to the positioning of different writers in relation to different historical experiences together with their estimate of the state of readerly sensibilities, in response to the general problem of finding a way to presence the supposedly unsayable. This inventiveness is visible in the range of conventional genres that find themselves appropriated: in this book, which has mainly concerned the catachresis of autobiographical modes like the diary and the memoir, we have also seen dance performance appropriated (by Bill T. Jones), TV soaps as (in *Longtime Companion*), the satirical musical *(Zero Patience),* and, last but not least, porn flicks (Guillaume Dustan). But witnessing's inventiveness also embraces the range of figural inventions and understandings of the etiquette of solecism that I have attempted to distribute, according to their rhetorical effect, along the continuum of cultural confrontation and assimilation, gloves off and gloves on. I think it is important to celebrate the ingeniousness and the capacity to improvise—what the Renaissance named *ingegno* and the Greeks, from a different angle, *metis* or practical skill—to which events of the most horrendous degree of cynicism, brutality, and inhumanity, on one side, and of terror, pain, and trauma on the other, have given rise. This infinite adaptability or wit is one of the most precious and remarkable of human talents; but it is regularly overlooked in intellectual circles because (I suppose) it resists theorization.

So let me conclude with a line of verse, one that I hope may encapsulate my argument in the way that the opening sentence of the *Communist Manifesto*—"A specter is abroad in Europe" [Ein Gespenst geht um in Europa]—establishes a tone that permeates, and a (hypo)thesis that subtends, that remarkable work. It comes from an early poem, "Heavy Breathing," by Essex Hemphill. I abstract the line from its immediate (most obviously, sexual) context in the poem, so as to allow it to function, like Alice's leg in *Auschwitz and After* (or the fragment of poetry Mado cites), as one of those detached parts, orphaned memories, or surviving remnants that occupy the landscape of aftermath and haunt us, as untimely returnees or revenants that offer themselves to, appeal for, our reading. "I prowl in scant sheets of latex." "Prowl" is a word that suggests haunting the outskirts, restlessly inhabiting them as the obscene haunts culture. It might well translate the verb *umgehen* (to circulate, to circle) that I rendered by "is abroad" in the Marx-Engels sentence. "Sheets" suggests ghosts as well as bed linen, linking the erotic and the thanatological. But it is the word "scant" that gives poignancy to Hemphill's line, and makes it hurt.

"Scant" suggests the sense of exposure that ensues whenever one's protectedness yields to an awareness of disaster. And in a reading consistent with my foregoing meditation on latex as a figure for conduction as the rhetoric of the "unpresentable," it points to the anxiety, arising from a sense of insufficiency or inadequacy, that attaches to what are inevitably symbolic responses to real and painful events, responses that nevertheless are held to qualify as our "best defense," or "our only strength." The act of haunting culture, for all its ingenuity, is an art of the scant. But finally, if it is the case, as I have tried to propose, that testimonial writing attempts in this way to pit some form of reinvented, reestablished but makeshift, *bricolé* community against the disaster(s) that destroy community, then the best gloss on Hemphill's line might be these lines—scant as they too are—from a later poem of his, in which the title word *heavy* recurs, or returns. The poem is "Heavy Corners":

> If we must die
> on the front line
> don't let loneliness
> kill us.

If "scant" is the alternative to loneliness, "heavy" is both the cause and the consequence of "scant's" scantness. The community to which these lines appeal is "scant" in the sense that it is an *exposed* community, open to danger and disaster, those "heavy corners" we have to turn. And also in the sense that such community is *insufficient,* inadequate in the face of the danger—the death, the loneliness—to which it might respond. But it *is* nevertheless a community of sorts, and my take on testimonial writing in this book has been, simply, that it is to such a scant community, a community of (and in) aftermath, that testimonial makes its appeal; such a community that it attempts to restore in the act of appealing to it. A community irrevocably damaged remains our only hope, our best defense, our sole strength, scant as the hope, the defense, the strength may be.

Essex Hemphill, a Black, gay, HIV-positive poet of extraordinary talent prowling the outskirts of American culture in more senses than one, and doing so in scant sheaths of latex in more than one sense also, died of AIDS complications in 1995. He was thirty-eight. You can see "him"—or is it his ghost?—giving heartbreaking performances of his verse and prose in Marlon Riggs's two, equally heartbreaking, video testimonials: *Tongues Untied* and *Black Is, Black Ain't.* Try to look at them sometime. Try to look, in order to see.

Notes

Preface

1. Italian distinguishes *animo,* masc. (pl. *animi*), "spirit" from *anima,* fem. (pl. *anime*), "soul."

2. The emphasis arises from the coupling of "What passing-bells for these . . ." and "And bugles calling for them . . ." in equivalent positions of line 1 and line 8, respectively, of the octet. In each case, the words "these" and "them" fall under a strong metric accent.

3. On indexicality, see especially Freadman 2004.

4. For an assessment and bibliography of the controversy that arose around the figure of Menchú and her *testimonio* in 1999, see Craft.

5. Here and elsewhere I use the vocabulary of denial (and in a moment counterdenial) heuristically, without necessarily alluding to the psychoanalytic concepts of repression and the return of the repressed. The theory I will develop (see chapter 1) is a theory of culture involving an analysis of the exclusionary character of genre and a rhetorical account of how that exclusion is eluded in testimonial writing. It is homologous with the psychoanalytic theory of denial/counterdenial but does not entail the idea of a personal unconscious.

Chapter 1

1. The best account known to me of "coming to witness" is Jorge Semprún, *L'Ecriture ou la vie.*

2. For the specific genre of AIDS diaries, this is the argument of Chambers 1999.

3. See Boulé 1995.

4. In the summer of 1997, two famous witnesses to the Resistance in occupied France, Pierre and Lucie Aubrac, whose bona fides had been called into question from the Right, asked for their case to be examined by a panel of famous historians. The newspaper *Libération* provided the forum and published a transcript of the proceedings, during which consternation arose from the inability of either the wit-

nesses themselves or the historians to disentangle the claims of factual accuracy from the character of witnessing truth. See *Libération,* July 9, 1997 (insert entitled "Le Débat"), and for commentary by the participants, *Libération,* July 10–13, 1997.

5. Recent work (2002) by Shoshana Felman points to the genre of the judicial trial as one of the key sites of intersection between culture's conventional genres and collective trauma (the obscene). She shows that "trials of the century," like the O. J. Simpson trial and the Eichmann trial, are so called because they tend to make apparent the dimensions of collective trauma (violence against women, the oppression of Blacks, the Shoah) from which individual crimes are inseparable. But the legal apparatus that defines the trial as a genre can ignore or dismiss the collective trauma (as the Simpson trial discounted the issue of domestic violence), or alternatively it may undergo a transformation as a result of the pressure of the traumatic (as in the Eichmann trial).

6. To identify an obscene reality as a fiction is, of course, the classic move of denial, exemplified by negationist ("revisionist") historians of the Holocaust. Like Moshe the Beadle in Wiesel's *Night,* witnesses may be disbelieved (declared mad or otherwise lacking in credibility), or the existence of (eye)witnesses may be denied, as negationists cynically deny the existence of eyewitnesses to the gas chambers.

7. I refer to Homer's hero as Odysseus, and reserve the Latinized version of his name for references to both Dante's and Levi's rewrite of the *Odyssey.* Direct reference to the *Odyssey* is quite rare in *Se questo è un uomo,* whereas the *Divine Comedy* is a partly subterranean but near-permanent intertext; conversely the *Odyssey* visibly underlies the whole of Levi's companion text, *La Tregua* (The reawakening).

Chapter 2

1. I write *im-pertinence* so as to foreground the idea of nonpertinence or incongruity, and *impertinence* as a synonym of impudence, reserving *im(-)pertinence* for cases in which both senses are simultaneously, and more or less equally, active.

2. See chapter 6. On the status of the symptom as simultaneously clinical and critical, see Deleuze 1993; and on the rhetorical status of witnessing writing as a troping of the symptomatic, see chapter 3 (on Pat Barker's *Regeneration*).

3. *Facing It* can be understood as an initial exploration of the genre of the AIDS diary (in which chapter 5 is devoted to *Unbecoming*). In this book, this chapter and chapter 4 (on Pascal de Duve's *Cargo vie*) return to the AIDS journal, while chapters 6 and 7 take up further generic extensions of autobiography in AIDS witnessing writing, viz. the "dual autobiography" and the "collective auto/biography" (or "farewell symphony").

4. On stammering and stuttering, as symptom and as trope, see chapter 3.

5. In a longer study of Australian AIDS writing, it would be necessary to

include Nigel Krauth's remarkable novel *JF Was Here.* It associates AIDS with the history of Australian colonialism in Papua New Guinea, and especially of "race" relations in that context; it also suggests interestingly that, in a racist context, the "inverse racism" of the im-pertinent (a gay white man and his protofeminist grandmother) can backfire and cause the same damage as racism itself.

Chapter 3

1. The other two novels are *The Eye in the Door* (1993) and *The Ghost Road* (1995). *Regeneration* was first published in 1991.

2. One cannot argue with any certainty from negative evidence, but the word *witness* (or *witnessing*) is absent from the two key prefaces—those of Owen for the *War Poems* (1920) and of Remarque for *All Quiet on the Western Front* (1928)—in which writers of the period attempted to indicate to readers the genre they considered appropriate to their texts. Remarque's preface is particularly eloquent: "This book is to be [*soll . . . sein*] neither an accusation nor a confession, and least of all an adventure. . . . It will try simply to tell of a generation of men [*über eine Generation zu berichten*] who, even though they may have escaped the shells, were destroyed by the war."

3. See Whitehead: "Barker's research for the novel coincided with the Gulf War"(692; also 693 n. 7).

4. Thank you to the auditor of my Toronto seminar of 1997 who drew my attention to this remarkable novel.

5. "Discomfort in culture" translates the German title *(Das Unbehagen in der Kultur)* of the book, published in 1930, that we know as *Civilization and Its Discontents.*

6. Thank you to Jacquie Millner for drawing my attention to the relevance of these poems.

7. Four drafts of "Anthem," including both drafts amended by Sassoon, are reproduced in Owen's *Collected Poems.*

8. Another such reverberation is Benjamin Britten's *War Requiem* of 1962 (see Herbert).

9. Line 3 ("Only the stuttering rifles' rapid rattle") anchors the main paradigmatic series in the poem, e.g.:

cattle, *rattle,* bugles, candles
stuttering, rattle, patter, glimmer, pallor, pall
stuttering, mockeries, voice of mourning, wailing, calling
passing, *stuttering,* mourning, wailing, calling, drawing
die, *rifles',* choirs, choirs, shires, eyes, shine, good-byes, minds, blinds
rapid, hasty, speed, slow
etc.

10. In recounting the episode of Orme's visitation, which begins with the rising wind and the tapping, Barker departs quite markedly from the episode of Ormand's appearance as Sassoon tells it, already in fictionalized guise, in *Sherston's Progress.* I surmise that she is responding to suggestions in Sassoon's Craiglockhart poetry (such as "Survivors" and "Sick Leave"), and probably also to the evidence, between the lines of the memoirs, of Sassoon's erotic interest in the man he calls Ormand and Barker Orme.

11. In her authoritative biography of Sassoon, Jean Moorcraft Wilson says oddly: "The title itself, for example, is almost solely due to Sassoon" (402).

12. For extremely helpful readings of this chapter in draft, I thank David Caron and Anne Freadman.

Chapter 4

1. I thank Jean Mainil for this suggestion, and for much help with de Duve and his work. (The name being of Flemish origin, the form *de Duve* rather than *Duve* is correct.)

2. As in the case of Pascal, de Duve's references to Baudelaire are recognizable to anyone with a French secondary level education. But my thinking about the relevance of Baudelaire's stay in Mauritius was triggered by a stimulating article by Françoise Lionnet.

3. I thank Dan for his brilliant seminar paper on puns and wit (1997).

4. *Sidéré* is partially synonymous with *foudroyé,* which suggests the *coup de foudre,* a metaphor for love at first sight (being hit by lightning).

5. Thank you to David Caron for this insight.

6. There is a famous essay by Roland Barthes (1964) titled "Ecrivains et écrivants," which provides a partial precedent for de Duve's distinctions. Thank you to Peter Edelmann for calling my attention to the Barthes piece.

7. French *simple* signifies simple but also single; i.e., it is an antonym of *double* as well as of *complexe.*

8. *Le Fil* is only distantly related to the writing of de Duve, Guibert, and Collard. It takes a more "clinical" perspective on the subjective experience of living with AIDS, tracing the narrator's fascination with his death, from aversion to entry into the stage of *agonie,* as the disease progresses. But its narrative follows the "thread of days" (89) as they build up a certain *entraînement* (rather than a *griserie*): a gradual letting go in the face of "misfortune's quiet approach" (49). And the writing mimes this *entraînement* so that it becomes contagious for the reader.

9. Arguably the scenes of *Les Nuits fauves* that are set in the Parisian night world, and particularly those that depict sexual encounters under the bridges, allude to the topos of the descent into the underworld.

10. Here the figure of Genet becomes crucial to the Rimbaud syndrome. Com-

pare also what is said in chapter 2 about the gay and lesbian ethical tradition as the tradition of the inversion of values.

11. This chapter revises and reconsiders an earlier essay (Chambers 1998c), which was itself an attempt to synthesize my previous positions on *Cargo vie.* My interpretations have shifted as I have become increasingly aware of, and have begun to understand, the equivocal character of de Duve's writing. Thus, on certain points of interpretation, I differ quite radically here from my earlier positions.

Chapter 5

1. I derive *untime* by back-formation from "untimely": aftermath writing is simultaneously un-timely (from the point of view of survivorhood) and untime-ly (from the point of view of survival). The word *Unzeit* exists in German (cf. *zur Unzeit,* "in untimely fashion," "inopportunely").

2. Mächler focuses on the biography of Bruno Dösseker. His report is fair, sensitive, and exhaustive; it does not question conventional understandings of personal identity, however, and predictably takes an either-or view of the truth-fiction dyad. The report stops just short of accusing Dösseker of fraudulence.

3. My thanks to David Caron for having drawn my attention to this item.

4. It's necessary to add, of course, that not being a *Muselmann* or a *sommerso,* in the camps, was a probably necessary but never sufficient condition of survival.

5. The corresponding German verb, *pflegen,* has a comparable double sense: it means to take care (*Pflegevater, Pflegemutter, Pflegekind,* "foster father," "foster mother," "foster child"), but also to be wont (*ich pflege zu sagen,* "I'm wont to say"), thereby suggesting habituation and acculturation. Cognate with French *plier* and English *to ply, pflegen* refers to a frequentative action, which is a seme common to both of its senses.

6. Anne Freadman reminds me that this uncanny alignment of referential lack and interpretive plethora is a way of describing the way language always works; signs refer only because they are readable, and reference is the mode of signification (readability) that is characteristic of language (which is therefore figural in character). The uncanny effect I am describing is thus that of the becoming evident of a semiotic truth in place of the illusion (that language refers "naturally," i.e. without semiotic mediation, to a preexistent world) in which people "normally" live. This illusion of linguistic transparency, I would add, is in turn a function of the smooth working of genres.

7. The peculiar aptness of this ditty from the point of view of testimonial—that is, its haunting quality—derives from its half-rhyming of demand and satisfaction *(Bettelbub/genug)* and its intensification of the stock phrase "noch einmal" (once more) by substituting "immer" (always) for "einmal" (once). Janeway's translation is neat, but obscures the point by transforming the song into specifically

anti-Semitic doggerel: "Beggar kid, beggar kid. / There's never enough for the yid" (138). Léa Marcou, the French translator, tries an effect of antiphrasis, a common figure in French (here: "jamais trop" for "toujours pas assez"): "Le petit mendigot, le petit mendigot./ Il en a jamais trop,/ le petit mendigot" (135). Perhaps: The beggar-kid, the beggar-waif./Can't never get enuf,/ The beggar waif?

8. I thank Aaron Nathan for showing me the relevance of the Lacanian categories to testimonial in general and aftermath writing in particular. See his unpublished paper on *La vita è bella* (Life is beautiful), "Lacan/Benigni." That the Lacanian Symbolic is identifiable with the figural and hence has an indexical character—more particularly the indexical character of the residual as a marker of loss—is a hypothesis that I propose here as a suggestive one, and one strongly supported by the text of *Fragments;* but my argument as a whole is a rhetorical and semiotic one and does not depend on such an equivalence or on psychoanalytic arguments in general. My conflation of the historical, the fictional, and the figural with, respectively, the Lacanian categories of the Real, the Imaginary, and the Symbolic is likewise proposed as a hypothesis worth following up.

9. Delbo's emphasis throughout the trilogy on solidarity and comradeship contrasts with other reports, particularly from the extermination camps, of the disintegration of ordinary moral values that occurred there. One reason for her emphasis is that she was deported to Auschwitz—more strictly Birkenau—as a political prisoner, not a "racial enemy," and in the company of 230 other French women with whom she shared a language and—very largely—a political philosophy. They were under the regime of *Nacht und Nebel,* not the *Endlösung.* That only 49 returned attests, nevertheless, to the severity of the conditions they endured. (See Delbo's *Le Convoi du 24 janvier.*)

10. It is worth noting that *specter* is from Latin *spectare,* a frequentative form of *specere,* "to see," that, like French *voyance,* appears to have implied heightened capacities of vision.

11. The difference between the date of the publication of the trilogy in 1970–71 and the period to which its account of math and aftermath refers is obviously crucial. After a flurry of early testimonial in the years immediately following the return of the survivors, a long period of discouraged silence ensued in France, as elsewhere, until the late fifties and early sixties (Wiesel, *La Nuit;* Schwarzbart, *Le Dernier des justes;* Langfus, *Les Bagages de sable),* and was broken finally only by the Eichmann trial in 1961, which Annette Wieviorka describes (117) as having "liberated" survivor testimonial by giving the survivor a "social identity" that had not existed before. Three of the Eichmann witnesses reappeared in Claude Lanzmann's *Shoah* (Wieviorka, 110). Much in Delbo's writing appears to predate its publication by many years; and *None of Us* had appeared in an earlier edition (Gonthier) in 1965, the same year Minuit issued *Le Convoi du 24 janvier* (Suleiman, 61). The publication of the trilogy thus occurred in a more welcoming climate than the period of dismissive reception of the survivors that *The Measure of Our*

Days describes, and it has become one of the classics of French *littérature de déportation.*

12. The question whether or not the line "Le temps que l'on mesure n'est point mesure de nos jours" scans depends on a relatively technical point. When the verse is written as a sentence, one has no guidance as to whether to pronounce or not to pronounce the final *e* of each occurrence of the word "mesure." The line, then, is a *vers démesuré,* both in the sense that it is unmetrical *(sans mesure)* and in the sense that it is, by any count, too long to scan as a regular line of French verse (having either fifteen, fourteen, or thirteen syllables). (It could, of course, be a line of "free verse.") Written as verse, however (a hemistich and an enjambed octosyllable), the sentence is regularly versified, but as a result the word "mesure" has two syllables on its first occurrence and three on its second. The line, then, is in *vers mesuré(s)* (metrical verse); but the discrepancy in the pronunciation of the word "mesure," required by the meter, remains as a marker of the difference between a scanned line and an unscanned line. The reason for this is that in French the pronunciation of unstressed *e*s that are elided in nonmetrical speech is the very sign of metrical (measured) language; i.e. two-syllable "mesure" would be normal in prose but arises in verse only because the word falls at the end of a scanned line; three-syllable "mesure" would be the normally expected pronunciation in most positions of a scanned line but would otherwise occur only exceptionally (e.g. for emphasis).

13. D. A. Miller claims the Broadway musical as a covertly gay male genre, a "place for us." That may well account for the appropriability it has displayed for purposes of AIDS witnessing. It would be instructive to compare *Zero Patience*'s flaunting style, however, with two other such appropriations of the singing-and-dancing treatment of a "star-cross'd lovers" plotline in the era of AIDS: Paul Rudnick's off-Broadway satirical play, then film, *Jeffrey* (text published 1994), and in France *Jeanne et le garçon formidable* (1998), a film by Olivier Ducastel and Jacques Martineau that pastiches the style of Jacques Demy.

14. An alternative formulation would present figuration, not as compensatory with respect to language's (preexisting) deficiency, but as the primary feature of language as a symbolic practice, and productive therefore, through the dynamics of reading, of the object as ghostly, i.e., incapable of being adequately represented. That is, one might say that it is the haunting quality of language as figurality that makes hauntedness recognizable, rather than, as in the formulation I have preferred (because it corresponds to a normalizing narrative grammar of before and after), that it is hauntedness that becomes haunting, and so recognizable, through the relay of troping.

Chapter 6

1. "Paradigmatic" is not intended to imply exemplary or normative: a genre is a set of differential relations, without a positive term, among texts that are

grouped for a specific purpose, in this case that of "reading out" some features of AIDS witnessing as aftermath writing in the United States, France, and Australia. Some further examples of texts having various features compatible with the genre of dual autobiography are those listed in the bibliography under the following author's names: Rafael Campo, René de Ceccatty, Clifford Chase, Christopher Coe, Mark Doty *(Heaven's Coast),* John Foster, Caroline Gréco, Hervé Guibert *(To the Friend),* Marie Howe, Joan Hurley, Jamaica Kincaid, Fenton Johnson, Bill T. Jones, Michel Manière, Thierry Mingot, Paul Monette *(Borrowed Time),* Barbara Peabody, Mark Senak, Yves Navarre, Ronald O. Valdiserri, Olivier de Vleeschouwer, David Wojnarowicz. Unusual in many respects—and therefore interesting—is Isabelle Muller, *Un Amour sérodifférent.* Except where there is a strong personal bond (Campo, Valdiserri), I have excluded writing by medical practitioners about their patients. My list is not intended to be exhaustive. For a related genre, see chapter 7 ("community auto/biography").

2. Both Monette and Doty followed the publication of collections of poetry concerned with the dying and death of a lover (Roger, Wally) with dual autobiographies in prose (*Borrowed Time, Heaven's Coast*) that furnish a specific reading context for the poems. (My convention here and elsewhere is to use first names—Paul, Bertrand, Amy, etc.—for characters, including narrators, and to indicate authors by their last name: Monette, Duquénelle, Hoffman.)

3. The concern with community that is readable in *L'Aztèque* and *Hospital Time* is not a necessary component of dual autobiography as a genre, but it links dual autobiography with community auto/biography (chapter 7) and is always implied by dual autobiography's critique of conventional autobiography's reliance on the ideology of the individual person.

4. Assuming that "Aztecs" is coterminous with HIV-positive people and people with AIDS, and that Hoffman's category of AIDS people refers to the gay (male and lesbian) community (since their "other" is defined by her as straight), the difference between the two definitions of the AIDS community (but Duquénelle's word is "peuplade," tribe, and Hoffman's is "family") is partly historical (grassroots support for people with AIDS was slow in being organized in France) and partly cultural: French understandings of citizenship and the public sphere (see Caron) have, until quite recently, excluded the idea of a "gay" (male or lesbian) community, defined by contrast with "straight" society, on which Hoffman relies. Clearly, both definitions have been superseded since the time (late eighties, early nineties) to which this writing refers.

Moreover, the categories themselves are quite fuzzy. AZT was given to some but not all HIV-positive people (those whose T-cell count had fallen below a specific threshold or who had broken through into AIDS). It is not clear where gay men (like some of Mike's friends) who shun people with AIDS fit in Hoffman's categories; and I do not believe she intends to exclude heterosexual people, whether as sufferers or as caregivers and survivors, from the community of those who "know the AIDS language." Thus I refer here, cautiously, to "AIDS people." (For the record, there is a body of writing, some it in the genre of dual autobiography, in which straight mothers, brothers, or sisters write in an intensely engaged fashion about the death from AIDS of a son or brother: see Gréco, Howe, Hurley, Kincaid, Peabody, Valdiserri.)

Chapter 7

1. My version of the story derives from information in the front matter of the Eulenburg score, signed Ernst Praetorius. I take it as authoritative, but it is obvious that the anecdote has a life of its own and circulates in many different versions.

2. Although the general outline of the story is well known, the detail of the "last solo" (see below) tends to suggest that Guibert might be White's source. White is a connoisseur of the Parisian literary scene, and indeed almost a French writer in his own right. Possibly the very dryness of White's brief account is intended to contrast with Guibert's romantic elaboration of the anecdote?

3. See *À l'ami,* 107; *To the Friend,* 91: "It wasn't so much my friend's last agony I was describing as my own, which was waiting for me and would be just like his."

4. The "Nacht und Nebel" order mandated that prisoners captured in Western European countries and *suspected* of being enemies of the Reich be transported secretly to destinations in Germany and neither their fate nor their place of detention be communicated to family or friends.

5. My understanding of infiltrational practices comes from Mireille Rosello, *Infiltrating Culture.*

6. "Ghetto" is the word habitually used by Dustan's narrator, Guillaume, for the Marais. It should be recalled that in the between-wars period and the occupation, the Marais was Paris's Jewish neighborhood. The rue des Rosiers (which traverses it, roughly parallel to the rue de Rivoli and the Seine) has retained its Jewish character, as has much of the neighborhood, and is still a metonym for Jewishness. (All translations of Dustan's French are by Ross Chambers.)

7. There is an ambiguity in this passage which cannot be captured in English, where "I'm not thinking" and "I don't think" are contrastive but each translates the French "Je ne pense pas." It is simultaneously suggested that Guillaume is *thinking,* "I am not thinking, etc." and *writing,* "I don't think, etc." For clarity's sake I split these two possible readings in my discussion, and for simplicity's sake I do not elaborate on the distinction between Guillaume's fictional writing of the text and Dustan's authorial redaction.

Chapter 8

1. This paragraph in particular, and the chapter as a whole, owes much to conversations with David Caron and his work on communities and the "founding" character of disasters for community. See Caron 1998b, 2001.

2. Rereading this account of a teaching disaster, which was written before the events of September 11, 2001, in New York and Washington, I am struck by a parallel between the microevent in my classroom and the macroevent in national and international history. Hijacking the familiar classroom in a way that the students took to be aggressive because it brought them face to face with the disaster of AIDS, I had been a kind of terrorist. They responded with an intellectual circling of the wagons that might be compared to the recourse to familiar themes of outrage, patriotism, and militarism that President Bush evoked in his declaration of a war of good against evil. In each case, something had been glimpsed—an abyss had been opened up—that it was vitally necessary to deny, and the violation of genre expectations was met by a reaffirmation of conventional (classroom, political) modes of discourse. What I did subsequently was to attempt to realign my teaching on the rhetorical model of testimonial rather than reproduce, even involuntarily, a terroristic model; and this chapter is a reflection on what such a realignment might entail.

3. The student was Charlie Snydner, who (to be accurate) wrote: "moderator of inborn pain," and whom I thank, both for his insights and for permission to quote his paper. He explained that by "moderator" he had intended to convey the sense of mediator (as in the so-called moderator of a discussion or debate), but with the additional suggestion that the teacher's role was to make the pain of reading more bearable. By "inborn" I took him to intend the idea that the students were led to acknowledge forms of pain within themselves of which they had previously been oblivious. I have been guided in this chapter too by conversations with Audrey Walton, an undergraduate who attended a graduate course on testimonial I taught at Northwestern University in the spring of 2000 and whose final paper, although I do not reproduce its argument, has inspired my thinking.

4. For a survey of this writing and an extremely shrewd appraisal of the deficiencies of the concept of hospitality in relation to immigration, see Rosello 2001, especially the introduction and chapter 1. For a thought-provoking fictional treatment of hospitality in the context of AIDS in Ireland, see Toíbín 2000.

5. Copi (Raul Damonte) was affectionately known in France for his fey drawings in *Le Nouvel Observateur.* He later turned to writing and, as both actor and playwright, the theater, before dying of AIDS complications in 1987. When his last play, *Une Visite inopportune,* was performed the following winter, it was frequently compared to Molière's *The Imaginary Invalid* in which, as every schoolchild in France knows, Molière was performing the title role when he died.

6. Willy Rozenbaum (cf. Dr. R. in *L'Aztèque*) is France's foremost AIDS physician. In his autobiographical meditation (1999), he describes his initial medical specialty—one of the few open to the child of poor Jewish immigrants from Poland—as resuscitation, and points out that from battling implacably against death in that role he was led by his involvement in treating AIDS patients to reconceive the relation of life to death, and to understand medicine as an art of rec-

onciliation rather than of combat. The unnamed doctor in *L'Accompagnement* is described as retaining helpful connections with the cardiac unit in which he had previously worked, and figures as an almost revered initiatory figure.

7. The rhetorical effect of this transparency, therefore, is not (as one might hastily assume) to protect the privacy of individuals so much as it is to index the production of allegory. Through being generalized, the particularity of certain real events is made widely significant.

. n.d. Symphony no. 45. London: Eulenburg.
6. *The Odyssey.* Translated by Robert Fagles. New York: Penguin.
, Willy. 1999. *La Vie est une maladie sexuellement transmissible, const*
telle. Paris: Stock.

d Theoretical Works

Theodor. 1976. *Noten zur Literatur.* Vol. 3. Frankfurt am Mai
amp.
n, Giorgio. 1998. *Quel che resta di Auschwitz.* Turin: Einaudi. Translate
aniel Heller Roazen as *Remnants of Auschwitz: The Witness and the Archiv*
w York: Zone, 1999).
, Pierre, et al. 1997a. "Le débat." *Libération,* July 9, 1–24.
—. 1997b. "Ce que cette table ronde m'a appris." *Libération,* July 10, 30–31;
ly 11, 30–31; July 12–13, 26–27.
es, Roland. 1964. *Essais critiques.* Paris: Seuil. Translated by Richard Howard
Critical Essays (Chicago: University of Chicago Press, 1972).
——. 1980. *La Chambre claire. Note sur la photographie.* Paris: Gallimard-Seuil
Cahiers du Cinéma). Translated by Richard Howard as *Camera Lucida:*
Reflections on Photography (New York: Vintage, 1993).
teson, Gregory. 1973. *Steps to an Ecology of Mind.* London: Paladin.
udrillard, Jean. 1981. *Simulacres et simulation.* Paris: Galilée. Translated by
Sheila Faria Glaser as *Simulacra and Simulation* (Ann Arbor: University of
Michigan Press, 1994).
Bayer, Ronald, and Gerald M. Oppenheimer. 2000. *AIDS Doctors: Voices from the Epidemic.* Oxford: Oxford University Press.
Becker, Alton. 1995. *Beyond Translation: Essays toward a Modern Philology.* Ann Arbor: University of Michigan Press.
Benjamin, Walter. 1977a. "Der Erzähler." In *Illuminationen: Ausgewählte Schriften.* Frankfurt am Main: Suhrkamp. Translated by Harry Zohn as "The Storyteller" in *Illuminations* (New York: Schocken, 1969).
———. 1977b. "Über den Begriff der Geschichte." In *Illuminationen: Ausgewählte Schriften.* Frankfurt am Main: Suhrkamp. Translated by Harry Zohn as "Theses on the Philosophy of History" in *Illuminations* (New York: Schocken, 1969).
Bennett, Scott. 1999. *White Politics and Black Australians.* Sydney: Allen and Unwin.
Benveniste, Emile. 1974. "L'Appareil formel de l'énonciation." In *Problèmes de linguistique générale,* vol. 2. Paris: Gallimard.
Bernard-Donals, Michael. 2001a. "Blot Out the Name of Amalek? Memory and Forgetting in the *Fragments* Controversy." *MMLA* 33, no. 3: 122–36.
———. 2001b. "Beyond the Question of Authenticity: Witness and Testimony in the *Fragments* Controversy." *PMLA* 116, no. 5: 1302–15.

Bibliography

Testimonial Writing

Antelme, Robert. 1957. *L'Espèce humaine.* Paris: Gallimard. Translated by Jeffrey Haight and Annie Mahler as *The Human Race* (Marlboro: Marlboro Press, 1992).
Barker, Pat. 1993. *Regeneration.* New York: Penguin.
———. 1995. *The Eye in the Door.* New York: Penguin.
———. 1996. *The Ghost Road.* New York: Penguin.
Borowski, Tadeusz. 1976. *This Way to the Gas, Ladies and Gentlemen.* Translated by Barbara Vedder. New York: Penguin.
Brett, Lily. 1999. *Too Many Men.* Sydney: Pan McMillan.
Bringing Them Home. 1997. National Inquiry into the Separation of Aboriginal and Torres Strait Children from Their Families. Canberra: Commonwealth of Australia.
Callen, Michael. 1990. *Surviving AIDS.* New York: Vintage.
Campo, Rafael. 1997. *The Poetry of Healing.* New York: Norton.
de Ceccatty, René. 1994. *L'Accompagnement.* Paris: Gallimard.
Chase, Clifford. 1999. *The Hurry-Up Song: A Memoir of Losing My Brother.* Madison: University of Wisconsin Press.
Coe, Christopher. 1994. *Such Times.* New York: Penguin.
Collard, Cyril. 1989. *Les Nuits fauves.* Paris: Flammarion, Coll. "J'ai lu."
———. 1993. *Les Nuits fauves* (Savage nights). Polygram Video.
Copi. 1988. *Une Visite inopportune.* Paris: Christian Bourgois.
de Vleeschouwer, Olivier. 1997. *La Vie des morts est épuisante.* Paris: Anne Carrière.
Delbo, Charlotte. 1965. *Le Convoi du 24 janvier.* Paris: Minuit.
———. 1970–71. *Auschwitz et après.* 3 vols. *Aucun de nous ne reviendra; Une connaissance inutile; Mesure de nos jours.* Paris: Minuit. Translated by Rosette Lamont as *Auschwitz and After* (New Haven: Yale University Press, 1995).
Doty, Mark. 1995. *Atlantis.* New York: HarperCollins.
———. 1997. *Heaven's Coast.* New York: HarperCollins.
Duquénelle, Bertrand. 1993. *L'Aztèque.* Paris: Belfond.

Dustan, Guillaume. 1996. *Dans ma chambre.* Paris: P. O. L.
———. 1997. *Je sors ce soir.* Paris: P. O. L.
———. 1998. *Plus fort que moi.* Paris: P. O. L.
de Duve, Pascal. 1993. *Cargo vie.* Paris: Livre de Poche-Lattès.
Foster, John. 1993. *Take Me to Paris, Johnny!* Melbourne: Minerva.
Fuad, Julie. 1999. *One of My Daughters: A Young Woman's Challenge with AIDS.* Bellingen, Aust.: J. Fuad.
Gréco, Caroline. 1996. *A Dieu, Julien.* Paris: Critérion.
Greyson, John. 1994. *Zero Patience.* Cinevista Video.
Guibert, Hervé. 1990. *A l'ami qui ne m'a pas sauvé la vie.* Paris: Gallimard. Translated as *To the Friend Who Did Not Save My Life,* translator not credited (New York: Serpent's Tail, 1994).
———. 1991. *Le Protocole compassionnel.* Paris: Gallimard.
———. 1992. *Cytomégalovirus.* Paris: Seuil, Coll. "Points."
Hemphill, Essex. 1992. *Ceremonies.* San Francisco: Cleis Press.
Hoffman, Amy. 1997. *Hospital Time.* Durham, N.C.: Duke University Press.
Howe, Marie. 1988. *What the Living Do.* New York: Norton.
Hurley, Joan. 1996. *How Far Is It to London Bridge?* Sydney: Millenium.
Johnson, Fenton. 1996. *Geography of the Heart.* New York: Washington Square.
Jones, Bill T. 1995. *Last Night on Earth.* New York: Pantheon.
Joslin, Tom. 1994. *Silverlake Life: The View from Here.* New York: New Video.
Kincaid, Jamaica. 1997. *My Brother.* New York: Farrar, Straus and Giroux.
Krauth, Nigel. 1990. *JF Was Here.* Sydney: Allen and Unwin.
Levi, Primo. 1998. *Se questo è un uomo* and *La tregua.* Turin: Einaudi. *Se questo* translated by Stuart Woolf as *Survival in Auschwitz* (New York: Collier Macmillan, 1961). *La tregua* translated as *The Reawakening,* translator not credited (New York: Collier Macmillan, 1995).
Manière, Michel. 1992. *A ceux qui l'ont aimé.* Paris: P. O. L.
Menchú, Rigoberta. 1993. *Me llamo Rigoberta Menchú y así me nació la conciencia.* Barcelona: Argos Vergara. Translated by Ann Wright as *I, Rigoberta Menchú . . .* (London: Verso, 1984).
Michaels, Eric. 1997. *Unbecoming.* Durham, N.C.: Duke University Press.
Mingot, Thierry. 1997. *Chronique d'un amour en exil.* Geneva: Zoé.
Monette, Paul. 1988. *Love Alone: Eighteen Elegies for Rog.* New York: St. Martin's Press.
———. 1988. *Borrowed Time.* New York: Avon.
Muller, Isabelle. 1995. *Un Amour sérodifférent.* Paris: Seuil.
Navarre, Yves. 1991. *Ce sont amis que vent emporte.* Paris: Livre de Poche-Flammarion.
Owen, Wilfred. 1964. *Collected Poems.* New York: New Directions.
Paley, Grace. 1991. *Long Walks and Intimate Talks.* New York: Feminist Press.
Peabody, Barbara. 1986. *The Screaming Room.* New York: Avon.

Remarque, Erich Maria. 1959. *Im Wes* Witsch. Translated by A. A. Whee York: Fawcett Crest, 1958).
René, Norman. 1990. *Longtime Companion*
Riggs, Marlon. 1994. *Tongues Untied.* Fran
Rousset, David. 1981. *L'Univers concentratio*
Salducci, Pierre. 2000. *Nous tous déjà morts.* Alain Stanké.
Sassoon, Siegfried. 1960. *Complete Memoirs of Ge ing Man; Memoirs of an Infantry Officer; Sher* Faber.
———. 1968. *Selected Poems.* London: Faber and
Semprun, Jorge. 1963. *Le Grand Voyage.* Paris: Gal Seaver as *The Long Voyage* (London: Weidenfeld a
———. 1994. *L'Écriture ou la vie.* Paris: Gallimard.
———. 2001. *Le Mort qu'il faut.* Paris: Gallimard.
Senak, Mark. 1998. *A Fragile Circle.* Los Angeles: Alys
Steinberg, Paul. 1996. *Chronique d'ailleurs.* Paris: Ram Coverdale with Bill Ford as *Speak You Also* (New Y [Henry Holt], 2000).
Tóibín, Colm. 1996. *The Story of the Night.* New York: Hen
———. 1999. *The Blackwater Lightship.* New York: Scribn
Valdiserri, Ronald D. 1994. *Gardening in Clay.* Ithaca, N.Y. Press.
West, Rebecca. 1990. *The Return of the Soldier.* New York: Carr
White, Edmund. 1997. *The Farewell Symphony.* New York: Knop
Wiesel, Elie. 1958. *La Nuit.* Paris: Minuit. Translated by Stella (New York: Hill and Wang, 1960).
Wilkomirski, Binjamin. 1995. *Bruchstücke.* Frankfurt am Main: Suh lated by Carol Brown Janeway as *Fragments: Memoirs of a Wart* (New York: Schocken, 1997). Text available in Mächler 2001, 3 under "Critical and Theoretical Works."
Wojnarowicz, David. 1991. *Close to the Knives.* New York: Vintage.
Yang, William. 1996. *Sadness.* Sydney: Allen and Unwin.

Other Primary Texts

Baudelaire, Charles. 1975. *Les Fleurs du mal.* In *Oeuvres complètes,* vol. 1. Paris: de la Pléiade.
Blanchot, Maurice. 1948. *L'Arrêt de mort.* Paris: Gallimard.
Dante Alighieri. 1982. *Purgatorio.* With facing translation by Allen Mandelbaum Berkeley and Los Angeles: University of California Press.

Bibliography

Bernard-Donals, Michael, and Richard Glejzer. 2001. *Between Witness and Testimony: The Holocaust and the Limits of Representation.* Albany: State University of New York Press.

Beyrer, Chris. 1998. *War in the Blood: Sex, Politics, and AIDS in Southeast Asia.* London: Zed Books.

Bianucci, Piero. 1972. "È una misteriosa necessitá, di tutti i popoli del mondo." *Il nostro tempo,* February 20. Repr. in *Primo Levi: Conversazioni e interviste,* ed. Marco Belpoliti. Turin: Einaudi, 1997. Translated by Robert Gordon as "A Mysterious Necessity" in *Primo Levi, The Voice of Memory. Interviews, 1961–1987* (New York: New Press, 2001).

Blanchot, Maurice. 1980. *L'Écriture du désastre.* Paris: Gallimard. Translated by Ann Smock as *The Writing of Disaster* (Lincoln: University of Nebraska Press, 1986).

Boulé, Jean-Pierre. 1995. "Hervé Guibert à la télévision: Vérité et séduction." *Nottingham French Studies* 34, 1: 112–20.

———. 1999. *Hervé Guibert: Voices of the Self.* Liverpool: Liverpool University Press.

Brison, Susan. 2002. *Aftermath: Violence and the Remaking of a Self.* Princeton: Princeton University Press.

Brophy, Sarah. 2002. "Angels in Antigua: The Diasporic of Melancholy in Jamaica Kincaid's *My Brother.*" *PMLA* 117, no. 2: 265–77.

Burton, Richard. 2001. *Blood in the City: Violence and Revelation in Paris, 1789–1945.* Ithaca, N.Y.: Cornell University Press.

Caron, David. 1998a. "Liberté, Égalité, Séropositivité: AIDS, the French Republic, and the Question of Community." *French Cultural Studies* 9, no. 3: 281–93.

———. 1998b. "Intrusions: Families in AIDS Films." *L'esprit créateur* 38, no. 3: 62–72.

———. 2001. *AIDS in French Culture: Social Ills, Literary Cures.* Madison: University of Wisconsin Press.

Caruth, Cathy. 1996. *Unclaimed Experience: Trauma, Narrative, and History.* Baltimore: Johns Hopkins University Press.

———. 2002. "The Claims of the Dead: History, Haunted Identity, and the Law." *Critical Inquiry* 28, no. 2: 419–41.

———, ed. 1995. *Trauma: Explorations in Memory.* Baltimore: Johns Hopkins University Press.

Chambers, Ross. 1991. *Room for Maneuver: Reading (the) Oppositional (in) Narrative.* Chicago: University of Chicago Press.

———. 1997. "The Suicide Experiment: Hervé Guibert's AIDS Video *La pudeur ou l'impudeur.*" *L'Esprit Créateur* 37, no. 3: 72–82.

———. 1998a. "AIDS and the Culture of Accompaniment in France." *French Cultural Studies* 9, 3: 399–409.

———. 1998b. *Facing It: AIDS Diaries and the Death of the Author.* Ann Arbor: University of Michigan Press.

Cohen, Stanley. 2001. *States of Denial: Knowing about Atrocity and Suffering.* Cambridge: Polity; Malden, Mass.: Blackwell.

Craft, Linda J. 2000–2001. "Rigoberta Menchú, the Academy, and the U.S. Mainstream Press: The Controversy Surrounding Guatemala's 1992 Nobel Peace Laureate." *MMLA* 33, no. 3 and 34, no. 1: 40–59.

Crimp, Douglas. 2002. *Melancholia and Moralism: Essays on AIDS and Queer Politics.* Cambridge: MIT Press.

Dekkers, Midas. 1994. *Dearest Pet.* Translated by Paul Vincent. London: Verso.

Deleuze, Gilles. 1993. *Critique et clinique.* Paris: Minuit. Translated by Daniel W. Smith and Michael A. Greis as *Essays Critical and Clinical* (Minneapolis: University of Minnesota Press, 1997).

Deleuze, Gilles, and Félix Guattari. 1975. *Kafka: Pour une littérature mineure.* Paris: Minuit. Translated by Dana B. Polan as *Kafka: Toward a Minor Literature* (Minneapolis: University of Minnesota Press, 1986).

———. 1980. *Mille plateaux.* Paris: Minuit. Translated by Brian Massumi as *A Thousand Plateaus* (Minneapolis: University of Minnesota Press, 1987).

Derrida, Jacques. 1967. *L'Écriture et la différence.* Paris: Seuil. Translated by Barbara Johnson as *Writing and Difference* (Chicago: University of Chicago Press, 1981).

———. 1993. *Spectres de Marx.* Paris: Galilée. Translated by Peggy Kamuf as *Specters of Marx* (New York: Routledge, 1994).

———. 1997. *Anne Dufournelle invite Jacques Derrida à répondre: De l'hospitalité.* Paris: Calmann-Levy. Translated by Rachel Bowlby as *Of Hospitality: Anne Dufournelle Invites Jacques Derrida to Respond* (Stanford, Calif.: Stanford University Press, 2000).

Dresden, Sem. 1995. *Persecution, Extermination, Literature.* Translated by Henry G. Schogt. Toronto: University of Toronto Press.

Egan, Susanne. 1999. *Mirror Talk: Genres of Crisis in Contemporary Autobiography.* Chapel Hill: University of North Carolina Press.

Eskin, Blake. 1998. "Wilkomirski's New Identity Crisis: A Swiss Writer Says Fragments Memoirist Is a Fraud." *Forward,* September 18, 1, 11–12.

Felman, Shoshana. 2002. *The Juridical Unconscious: Trials and Traumas in the Twentieth Century.* Cambridge: Harvard University Press.

Felman, Shoshana, and Dori Laub. 1992. *Testimony: Crises of Witnessing in Literature, Testimony, and History.* New York: Routledge.

Frank, Joseph. 1995. *The Wounded Storyteller: Body, Illness, Ethics.* Chicago: University of Chicago Press.

Freadman, Anne. 1988. "Untitled: On Genre." *Cultural Studies* 2, no. 1: 67–99.

———. 1990. "Genre Again: Another Shot." *Southern Review* 23 (November): 251–61.

———. 2004. *The Machinery of Talk: Charles Peirce and the Sign Hypothesis.* Stanford, Calif.: Stanford University Press.

Freadman, Anne, and Amanda Macdonald. 1992. *What Is This Thing Called Genre?* Mount Nebo, Aust.: Boombana.

Frow, John. 2001. "A Politics of Stolen Time." In *Timespace: Geographies of Temporality,* ed. John May and Nigel Thrift. London: Routledge.

Fussell, Paul. 1975. *The Great War and Modern Memory.* Oxford: Oxford University Press.

Ganzfried, Daniel. 1998. "Die geliehene Holocaust-Biographie." *Weltwoche,* August 27–September 3.

Gilmore, Leigh. 2001. *The Limits of Autobiography: Trauma and Testimony.* Ithaca, N.Y.: Cornell University Press.

Girard, René. 1982. *Le Bouc émissaire.* Paris: Grasset. Translated by Yvonne Freccero as *The Scapegoat* (Baltimore: Johns Hopkins University Press, 1986).

Gordon, Avery. 1997. *Ghostly Matters: Haunting and the Sociological Imagination.* Minneapolis: University of Minnesota Press.

Gourevich, Philip. 1999. "The Memory Thief." *New Yorker,* June 14, 48–68.

Griffin, Gabriele. 2000. *Representations of HIV and AIDS: Visibility Blue/s.* Manchester: Manchester University Press.

Gubar, Susan. 2001. "Prosopopoeia and Holocaust Poetry in English: Sylvia Plath and Her Contemporaries." *Yale Journal of Criticism* 14, no. 1: 191–215.

———. 2003. *Poetry after Auschwitz.* Bloomington: Indiana University Press.

Halliday, Michael. 1978. *Language as Social Semiotic.* London: Edward Arnold.

Herbert, James D. 1999. "Bad Faith at Coventry: Spence's Cathedral and Britten's *War Requiem.*" *Critical Inquiry* 25, no. 3: 535–65.

Hungerford, Amy. 2001. "Memorizing Memory." *Yale Journal of Criticism* 14, no. 1: 67–92.

Jakobson, Roman. 1960. "Linguistics and Poetics." In *Style in Language,* ed. T. A. Sebeok. Cambridge: Technology Press of Massachusetts Institute of Technology.

Jarroway, David R. 2000. "From Spectacular to Speculative: The Shifting Rhetoric in Recent Gay AIDS Memoirs." *Mosaic* 33, no. 4: 115–28.

Jelin, Elizabeth. 2002. *Los trabajos de la memoria.* Madrid: Siglo XXI de España.

Jenny, Laurent. 1990. *La Parole singulière.* Paris: Belin.

Kaempfer, Jean. 1998. *Poétique du récit de guerre.* Paris: Corti.

Kaplan, Robert. 1999. *The Nothing That Is: A Natural History of Zero.* Oxford: Oxford University Press.

Kristeva, Julia. 1980. *Pouvoirs de l'horreur.* Paris: Seuil. Translated by Leon S. Roudiez as *Powers of Horror: An Essay on Abjection* (New York: Columbia University Press, 1982).

LaCapra, Dominick. 1998. *History and Memory after Auschwitz.* Ithaca, N.Y.: Cornell University Press.

———. 2001. *Writing History, Writing Trauma.* Baltimore: Johns Hopkins University Press.

Langer, Lawrence. 1975. *The Holocaust and the Literary Imagination.* New Haven: Yale University Press.

———. 1991. *Holocaust Testimonies: The Ruins of Memory.* New Haven: Yale University Press.

Lappin, Elena. 1999. "The Man with Two Heads." *Granta* 66:9–65.

Lecercle, Jean-Jacques. 1998. "Bégayer la langue—Stammering Language." *L'Esprit Créateur* 38, no. 4: 109–23.

Lejeune, Philippe. 1975. *Le Pacte autobiographique.* Paris: Seuil. Translated by Katherine Leary as *On Autobiography* (Minneapolis: University of Minnesota Press, 1989).

Leys, Ruth. 2000. *Trauma: A Genealogy.* Chicago: University of Chicago Press.

Lionnet, Françoise. 1998. "Reframing Baudelaire: Literary History, Biography, Postcolonial Theory, and Vernacular Languages." *Diacritics* 28, no. 3: 63–85.

Lyotard, Jean-François. 1976. "La Force des faibles." *L'arc* 64:4–12.

———. 1983. *Le Différend.* Paris: Minuit. Translated by Georges Van der Abbeele as *The Differend: Phrases in Dispute* (Minneapolis: University of Minnesota Press, 1988).

———. 1988. *L'inhumain: Causeries sur le temps.* Paris: Galilée. Translated by Geoffrey Bennington and Rachel Bowlby as *The Inhuman: Reflections on Time* (Stanford, Calif.: Stanford University Press, 1991).

Mächler, Stefan. 2000. *Der Fall Wilkomirski.* Zurich: Pendo Verlag. Translated by John E. Woods as *The Wilkomirski Affair: A Study in Biographical Truth* (New York: Schocken, 2001).

McGlothlin, Erin. 2003. "No Time Like the Present: Narrative and Time in Art Spiegelman's *Maus.*" *Narrative* 11, no. 2: 177–98.

Mellamphy, Dan. 1998. "The Wit in Witness." University of Toronto. Typescript.

Ménil, Alain. 1997. *Sain(t)s et Saufs. Sida: Une épidémie d'interprétation.* Paris: Les Belles Lettres.

Miller, D. A. 1998. *Place for Us: Essay on the Broadway Musical.* Cambridge: Harvard University Press.

Nancy, Jean-Luc. 2000. *L'Intrus.* Paris: Galilée.

Nathan, Aaron. 1999. "Lacan/Benigni." University of California, Berkeley. Typescript.

Novick, Peter. 1999. *The Holocaust in American Life.* New York: Houghton Mifflin.

Ramazani, Jahan. 1994. *The Poetry of Mourning: The Modern Elegy from Hardy to Heaney.* Chicago: University of Chicago Press.

Rancière, Jacques. 1987. *Le Maître ignorant: Cinq leçons sur l'émancipation intellectuelle.* Paris: Fayard. Translated by Kristin Ross as *The Ignorant Schoolmaster:*

Five Lessons in Intellectual Emancipation (Stanford, Calif.: Stanford University Press, 1991).

Rand, Nicolas. 2001. *Quelle psychanalyse pour demain? Voies ouvertes par Nicolas Abraham et Maria Torok.* Paris: Erès.

Rosello, Mireille. 1996. *Infiltrating Culture: Power and Identity in Contemporary Women's Writing.* Manchester: Manchester University Press.

———. 2001. *Postcolonial Hospitality: The Immigrant as Guest.* Stanford, Calif.: Stanford University Press.

———, ed. 1997. "The Politics and Ethics of Contamination and Purity." *L'Esprit Créateur* 37:3.

Rothberg, Michael. 2000. *Traumatic Realism: The Demands of Holocaust Representation.* Minneapolis: University of Minnesota Press.

Sarkonak, Ralph. 2000. *Angelic Echoes: Hervé Guibert and Company.* Toronto: University of Toronto Press.

Schehr, Lawrence. 2002. "Writing Bareback." *Sites* 6, no. 1: 181–202.

Shilts, Randy. 1987. *And the Band Played On.* New York: Penguin.

Sontag, Susan. 1989. *AIDS and Its Metaphors.* New York: Farrar, Straus and Giroux.

Spoiden, Stéphane. 2001. *La Littérature et le sida: Archéologie des représentations d'une maladie.* Toulouse: Presses Universitaires du Mirail.

Suleiman, Susan Rubin. 1995. "War Memories: On Autobiographical Reading." In *Auschwitz and After: Race, Culture, and "The Jewish Question" in France,* ed. Lawrence D. Kritzman. London: Routledge.

———. 2000. "Problems of Memory and Factuality in Recent Holocaust Memoirs: Wilkomirski/Wiesel." *Poetics Today* 21, no. 3: 543–59.

———. 2002. "History, Memory, and Moral Judgment in Documentary Film: On Marcel Ophul's *Hôtel Terminus: The Life and Times of Klaus Barbie.*" *Critical Inquiry* 28, no. 2: 509–41.

Tal, Kalí. 1996. *Worlds of Hurt: Reading the Literature of Trauma.* Cambridge: Cambridge University Press.

Thatcher, Nicole. 2001. "La Mémoire de la deuxième guerre mondiale en France et la voix contestataire de Charlotte Delbo." *French Forum* 26, no. 2: 91–110.

Theil, Stefan. 1998. "A Classic or a Hoax?" *Newsweek,* November 16, 84.

Tougaw, Jason. 2002. "Testimony and the Subjects of AIDS Memoirs." In *Extremities: Trauma, Testimony, and Community,* ed. Nancy K. Miller and Jason Tougaw. Urbana: University of Illinois Press.

Treichler, Paula. 1999. "AIDS, Homophobia, and Biomedical Discourse: An Epidemic of Signification." *How to Have Theory in an Epidemic: Cultural Chronicles of AIDS.* Durham, N.C.: Duke University Press.

Trezise, Thomas. 2001. "Unspeakable." *Yale Journal of Criticism* 14, no. 1: 39–66.

———. 2002. "The Question of Community in Charlotte Delbo's *Auschwitz et après.*" *MLN* 117, no. 4: 858–86.

Wajnryb, Ruth. 2001. *The Silence: How Tragedy Shapes Talk.* Sydney: Allen and Unwin.

Waller, Margaret. 1993. *The Male Malady: Fictions of Impotence in the French Romantic Novel.* Camden, N.J.: Rutgers University Press.

Wieviorka, Annette. 1998. *L'Ere du témoin.* Paris: Plon.

Willett, Graham. 2000. *Living Out Loud: A History of Gay and Lesbian Activism in Australia.* Sydney: Allen and Unwin.

Wilson, Jean Moorcroft. 1998. *Siegfried Sassoon: The Making of a War Poet.* New York: Routledge.

Yaeger, Patricia. 2000. *Dirt and Desire: Reconstructing Southern Women's Writing, 1930–1990.* Chicago: University of Chicago Press.

Index

Index

Index

Index

Index

Index

Index